Woke ... .. .. ....    .  ...  .  ̶ ̶ .κ gospel s

# WOKE ME UP THIS MORNING

# WOKE ME UP THIS MORNING

**Black Gospel**

**Singers**

**and the Gospel Life**

**Alan Young**

University Press of Mississippi ❧ Jackson

Lyrics on pages 26, 27, and 28 © Roma Wilson; "He Works That Way"
© Rev. Willie Morganfield; lyrics on page 261 © James Holley.
All photographs were taken by Alan Young.

Copyright © 1997 by the University Press of Mississippi
All rights reserved
Manufactured in the United States of America
00  99  98  97      4  3  2  1
The paper in this book meets the guidelines for permanence and durability of
the Committee on Production Guidelines for Book Longevity of the Council on
Library Resources.

Library of Congress Cataloging-in-Publication Data

Young, Alan.
    Woke me up this morning : Black gospel singers and the gospel life / Alan
Young.
        p.   cm.
    Includes index.
    ISBN 0-87805-943-1 (cloth : alk. paper). — ISBN 0-87805-944-X (pbk. : alk.
paper)
        1. Gospel musicians—United States—Biography.   2. Gospel music—His-
tory and criticism.   I. Title.
ML394.Y68   1996
782.25'4'092276
[B]—DC20                                                        96-28054
                                                                    CIP
                                                                     MN

British Library Cataloging-in-Publication data available

*To my wife, Beverley . . .*
*and to Elder Roma Wilson*

# CONTENTS

# PREFACE

*"He woke me up this morning . . ."*

As the Dixie Hummingbirds swung into song at the Newport Folk Festival in 1966, they brought a new experience to many in the large audience—the excitement of seeing an African-American gospel quartet in performance. And while the enthusiastic throng may not have realized it, the words the 'Birds sang offered an instant insight into the basic credo of black religion:

> The Lord woke me up this morning
> Right on time
> When my eyes came open
> I was clothed in my right mind . . . *

"He woke me up this morning" is a simple, direct and potent expression of faith, summarizing the fundamentalist African-American Christian belief in the omnipotence of God and the control he has over every part of life. "He woke me up this morning, clothed me in my right mind. He put shoes on my feet, clothes on my back, food on my table. . . ." These words are used frequently and in many different expressions of belief—in prayer, in sermon, in testimony and in gospel song. For this reason, they also serve as the title of this book, which is primarily about gospel music, although other facets of African-American religious culture are examined as well.

*The Dixie Hummingbirds, *I've Got So Much To Shout About*, on *The Gospel at Newport*, Vanguard 77014–2 (U.S.; CD; 1995).

One of these facets is the relationship between black America's two seminal music forms, gospel music and the blues. And, as a peripheral irony, the blues has a similar catchphrase, so well known that it, too, has been used as the title of a book.* Where the gospel singer uses "The Lord woke me up this morning" as a prelude to a catalog of blessings, the blues singer says, "I woke up this morning," following it with an observation or a declaration—"I woke up this morning/Blues all around my bed"; "I woke up this morning/Looking 'round for my shoes"; "I woke up this morning/Feeling so bad."

The two expressions are similar, but their philosophies are quite different. While the gospel singer's "He woke me up this morning" affirms belief in a higher being and his dominion over every aspect of human existence, the blues singer's "I woke up this morning" characterizes a bleaker outlook in which the singer is troubled and knows—and accepts—that nobody except he or she can (or will) do anything to alleviate the problem. Whatever points of similarity may exist between gospel music and blues, the differing ways of waking up illustrate one vast difference. Gospel singers know they are not alone; blues singers know they are.

TRADITIONALLY, the preface is the section in which the author thanks the people who have contributed to the work. Despite the feint of first explaining my title, this preface is no exception; like the gospel singers, I have definitely not been alone. First on the list must be my wife, Beverley, who probably now knows more about gospel music than any other British/Celtic traditional folk singer. Without her constant support, the book would not have been written. She kept the household going while I went off on the great adventure of doing the interviews and research. She was my "first reader," checking chapters and making valuable suggestions as the work progressed. And she accepted the constant monopolization of the household stereo by quartets, soloists, groups and choirs, as well as the constant monopolization of my time by the book.

Also at the top of the list are the people whose words make up the bulk of this work. All gave of their time to submit to my interviews; all spoke freely and candidly, responding frankly even to quite personal lines of questioning; all were gracious, friendly and helpful. I count myself

---

*A.X. Nicholas, ed., *Woke Up This Mornin': Poetry of the Blues* (New York: Bantam Books, 1973). The book is a collection of blues lyrics.

privileged to have met them. The same applies to the many other people who, although not directly part of the book, provided me with valuable information and assistance. Melvin Mosley, lead singer and manager of the Spirit of the Memphis, told me: "There are no strangers in gospel music. Anyone that comes here and is interested is a friend." The truth of this was proven to me many times over.

Doing background research for a project such as this is never easy, and I have made it more difficult for myself by living in New Zealand, thousands of miles away from my subject. Occasionally, I found it necessary to contact researchers in other countries. Not all responded, but my thanks go to Kip Lornell in Washington, Doug Seroff in Nashville and Opal Nations in San Francisco for the help they so willingly gave.

In this area, I have to single out for special mention the assistance I have received from David Evans, professor of music at the University of Memphis. As editor of the book, he has done everything from identifying my difficulties with American spelling and wrestling with the vagaries of my two-finger typing to offering invaluable information, criticisms, and suggestions, some of which prompted radical revisions. As mentor, he gave assistance at the genesis of the book, when he provided me with contacts, ideas and thought-provoking discussions. And as friend, he and his wife, Marice, welcomed me to their home—the importance of clean laundry and home cooking to projects such as this is not always recognized—let me loose on an awe-inspiring record collection, and showed me where to find the best barbecue in Memphis.

Writing a book is one battle; finding a willing publisher is another. I have been fortunate in having the support of JoAnne Prichard, executive editor of the University Press of Mississippi, who saw potential in the work at a stage when it bore very little resemblance to this finished product. Her perceptive comments and suggestions, and her encouragement, were of great assistance.

To all these people go my thanks and my heartfelt gratitude. The clichéd phrase "I couldn't have done it without them" is completely true.

# MUSIC IN THE AIR:
# AN INTRODUCTION

*"We have to preach so everybody knows
what we're talking about . . ."*

Blues. Rock 'n' roll. Memphis. Mississippi. On one level, this is a collection of nouns; two are forms of music, and two are locations in the southern United States. But words can take on powers beyond their meaning, and these four (allowing rock 'n' roll as one) are among the most potent in the lexicon of American popular music. Blues and rock 'n' roll are venerated and vital elements in the fabric of American culture, and Memphis and Mississippi are geographic icons throughout the world because of their links with the music. Today, the old hip-swinging guitar and piano-based rock 'n' roll of Memphis is a memory, but the faithful still come to the Sun recording studio on Union Avenue where Elvis Presley, Jerry Lee Lewis, Carl Perkins and other founding fathers made their first recordings. Traditional blues is moribund, virtually severed from its African-American roots and sustained almost entirely by the life-support system of white patronage. Yet the tourists come to inspect the grave sites of yesterday's greats and to seek out what little remains of the "authentic" blues.

But as the misty-eyed Presley worshippers queue to view their idol's grave in the grounds of his Graceland mansion on Elvis Presley Boulevard in Memphis, and the blues fans go from the ruins of Muddy Waters's cabin in Stovall, Mississippi,* to the place near Greenwood

---

*Since this was written, Muddy Waters's cabin has been refurbished, uprooted and taken on tour to blues events—so it is now possible for the cabin to come to the blues fans rather than vice-versa.

where Robert Johnson might be buried, the air around them is filled with the vibrant sounds of a music alive, evolving, and still totally the property of the culture which developed it. Gospel music. African-American religious music. The unique blend of entertainment and spirituality with which black Americans praise God and raise their own spirits.

This is a book about gospel music. Or, more accurately, it is about gospel music people. Although some excellent studies have been done, the literature on gospel music is not extensive, and most of it is quite tightly focused, either on history or on specific elements of the music. The aim of this book is to look at gospel from a broader perspective, exploring a range of views and explanations on various aspects of the music and its culture and presenting it as a continuing tradition and an integral part of current African-American religious life. In the seventeen interviews around which the book is built, people involved with gospel music and religion talk at length about their lives, their music, their feelings about it and the effect it has had on them. If the book has a core thesis, it is that the heart of gospel music lies not in concert chambers or recording studios but in churches, local auditoriums and religious homes.

For this reason, I talked to people near the grassroots of gospel music in the contiguous areas of southwest Tennessee and north Mississippi, both strongholds of the music. No great master plan governed the selection of interview subjects—it would not be too much of an exaggeration to say that I embarked on the project armed with little more than an idea, a tape recorder, a camera and high hopes—but the people profiled do have things in common. All have a demonstrated long-term commitment to gospel music and/or "church work." Their taste in gospel music is firmly on the side of what the community regards as "traditional"; all who perform do so in this style. Most are Baptists, which is not surprising, considering the dominance of this church in the South, although the "sanctified" pentecostalist churches are also represented. And the close-knit nature of the gospel community is well illustrated by the fact that each person interviewed knows, or knows of, at least some of the others.

I have reproduced their stories, their observations and their views in their own words, with my interpolations establishing contexts or bridging topics of discussion. Obviously, taped conversations have been edited, as verbatim speech does not easily transfer to the printed page, but editing has been kept to the minimum needed to facilitate coherency.

Almost all the interviews were done in one concentrated period from late summer to early fall of 1992. For this reason, time is frozen throughout the interview sections; ages given are correct for late 1992, and the word "now" refers to that period. Some interviews required follow-ups, which were done over the subsequent two years. Rev. Dr. David Hall, of Temple Church of God in Christ in Memphis, is the only person whose full interview, done in October 1994, falls outside the 1992 time frame. Most of the interviews were done in private homes. Apart from making sure I obtained at least the basics of each person's biography, I allowed each interview to go wherever the conversation took it, with a minimum of overt "steering." However, I did have areas in which I wanted to get a variety of opinions on single topics, and these were raised with most of the people interviewed.

The main such area was the relationship between gospel music and blues. A "good versus evil" social schism is seen as existing between the two, yet they developed concurrently and share common musical roots. Much has been written from the blues side; I wanted to obtain a perspective from the sacred side. Many of the people interviewed grew up in an era when blues was the main African-American secular music, especially in the South. Today, it appears that the word "blues" is sometimes used as a catchall for black pop music—most of the people interviewed, even younger ones, used the words "blues" or "R&B" (or occasionally "jazz") when talking about secular music. Also, though, blues is still an active part of southern African-American life. Older, traditional styles have no relevance today, but support for the soul-based blues of artists like Bobby Bland, Bobby Rush, and Denise LaSalle remains strong, and blues veteran B. B. King is still a popular figure.

Another area discussed with many of those interviewed is the euphoric state known as being "in the spirit" and their experiences with it. Being "in the spirit" can range from a feeling of happiness to a state in which a person is completely overcome by religious fervor, shouting, leaping and sometimes passing out—known as "falling out." To the uninitiated, having someone nearby fall out at a gospel performance or in church can be an unnerving experience; to those in the culture, it is a fact of life. To the outsider, it may appear an extreme manifestation of hysteria; to the believer it can only be the Spirit of God coming down. It is a phenomenon not extensively discussed in most writing on gospel music, yet a gospel music performance without people "in the spirit" is rare and would almost certainly be deemed a failure by performers and audience alike.[1] To view gospel purely as a style of music is to miss the point of its existence. The reason for the passion which makes it unique is the singers' belief in God and faith in his blessings; the reason for its continued well-being is that this message appeals to the African-American churchgoers who attend the performances and buy the records.

This book is divided into sections, each dealing with a facet of gospel music and its culture. Introductory remarks give some history to place the interviews in context. The sections dealing directly with the performance of gospel music are divided into soloists, quartet-style performers, and solo and group female singers. The others cover gospel radio, preaching and the experiences and views of two musicians who gave up gospel to play secular music, but subsequently returned to gospel. Some of those interviewed fall into more than one category. Rev. Willie Morganfield is a preacher and a singer; Rev. J. W. Shaw owns a radio station, and is also a singer and a minister. While they have to be placed in single sections—Rev. Morganfield as a preacher, Rev. Shaw as a broadcaster—all aspects of their gospel lives are explored.

The book is not intended to be an all-encompassing study of gospel music, and two styles not directly represented are modern "contemporary" religious music and gospel choirs. My decision to focus on traditional styles accounts for the absence of "contemporary." This to a degree reflects my own tastes, although I also felt it important to document people with long-standing involvement in gospel music. These people favored traditional styles, and many of those to whom I spoke were quite dismissive, sometimes to the point of contempt, about modern gospel. Focusing on traditional styles cannot be used as a justification for omitting choirs, which have been in existence for as long as there has been a separate African-American church. However, allied with my desire to seek out the traditional was a wish to focus on the more "personal" styles of soloists and small groups rather than on the highly arranged performances of larger, often church-based, choirs. But the absence of choirs in this study is not an expression of bias or an attempt to deny their importance in the gospel spectrum.

Two contradictory schools of thought exist on social and cultural studies. One holds that the best research is done by people working completely outside their own culture, mainly because they will take nothing for granted and have no preconceptions which can color their work.

According to the other view, valid research can be done only by someone directly involved in the culture under examination.[2] Under this regime, I would have to be a committed African-American Christian. I fulfill none of these requirements—in fact I am probably as "outside" as one can be. I am a white New Zealander (aged 45 in 1992) and a newspaper journalist, whose relationship with any church ended in my teenage years. My first exposure to gospel came through phonograph records. I started collecting blues in the mid-1960s, about the same time I started playing guitar and singing blues, an activity with which I have had some performing and recording success in New Zealand and Australia. Among the "reissue" albums of mainly 1920s and 1930s material on which I concentrated in my early collecting days were fine examples of religious music and preaching by artists such as Blind Willie Johnson, Rev. D. C. Rice, Edward W. Clayborn, Washington Phillips and others. Although they were marketed as a subspecies of blues, they stimulated my interest in African-American religious music, and I began seeking other recordings. In the process, I discovered the excitement of the "hard" quartets like the Sensational Nightingales and the Blind Boys of Mississippi and Alabama, the suave elegance of the Soul Stirrers and the Harmonizing Four, the understated beauty of the Staple Singers, and the raw-edged sincerity of the Consolers—a panorama of beautiful, skilled and, above all, passionate music of faith and conviction.

My first visits to the United States, in the late 1980s, were largely as the archetypal blues tourist, seeking out the isolated pockets of authentic blues still to be found and visiting the tangible relics of the masters who now exist only as recorded voices. I went to clubs and juke joints, grave sites, Mississippi Delta townships, blues museums—and to the Sun studio in Memphis. There was also gospel music, at the New Orleans Jazz and Heritage Festival, at the Northeast Mississippi Blues and Gospel Folk Festival in Holly Springs, and on one memorable night at the Civic Center in Clarksdale, Mississippi, where the Pilgrim Jubilees of Chicago performed to an audience of fewer than a hundred people in a six hundred-seat hall as though it were a Carnegie Hall sell-out.

How does someone more than eight thousand miles from home in a foreign country track down something so completely off the tourism trails? Start by turning on the radio. Memphis has around thirty radio stations; five are devoted exclusively to African-American religious programming. Drive through Mississippi; as one gospel station fades from the car radio, another comes into range. Some cover only twenty or thirty miles, while others, such as WXSS or WLOK in Memphis, have a multistate reach. As well as playing music and excerpts from church services, the gospel stations advertise "programs," the unique mixtures of church service and entertainment that constitute gospel music concerts. Programs are also often advertised in newspapers and at some Christian supply stores. The other way of finding gospel music is simple. Go to church. Witness and join the exuberant mixture of song and oratory that is a traditional African-American religious service. The two main denominations for the gospel lover are the Baptist and the Church of God in Christ. The Baptists are by far the biggest denomination in the South; the pentecostalist Church of God in Christ has a commitment to music that goes back to its establishment in 1907. Every church will have at least one choir; many will also have a junior choir and possibly other musical ensembles. In both denominations, music and preaching make up the bulk of services.

A foreigner seeking out African-American music in its community environment enters a doubly alien world. America at large has its idiosyncrasies for the Antipodean visitor, ranging from the obvious (drive on the other side of the road) to the subtle (eat the salad *before* the main dish, not with it). But beyond these, it is impossible to spend any time in the South without realizing that thirty years after the worst bitterness of the civil rights struggle, skin color continues to be a socially and economically divisive factor. Veteran social commentator Studs Terkel describes race as "the American obsession,"[3] and one of his informants uses a vivid analogy to describe African-American life: "Being black in America is like being forced to wear ill-fitting shoes. . . . It's always uncomfortable, but you've got to wear it because it's the only shoe you've got. . . . Some people can bear the uncomfort more than others. Some people can block it from their mind, some can't. When you see some acting docile and some acting militant, they have one thing in common: the shoe is uncomfortable. It always has been, and it always will be."[4]

Religion is obviously a device used by many African-Americans to ease the discomfort of the ill-fitting shoe. White America seldom intrudes into black worship, so a Caucasian foreigner would have to be singularly insensitive—to history, if nothing else—not to feel a little ill at ease entering this seemingly exclusive domain. However, in none of the churches, programs and private homes I visited was I ever made to feel less than completely welcome, sometimes to the extent of being singled out for a personal greeting from the pulpit during services. I encountered occasional instances of racially motivated antipathy at blues functions, but the gospel world was totally hospitable. When the Spirit of Memphis invited me to go with them to a program in a small Memphis church, I said I would very much like to go, as long as the church members didn't mind my being there. "Mind?" said manager and lead singer Melvin Mosley incredulously. "If they mind, we don't play!" (My naive misgivings were entirely unjustified.) My journalistic background undoubtedly aided me in conducting my interviews, but as my project progressed, I realized that being a non-American was also helping me.[5] The fact that a foreigner from a country little known to many Americans knew about gospel singing and was eager to learn more served as a very effective icebreaker. The exception to this was the Watson Family in Memphis. They were every bit as accommodating and cordial as any of the other people I met, but their initial enthusiasm stemmed from the fact that, in 1987, they were featured in a television documentary shot in the United States by a film crew from New Zealand. The coincidence of being interviewed again by someone from this small South Pacific country provided much amusement. Another benefit of being non-American was that many people saw me as an outsider to the U. S. social system. During an interview (not part of this book) near Vicksburg, Mississippi, an elderly pastor told me an anecdote which made it clear he regarded Caucasian foreigners as being neither "white" nor "black"; to him, the terms carried connotations beyond skin pigmentation.

DEFINING gospel music is not an easy task. The South has its own code. "Southern gospel" refers to songs performed by whites and based on folk and country music. The term "gospel music," without a qualifier, is African-American. Ethnomusicologist Kip Lornell describes *gospel* as "a word with many meanings for different people. Black singers occasionally use it when referring to any type of religious music. . . . For these singers, the phrases 'gospel music' and 'religious music' are interchangeable." University of Memphis music professor David Evans says gospel "can incorporate all types of religious music," and "serves as entertainment as well as a religious experience . . . and tends to be innovative in content and style."[6] In a study of the relationship between preaching and gospel music, Marion Joseph Franklin says that "the free-style collective improvisations of the Black church as a collectivity and the solo singing of the Black pulpiteer are all part of Black gospel music."[7]

The sum of this expertise seems to yield a definition which excludes only the formal music of mainstream churches and older styles such as shouts and spirituals. But not all black religious music is "gospel." A key component of the genre is entertainment. Gospel music is firmly based in religion, but it is composed and/or arranged with performance in mind, and a conscious professionalism exists in the performances of all artists, from local groups who sing only within their community to those who make their living from their music. Imposing this criterion narrows the field considerably, but pitfalls exist. Many songs are specifically composed for gospel performances, but these events can also include arrangements of church hymns. Conversely, gospel songs have migrated to the churches. Is "Oh, Happy Day" a gospel song on a stage, but not when sung by a congregation? Pinpointing the beginnings of gospel music is also difficult. The university-based "jubilee" groups of the 1870s sang religious songs to entertain, but their songs lacked the element of performance-oriented original composition. While some authorities credit composer Thomas A. Dorsey with introducing this element in the 1930s, it was already present before him, although his compositions did lay the groundwork for the overt evangelizing which is part of modern gospel music. The origins of gospel music probably lie midway between the 1870s and the 1930s, in the first decade of the twentieth century, when the songwriting of Charles A. Tindley added performance-oriented composition to the existing entertainment ethic of the jubilee groups.

What is beyond dispute is the influence gospel music has had on American popular music, especially soul music. Well-known examples include Aretha Franklin, who as a child sang in the Detroit church of her father, Rev. C. L. Franklin (noted in his own right as an oft-recorded preacher), and Sam Cooke, who moved from the Highway QCs to the Soul Stirrers before finding fame and an untimely death as a pop singer. Lou Rawls, Dionne Warwick, and Wilson Pickett all left gospel groups for secular careers. Yet, despite a few isolated exceptions—Mahalia Jackson's later recordings, "Oh, Happy Day" by the Edwin Hawkins Singers—the music which gave them so much of their chart-topping styles has never achieved a similar fame. Big-production pop records have to sell millions of copies to be counted as a success; Alan Freeman, president of one of America's biggest independent gospel record companies, Atlanta International Records, says his best-selling album sold about four hundred thousand copies.[8] Most sell far fewer. Gospel's minority status is also reflected in the amount of generally available research and writing on the subject—a bibliography which, despite the dedicated efforts of a handful of researchers, is markedly at odds with the music's importance as a cornerstone of other musical forms and as a foundation stone of African-American culture.

Most writing on gospel music concentrates on factual and/or specific aspects. Anthony Heilbut's twice-reprinted *The Gospel Sound: Good News and Bad Times* provides an overview of various styles and gives biographies of a wide range of gospel artists.[9] Viv Broughton's *Black Gospel* also concentrates on history and biography.[10] Kip Lornell and Ray Allen step into sociology with excellent studies of quartets, Lornell in Memphis,[11] Allen in New York.[12] British researcher Paul Oliver's *Songsters and Saints* includes sections on pre-1943 preachers and singers.[13] Mahalia Jackson is the subject of two biographies;[14] Michael Harris's biography of Thomas A. Dorsey highlights the difficulty Dorsey had getting his new sound into established churches, and examines the relationship between Dorsey's earlier blues and his gospel.[15] *We'll Understand It Better By and By*, edited by Bernice Johnson Reagon, is primarily an examination of the lives and work of six leading African-American gospel composers.[16] A number of articles (academic and journalistic), theses, and dissertations have also been written on gospel music.

FROM this work can be obtained a history of gospel music, including its genesis in slavery, when masters gave their human property a distorted Christianity, based strongly on St. Paul's injunction (Colossians 3:22), "Servants, obey in all things your masters . . ." while ignoring the corollary in 4:1: "Masters, give unto your servants that which is just and equal. . . ."[17] The Great Awakening religious movement which started in the 1730s spread the influential hymns of English cleric and songwriter Isaac Watts, and the first black church was established in 1773. Slavery produced the spirituals; the 1870s brought the era of the "jubilee" singing groups, spearheaded by the Fisk Jubilee Singers, from Fisk University in Nashville, Tennessee.

The evolution of black religious music in the twentieth century is easier to follow, thanks to the phonograph record. The fact that most of the best gospel artists have been recorded means a map exists from which changes in styles and fashions can be charted. Probably the first African-American group to record was the Unique Quartette, from New York, in 1890. Only one of its cylinder recordings is so far known to have survived, the secular "Mamma's Black Baby Boy," recorded for Edison in 1893. It is performed in a close harmony style, staid and formal by latter-day standards, but still a quartet style. In early 1894, the Standard Quartet made twenty-two cylinder recordings for Columbia. Most were popular songs of the era, but five were religious songs, spirituals arranged for formal performance.[18] During the 1890s and 1900s, other groups also recorded. The introduction to one such recording, made in 1902, provides an insight into social attitudes of the time; "Praying On the Old Camp Ground" is introduced by a stentorian (and anonymous) voice proclaiming it to be a "coon shout by the Dinwiddie Colored Quartet."[19]

In the 1920s, recording companies ventured from blues and jazz into sacred music as part of their search for material which would appeal to the newly discovered African-American "race" market. The Okeh and Paramount companies led the way with recordings of unaccompanied male quartets singing secular material, some of which enjoyed considerable sales in the white market.[20] One such group was the Norfolk Jazz Quartet, first recorded in 1921, by Okeh. When it moved to Paramount, in 1923, its first session produced eight songs, including two religious numbers, issued as by the Norfolk Jubilee Quartet. One of them, "My Lord's Gonna Move This Wicked Race," sold very well, and of the ten tracks the group recorded at its next session, eight were religious. The success of the Norfolk group was noted by other recording companies and, except for the depression years of 1933–34, at least thirty quartet records were issued annually between 1927 and 1941.[21]

Another possibly unexpected success came from the decision to record sermons. The first such records featured only speech—preachers presenting cut-down versions of the messages they delivered from the pulpit. In 1926, Columbia recorded four sermons by Atlanta Baptist pastor J. M. Gates. As well as the preaching, the records featured singing by Gates and two unidentified women. The first Rev. Gates record, "Death's Black Train Is Coming," was a commercial success, and led to a proliferation of singing preachers, usually accompanied by backing singers, often label-credited as " . . . and Congregation," who also provided interjections and support during the preaching.

Soloists, often providing their own accompaniment, were also recorded. Among the most popular were artists accompanying themselves on guitar in a style closely related to the then-popular "country blues" style. This style also characterized a number of small groups from sanctified churches which performed religious music accompanied by instruments used in the jug bands of the era. (The jug is usually an earthenware demijohn; the performer sounds vocal notes forcefully across its mouth to produce a booming breathy bass. Other jug band instruments include guitar, harmonica, mandolin, and washboard.) The most prolific performer in this style was Elder Richard Bryant, a Mississippi Delta preacher who recorded in Memphis between 1928 and 1930. Two other contemporary groups, Brother Williams Memphis Sanctified Singers and the Holy Ghost Sanctified Singers, also used the jug in their accompaniments.[22]

The late 1920s also brought the Dorsey era. While establishing when gospel music first appeared is not an easy task, the songwriting of Thomas Andrew Dorsey established "gospel" as a genre of African-American religious music. Dorsey (1899–1993) was a Georgia preacher's son who, by the 1920s, had gained impressive credentials as a jazz and blues pianist, composer and arranger. As "Georgia Tom" Dorsey, he toured as leader of Ma Rainey's band, recorded on his own and with other artists, composed songs for other singers, and, with guitarist Tampa Red (Hudson Whitaker), launched the "hokum" craze with the double entendre ditty "It's Tight Like That." He wrote his first religious song, "If I Don't Get There," in 1921; in that year, it was included in the National Baptist Convention's *Gospel Pearls* songbook.[23] But through the 1920s, he was primarily active in jazz and blues. In 1928, after a period of clinical depression, he underwent a religious conversion and started writing sacred songs again, employing a new technique of using blues-based tunes to accompany sacred words (although 1928 was also the year in which he and Tampa Red recorded "It's Tight Like That"). The first two songs he wrote in this vein were "If You See My Savior (Tell Him That You Saw Me)" and "How About You?", still among his better-known pieces. Dorsey initially had little success selling his compositions or getting them performed, and continued to make his living from blues until 1932. From then on, he devoted himself to writing and promoting gospel music. He wrote more than five hundred songs, and played a leading role in moving Chicago's mainstream African-American churches away from copying white religious ceremony and music and back into a distinctively black style of worship.[24] His name is attached to many of gospel's most popular songs—"Precious Lord," "Remember Me," "The Old Ship of Zion," "Peace In the Valley," "Today,"

"I'm Going to Live the Life I Sing About In My Song"—many of them so well known they are sometimes assumed to be traditional.

In Chicago, his new sound attracted a number of talented singers. The first was Sallie Martin (1895–1988), who joined Dorsey's group at Ebenezer Baptist Church in 1932 and became his business partner, helping to demonstrate the songs and sell the sheet music. Dorsey and Martin established the Gospel Singers' Convention, and Martin traveled through the South and to California, indoctrinating other singers and organizing gospel choruses at churches. The most famous convert was made at home in Chicago. Mahalia Jackson (1911–1972), widely regarded as the greatest gospel singer of all, first impressed Dorsey when he heard her singing as a seventeen-year-old in 1928, soon after she arrived in Chicago from New Orleans. Long before she joined Columbia records and became an international star, she was touring with Dorsey, astounding congregations with her vocal abilities and helping her mentor move the product.

The Dorsey-Jackson coalition was formed after Sallie Martin and Dorsey quarreled and parted company in 1940. Martin went into partnership with composer Kenneth Morris to form the Martin and Morris gospel music publishing business, and joined forces for a while with Roberta Martin (no relation) to form the Martin and Martin Gospel Singers. The partnership didn't last, and soon the Sallie Martin Singers and the Roberta Martin Singers were each on the road, one singing only songs published by Martin and Morris, the other singing only songs published by Roberta's Studio of Music. The Roberta Martin Singers included some of Chicago's finest male singers, among them Robert Anderson, Norsalus McKissick and Eugene Smith. Martin, Anderson and especially Eugene Smith were the principal influences on another giant of the gospel field, Rev. James Cleveland (1931–1991), founder in 1968 of the Gospel Music Workshop of America. Alex Bradford (1927–1978) also started his musical career under Roberta Martin's influence, making his first records in 1951 with a group that included Willie Webb, an original member of the Roberta Martin Singers. Bradford went on to a successful recording career, and achieved wider fame for his involvement with the gospel musical *Black Nativity.* From 1960 until his death, he was minister of music for the Abyssinian Baptist Church in Newark, New Jersey, leading the church choir on one of the few gospel choir recordings to achieve sales outside the gospel market, aided considerably by the fact that it was on the major Columbia label (Columbia CL-1548, reissued in 1991 as compact disc Columbia CK-47335, *Shakin' the Rafters*).

Propagated by the travels of Dorsey with Sallie Martin and Mahalia Jackson, the Chicago influence spread well beyond the city. Willie Mae Ford Smith (1904–1994), born in Mississippi but raised in St. Louis, Missouri, started singing with a family quartet, the Ford Sisters, in the 1920s and was performing as a soloist in 1932 when she met Dorsey and Martin. Although she made only six commercial recordings in her prime, she was very influential as a singer and as an evangelist of the "new" style. One of her converts was Joe May (1912–1972), who sought tuition from her. May's first recording, "Search Me Lord" (1949), was from Smith's repertoire and gave him the first of his many hits. He toured and recorded extensively, earning the nickname "The Thunderbolt of the Middle West," and died of a stroke at the age of sixty while driving to sing in a program in Georgia.

Cleophus Robinson (b. 1932) says he started singing at the age of three, and cites his mother as his main vocal influence.[25] Mrs. Lillie Robinson's singing was likened by locals around the family home in Canton, Mississippi, to that of Mahalia Jackson, but Cleophus was more strongly influenced by Jackson herself, after he left home and traveled to Chicago in 1948. He stayed in Chicago for eighteen months, singing on programs and in churches with Jackson and the Roberta Martin Singers, and making a single unsuccessful recording session in 1949. He did not record again until 1953, when he joined the Peacock label. His sales rose as he found his style, and, by 1964, Peacock was label-crediting his singles to "Reverend Cleophus Robinson, World Famous Preacher and Singer." (When his wife recorded in 1967, she was credited "Sister Bertha Robinson, Wife of Rev. Cleophus Robinson.") He remains active in the 1990s.

While the Chicago-influenced stylists are powerful singers with the skills and the rhythm to move their audiences, their sound is often stately and almost classical, especially in comparison to what developed elsewhere. While Dorsey and his disciples were spreading their word, the Golden Gate Quartet of Norfolk, Virginia, was on its way to becoming the first "star" gospel group. William Langford (first tenor), Henry Owens (second tenor), Willie Johnson (baritone), and Orlandus Wilson (bass) formed their close-harmony "jubilee" group in 1934. Their singing style borrowed heavily from the top-selling secular harmony singing group the Mills Brothers, and they created a fast-moving intricately arranged style. On stage, they wore matching tailored suits, and their performances introduced a new level of professionalism into gospel. In a 1980 interview with researcher Doug Seroff, Willie Johnson said: "We were singing in every church that let a quartet sing in it. And the main churches that got to me were the Holiness [pentecostal] churches, because they sang with a beat. And . . . I'd give our things a beat, upbeat it, you know. That, in some churches, the preachers wouldn't allow you to do. That was sinful stuff! You were singing the Lord's music with a beat, and that was like dancing. . . . I think with this quartet, what we tried to create was what I called 'vocal percussion.' It was just like a drum, but it had notes to it, had lyrics to it."[26]

The group made its first recordings in 1937. By the end of 1938, it had appeared on a national NBC radio broadcast and in the first *Spirituals to Swing* concert, promoted by entrepreneur and Columbia Records executive John Hammond to display jazz, blues, and gospel to a predominantly white audience at Carnegie Hall in New York. In 1955, the Quartet toured France. Orlandus Wilson was the only original member left, but the sound was as highly polished as ever and the Gates were feted in Europe. In 1959, they took up full-time residence in France, attracted by the amount of work available and by Europe's more liberal racial attitudes.

The Golden Gates, with other groups such as Mitchell's Christian Singers and the Heavenly Gospel Singers, helped establish "quartet" as the dominant gospel style. But the years immediately after World War II brought a new approach to singing and presentation. The "jubilee" emphasis on a smooth sound with sweet harmonies and often no definable lead singer was replaced by the "hard quartets"—groups led by one or two powerful lead singers and aiming to "wreck the house" by producing such an overpowering performance that the audience was reduced to shouting hysteria. This era produced names still revered in gospel forty years later—Archie Brownlee of the Five Blind Boys of Mississippi, Julius Cheeks of the Sensational Nightingales, Silas Steele of the Famous Blue Jay Singers and the Spirit of Memphis, Ira Tucker of the Dixie Hummingbirds, Clarence Fountain of the Five Blind Boys of Alabama, Rebert Harris and Sam Cooke of the Soul Stirrers, and many others. Harris is credited with devising the "twin lead" system which helped give the hard groups their power, setting up arrangements in which one lead took the basic melody, and the other provided an overlay of interpolation and ornamentation, often taking over the lead mid-song at a higher pitch and with a higher energy level.[27] A side effect of this development was that the true quartet became a rarity as groups took on more members to fill all the parts; the Spirit of Memphis Quartet, for example, has belied its name throughout most of its career by having five or six singers. But they sang in the traditional lead/tenor/baritone/bass harmonies, and the style was—and is—still known as "quartet."

The other change which the hard groups introduced was extravagant on-stage movement. Earlier groups often choreographed songs, but the movements were restrained and formally arranged. Now the groups, especially the lead singers, would use all the stage room available, running from side to side, falling on one or both knees or even leaving the stage to sing among the audience. Some doubt exists as to who pioneered off-the-stage performing. Ira Tucker, of the Dixie Hummingbirds, is often credited with being the first, in 1944.[28] But another Dixie Hummingbirds member, Beachey Thompson, says Jimmie Bryant, bass singer for the Heavenly Gospel Singers, was doing it in the 1930s.[29] Silas Steele, of the Famous Blue Jay Singers, is also said to have been an early aisle walker. One of the most famous was Archie Brownlee, lead singer with the Five Blind Boys of Mississippi. In *Black Gospel,* Viv Broughton quotes an unidentified singer who saw the totally blind Brownlee in action: "I seen him . . . jump all the way off that balcony, down on the floor—*blind*! I don't see how in the world he could do that."[30]

The first quartets performed without instrumental backing. But during the 1950s, instruments infiltrated, probably in imitation of the secular "doo-wop" singing groups. Just a guitar was used at first; then drums appeared. The Sensational Nightingales added piano, and the organ came soon after. The drive towards accompaniment was in part fueled by record companies, which felt that instruments filled out the quartets' sound and made them more competitive with other recorded music. Don Robey, owner of Houston-based Peacock records, claimed to be the one who "put the beat" into gospel records. "I was highly criticized when I started it," he said. "But I put in the first beat—which was not a drum—then after the public started to buy the beat, why, then I put a drum into it. . . . I found that the public wanted something new in religious music, and I tried it with different instruments to see which they would take to. They did not take to the trombone, but they did take to the guitar and the drumbeat, and it got to a point where if you didn't have a beat in a religious record, you had no sales."[31] Robey's claim is somewhat egocentric; a more realistic assessment is that he was quick to recognize a developing trend. Another major gospel label of the 1950s, Specialty, would sometimes overdub extra accompaniment if it was felt the track needed a boost, a process label owner Art Rupe called "sweetening." The advent of instrumentation marks the end of a golden era for many quartet aficionados, but quartets remained prominent well into the 1960s, and are still an integral part of gospel music. The use of instruments has continued to evolve, and a typical lineup now includes one or two guitars, a bass guitar, drums and keyboards ranging from piano and organ to electronic synthesizers capable of reproducing the sound of a brass or string section. This full backing has brought a change in singing style—the bass singer has all but gone, replaced by the bass guitar and the lower register of the keyboards, and the vocal structure is now usually one lead singer with a narrow-range harmony backing.

The 1950s were also rich in other styles of gospel. Roebuck "Pop" Staples learned to play guitar by listening to bluesmen like Charley Patton around the town of Drew in the Mississippi Delta. In 1935, at the age of twenty-one, he moved his young family to Chicago, where he and his children started singing gospel music, dropping the final "s" in their name to perform as the Staple Singers. Staples played a stark blues-based guitar style, using a very heavy "tremolo" vibrato effect, while his daughter Mavis sang a rich velvet lead. "We just sang like we did down south," Staples said in 1992. "I played the blues down south, and my gospel singing has got a kind of a blues feeling to it. It's different."[32] Their 1956 song "Uncloudy Day" became a hit, and many others followed. In the 1960s, the Staples began to shift from gospel, becoming among the first sacred artists to move into "inspirational" music, songs which have uplifting messages but no direct religious references. In 1968, they joined the Memphis-based Stax soul label and had the biggest hit of their career, "Respect Yourself," in 1971. As soul music's popularity waned, the Staples made a partial return to their religious roots—not without some criticism from Christians, who saw the group as having "sold out"—performing a mixture of their old gospel hits and more recent inspirational material.

The Consolers, a duo from Miami, Florida, were the opposite side of the coin. Sullivan Pugh also played a heavy blues-inflected guitar style, which he used to back his wife, Iola, and himself as they sang songs full of piety and old-fashioned values in raw voices bereft of technical finesse but resonant with sincerity. The Pughs also performed from the 1950s to the 1990s (Iola Pugh died in 1994) but, unlike the Staples, never deviated from their fundamentalist Christian message and their "down-home" sound. As a result, they found no fame in the white or pop markets, but retained their nationwide popularity in the church-and-program constituency that provided them with steady work for nearly fifty years.

The quartet "boom" waned in the 1960s, and many of the old groups came "off the road," disbanding or returning to regular jobs and singing parttime. Some of the big-name groups, including the Soul Stirrers, the Sensational Nightingales and the Dixie Hummingbirds, kept going, but often their sound was weakened by personnel changes and sometimes unsuccessful attempts to adjust to new styles. Soul music drew young performers and audiences alike, leaving gospel floundering (with blues) in its wake. Some gospel artists tried to ride the new wave, creating a style which critics have labeled "gos-pop." In extreme form, the singing in a gos-pop recording becomes merely another part of the arrangement along with the instruments, nullifying one of the most important parts of gospel song—the lyrics' message—and creating an empty exercise in bass-heavy rhythm.

Gospel's next major development was the rise of the choirs, an ascendancy which continues into the 1990s. Traditionally, choirs are affiliated with churches, and range in size from twenty or thirty voices to ensembles of two hundred or more, such as the Southwest Michigan State Choir of the Church of God in Christ, which recorded in the 1960s under the direction of Mattie Moss Clark. Although choirs were recorded before World War II, researcher and gospel singer Horace Clarence Boyer says the first choir to "reach renown within the gospel field" was the St. Paul's Church Choir of Los Angeles.[33] It was already established in radio broadcasting when, in 1947, it recorded under the direction of Professor J. Earle Hines, an émigré Chicago singer, whose baritone lead on "God Be With You" produced a hit. A second song from the same session, "If We Never Needed the Lord Before," was issued soon after and was equally successful.

Community choirs, often created by a choir director and not affiliated with any one church, have also evolved. An early community choir was the Wings Over Jordan, an ensemble of about fifty voices, formed in 1936 by Rev. Glenn Settles in Cleveland, which made records, broadcast on radio and went on national tours. Some, such as the one hundred-voice Mississippi Mass Choir, founded by Frank Williams in 1982, or the Chicago Community Choir, led since 1964 by Rev. Jessy

Dixon, are among the most popular gospel recording artists of the 1980s and 1990s.

Choirs also serve as foundations on which a wide range of talented soloists have built some of gospel's most successful songs. Singers who have performed in front of choirs range from Mahalia Jackson (and many other Chicago artists) to Sam Cooke and the Soul Stirrers. The doyen of choir directors was James Cleveland, whose thirty-year reign started when he recorded a Soul Stirrers song, "The Love of God," with the Voices of Tabernacle, the choir of the Prayer Tabernacle in Detroit. Cleveland was raised in Chicago and sang as a child in the choir of the Pilgrim Baptist Church, where the minister of music was Thomas A. Dorsey. He had been a recording artist for ten years when he made "The Love of God," and was known and respected in the Chicago gospel community. But "The Love of God" made him a star. Soon after, he signed a contract with the Savoy label, which in 1962 teamed him with one of the era's most successful choirs, the Angelic Choir from the First Baptist Church in Nutley, New Jersey directed by Rev. Lawrence Roberts. Their first album, *Christ Is the Answer* (Savoy MG-14059), sold more than one hundred thousand copies,[34] but it was the third, *Peace Be Still* (Savoy MG-14076), which set new records, selling more than eight hundred thousand copies.[35] Over the next ten years, Cleveland became the leading figure in choir-based gospel music and was responsible for furthering the careers of a number of performers. One was Texas-born Jessy Dixon, who was living in Chicago when Cleveland hired him as a musician: "James hired me and [organist] Billy Preston at the same time to play for him. He was big then—he would go to the Apollo [Theater in New York] and different places. He hired me as a keyboard player, more than as a singer. But I had written these little songs and he liked them, so he let me sing, just on a whim. And he saw the audience liked me and he was not jealous. So he began to push me."[36]

Cleveland's influence was also felt in the selection of artists by Savoy, which by that time was a leading gospel label. Predictably, it specialized in choirs and choir-backed soloists, rather than the quartets of labels like Specialty and Peacock. Equally predictably, not everyone was happy with the influence he wielded. One singer, discussing the politics of making records, said: "I think Reverend James Cleveland was a great man because he opened the door for a lot of people. But he was nothing near like one of the greatest singers. I know people in my home town that could sell more records than James Cleveland ever sold—if they had a chance. And this is the kind of thing I'm talking about . . . the politics. If you knew James Cleveland, you could get on Savoy. But if you didn't know James Cleveland, it didn't make any difference how well you could sing, nine times out of ten you wouldn't get on Savoy. That's what I mean about politics."[37]

Whatever the "politics," Cleveland did assist a great many artists, especially through his Gospel Music Workshop of America, which held its first annual convention in 1968. The workshop conventions feature classes on many different facets of gospel music, with the accent on choirs, and have spawned a proliferation of groups across the United States, especially in the South and in California, where Cleveland moved around 1969, establishing a church in Los Angeles. One of the most successful was the Southern California Community Choir, with which Cleveland did much of his later work.

In 1969, gospel music made one of its rare penetrations into the wider musical world with the release of a privately recorded album by a Church of God in Christ youth choir from Oakland, California, led by a teenage interior design student. The choir director was Edwin Hawkins; the stand-out song was a reworking of the Baptist hymn "Oh Happy Day," by Philip Doddridge (it is now also in the Church of God in Christ hymnal). "We cut it privately with a local recording enterprise who turned out 500 records in the first order," Hawkins recalled. "The next order, for 1000, also sold quickly. Then things began to happen."[38] The record became an international hit, and the Northern California State Youth Choir, renamed the Edwin Hawkins Singers, found itself transported from the Ephesian Church of God in Christ to venues ranging from Madison Square Garden in New York to casinos in Las Vegas. The impact of the Hawkins Singers on the wider music market was fleeting, but it opened the way for a more modern choir style, foreshadowed by some of James Cleveland's work, in which traditional material was replaced by modern arrangements and harmonies, drawing from sources as diverse as bossa nova and jazz. The continuing popularity of choirs was amply demonstrated in 1989, when the Mississippi Mass Choir's first album stayed at Number One on the *Billboard* gospel chart for forty-five weeks. Two subsequent albums also spent lengthy periods on the chart, in 1991 and 1993.[39]

The choir sound has influenced other styles of gospel. Frank Williams, founder of the Mississippi Mass Choir, was also a long-time member of the popular Jackson Southernaires quartet. He explained why the group moved away from the "hard" sound it had been using since its inception in 1945: "We were trying to develop a type of gospel that would appeal not only to quartet fans but to church people, choirs. There are two totally different audiences. Every church has a choir, a few have quartets. So church people, to me, prefer choirs, the sound of choirs."[40]

Choir and quartet is one demarcation in modern gospel music. The other, which arouses more passions, is between "traditional" and "contemporary." To many in gospel and the church, contemporary singers have abandoned God for Mammon; Anthony Heilbut acidly describes the name for the style as "an amalgam of 'con' and 'temporary'."[41] The contemporary singers see themselves as using worldly styles and sounds to spread the gospel message to an audience that the traditionalists cannot reach. Their music owes little to traditional gospel styles, and much to post-soul music developments, including disco and rap. One of the pioneers of the modern sound is Californian Andrae Crouch. The polished production of his records and the modern "fusion" sound of his music enabled him to cross over into the white market to the extent that, from 1970 until 1991, he was contracted to the white-oriented religious record label Light. But although he is a leader in the contemporary style, Crouch covers as broad a spectrum of gospel music as it is possible to cover. At one extreme, songs he has written are in the hymnals of the Church of God in Christ and the Baptist church;[42] at the other he has sung backup for pop stars Michael Jackson and Madonna. Of his singing with Madonna, he said, "I never did it for popularity for myself, but I saw it as an opportunity to share the Lord with them."[43] Other leading contemporary performers include the Winans family, from Detroit, and Take 6, a group of young men from Nashville who sing in a modern style without instrumental accompaniment.

The clash between old and new has less to do with the sound of the modern style (although some criticize the emphasis on rhythm) than it does with the lyrics. As the Staple Singers did twenty years earlier, many contemporary singers aim to please a wider market by softening the message, sometimes to the extent that it is difficult to tell whether a lyric is about God or a lover. Shirley Caesar, a gospel star since the 1950s when she performed as "Baby Shirley," explained her view on contemporary gospel in 1992: "We have to keep up with the times. I'm a traditional singer, but I know how to put a contemporary flavor to it. Whatever it takes to reach men and women, we have to do. But we have to preach so everybody will know what we're talking about. . . . Anytime you've got a song and the Lord is not mentioned to the extent that it's going to help somebody, you're not listening to a gospel song."[44] Even Andrae Crouch has spoken against dilution of the message: "To me, it seems more people [in gospel music] are concerned with their own promotion than with sharing the Word. We've reached the mainstream, but instead of fishing for men, we're panning for gold. . . ."[45]

CROUCH's comments encapsulate the difference between gospel and other forms of music. Gospel isn't meant to be pure entertainment. Its purpose is to praise God, uplift the faithful and convert the sinful. It opposes worldly practices, from lying and boasting to drug taking and violence. But if it doesn't entertain, it cannot succeed in its other aims. The resolution of this conflict has produced a performance style which to outside eyes might appear as showy and glitzy as a James Brown soul revue, but which conforms completely to the gospel ethic as it has evolved. The performers wear elegant and sometime ostentatious stage clothes—but who wants to sing the Lord's message dressed in rags? The rhythms are powerful and compelling—but this helps bring down the Holy Spirit and get the message across. The artists shout, scream, and exhort the audience, pushing towards an atmosphere of apparent hysteria—but this is the Holy Spirit at work. If people in the audience like what they are hearing, they will clap, shout encouragement and rise from their seats—the Holy Spirit again. The atmosphere may resemble a pop or soul music concert, but it is religion. This may sound cynical, but it isn't. While gospel singers take pride in their ability to move an audience, most also firmly believe that they give their best performances when their "help comes down" and the Holy Spirit inspires them. Most musicians have had special nights when everything combined to produce an out-of-the-ordinary performance. The secular artist will attribute this to a variety of factors—a receptive audience or a good venue, feeling relaxed and confident and playing well. The gospel artist *knows* the Spirit of the Lord is responsible.

This mixture of sacred and secular is most graphically seen at a gospel "program." On the surface, a program is a gospel concert, almost always featuring a number of different acts. In fact, it is a unique blend of church service and concert, enabling those attending to be entertained and uplifted. The venue is usually a church or an auditorium. Expensive musical equipment—guitars, amplifiers, synthesizers and other keyboards—festoons the stage. The atmosphere is festive. But the differences between a gospel program and a secular concert appear as soon as the show starts. Instead of an MC urging a great big welcome for the first act, the audience is invited to join in singing a "church song," a well-known standard, usually with a repetitive verse structure that makes it easy to learn—"Jesus Is On the Main Line" and "(Glory Glory Hallelujah) When I Lay My Burden Down" are favorites. A pastor offers a prayer, after which may come another audience-participation song, led by the MC or a specially invited song leader. Only then does the entertainment start. This part of the program is also viewed by audience and performers as having a religious aspect. At a program in Mississippi, singer Leomia Boyd became upset at the bright lighting being used by a camera team. She stopped her performance, strode to the edge of the stage and demanded, "How can we have church here with those lights on?" The lights went off, and the camera was subsequently unable to capture Mrs. Boyd as she left the stage to sing among the audience, at one point sinking to her knees in the aisle.

Programs illustrate other differences between gospel and secular music. While some are presented by promoters as money-making ventures, in the same way secular concerts are—and sometimes with a nonreligious attitude towards paying the performers—others operate as part of an informal cooperative approach among gospel groups. One of the more common forms of program is the "anniversary," organized by a group to mark the passing of another year since its foundation, and to make some money. Sometimes a "name" group will be engaged as the headline act; otherwise the group celebrating its anniversary will head the bill. The rest of the acts will be local groups, mainly quartets and soloists, with the occasional choir. An out-of-town group will be paid, but the local acts will perform without payment or for expenses only. The reason for this philanthropy is simple. Profits from the program go to the anniversary group—and the other groups appearing will also be planning anniversaries, for which they will require performers.

Many of the differences between gospel and secular music are easy to identify. The most significant difference is not so obvious, although the format of many gospel programs offers a clue. At the Clarksdale program referred to earlier in this chapter, the Pilgrim Jubilees were the main act. Also on the bill were another top Chicago quartet, the Salem Travelers, and the Deltalettes, an all-female group from Cleveland, about thirty miles south of Clarksdale. The Deltalettes didn't have a good night. Their arrangement of Alex Bradford's "Too Close To Heaven" proved too tough for them, and the song trickled to an ending so disorganized that the small audience didn't realize it was over and didn't applaud at all. Then the group suffered the ignominy of sitting in the front row while the Pilgrim Jubilees sang the same song superbly. But the promoter, local trenching contractor James Williams, explained that the Deltalettes were an important part of the program—they were a local group, and their presence was intended to boost attendance. Therein lies a difference between gospel and virtually every other form of music. Gospel still belongs to its community. It has national stars, big recording companies, and television and radio shows, but its foundation is still in thousands of churches throughout the United States, especially in the South.[46] Church is a social as well as a religious occasion, and the church membership makes up a close-knit group within the larger community. Every church has a choir, and most have members who sing in groups. People like to see the big name groups, such as the Pilgrim Jubilees or the Mighty Clouds of Joy, but they also like to see their own singers.

The community-based nature of gospel also shows in the two-tier recording industry which operates in the genre. On top are the name acts, signed to established labels and receiving national promotion. Local performers cannot aspire to this, but they can still make records or tapes (since the demise of the vinyl LP, few can afford compact discs). They do this by financing the project themselves, hiring the recording studio and engineer, then paying to have the tapes or records manufactured and packaged. A number of small companies specialize in producing these recordings. Usually, the artists will pay for a few hundred copies which they will sell themselves at programs and through local outlets. Copies will also go to local radio stations, and it is possible for a group or artist to have a home-town hit from a self-financed record.

Gospel in the community is not always the same as gospel on the big shows or on nationally selling records. While the fashion in radio listening and record buying may be for choirs or contemporary performers, all styles of gospel music coexist within the community. Unlike pop music, where a new fashion will banish the previous vogue, gospel's successive new developments find their own place in the structure alongside the older ones. The sheer number of grassroots performers, many highly skilled despite their anonymity, means that gospel always has a substantial pool of potential new stars. And they do not sing in vast arenas to an anonymous mass. Their venues are churches, schools, and small community centers, where they perform to the people they will meet in church on Sunday. It is a world far away from the taste manipulators and trendsetters who infest other forms of music. Gospel music continues to develop because it is not only still in touch with its community, but still belongs to it.

WOKE ME UP THIS MORNING

# 1 THE GOSPEL EVANGELISTS

*"We want to sing a song. . . ."*

The itinerant musician is a recurring figure in the history of southern African-American folk music. Traveling from town to town with only a few possessions, such singers made a living performing for tips on street corners and at social gatherings. Typically they were blues singers, and the history of the blues contains more than enough footloose minstrels to validate the stereotype. But not all were singing blues. A number used the same instruments—usually guitar or piano—as the blues players, performed in a similar style, and sang religious songs. The need to make a living was common to all such performers, secular or sacred, but the religious singers also had another motivation: they wanted to "spread the word," evangelizing in song (and sometimes speech) their fundamentalist Christian faith. A very few such singers, male and female, still exist today, playing their songs and testifying on sidewalks or in public places, mainly in the larger cities of the US. But they have no role in the music industry, which has lost interest in solo performers accompanying themselves on acoustic instruments, whether in the studio or on stage. It wasn't always that way. Religious music runs as an undercurrent throughout the formative years of jazz and blues, primarily because it was something much stronger than that in the lives of the people creating the music.

The biographies of many secular African-American musicians detail childhood church attendance and influence. Blues artists as disparate as Muddy Waters and T-Bone Walker have cited church music as an influence. "I was a good old Baptist, singing in church," Muddy Waters told James Rooney. "I got all my good moaning and trembling going on for me right out of church. Used to be in church every Sunday."[1] Two of the great pioneer Delta blues singers, Charley Patton and Eddie "Son" House, retained contact with the church throughout their lives. The strongest religious influence on the rural musicians of the South in the early years of the twentieth century came from the Baptist church, then as now the largest African-American denomination. Other major denominations were the Church of God in Christ, which was the biggest and most influential of the "sanctified" pentecostalist groups, and the Methodists.

Students of blues and gospel music have a ready-made reference library going back to the beginning of the 1920s (with a few examples from as far back as the 1890s), thanks to the recording industry's decision—for strictly commercial reasons—to issue recordings by African-Americans for African-Americans.[2] The earliest blues recordings, from 1920, were the "vaudeville" or "classic" stylings of female singers backed by jazz-oriented musicians. In 1924, the Okeh company ventured onto new ground by recording Ed Andrews, a Georgia singer who accompanied himself on guitar and sang what is now known as "country blues." His one record does not seem to have been a great success, but it charted the direction blues recording was to follow until the upheaval of the Great Depression, with rural singers sweeping the jazz-based vaudeville singers from the limelight. The advent of this style also opened the door for the religious "guitar evangelists."

The number who stepped through that door indicates that solo religious singers, although not as plentiful as blues performers, were by no means scarce. Most played in styles closely related to the blues; a number of the guitarists used the "slide" style, in which the guitar is tuned to an open chord and noted with a glass or metal object, usually a cylinder slipped over the little or ring finger. The material they performed ranged from self-composed songs to reworkings of standard hymns. Many were professional street singers. As a career, street singing is not easy. It is physically demanding, the income is erratic and seldom large, and the performer daily faces the hazards of the street, ranging from being forced to move by police to assault and theft. Religious singers would almost certainly have found it a tougher struggle than did the blues singers, whose music had a greater entertainment value. While some took to the streets primarily to proselytize their faith, most were there because they had to sing for a living. Some were hit by the Depression as it slashed employment opportunities; many suffered afflictions, which meant they could do no other work. The most common was blindness, and a disproportionate number of black folk musicians in the era were without sight. They included some of the most skilled performers—in blues, Blind Lemon Jefferson, Blind Blake, Blind Boy Fuller, and Blind Willie McTell; in religious music, Blind Willie Johnson, Blind Gary Davis, Blind Joe Taggart, and Arizona Dranes.

Dranes, from Fort Worth, Texas, was twenty-one years old in April 1926, when she made her first recordings. She was already well established in the Church of God in Christ around Dallas-Fort Worth, and her raggy piano style and impassioned singing later had a widespread influence on the church's music. Joe Taggart, a street singer, was playing around Greenville, South Carolina, when he was first recorded, in November 1926. Like a number of blind singers, Taggart employed a sighted youngster who helped him navigate his way around the streets. His "lead boy" during the mid-1920s was Joshua White, who would later record as a blues singer—he also recorded some religious material— before crossing over to a wider audience via the folk music boom of the late 1940s. White made a boyhood career of leading blind singers, starting in 1922 when John Henry "Big Man" Arnold paid White's mother four dollars a week for her eight-year-old son's services. He traveled as far as Florida with Arnold, but was back in Greenville in 1924 when he joined Joe Taggart.[3] When Taggart recorded in Chicago in 1928 and 1929, White played second guitar and sang with him.

Taggart's street repertoire and the recordings he made under his own name were exclusively religious. He would reportedly play blues at parties, and in 1928 made two blues recordings under the name Blind Joe Amos. But his first recordings clearly show his familiarity with the church and indicate a commitment to it. "Sing, church, sing," he interjects before each chorus of "I'll Be Satisfied," suggesting that he was used to singing before a congregation which was expected to join in, or that he wanted to create this effect on his recording. The introduction to "I Shall Not Be Removed"—the first appearance on record of the song that was to become an anthem of the civil rights struggle—gives a clearer indication of his religious conviction. "We want to sing a song this afternoon," he says, "which should be the testimony of every true Christian. Not one of those who have attached their name to the church roll, went into the water a dry sinner and come out a wet sinner, but one that have been really regenerated." Although Taggart was a competent guitarist, he and his wife, Emma, sing their harmonized song without accompaniment, another pointer to a (probably Baptist) church background.[4]

A month after Taggart made his first recordings, Vocalion recorded Rev. Edward W. Clayborn. Biographically, Clayborn is an even more shadowy figure than Taggart; nothing is known about him apart from the suggestion that he may have been from Alabama.[5] His first record sold well, and was re-pressed several times. On one side was Clayborn's version of the popular "The Gospel Train Is Coming"; on the other was the probably self-composed "Your Enemy Cannot Harm You (But Watch Your Close Friend)." This song, which bases its cynical view of human relationships on Judas Iscariot's betrayal of Christ, was enough of a success to prompt two further Clayborn songs on the theme. Clayborn's repertoire was a mixture of well-known songs and moralistic warnings. Popular themes are found in "Let Jesus Lead You," "Bye and Bye [sic] When the Morning Comes," "Then We'll Need That True Religion," and a version of "I Shall Not Be Moved." The titles of his homilies speak for themselves. As well as the friendship trilogy, they include "Let That Lie Alone," "Everybody Ought To Treat Their Mother Right," "Men Don't Forget Your Wives for Your Sweethearts" and "The Wrong Way to Celebrate Christmas" (by "roaming the streets and drinking their soul away" instead of going to church).[6] Clayborn's label credit was The Guitar Evangelist (Rev. Edward W. Clayborn)—later reversed to Rev. Edward W. Clayborn (The Guitar Evangelist)—which gave historians and collectors the generic name now commonly used to describe self-accompanied folk-style religious singers.

Judged purely on performance standards, Clayborn was not best-seller material. His singing was almost dispassionate, and he handicapped himself by recording all his songs in a "Spanish" open guitar tuning, which means that every one of his thirty recordings is in the key of A. He used a rigid alternating bass, overlaid with skillful treble-string slide playing, from which he detracted by ignoring all chord changes in his songs, producing striking discords in the guitar passages and at times forcing his voice well off the melodic beaten track. But to the original buyer of his paper-sleeved 78 rpm records—and to anyone listening to him in person—the nuances of performing technique were secondary to what the songs were saying. Clayborn might never have made a chord (apart from the open-string tonic) on his guitar, but the listener empathized when he sang, "You may search the whole world over / But it's hard to find a true friend." His bass line was relentlessly metronomic, but it didn't detract from the warning: "If you don't want to get in trouble / You better let that liar alone."

By 1926, recording companies were casting their nets over the South for rural blues performers. They had no real idea of what would sell, so anyone judged competent (and some who strained even the most liberal interpretation of this requirement) would have two or four songs recorded, pressed and put on the market. If they sold, the artist would be recalled to make more recordings. The success of Taggart and Clayborn's recordings showed that a market for "down home" religious recordings existed, so between 1927 and 1930 the industry applied the same "try it and see" approach to sacred music. A number of guitar evangelists were among those tested. From the streets of Memphis came A. C. Forehand and his blind wife, Mamie. Atlanta produced Luther Magby's hard-edged singing and harmonium accompaniment, combining the sounds of church and street. William and Versey Smith were a husband-and-wife team whose shrill-edged driving style and anachronistic material—one of their four 1927 recordings was about the sinking of the Titanic in 1912, and another exhorted listeners to "help the boys come home" from World War I—bespoke tough years of street singing.[7] Other guitar evangelists of the era included the probably pseudonymous Rev. I. B. Ware, Blind Benny Paris and his un-named wife from Georgia, Blind Willie Harris from New Orleans, Blind Willie Davis, Eddie Head, Mother McCollum, Sister Cally Fancy, and Lonnie McIntorsh.[8] None had more than half a dozen songs issued.

Two of the best-selling 1920s soloists came from Texas. Washington Phillips accompanied himself on the dulceola, an invention patented in 1902 which attached a keyboard to a zither-style frame.[9] Phillips is another biographical blank; although he is solo and self-accompanied, his gentle tenor and restrained accompaniments do not suggest a street singer.[10] The opposite is true of Blind Willie Johnson, whose driving guitar style and strong (often artificially deepened) singing were ideal for his street-singing career, which by 1927 had taken him from his small hometown of Marlin, Texas, to Dallas. Phillips and Johnson are artists whose material found favor with listeners of their time and those of forty and more years later. Johnson's dazzling slide guitar technique places him among the best of the pre-war instrumentalists, sacred or secular, while Phillips's flowing ethereal sound has a more cerebral but equally universal appeal. The Depression ended both men's recording careers. Phillips left eighteen recordings, four from his last session unreleased. Johnson left thirty songs, all issued.[11] Phillips vanished into obscurity; Willie Johnson lived the rest of his life in Beaumont, Texas, playing on the street and for church occasions. He died of pneumonia around 1949.

Virtually all the guitar evangelists were from the South, and little to nothing is now known about most of them. Some, such as Joe Taggart, the unrecorded "Big Man" Arnold, and Willie Johnson, traveled; most seem to have played mainly around their home areas. In most cases it is not even known to which church they belonged. Blind Willie Johnson apparently worshipped with the Baptists and the Church of God in Christ at different times in his life; Washington Phillips's astringent criticisms of church leaders ("The Church Needs Good Deacons"), poor parenting ("Train Your Child") and the fragmentation of the church ("Denomination Blues") point to a fundamentalist background. But virtually all the religious singers held to a faith which enabled them to spurn the potentially greater rewards of secular music. A rare portrait of one such singer is found in Rev. Charles Walker's biography of gospel songwriter Lucie E. Campbell Williams, when he tells how she came to write the popular "Something Within" in 1919:

> The song was dedicated to a blind gospel singer named Connie Rosemond, who inspired it. Mr Rosemond customarily played his guitar on Beale Street, and people put coins in his little cup and wished him well. Miss Lucie had come to the fish market to purchase some fish. There sat Connie Rosemond, playing hymns and spirituals, as was his custom. It was winter—cold, damp, rainy. Mr Rosemond's feet were wrapped in burlap bags as he sat and played. Some of the neighborhood men came out of the bar and listened to the musician play and sing. One of them called to Mr Rosemond . . . "Hey Connie! I'll give you five dollars to play 'Caledonia' or some other blues," and Mr Rosemond replied, "Oh, no, I can't do that." The man's partner taunted him. Connie Rosemond stood his ground and responded again, "I can't do that; all I know is that there is something within." Campbell, witnessing this scene, was taken with Rosemond's conviction and the image of having "something within." It moved her to write the hymn that brought her to national attention as a gospel hymnodist.[12]

At the 1919 National Baptist Convention in Memphis, Lucie Campbell introduced "Something Within," as well as Blind Connie Rosemond, who sang it to the convention. Eight years later, in June 1927, he recorded it, accompanying himself on piano rather than the guitar he was playing when Lucie Campbell first saw him.[13]

Singers' attitudes towards secular material were to a degree shaped by their denomination. Even today, many Baptists will acknowledge listening to and enjoying blues, while members of the Church of God in Christ (COGIC) are more likely to reject what was once known as "the devil's music." But if the Church of God in Christ was theologically more conservative than many other denominations, its attitude to music in church was liberal. Its founder, Bishop Charles Harrison Mason, adopted the "why should the Devil have all the good tunes?" philosophy attributed to Salvation Army founder General William Booth, and encouraged musical backings to church music at a time when the Baptists were still opposed to it. COGIC performances were also more uptempo and fiery, a trend often mirrored in solo performances.

The wall between blues and religious song was by no means impenetrable in the 1920s and 1930s. Very few sacred artists ventured into the blues field; Blind Joe Taggart (alias Blind Joe Amos) is one exception, and it has long been suspected that two unissued and untitled songs recorded by "Blind Texas Marlin" may be Blind Willie Johnson, because they were recorded immediately after one of his 1928 sessions and because he came from Marlin, Texas. But a number of 1920s and 1930s blues singers recorded sacred material, both in rural and in vaudeville styles. The first recordings made by one of the stars of the 1920s, Blind Lemon Jefferson, were the religious standards "I Want To Be Like Jesus In My Heart" and "All I Want Is That Pure Religion." They were not his first issued record; the Paramount label held on to them for about ten months, issuing them in October 1926 under the pseudonym Deacon L. J. Bates. This was a common device, presumably used to aid sales of the records to religious buyers who might shun sacred material by blues singers. Charley Patton became Elder J. J. Hadley, and Blind Boy Fuller became Brother George and His Sanctified Singers, a name also used for Brownie McGhee after Fuller's death in 1941. For the Atlanta singer Robert Hicks, the process was reversed. His blues songs were issued under his nickname, Barbecue Bob, so when he recorded two religious songs in 1927, they were issued under his proper name.

The effectiveness of these "noms de disc" is doubtful, as the singers camouflaged in this way had well-known and distinctive styles. And many singers combined blues and sacred recording without disguising their identity. Booker White's first session, in 1930, produced titles as disparate as "Women Shootin' Blues" (which was not issued) and "I Am In the Heavenly Way" (which was). Two records were issued from the session, one sacred, one blues, both under the name Washington White. (The singer's full name was Booker T. Washington White; he later became known as Bukka White.) Charley Patton continued to record religious songs, and the Elder J. J. Hadley disguise was dropped after one issue. Bessie Smith recorded "On Revival Day" (subtitled "A Rhythmic Spiritual") and "Moan Mourners." Smith's approach to the songs differs little from her blues style, and both—especially "On Revival Day"—edge towards being burlesques. However, biographer Chris Albertson notes that Smith grew up in a religious household, and quotes a contemporary, drummer Zutty Singleton, describing her as "real close to God, very religious. . . . That's why her blues seemed almost like hymns." Guitarist Danny Barker spoke of "a similarity between what she was doing and what those [southern] preachers and evangelists did."[14]

Others who recorded sacred and secular songs included John Hurt, Skip James, Brownie McGhee, Frankie Jaxon, Sara Martin, Memphis Minnie (under the transparent pseudonym Gospel Minnie), Blind Willie McTell, and John Estes. Virtually all these singers had exposure to the church somewhere in their backgrounds, but could seldom sing religious material in public performance, as it would usually be inappropriate for the occasion. Recording enabled them to place their religious music before a wide audience, bridging the gap between blues and sacred—and presumably gaining them some community approval for so doing. Says researcher Portia Maultsby: "Many blues performers received their musical training in the Black church. This, coupled with their religious beliefs, motivated many to include religious songs in their repertoire. Generally, these songs were not performed in public, but were recorded and sold in the Black community. Thus, the religious message of the bluesmen was heard by all—whether churchgoer or not."[15]

Some singers, while never abandoning blues, had a continuing relationship with the church. They included Charley Patton, Son House, Skip James and Blind Willie McTell, a singer and twelve-string guitarist from Atlanta. McTell recorded extensively from 1927 until 1949 (with a final, privately recorded session in 1956); from 1935 on, his recordings include sacred songs. One was "Ain't It Grand To Be a Christian," which he also performed in church. His cousin, Horace McTear, told David Evans: "He could really sing them church songs. We'd carry him to church, and he really sung for them in church and everybody was getting happy. He'd sing one song every time I'd carry him to church. He loved to go to church. He'd go there and he'd sing. He sang a song about 'Ain't it grand to be a Christian, won't it be grand?' He'd sing that, and oh man, there'd be some preaching then."[16]

One leading sacred performer who started as a blues player was Blind Gary Davis, a guitarist of awe-inspiring skill who in his later years became one of the most widely known guitar evangelists. In July 1935, Davis went to New York as part of a trio assembled by white talent scout J. B. (James Baxter) Long, who ran a store in Durham, North Carolina. The other two were bluesmen—guitarist, and singer Blind Boy Fuller and washboard player, guitarist, and singer George Washington, nicknamed Bull City Red or Oh Red. All three were Durham-based street singers making their first visit to a recording studio.[17] Davis was probably also meant to be a bluesman—the first two songs he recorded, "Cross and Evil Woman" and "I'm Throwing Up My Hand" were blues. But by 1935, he was a Baptist convert, and was replacing his blues repertoire with a religious one. The remaining thirteen titles he made, including a guitar backing to George Washington's singing of "I Saw the Light," were all religious,[18] and it seems likely that this was his idea, not J. B. Long's or the American Recording Company's. Davis did not record again until 1945. He and Long had a disagreement over the money he was paid for the 1935 session, but also, blues singer Willy Trice recalled, "Mr Long didn't take him back on account of . . . Gary wanted to play spirituals."[19]

The most sophisticated and successful of the guitar evangelists was Rosetta Tharpe, daughter of traveling Church of God in Christ evangelist Katie Bell Nubin. Like Gary Davis, Tharpe in her early days used a powerful metal-bodied National resonator guitar; like Davis, her guitar playing was aggressive and skillful, with strong blues overtones; like Davis, she started her recording career in the 1930s. But there the similarities end. Davis's records sold poorly, and he continued his life as a street singer, moving to live and work in New York in 1944. Tharpe's bouncy melodies, instrumental skill and worldly performance style took her from playing holiness churches with her mother to international gospel stardom.

The guitar evangelists were never a particularly strong force in commercial gospel music, and as tastes and styles changed after World War II, they became more of a minority. But good performers were still around. One of the best was Rev. Utah Smith, a Church of God in Christ minister from Shreveport, Louisiana, whose travels took him over much of the United States. He was first recorded in New York in June 1944, singing "God's Mighty Hand" and his theme song, "I Want Two Wings"; the songs were label-credited to Rev. Utah Smith (The Traveling Evangelist). Accompanying himself with flashy guitar pyrotechnics on an electric instrument (which he started using in 1942), Smith produced a powerful sound. In performance, he played the guitar behind his head and between his legs, while the notes showered from his fretboard with dramatic shifts between treble and bass. He did not record again until 1953, when he did a session for the Checker label during a visit to Chicago. He made eight tracks, though only two, including another version of "I Want Two Wings," were released. Smith had his own church in New Orleans, the Two Wing Temple, and soon after the Chess sessions, he issued two songs—"Glory To Jesus, I'm Free" and a third version of "I Want Two Wings"—on his own Two Wing Temple label.[20]

The 1950s brought the first sign of another factor that was ultimately to have an influence over the performing and recording careers of a number of guitar evangelists. The urban folk music boom, which had started in the 1940s as a predominantly left-wing phenomenon, brought white audiences to hear black performers. Early beneficiaries of this were blues performers Huddie Ledbetter, Josh White, Brownie McGhee, Sonny Terry—and, a little later, Blind Gary Davis. In 1954, Davis, who was playing the streets of Harlem for donations from passers-by, recorded eight songs for the pioneer folk music label Stinson, accompanied by harmonica virtuoso Sonny Terry.[21] Technically, the recordings are poor, but the album exposed Davis to a new audience of mainly white, college-based, folk music fans. It was an audience that was to increase dramatically over the next decade, and Davis acquired elder statesman status as an original oracle in a field dominated by imitators. In 1960 and 1961, he recorded for Bluesville, another early label set up to sell American folk music—mainly blues—to a predominantly white audience.[22] His Bluesville albums are easily the best work of his folk era, but he continued recording until shortly before his death in 1972 at age seventy-six.

Since the 1960s, most guitar evangelists who have made it on to commercially distributed records have done so on labels aimed at the white folk and collector market. In 1961, Philadelphia street singer

Blind Connie Williams recorded a mixture of blues and religious songs which eventually appeared on the Testament label in 1974. Williams told Pete Welding he sang only "spirituals" on the street, partly because he enjoyed singing them, but mainly because "the police rarely would bother him if he confined himself to this sort of material."[23] From Americus, Georgia, came Rev. Pearly Brown, another blind singer and guitarist who was recorded in 1961 and again in 1974.[24] Former Library of Congress folklorist Alan Lomax recorded several religious singers during a 1959 trip through the South;[25] in 1975, the Advent label issued a field-recorded "survey of rural black religious music."[26] This included guitar evangelists, the most striking being Willard Artis ("Blind Pete") Burrell, of Bogalusa, Louisiana, singing over delicate high-capoed open-tuned guitar playing.

While these artists were devout Christians, they were not being hailed by their new audience because of their religious convictions. This was an audience interested, in the words of British writer Viv Broughton, "in the music, but not the message."[27] The performers reacted to this in different ways. Gary Davis was occasionally persuaded to resurrect some of the blues and pre-blues pieces he had learned fifty years earlier, although these feature much more in his recordings than they did in his concert performances.[28] But to most performers, the songs and the performance remain spiritual, whatever the audience or the venue. During the 1989 New Orleans Jazz and Heritage Festival, Clarence Fountain, veteran lead singer of the Blind Boys of Alabama, stood on the stage of Tipitina's, a popular blues and rock venue. "We haven't come here to bring Jesus to you," he proclaimed as two bars served liquor and cigarette smoke hazed the lights. "He's already here!"

The folk boom of the 1950s and 1960s also created an interest in the original recordings of older singers who were being "rediscovered" and thrust onto concert stages in the United States and Europe. This interest led to the issuing of albums containing scratchy dubs of the 78 rpm records issued in the 1920s and 1930s. The accent was on blues, but religious singers also appeared, spearheaded by the ones who sounded most like blues singers. In this way, Blind Willie Johnson, Blind Joe Taggart, Rev. Edward Clayborn and many other lesser figures found a posthumous international market, often marketed as "holy blues." By the mid-1980s, reissue albums of gospel music from the 1940s and 1950s were also appearing. The main focus was on quartets, but guitar evangelists of the era were also presented.

They include some stunning performers. From the early 1950s came the swinging slide guitar and strident singing of Sister O. M. Terrell. Willie Mae Williams, another slide guitarist, was represented by two 1949 recordings, her entire recorded legacy.[29] The early 1960s recordings of Rev. Lonnie Farris, originally issued in Los Angeles as 45 rpm single releases on his own Farris label, made a brief appearance on a limited edition reissue in the 1970s, and have since been reissued on vinyl and compact disc.[30] The impassioned singing and playing of Rev. Charlie Jackson, first issued on singles by New Orleans preacher Rev. Robert Booker on his Booker label, came out again on a tape produced in Scotland in 1988.[31] All these soloists were guitarists, with a surprising number playing slide guitar or even, like Lonnie Farris, the Hawaiian-style lap steel guitar. But one of the hits with the new nonreligious gospel audience was a harmonica-playing group credited on its sole early 1950s record as Elder R. Wilson and Family. The performances were vibrant, dynamic, and exciting; the artists, like so many other evangelist singers, were complete mysteries.

# ELDER ROMA WILSON

*"We were having a good time..."*

ROMA Wilson never intended to become a mystery man, and nothing in his appearance, his manner or his life offers any hint of his years as an international enigma. He's a working man and a preacher with a talent for singing religious songs and playing them on the harmonica. It was this ability which created the mystery. In the early 1950s, the Philadelphia-based Gotham Record Corporation issued a 78 rpm disc credited to "Elder R. Wilson and Family." Both songs on the record were religious, and featured a single singer accompanied by three or four harmonicas. In 1968, the A side of the disc, "Lily of the Valley," appeared (correctly retitled

*Elder Roma Wilson on stage at the Northeast Mississippi Blues and Gospel Festival in Holly Springs, Mississippi.*

"Stand By Me") on the Blues Classics label, an offshoot of Californian Chris Strachwitz's Arhoolie label set up to reissue early blues recordings.[1] The anthology album's notes gave brief details on all the performers featured, but offered virtually nothing on Elder R. Wilson, saying only that his record was made in Detroit in about 1949 and was "one of the most unusual and striking of post-war religious recordings."

Eventually a few details emerged. The "R" stood for Roma; the harmonica players were Walter Mitchell and Robert and Howard Richard. Then Mitchell and the Richards disappeared from the plot; the backing musicians were Elder Wilson's sons. But when another Gotham track was issued in England on a 1992 compact disc,[2] it seemed even less was known about Wilson and his recording career. It had been thought that he was recorded in Detroit; now clues offered by a Gotham master tape suggested it might have been Philadelphia. Roma Wilson was not able to answer the questions. He didn't know about the reissue albums and their biographical blanks. He didn't know he'd had a record issued in the early 1950s. He didn't even know he'd been recorded.

Forty years after the creation of the mystery, Roma Wilson lives in Red Hills, a small settlement a couple of miles from Blue Springs, which is near New Albany in Union County, in northeast Mississippi. His low-slung, gray-painted brick house is built behind two pines on a large expanse of lawn. Family photographs adorn the walls of the living room; more are on and inside a glass-fronted cabinet against one wall. Incongruous among the glossy color prints is a small creased black-and-white snapshot of a much younger Roma Wilson, dapper in a double-breasted suit and posing with a harmonica to his lips. Today, the thin moustache is gray, matching the receding hair. The eyes look through spectacles, and the face bears the lines and wrinkles of a man well into his sixties. Elder Wilson is eighty-one. And he mows all that lawn himself, with a hand mower.

"It doesn't take me hardly a little over a day if I get out early and just keep at it. You see, I was saved young, and I always took good care of myself. I'm just blessed. I never served but one week in the hospital in my life, and that wasn't serious. Apart from that, I've never been under the care of a doctor. I mostly just use herbal medicines—sometimes I go out and get plants and things. I was raised up that way. My father was half Creek Indian, and he did that a lot. So I just believe in that and watch what I eat and how I carry myself, and that keeps me pretty healthy. My father was ninety-two, and he never had a day's sickness. But then he fell from a high step and broke some bones in his neck. He didn't live too long after that.

"I was born in Hickory Flat, before you get to Holly Springs on Highway 78. Hickory Flat, Benton County, Mississippi. On December 22, 1910. And I was raised back there at a little place called Myrtle [a few miles closer to New Albany than to Hickory Flat], then in New Albany. That's where I was raised up until I was a grown man. But before that time, my father . . . he was poor and he tried to make a living for us all by working in sawmills and farming in the red hills. He couldn't make much from that because the land was too sterile. But he did the best he could in bringing us up. This was out in the rurals. We had to walk to school, I guess a couple of miles, and walk back home every day. And sometimes we wouldn't have nothing but cornbread and molasses in a bottle to carry for our lunch at school. We were just that poor. Not like it is today, children having the advantages they have today. Buses to carry 'em, and parents having plenty for 'em

to eat, plenty clothing for 'em to wear and shoes for 'em to wear. We
didn't come up that way. Sometimes, with so many of us—there was
ten of us children, six boys and four girls—my father could hardly buy
enough shoes for us during the winter. If he bought one pair, that was
just about it. And if those shoes busted up . . . I have walked on frozen
ground barefooted.

"Then in March, we had to go in the fields. We didn't have the chance
for an education like the children have now. School didn't last too long.
It would start mostly when people were through picking cotton. That
may be in November. When winter was over and March come, we had
to go right back in the fields, go to work. Cutting briars back off ditch
banks and cutting cornstalks. Didn't have a chance for education. And
so that's the way we came up. I try to sense it into the young people
now. Y'all have a golden opportunity, and they oughta try and make all
out of it that they can.

"When I was ten, my mother left home. Just ran away. Well, she ran
away, really, with another man. My father was awful good to her, but
it just seemed like the other women around her were coaxing her into
it. My father did the best he could, but eventually, when I was fifteen,
he broke up housekeeping and put my two youngest sisters and me
[Roma was the second youngest in the family] with the oldest ones that
were married. Then we had to get out and do work to help pay for our
board—we didn't just want to stay with our brothers for nothing. So
we couldn't attend school like we should have. At fifteen years of age, I
had to start working for myself. I was working on the railroad, helping
lay steel and putting crossties under the track and all of that. And also
I was logging, down in Lafayette County [immediately south of Union
County], hauling logs, working at a mill. And I had to do the best that
I could from that age up until I got married. But before I got married,
I lived with a gentleman and a lady, they didn't have any children and
they wanted me to live with them. She was a retired schoolteacher, and
she taught me up until my nineteenth year. I was in the fifth grade when
she took me up and started teaching me. She recited me at home and
made me study my books. And so I guess I made a good seventh or
eighth grade. I got married when I was nineteen. My wife's name was
Birdie, Birdie Wilson.

"I started blowing harmonica at age fifteen or sixteen. At that time,
there were many harmonica players, just young folks together. We played
for fun and for amusement. We were on farms and working on farms,

and that's the biggest amusement we had then. We didn't know anything to play much but just tunes, not songs but just tunes, while we found out how to get sounds out of the harmonica. It wasn't music, but just tunes, just . . . I'd say, a noise. They called it 'Lost John,' and there wasn't no singing in it.3 Just an old tune on the harmonica. We learned from the older harmonica players before us. There was some old men, about fifty years old, that played harmonica. But that's all they would play, just tunes. Something that would keep people in motion. They would have these old breakdown suppers, and they'd be out there circling and just making that noise. But then after I knew where the notes were on the harmonica, I went to practicing on church songs. And when I started on church songs and began to play so well, I began to play in churches here and there. On different things. Like we had anniversaries and concerts to raise money to help the church. And so from then on I have been playing up until this time.

"I was saved in 1928. Called to preach at seventeen. I started out as an evangelist. At that time, we used to build what they called a bush harbor. Get four good poles and cut 'em off, dig post holes and put 'em [the poles] down in the ground. Then lay poles in them across the other way and build something like a pen. We'd cut bushes and throw them up until it became a solid roof. Then we'd put seats in there, planks across blocks, and we'd get under. Out of the sun in the summer time. It was about the size of a room. There were lots of people living in the country then, and they just loved to come to the bush harbor service. People would get saved under those bush harbors. And that's where I first started. We had bush harbors because we didn't have many buildings then.4

"After that, I was called over to Guntown settlement [fifteen miles north of New Albany], and we started meeting from house to house. People would take all the furniture out of one room, and we'd put in planks on blocks for seats. I'd be preaching in those rooms. Sometimes it would be so crowded people would be standing all around the walls and out the doors and looking in through the windows. We would have a little table for a pulpit, or sometimes just a sewing machine. Have a Bible laying on a sewing machine. And people would be getting saved in there. Oh, they'd be getting saved by the dozens. Lots of people got saved under my ministry.

"I started with the Glorious Church of God in Christ. But after it deteriorated and went out—it didn't last very long—I united with the

Church of the Living God the Pillar and the Ground of Truth. Today, it's all over the country. But in those days, when I went to Arkansas [in 1937], it wasn't there. So I united with the Church of God in Christ because it was the only holiness church there I knew of. Then, when I came back here to New Albany [in 1976], I found the original people I was with, and I just came back to my original church, the Church of the Living God.

"From Guntown, I went to . . . well, the whole state of Mississippi, really. I just mostly went round all the missions and the churches that we had in the state at that time, which was very few. Then afterwards, in 1937, I moved to Arkansas. I went out there with my family. I had about five or six children at that time. I farmed in Arkansas, sawmilled some there. I always did work for my living. I was a farmer and a minister. And when the farming work was down, I went to the sawmills to work to support my family. I first lived in a little town called Madison, Arkansas. Then we went to Wynne, then to Crawfordsville, then to Blytheville [all in northeast Arkansas]. During my time in Arkansas, my occupation was mostly a cotton farmer. And I raised corn for my own bread, raised hogs and I raised chickens. We had to generate our own living, like chickens and hogs, cows—I had a couple of milk cows. They exempted me during the war because I was farming. And I had about seven kids.

"I was mostly on a share.[5] But one or two years I rented. I bought some mules and plows and rented. But about the time I started renting, well, things turned all so bad. Bad crop years. So I sold all my stock, shareworked one more year, and after that I quit completely. Went north, to Muskegon, Michigan. That was in 1950. See, I'd always find somewhere I could make a living for my family. And I depended so much on my own labor, so if it wasn't good here, I'd just move where I could find other jobs to do. Just dependent on my own self. So [in Muskegon] I worked in a foundry where they made automobile cylinder heads and things like that. I was working where they made cylinder heads, on the shakeout chain, where I had to pull 'em off, red hot heads, put 'em behind me on that rack, then shake the sand out of the mold. That kept me jumping around all day. Of course I was still in the ministry. I wasn't pastoring, but I was having revivals at various churches.

"By that time, a lot of my children were big enough to work in the harvest. So they went picking cherries, picking cucumbers and things like that, 'way up in north Michigan. Then when the harvest ran out, we moved to Detroit [in 1952]. I worked in the foundry there. And I was pastoring a church. But I was working for my living. I never have relied on the people for my support. I'd always tell the people [in his church]: 'Now, whatever you want to give me, I appreciate it. But I'm going to tell you this. I'm a working preacher. I don't want my biscuit in your pocket. 'Cause you can take it away from me when you get ready. I make my own biscuit. 'Cause I work for myself.' "

*Use of the harmonica is not widespread in gospel music, but it is by no means rare. On record, it was used as early as 1924 by Sam Jones, a one-man band from Cincinnati, who recorded as Stovepipe No 1. (The name was taken from one of his instruments, a length of wide pipe which amplified and deepened the buzzing hum of the kazoo wired inside it.) He recorded sacred and secular songs, accompanied by his own guitar, stovepipe, and a harmonica that was suspended in a rack around his neck so he could play it and his guitar together.[6] The same arrangement was used by Blind Roger Hays, a New Orleans street singer who recorded two songs with guitar and harmonica in 1928.[7] In Memphis, the Holy Ghost Sanctified Singers and the blind street singer A. C. Forehand used harmonica in their accompaniments, as did Elder Richard Bryant's Sanctified Singers from Mississippi. In 1942, Library of Congress collector Alan Lomax recorded an elderly blind singer, Turner Junior Johnson, after chancing on him playing harmonica and singing in the streets of Clarksdale, Mississippi.[8] Johnson recorded sacred songs, accompanied by harmonica, as well as folk tales and a couple of blues, which, he told Lomax, he played only because they made money for him. "I get out here on the street and play good Christian songs and the folks'll pass me on by," he said.[9] One striking example of the use of harmonica in more modern gospel can be heard on a version of "Holy Ghost" made in San Francisco, probably in the 1970s, by "Rev. Billingsley and His Gospel Harmonica—With the Christian Love Singers of Oakland" and issued on a small local label. Billingsley's style is a fusion of country and the more driving sound developed by Chicago blues harmonica players from the 1950s, and the overall accompaniment, with electric guitar and bass, organ and drums, owes much to the blues.*

*Roma Wilson played his harmonica for churches and at church-related functions. While the family was in Arkansas, some of his children followed their father's example and took up the instrument. When they moved to Detroit, Roma, Robert Lee, Clyde, and Sammy Lee went on the city streets, performing their music for tips. Sammy Lee was thirteen, Clyde was eleven, and Robert Lee was nine.*

"Robert Lee was just a little bitty fellow. When he was blowing, you could pick him up in your arms and he would keep blowing. The people were so amused. We'd go up and down the streets, on vacant lots and so forth, and we'd have such crowds around us that sometimes the police would run up. They wouldn't know what was happening. They'd jump out of the car and run through the crowd. When they saw what was happening, they'd stay and listen. They would say to me, 'Are those your children?' I'd say, 'Yessir.' 'Well, don't let them get hurt.' I'd say, 'Ain't nobody going to bother them.' Because if anybody came up disorderly, the people would just take 'em and make 'em leave.

"So we played on the streets a lot. And the people would give us good money. We didn't ask for anything. Just had a cigar box wired to the amplifier. Had a hole cut in the lid and people would put money in it. Sometimes on a Saturday, we would gain three hundred dollars or more in a couple of hours. That's true! Then sometimes the boys would take off by themselves. They'd come back with their little pockets full of money that people gave them, sometimes a couple of hundred dollars. They'd put it in their mother's lap and go back out again. Yeah, we were having a good time. A good time!

"There was a fellow named Joe Battle and he had a record shop, 'way down at the lower end of Hastings Street.[10] And we would pass his shop, going up and down Hastings Street. One day, he called us in and told us he wanted to hear a little bit of what we were doing. So we played a little bit, and he had a tape going and he taped it and played it back. Just a little bit of, I think, two songs. One was 'Up Above My Head.' We passed again, and he called us in again. He said, 'I just want to hear y'all again.' Then he said, 'Boys, if you just had a little music [other accompaniment] in there, a little drum or something tapping along with you, y'all could make a good record.' That was the last time. He didn't ever let us know that he was going to record us. We just went on and we never did go back there any more. And we didn't even know he'd recorded us."

*Obviously, Roma and his sons knew they had been taped. But they didn't regard it as a proper recording session. And they didn't know that the music they played so Battle could "hear y'all" was soon to be sold to Ivin Ballen, owner of the Gotham label. Battle recorded six songs from the Wilsons— "Lily of the Valley" ("Stand By Me"), "Better Get Ready," "Gonna Wait Til a Change Comes," "This Train," "Got Just What I Wanted" and "Troubles Everywhere" ("Up Above My Head"). Ballen issued "Lily of the Valley" and "Better Get Ready." The other tracks remained unheard until they appeared on a 1983 German reissue album.*[11] *Roma Wilson says he found out they existed when he performed at the New Orleans Jazz and Heritage Festival in 1991.*

"A fellow from Germany said to me, 'You know, I've got an album here with your songs on it.' I said, 'You have?' That album had my songs on it, with a whole lot of blues singers. I was took off my feet! Joe Battle misrepresented me, and I didn't even know it until I saw the album.* But sometimes now I play it and listen to it. My boys, my little boys and myself. And I didn't even know about it. But I was talking to my daughter in Detroit about it, and she said, 'He didn't only do you bad.' She said he [Battle] would slip around the churches and steal what they were doing—singing or praying—and he'd put it on records. He'd go in like he was listening just for amusement, you know, like people do with a tape recorder. Then he'd go on back to his shop and make it up. We didn't know what was going on.[12]

"I stayed in Detroit until 1976. I was working construction work with my son. But then my wife died and my children were all grown, so I came back here to Mississippi, where I was raised up. Then in '77, I married again. See, this lady—her name is Esther Ruth, she was a McCoy—she had lost her husband and I had lost my wife. She had known me from the beginning of my ministry here when I was real young. But we had gotten away from each other. So when I came back and she heard about me, she came up to where I was conducting a service, and we found we had known each other 'way back then. So in just a little while, we got married. She's an ordained elder in the church also, a minister too. She was an ordained elder before I came back here.

"So now I'm presiding elder, and we just go from church to church. I have nine churches that I visit once every three months, every quarter. I

---

*In notes to *Religious Music—Solo and Performance,* Library of Congress LBC-15 (U.S.; vinyl; 1978), which reissues *Better Get Ready,* Richard Spottswood writes: "In 1969, Mack McCormick talked informally by telephone with Elder Wilson. . . . Wilson said that in 1948, he had moved from New Albany, Mississippi, to Detroit with his family. Not long afterwards, a friend put him in touch with someone on Hastings Street named Joe. . . . Wilson made some tests of gospel songs which he sang to the accompaniment of four harmonicas—his own and those of his three young sons. Wilson was never contacted again, and he was amazed when McCormick told him that a record of two of his songs had been released."

go round and make investigations. There's twenty-two questions I have to ask—information about how many members have been received and how many have been baptized and so forth. Then when our state meeting convenes in July, I carry them a complete record of all our churches. I've been presiding elder for . . . it's been about three years now. See, being a minister in this church and one of the oldest, with more information to give than anyone else in it . . . they picked me because I had information and because I've been in the ministry for so long, and so I'm qualified. So they made me presiding elder. And it was also to give me an easy job without having to be constantly preaching so long. See, I sing a lot, too, and play the harmonica. So I don't have to preach so much when I go round the churches unless I want to. I still do preach, but not as much as I used to. The biggest church I have has about 255 members, at Amory. Then the next one has maybe 150 or 160 members. Then right on down to sixty members and thirty members. They're just building, just building up." [His nine churches are spread over about one hundred miles, from Blue Mountain in the north, to Aberdeen in the south.]

*In 1989, Wilson was reunited with another face from the past. Rev. Leon Pinson, a virtually blind singer and guitarist, was living in New Albany and performing religious music. Like Wilson, Pinson played for local black churches, but he had also been "discovered" by white folk music enthusiasts, and was performing at festivals and concerts. Many of these bookings were arranged by his manager, ethnomusicologist Worth Long, from Atlanta, Georgia.*

"Now Rev. Pinson . . . I didn't know Rev. Pinson to ever preach a sermon. I asked him one day, 'When did you get to be a preacher?' He said, 'Well, they just call me Rev. Pinson. I'm a minister of music.' They were calling him 'Reverend' when I came back here and found him. I knew him from 'way back when I lived in Arkansas, in the year of '49. He came out there and he played. My children were small then; they had just started blowing harmonicas. And so he and I would be together with them and he'd be singing and playing his guitar and we'd be blowing the harmonicas. Then he came back to Mississippi and I didn't see him any more until I came back here from Detroit. He was living in Cleveland, Mississippi, at that time, and I didn't know how to get in touch with him. But when he moved back to New Albany, he found my phone number through some friends of mine up there and he called me. He told me he wanted to see me again and get with me. He said, 'I'm making tapes up by myself and selling 'em.' He said, 'Come on up and let's rehearse together some.' So I went up there to his house, and we rehearsed on the songs we play now. And they did so well we made some tapes of them. I think he made up about eleven tapes, and he said, 'I'm going to sell these tapes, and when I sell them, I'm going to give you your part of the money.' Well, I didn't think too much about it, but in a week he called me and told me, 'I done sold every one of them. Sold 'em eleven dollars each. Come on up here and get your money.' Well, that sounded so good to me and I went on up there. He said, 'Now Worth Long has heard the tapes, and he wants you to come with me to New Orleans.' I said, 'All right.' "

*The two men have traveled widely, performing in Chicago and Florida, Washington, D.C., New Orleans, and Birmingham, Alabama. Closer to home, they have played at the University of Mississippi in Oxford, at Rust College's annual Northeast Mississippi Blues and Gospel Folk Festival in Holly Springs, and at the Delta Blues Festival in Greenville, Mississippi. In 1993, Wilson's first new commercial recordings in forty years appeared, six tracks with Leon Pinson on an anthology tape, recorded during a tour that included venues in Mississippi, Louisiana, North Carolina, and Alabama.[13] Wilson's harmonica is showcased on a new version of "This Train" and on "Three Ways To Play the Harmonica," an explanation of some of the techniques he uses. He plays in a style recognizably related to the rural blues sound of which Sonny Terry is the best-known exponent, but with a more relaxed feel; the overblown treble notes which players like Terry used to create high points of tension are not a major part of Wilson's playing. Probably because he is used to playing without other accompaniment, he has a full sound, using the bass side of the harmonica and often playing chords rather than single notes. He usually plays in the "cross" style, using a harmonica in a key a fourth above that in which he is playing—a technique which makes it easier to "bend" notes, giving a more expressive sound to the harmonica. But he can also—as he demonstrates in "Three Ways To Play the Harmonica"—play "straight" style, using a harmonica in the same key as the piece being played. (Wilson refers to this as "blowing the harmonica flatly." The third style he demonstrates is a variant of the "cross" style.) In 1994, he was recorded by Arhoolie, which issued the compact disc This Train (Arhoolie ARHCD-429). It contains the six Battle tracks and fourteen new recordings, including two of Wilson playing at Johnson's*

*Chapel, Church of the Living God, in Aberdeen, Mississippi, and two vocal duets with his wife.*

"It's a great joy and amusement to me. When I blow that harmonica, there's something comes over me—the Spirit. It's within me. And I enjoy it as much as the people do. I believe what the Bible said: 'All you do, do it in the name of the Lord.' We don't do it to be seen as people. We do it because we want the folks to feel as good as we feel doing it. So everywhere I tell the people, 'Get with us, get in the spirit. We're not here to make a big show. We're doing it in the name of the Lord.' And maybe the words of a song will help somebody, lift somebody, motivate somebody. We don't have time for no blues. I don't have the blues, I only have joy. Got no blues, but we got respect for them—if people wanna play 'em, that's their business. We don't discriminate against them. But we play all gospel. See, some publishers have mistaken us, and have put in there that we have been playing . . . one lady said, 'They got y'all up there in the Oxford paper, it said y'all playing the blues.' I said, 'Well, the folks should know better than that! All the people know we don't play no blues.' What we do, we believe in doing it as unto the Lord and dedicated to him and for his purpose. But those [blues] songs are dedicated on the other side, not the spiritual side. That's all that turns us against it. We're not against the people that do it—if they want to do it, that's their business.

"And if I'm up there playing with blues singers, I'm there working. I'm working for what I'm doing and for my pay, just like if you're in a factory, working with all kinds of folk. You're there making your living. You're working, you're doing what you do. If I go to playing blues, then somebody can say, 'That old preacher playing blues!' But they can't say that because we don't do it. And I have lectured to big crowds and they have applauded me for it when I said, 'This ain't no time to have the blues, seeing the condition of the world. We need to get some of the spirit of God, and God on our side.' So if you think you're going to hear us playing the blues, you'll be disappointed.

"The same instruments that play gospel play the blues. And some of the same sounds that you make on the instruments playing gospel, they make in blues. So that's why someone in a misconception says we play from a blues background. But we don't. It's a musical background that we play from. 'Cause the same chords that play blues play gospel music. Some of the sounds and slurs maybe sound like blues. But it's not. We're playing the gospel. We're doing this as unto the Lord. So the sound we're making is all dedicated to him. To his glory. It's not only good for entertainment, but for your health. God gets in you and helps you to live strong and healthy. I tell a lot of people in church: 'You talking about old arthritis; you get enough of God in you and your limbs aren't going to be hurting you all the time.' So we hope that we could say something to change the minds of some of them [secular audiences]. But if we can't, then that's just like preaching. Don't care how you preach, you never will change some folk. Noah couldn't do it, Lot couldn't do it at Sodom and Gomorrah, Jesus couldn't do it. So we can't."

*Many of the songs Wilson sang into Joseph Von Battle's microphone with his sons playing in the background are still in his repertoire today. They encapsulate his style, which is based firmly on traditional songs, but with some Roma Wilson reworking. "Troubles Everywhere" is "Up Above My Head," which he recalls recording on the first visit to Battle's record shop; the song was presumably retitled by Battle or Ivin Ballen. One of the best-known versions is by Rosetta Tharpe. "Lily of the Valley" is another arbitrarily assigned title, for "Stand By Me," written by Charles A. Tindley and published in 1905. "This Train" is a version of the standard "This train don't carry no liars / gamblers / hypocrites, etc.," and may be based on a Rosetta Tharpe recording. The Battle recordings were obviously made with only one microphone—Roma's singing and playing are to the fore; the other three harmonicas, which provide a rhythmic foundation, are echoey and very much in the background.*[14]

"The leading harmonica that you hear in all the songs is me. My sons can only be heard in the background. That song 'This Train' is my arrangement. Of course it's been sung before, but it wasn't arranged like I play it. And that song about 'You just as well to get ready, you got to die,' I wrote all the verses of that song. I composed them myself."[15]

> You just as well to get ready,
> To meet your God on high.
> While you plan to live here,
> You better prepare to die.
> Don't let the setting of the sun,
> Catch you with your work undone.
> You just as well to get ready,
> You got to die.

You may be a rich man,
With all your silver and gold,
But this whole world full of money,
Won't save your dying soul.
You've got to be free from sin,
And have the Holy Ghost within.
Just as well to get ready,
You got to die.

"So all of those verses I wrote. I wrote it up in Detroit, Michigan, then when I came down here I just kept playing the tune and singing it. And there's one song I haven't recorded; I composed it, but I haven't been playing it yet."

Ain't it a shame, ain't it a shame,
How the people do.
The streets are full of violence,
The streets are full of crime.
Every time you turn the radio on,
It's bad news most of the time.
The white race hating the black race,
The black race hating the white,
They oughta throw their race hate down,
And walk in the gospel light.
Ain't it a shame.

Our young men are dying
On a rugged battlefield.
Mothers and fathers are losing their sons,
I know about how they feel.
Their hearts are filled with sorrow,
Their eyes are filled with tears.
This wicked fighting oughta be stopped,
That's going on through the years.
Ain't it a shame.

Fighting is not the answer,
Not ammunition and guns.
If we would all live right and turn to God,
That would put the Devil on the run.
They talk about rioting and burning,
They shouldn't be thinking of such.
They have the whole world living in fear,

Because they are killing too much.
Ain't it a shame.

"See, all of that I composed. I haven't been playing it yet,[16] but some few people have been singing it around here. And my boys made a little record of it. In Detroit. They're still in Detroit. And they still play. About four or five of them [including Clyde and Robert Lee] are in a quartet, and Sammy Lee—we call him Sam for short—he's become a minister. He's pastoring a church. They're kinda scattered now. But every once in a while they get together and sing. And when they're not together, Sam plays on his own, just like I do. Three of my daughters play piano. And I have a daughter plays the guitar. Esther. She plays with the Trumpelettes of Detroit, Michigan, and she plays like this. . . . [He mimes overhand style, played with the guitar laid face up on the lap. The style is usually associated with steel guitar playing, but a few non-steel guitarists learn to play this way, with the fingers pressing down on the strings. One prominent gospel artist who plays in this manner is Sullivan Pugh, of the Consolers. He plays standing up with his guitar on a strap around his neck, but tilts the instrument so it faces up and frets the strings from above.] She plays it that way because when she was small, when she was about nine years old, she played it like that, and when she grew up she wasn't used to putting it up the other way. And I have one grandson, he's a great organist, and another plays the drums. I have eleven children. Six boys, five girls. Must have about thirty-five grandchildren and twenty-odd great-grandchildren. And one great-great-grandchild. They're all in the North. It's been about two or three years since I've been up there, but some of them come down here every once in a while. They stay in touch, though—call me, talk to me."

*As well as looking after his nine churches, playing his music, mowing the lawn and tending his extensive vegetable garden, Roma Wilson has another occupation in his "retirement"—his own church, based in a trailer home across the road from his house. He started it when people he had pastored before he left Mississippi heard he was back in Blue Springs and wanted to rejoin his flock. Most have since drifted away, and today the little church has no formal members and no meetings schedule. Many who attend belong to the Church of the Living God. But they don't have to— Elder Wilson doesn't believe in denominations. It's not the only area where, despite his senior position in the Church of the Living God, his personal theology differs from that of the church.*

"I'm not a denomination man. I don't care if you say you're Baptist, Methodist or what you are, we're all in one body when it comes to Christ. It's the one church! This denomination is gotten up by man. The Lord has no division because of denomination. I preach for Baptists. . . . Church of God in Christ people come and worship with us. We just don't believe in the division called denomination. And neither race. White or black, it doesn't matter to us. And we don't put no assessments, no charges. Our folks [Church of the Living God], they teach tithing. But I don't stress on it too much. Jesus didn't stress too much on tithes. He just said, 'Give and it shall be given unto you; good measure, pressed down, and shaken together, and running over.'[17] So a lot of the preachers fight me on it, but when I pull up the Bible on them, they can't fault it. God never lies.

"And another thing I stress on. I see in the Acts of the Apostles that day when so many souls were added to the church, it says they had so much love for each other and cared so much that they sold their possessions and laid it at the apostles' feet to be distributed among the poor saints.[18] What kind of charity do you see like that today? You don't see none of that. You see a lot of these preachers getting thousands of dollars, another poor preacher can't hardly get a nickel. You know that ain't right. That's why they don't have me in the pulpit so much, running over Bible quotes. [He laughs; it's a light-hearted remark with a kernel of seriousness.] I must say I don't care, 'cause they ain't giving me my living nohow."

*Although his partnership with Leon Pinson has exposed him to a new audience for his music, Roma Wilson still goes out on his own to play at churches. He enjoys doing it, and it helps keep him in practice.*

"Sometimes I'll have a spell of playing at home, but not often. I have so much to be doing. But I have a good many calls from various churches for myself alone to come in and play, maybe for an anniversary or something of that kind. I don't make any charges for that. They might give me something, but I don't make any charges. I play just to keep in practice—and because I like it."

*In August 1994, Roma Wilson was awarded a National Heritage Fellowship, recognizing him as "a master traditional artist." The award, which carried a ten thousand dollar cash grant, was signed by President Bill Clinton and presented to Elder Wilson by First Lady Hillary Clinton at a ceremony in Washington, D.C.*

# REV. LEON PINSON

*"My own style, I call it . . ."*

AMONG the community-based evangelist singers who have found wider fame in the white-oriented festival and concert world, Rev. Leon Pinson is a veteran. He first played at the Smithsonian Institute's Festival of American Folklife in Washington in 1974; he's been back several times, and now has a manager and a small but steady flow of bookings at a variety of venues. But when he's at home in New Albany, he still plays most Sundays at the Union Grove Baptist Church, of which he is a member. And he still answers the call to go out and play for other small local churches.

*Rev. Leon Pinson at his home in New Albany, Mississippi.*

At seventy-three, Pinson is snowy-haired, solemn and carefully spoken. A childhood attack of meningitis left him crippled in one leg and almost blind. Six feet tall and slightly stooped, he walks with the aid of a cane. He lives alone in what he calls a "handicap" apartment on the outskirts of New Albany in the Fairground Community housing estate, and looks after himself, apart from having someone in occasionally to do housework. Prominent in his living room is his new piano, with its lid locked shut. When he wants to play the instrument, he unlocks the lid with a small key he carries in his pocket. "There's nobody here but me," he explains, "but sometimes people come in and want to play it. When that happens, I can just say, 'It's locked.' A lot of people just want to bang on it."

"I'VE lived on my own most of my life. Never have married. I used to stay with some of my people. Coming up, I lived with my brother and his wife, then I used to live with my sister and her husband while he was living. Then he passed, so I just got up and got going to myself. I came up playing gospel music. I just always liked sacred music. I never did worry about trying to play no blues or rock and roll stuff. I just played all of mine in religious style. That's what I started out on, and that's what I'm still holding out. I was born in Union County [in 1919]. There was eight of us children, and all of them have passed except my sister and me. I'm the baby, the youngest one of them, and my sister is the third child. We were raised out in a community they call St. Mary. Out in the rural. My father was a farmer, on a share. He grew cotton, sorghum, and everything. Potatoes, peanuts.

"I had meningitis when I was a baby, what they call spinal cord meningitis. I'm crippled in one leg—my right leg, it's short—and can't see well out of my eyes. I can see just . . . barely a little, just barely a little bit. Places I don't know, I don't try to go at. Not by myself. But I can go to some few little places around here [his home]. I can go out to my mailbox and come back to the house. But my eyes have been bad ever since I can remember. When I was a little boy going to school out at St. Mary . . . there was a church out there, and a little old two-room school building. We had three teachers. Two taught school in the two-roomed building. Then the principal teacher taught in the church, next to the school. And they had an organ in there, one of those old ones that you pedal with your foot. And by me not being able to see to read, she would give me a little recess and I would go out and try to play a little on the organ. That's how I came to play the piano. Just learned it myself.

"The guitar . . . well, I started out playing a little old . . . what they called David's harp, like in the Bible. It was a three-cornered thing, flat, made out of wood. It had eight strings, with the bigger ones on the long side and the little strings on the shorter side. My sister worked for some white people and they gave it to her for her little daughter. But she couldn't play it, and I got it. [The triangular David's harp is a form of psaltery; to play it, one plucks the strings or uses a small bow. It is usually tuned with a key similar to that used for a zither or an autoharp.] I'd take pliers and tighten the strings up where I wanted them. Then I'd lay it down flat on my lap and play it. I had some old scissors that had the point broken off them and I'd run them up and down the strings [in a style based on slide or steel guitar]. It mightn't be the way you're supposed to play it, but that's the way I did it. It had eight strings and all of 'em broke but three—that's when I got a little ukulele. Had four strings on it. I played it with a knife, same way as the harp. And my daddy would complement me on the guitar. He didn't play too much on his own, but he would complement me and we played that way. All sacred songs.

"I bought me a guitar in 1937 from my sister. She was working for some white people. She bought that guitar from the man she was working for to give to her little boy. And he died at the age of six, so he didn't get to use it and she let me have it. So I started out trying to learn how to play my guitar. I'd be sitting up at night sometimes . . . see, in wintertime we'd have a big fireplace there, and we'd throw a lot of sticks on there and let it burn. I'd be sitting up a lot of times when everyone had gone to bed, trying to learn how to play my guitar. Sometimes my father would wake up and say, 'Boy, why don't you put that thing down and go to bed?' I was still in my teens, 'cause my daddy died when I was about nineteen or twenty. But I just taught myself. The Good Master gave me the talent, the gift, and I just went on my own. See, I don't play nohow like the rest of the people play. I play in my own style and they play in theirs. I play by sound; 'ear' I call it. And I try to go to playing what I want to play. Make my runs and make it sing like I want it to sing. When I play slide, I play with a knife where other people use a bottleneck. Change the guitar over to what they call 'cross E.' I play with the back of my pocket knife, make a sound like somebody singing. Then I play in natural. I make some runs up and down on the guitar strings, make the guitar set a bass part while I sing. So it's two voices in a way, the guitar voice and my voice."

*"Make my runs" summarizes Pinson's guitar style. He plays with a loose-fingered technique, brushing the treble strings with his fingers and using his thumb to make bass-string runs which connect or replace his chords. Like many self-taught guitarists, especially in the rural South, he plays all his material in one key. Most single-key guitarists use a capo, a clamp which locks on to the neck of the guitar and blocks all six strings so the same chord positions can be used in a higher key. Pinson never uses a capo, so his guitar-accompanied songs are all in the same key, even when it doesn't particularly suit his voice. The key he uses is E♭, a difficult key on a guitar tuned in concert pitch, and one seldom used for solo playing. But Pinson tunes his guitar so low that the open bass string is a C note, rather than the standard E—the bottom-to-top tuning is C-F-B♭-E♭-G-C instead of the standard E-A-D-G-B-E—and when he plays in E♭, his fingers are fretting positions that would play the key of G on a concert-tuned guitar. These positions are not difficult to play, and lend themselves to the use of chord-*

*connecting runs. Such runs are widely used in country music, especially in bluegrass, and some of Pinson's runs have similarities to those used in bluegrass, although he phrases them quite differently. When he plays slide guitar, he rejects the commonly used glass or metal cylinder slipped over a finger in favor of a more archaic technique in which he grips a pocket knife between the fingers of his left hand and stops the strings with the knife's metal back. He refers to the tuning he uses for this as "cross E," but in fact the instrument is tuned to a C chord, although the intervals between each string are the same as for an open E tuning in concert pitch. (Pinson's open tuning is C-G-C-E-G-C; open E tuning is E-B-E-G#-B-E.) Because they are tuned so low, the strings on his guitar are loose, and he has difficulty keeping them in tune. When he plays piano, Pinson holds his hands in an unusually flat position over the keyboard, with his wrists sometimes below the level of the keys and sets up a simple but strong bass to underpin his treble chord and melody playing. It's a basic driving style, reminiscent of Arizona Dranes and other pentecostal pianists. As with the guitar, he plays everything on the piano in one key. He doesn't know what it is, but thinks it may be G; it is in fact F#, which he uses almost certainly because it employs all the black keys, which are easier to locate by touch than the white ones.*

"I was playing for churches, religious programs and things like that. That's what I wanted to be doing. I was saved in 1936. Out there at St. Mary, in that church out there. It was a Methodist church. All of my family went to church, but they didn't all involve themselves in it like I did. And then I had a little singing group, a quartet. That was back in about 1940-something. I named it the Silvertone Quartet, but we never did put out any records.[1] I got them when they was young, starting up in their teens—about thirteen and fourteen, fifteen. I sang lead most all the time and played the guitar. But after a while they got scattered. Some of them got married, and others of 'em got gone . . . it got so that sometimes people would tell me they wanted my group and myself to do a program at a church, and I'd have to tell them I couldn't promise them about the group, 'cause the group might be gone.

"I always have played music [for a living]. I never had no job. I used to go to Arkansas, Tennessee, St. Louis, a lot of different places. Wisconsin and Illinois. I'd go to a lot of places like that and sing. I was in Racine in Wisconsin when I bought my first electric guitar, in '44.[2] I was visiting my cousin up there. And I was up in Arkansas when I met Elder Wilson.

I've been knowing him a long time. I was up there playing with some fellows, and I went to his home and we played some together. Then he got away from me and I didn't see him in a long time. But when he lost his wife and came back here and married again, I got after him about playing with me. See, Worth Long [his manager] wanted me to get different people that played music. And so I went to Elder Wilson about playing with me. It didn't look like he wanted to get hooked on up on it for a while, but he finally got with me and I think he kinda likes it now. And it helps him out a little, too.

"I used to play at WDIA radio station in Memphis. That was in 1950. Every morning, Monday through Friday. For quarter of an hour. I played all gospel music, on the guitar—I didn't use the piano like I do now. All of my playing was mostly guitar—that's what I had, and that's what I played. I stayed up there [in Memphis], with some people. I'd stay about a couple of weeks, then I'd come home. But I'd be back up there on Monday morning. I didn't do it for too long, though. See, they had different ones come on at a certain hour, and when they changed the days, that made my time run out. [Pinson's segment was dropped in a programming reshuffle.] But they asked me if they wanted me to come back, would I come. And I said, 'Yeah, if I'm not being somewhere else.'"

*Pinson never did return to WDIA. He remained based in New Albany, playing for churches and related functions locally and further afield until 1964, when he moved from north Mississippi into the Delta to live in Bolivar County, near Cleveland and about one hundred miles from New Albany.*

"There was some people that I knew. They used to live up here [in New Albany] and they had moved down in the Delta. They had some children that were big enough to go to school, and two more little younger ones, twins, under them. And the man and his wife wanted to work to pay their bills and things that they owed. So they asked me what I was doing up here, and I told them not anything much but going from place to place singing and playing at churches and different places. They said to me, 'Well, you can do that down here. You can come and sing and play at the churches down here.' They wanted me to stay and see after those two smaller children while the other three went to school. 'Cause if I didn't, one would have to stay and see after the two smaller children one day while the others went to school, then the next day they'd change and another would see after the children. That's the way they had it fixed until I went down there and was staying with them. Then that gave the three that were big enough a chance to all go to school.

"So I stayed there and looked after those children until they got big enough to go to school. And then I left them. They were living kinda out in the rural, and I came on over to Cleveland [Mississippi] and stayed there. Then there was an apartment house being built there at Cleveland. It wasn't ready, so I moved to Greenville and found me a little house there to stay in 'til they got that apartment at Cleveland completed and I could move in. When they got it completed, they let me know and I came back to Cleveland. I reckon I stayed in Greenville about five or six months. I bought that electric guitar I have now in Greenville. That was in 1974. It's a Gibson." [The instrument is a cherry red Gibson ES-335 semi-acoustic guitar. In Cleveland he moved into a "handicap" apartment, part of a public housing project.]

*During his time in Cleveland, Pinson found himself being asked to perform at musical engagements outside his regular round of church-related work. Although he was not a recording star, he was well known locally, and his name cropped up when folklorists and other people—mainly young whites—started coming to Mississippi to seek the musical descendants of the Delta voices they had heard on records.*

"I went to the Smithsonian [Institute]. The first year I went there, that was in '74, I went there and played at Washington, D.C., out on the Mall [at the Festival of American Folklife]. Then I went in '75, then I went back in '76, the bicentennial year. That was the last time I went there until '91. And I went back there in '91—that was the Smithsonian again. I went to the World's Fair in '82, in Knoxville, Tennessee. Then in 1984, I went to the World's Fair again. That was in New Orleans, Louisiana. Last year, we [Pinson and Wilson] went to Vero Beach in Florida. Down on the beach. Then we had a big tour. We went around a lotta different places. Down in Lafayette, Louisiana, went to Shreveport, Louisiana, went to Port Gibson, Mississippi, come to Oxford, Mississippi, and we left there and went to Raleigh, North Carolina, and we left there and went to Winston-Salem, North Carolina, then we came back to Montgomery, Alabama.³ And I had been down to Atlanta a few times before that time. I've been to Gary, Indiana . . . I've just been playing a whole lot all around.

"I've been at the Delta Blues Festival, in Greenville, and at Rust College.[4] At Rust College, when they asked us to play, we knew it was the Blues and Gospel Festival. But down there at Greenville, they just said 'the blues festival.' They don't tell us nothing about no gospel. So one time when I was living at Greenville, they sent a man, and he came at me and said, 'They sent me after you to see if you'll play.' I said, 'Hey no! I don't play no blues.' He said, 'They know what you play, but they told me to come here to ask you could you come down and play. They'll give you so much to come and play.' So I went down and played for them.

"But I have never played blues. I don't sing 'em, I don't play 'em and I don't have 'em. Down at Greenville, that guy Malcolm Walls [the Delta Blues Festival director], when he makes his talk, he says, 'Everybody has the blues sometime.' But I don't. I have the spirit with me, but I don't have no blues. There ain't no need of them. That ain't the Good Master's way. I hear blues a lot, but they ain't my type. I hear some people say I'm singing the 'gospel blues.' Gospel blues! I never heard of 'em. Gospel blues! Ain't no blues in gospel. I guess it's just that they like what I do right well, so they say, 'Well, you can tune your guitar in the same tuning and maybe play blues.' But I never did try to play 'em. If they asked me to play some blues now, I wouldn't know what to do. I wouldn't know how to play 'em. I've just been used to playing spirituals all the time. But everybody's gonna play what they want to play. It's like if you play blues and I play spirituals. Well, I don't stop you—unless my spiritual hit you well enough to make you stop. You're still gonna play your blues, but I'm gonna stay on my religious style. Gospel is just uplifting. It's the spirit. It's just a good feeling that the good master gives you. A spiritual feeling. It's not a blues feeling. You don't have no need of the blues if you're saved."

*While he was in Cleveland, Pinson recorded a self-financed seven-inch 45 rpm single, so he would have records to sell at his performances. He also returned to radio work, doing a half-hour show once a week on a local radio station.*

"I got me a few little small records made, and I'd sell them on my personal appearances. That was in about '76 I believe. I had two songs on there—one on each side. One was 'If You Are a Witness, Let God Abide.' And the other one was an instrumental. It was what they call a Doctor

Watt,[5] and it was called 'Before This Time Another Year.' I played that one with my knife on the strings. But I don't have any of those records left. I got shed of 'em, and I didn't buy any more to keep 'em going. And I had a radio program in Cleveland. Every Sunday morning, from 8:30 until 9. On WCLD. That was from about '82 until '88, when I left to come up here [to New Albany]. I came back because . . . after my other sisters and brothers had passed, my sister that lives up here—her name is Irma Lou Hill—she wanted me to move up here since there wasn't but the two of us left. So I just made up my mind and came on up here.

"When I came up here, I joined up with my sister at her church. I was baptized in a Methodist church, but in New Albany, my church was the Church of God. Then when I went down to Cleveland, I didn't find no Church of God, so I switched over to the Baptist church. I belonged to Old St. Phillip Baptist Church down there. Then when I came up here, I joined up with my sister at Union Grove. It's the same faith, Baptist. That's my membership now. And I play at that church. I mostly play the piano there because they have one, so I don't have to carry my guitar and amplifier up there and hook them up. All I have to do is walk to the piano and raise its lid. But I play guitar if I go to other churches. Then every once in a while, I change over and play a number or two on the piano. I play certain songs on the guitar, and certain songs on the piano. But some songs I play on both.

"I'm a minister. But I haven't been ordained. I don't preach none, or pastor a church or anything. 'Cause I can't see well. But when I go out and sing gospel music, well, some of those songs are kinda like a sermon. That one 'bout 'The Handwriting On the Wall.' "[6]

> There's a handwriting on the wall
> Handwriting [instrument finishes line]
> I see a handwriting on the wall
> Oh oh oh Lord [instrument finishes line]
>
> Well you read your Bible, you read it well
> You know about the story that I'm 'bout to tell
> Belshazzar was sitting at the banquet hall
> Drinking out the vessel of Israel's God
> They tell me that his eyes got red with wine
> When God came a-jumping on the wheels of time
> He rode on down to the banquet hall
> Set the hand writing on the wall

Belshazzar looked up at the banquet hall
He saw that writing of Israel's God
Go get old Daniel, I heard him yell
Tell him to read that writing and read it well
Gonna make him the ruler of the land
If he'll only read the writing that's written by the hand

There's a handwriting. . . .

When Daniel came jumping with the power of God
Began to read what he saw on the wall
Read in Ezekiel that you God's son*
Great God almighty, your days are done
God's done got tired of your wicked ways
The angels in heaven done numbered your days
Your evil deeds, God's done got tired
You've got to go to judgment to stand your trial
You've got to go to judgment to stand at the bar
For drinking out the vessels of Israel's God

*Pinson's 45 rpm record of "If You Are a Witness/Before This Time Another Year" was recorded professionally, although no recording company was involved—he paid for the studio time and the record production costs. (He was reportedly also recorded in 1967 by folklorist George Mitchell; no tracks were ever issued.) These days, he carries cassette tapes for sale at concerts and other performances. But he has eliminated the recording studio and the need for professional duplication. When he decides to make some tapes, he sets up his portable recorder and sings and plays into it.*

---

*Pinson's version of "Hand Writing On the Wall" is almost identical to that recorded by the Trumpeteers in September 1947 (Score 5001). The only significant deviation is in the third line of the second verse. The Trumpeteers quote the words written on the wall, "Mene mene tekel upharsin" (dropping the second "mene" to make the line fit); Pinson's rendition of the same line is indistinct in the two versions of the song available to the author, but is almost certainly as transcribed. The book of Ezekiel tells how Nebuchadnezzar laid siege to Jerusalem and triumphed with the help of God, but has little relevance to "Hand Writing On the Wall," and Pinson's line is very probably a mishearing of the Trumpeteers' line ("Mene tekel . . ."/"Read in Ezekiel . . ."). Lines 5–8 of the second verse are identical to lines in the very popular "Jezebel," recorded by the Golden Gate Quartet in 1941 and subsequently sung by many other groups.

*When he has filled a sixty-minute cassette tape, he uses another twin-deck recorder to run off a dozen or so copies. He sell them at eleven dollars each; when they're all gone, he loads his little red portable recorder, sets up his instruments and makes another tape. He keeps no store of "master tapes"; each batch of tapes he makes contains new recordings.*

"I just go into my back room and plug up my guitar and amplifier and set that little tape recorder on the end of the bed. Then I just turn to it and sing. If I'm playing the piano, I have to sit it closer to me. Then when I go out to play, I carry some [tapes] with me. Sometimes people ask me do I have a recording or a tape, and I just have some with me. See, I do all my own arrangements. All my own playing, too. But I don't write songs, I don't write at all. I just get songs and sing 'em and just play 'em myself. I play in my own arrangement. My own style, I call it."

*Leon Pinson has no idea how many songs he knows. But much of his material is firmly traditional. His slide guitar version of "Your Close Friend" is a direct descendant of Edward Clayborn's "Your Enemy Cannot Harm You" from 1926. He has never heard of Arizona Dranes, but his piano-accompanied "Don't You Want To Go" was the last song she recorded, in 1928. Some of his songs, such as "This Little Light of Mine," or "Jesus Is on the Main Line" are staples of African-American gospel song. Others come from single sources, identifiable because his versions often remain close to the source. "Shame on You" follows the 1974 hit by Slim and the Supreme Angels closely enough to retain Howard "Slim" Hunt's vocal asides between the lines. "Only Believe" has a structure and somewhat uncomfortable falsetto singing that point strongly to the Gospelaires of Dayton, Ohio, and their stratospheric high tenor, Charles McLean.*

*His piano and guitar repertoires are mainly separate, but there is some overlap. Some songs retain the same feel and tempo whatever the accompaniment. Others change markedly. His piano version of Thomas A. Dorsey's "Precious Lord" is slow and stately in the manner of the big-voiced soloists of the 1950s; when he performs it with the guitar, it is faster with an altered tune and a delivery that suggests a quartet origin. "What a Friend We Have in Jesus" is also done hymnally on the piano, but acquires a faster tempo and a modified tune on guitar.*

*When Pinson and Roma Wilson go out to play what Wilson calls "an engagement," they wear dark suits, white shirts and neckties, standing out in sober contrast to the often more flamboyantly dressed artists sharing the bill with them. The job of introducing the songs is shared, but Pinson does much of the lead singing. His song introductions have an old-fashioned formality. "Thank you very much. We hope that you enjoyed that number. Now Elder Wilson is going to play you a number of his own choice," he intones in a delivery that harkens back to Joe Taggart's "We want to sing a song . . ." of 1926. Elder Wilson's introductions are also formal, but the occasional note of wry humor creeps in. Introducing "This Train," he tells how the train carries "no liars, no hypocrites, no backsliders. No gamblers, no hobos, no midnight ramblers." A short pause. "So you see, there's very few on it." His quips sometimes slide past audiences, which don't always seem to expect the serious business of religion to be leavened with humor.*

# BOYD RIVERS

*"I've got that little touch. God gave it to me . . ."*

BOYD Rivers is a singer and guitarist.* He sings in local churches around his home in Madison County, Mississippi; he's also played in France and Italy.[1] He is an amiable conversationalist who, with little warning, will erupt into full-blown preaching, driving his words out with almost intimidating force and intensity. He has a store of biblical anecdotes to illustrate the points he is making, but many are tangled and quite at odds with the source being quoted. He's a gregarious man who enjoys hanging out with his friends at JoJo's gas station and convenience store on Highway 51, which for a few hundred yards is also the main street

*Boyd Rivers at his home near Pickens, Mississippi.*

of Pickens, Mississippi. But he lives alone, apart from two pet dogs, in an isolated small house at the end of a rutted two-mile clay and roughly graveled track, about five miles outside Pickens.

Inside, his house has the spartan neatness of an orderly man living alone. His guitar and amplifier are in one corner; on the wall above are a calendar from a local undertaker, the faded cover of an Angelic Gospel Singers record album, and a large color photograph of a young man in U. S. Marine Corps uniform. Rivers, stocky and clean-shaven except for a closely trimmed mustache, sits on the couch, his cigarette burning in the ashtray in front of him. His pressed dark-brown trousers and shirt of nearly identical shade give the impression of a uniform. On his head is a white hat, a cross between a panama and a Stetson. His smile reveals that several of his front teeth are missing.

---

*Boyd Rivers died of a heart attack on November 22, 1993, aged fifty-eight.

"My name is Boyd H. Rivers. I was born on December 25, 1934, Christmas Day, here in Madison County. And the way I started in music, I nailed two nails to a wall, put a wire on them.[2] That's the way I started playing music 'til I got able to buy a guitar. I was about eleven or twelve. Then I got me a little common guitar for seventeen dollars. I never will forget it. I bought it in Pickens from a man that ran the store. Paid him three dollars a week on it until I got it. I first started picking the blues, but something changed me from that. I used to go to sleep at night and dream I was in church where the people were shouting. And I liked that more than I did looking at people dance half the night in clubs, some of them getting hurt, getting killed. They'd be drinking at those things. And that changed my whole attitude. I used to play everywhere, in the jukes and everywhere. Until I was about nineteen years old. But it never did make sense to me. 'Cause when it's cut off, looks like it leaves you lonely. That's what makes people drink—to be where the herd is. As long as you're drinking, it's all right. But when you leave it, you feel lonely. So I had to find something to make me happy here on earth. And I switched over to the spiritual.

"I sought the Lord down in Mary Magdalene Missionary Baptist Church [in Pickens]. I prayed and I prayed until the preacher closed out. My grandmother, her name was Mary Boyd, always told me, 'Don't lie! If you don't feel nothing, don't move.'[3] So I stayed right there until they closed out. But that Tuesday evening in the next week, the Lord let me know he heard me. He let me feel it. And I haven't felt like that since. I went home that night and I slept better than I did any night. Never did play the blues no more. And I ain't gonna play them no more. Not in public. Sometimes I'll be sitting here [at home] alone and. . . . Now don't misunderstand me! We ain't read where the blues is a sin. We ain't read it in the Bible—it's not in there! Music's music.

"So I got growed, I done growed on up and got powerful and powerfuller. Now I can pick it [the guitar] in the dark. See, it's in my heart now. I've held it. I'm always dreaming that I'm in church. I've been to every church in this district, singing God's praises. My wife, when we were together, we used to do it together, but . . . remember, when you marry, y'all got to be on the same accord almost. You can't be pulling east and west, you won't stay together. My wife left me. I don't too much want to talk about it, but . . . when you marry, you marry one, not the whole family. You and her have to agree on things. I loved my wife, but her mother kept on talking to her, telling her the same thing. So she left. That's my son [the photograph on the wall]. His name's David Rivers. He's in the marines. My wife left when he was thirteen. He got grown, said, 'Daddy, I'm going to do something for myself.' He went to the marines. Now he's been in the marines going on seven years. I got one other son. He's in Baton Rouge, Louisiana. He went with his momma, and that's where she's at. You know, children are like that. If David hadda wanted to go with his mother, I wouldn't care. I can make it. God'll take care of me. He always has. You know, I'm glad I'm like I am. I don't worry about nothing.

"See, when Jesus risen from the dead, it was two women standing there. Mary and Martha. One wanted to touch him. He said, 'Touch me not! I've got to go to my father. If I don't go, the comfort won't come. Go tell them to wait in the upper room.' Simon Peter come running down in the grave. Got in the tomb there and picked up some of the garments. Said, 'Surely this man must be the son of the living God— here's the garments we wrapped him in. Where is he?' Do you know what she said? She said Joseph had stolen the body! That's the reason they don't want women preaching today. They can teach, but they don't want a woman preaching. 'Cause they lied in the first, in the beginning, and people been lying ever since!"

*It's an impassioned speech, giving a firm biblical justification for the refusal of some denominations to ordain women and for Rivers's own misogyny. But he's wrong. The quotation he ascribes to Mary Magdalene comes from St. Matthew's account of the resurrection of Christ. However, it is spoken not by Mary to Simon Peter, but by the chief priests to whom the soldiers of the watch report the mysterious events at the tomb of Joseph of Arimathea. "And when they were assembled with the elders and had taken counsel, they gave large money to the soldiers. Saying, Say ye, His disciples came by night and stole him while we slept" (Matthew 28:12–13).*

*While religion is obviously a mainstay in the lives of gospel singers, Boyd Rivers's faith is at a stage beyond that of most. He is completely immersed in his religion, driven and consumed by it to the extent that answers to questions about his life and his music often turn into full-blown sermons.*

But ooooh, you've got to wait on him
And call the Lord every day

If you call him every day [handclap] and mean it
Then things'll look brighter to you when you wake up in the morning.
Look out there every d-a-a-a-y-y
I know he'll make a way for you, yes he will
He loves you
Just like he loves everybody
S-o-o-o-m-e people,
Seems like the Lord don't love nobody but them but that's a lie
He loves everything he made.
He said, "Everything I made I love it,
And everything I made is good
And very good." Didn't he say it?
Oooohhhh don't put off today for tomorrow [handclap]
Because tomorrow ain't promised to you.
Ohhhhhhh Lord,
Ohhhhhhh I'm so glad this evening.

*It is the hypnotically rhythmic oratory of a fundamentalist preacher nearing the peak of his peroration. From the pulpit, it would be stirring. In Boyd Rivers's living room, it is overpowering—especially as part of his answer to the question "Do you ever sing the blues today?" The cords in his neck stand out as the words tumble in a rasping shout. His right arm is extended at a forty-five-degree angle, his fingers widespread and fluttering. The delivery is in urgent cadence, flowing in couplets, with the first line stressed hard, the second delivered more quietly. In a moment, he will stop and sit in silence before shaking his head as though coming out of a trance and resuming normal conversation.*

"I'm still a member at the Mary Magdalene Church, but I won't tell you I go like I'm supposed, because the building don't mean nothing. I get the spirit of God on me here at home. I've been living here since I got married. I bought this acre from my daddy-in-law and had my house built. I paid for it. Glad I did. 'Cause otherwise, when my wife left that morning, I'da had to leave the next morning. They wanted me to go, but thank the Lord, I didn't get in no trouble. I have a sister in Pickens, named Ella Mae Rivers. And I have two in Chicago. Got a brother in Magee, Mississippi, Rev. Eugene Rivers. He's a preacher. I see my sister; the others hardly come 'round. But as long as they're doing all right, I'm all right. Sometimes it's best not to visit too much. Makes a better relationship.

"I used to work for the Canton Casket Company in Canton [sixteen miles south of Pickens]. I worked there for about twelve years, then I got hurt. Little old ripsaw hit my hand. [He displays his right hand; the little finger and part of the side of the hand are missing.] I thought I wouldn't be able to play my guitar, but God brought it back. And they paid me good for it, and I haven't worked since. That was in 1972. We made caskets for the dead people. It was a good job. Because you're gonna die, sooner or later. I had to think about it when I first started to work there. Dreamed one night I was in one of them caskets. Dead, man! I jumped up, hit my head upside the wall. Scared! I had just started work there then. And after that, I never did worry about it no more."

*Like Leon Pinson, Boyd Rivers uses only one set of chord shapes on the guitar. His basic key is E—widely used, especially by blues players, because of its open bass tonic, full-sounding open-string first position chords, and straightforward inversions—but unlike Pinson, he uses a capo to move the shapes up and down the neck, varying the keys in which he plays. Not surprisingly, his playing has strong blues overtones. One of his early influences was L'il Son Jackson, a Texas blues player who also later spent time as a church member. Rivers saw him once in a Canton nightclub and studied his playing so closely that when Jackson laid down his guitar to take a break, he was able to pick it up and duplicate the star's sound.4 Rivers's own style has a lurching bounce, with sudden shifts between treble and bass figures. He adjusts standard tunes to fit his distinctive style, and also varies the keys in which he performs individual songs to suit the context in which he is playing.*

"Maybe you heard that song 'You Got to Take Sick and Die'? [It's one he has recorded.] On that album, it's in middle tone. But I can do it better than that. You oughta hear me do it in high tone. I'm gonna show you what a high tone mean, and I don't mind doing that. Because you ain't been 'round nobody like me. You been around pretenders. See, there's a difference between a pretender and somebody that means business. I'll show you what high tone is. [He connects the guitar to the amplifier, turns it on and plays a flurry of notes.] That's a standard tone. Now I put it in high tone. That's the way I pick it for the congregation so they can hear."

*He puts the capo on the neck of the guitar at the fourth fret and plays the same pattern. The technique is not as esoteric as he presents it—all he's done is use the capo to shift the key from E to A♭. But the change pushes his voice towards the top of his range, and although he has the guitar volume turned up so his notes will sustain, his unamplified voice rasps easily above the strident treble patterns he is picking. "High tone" is the technique he has evolved to make his words audible above the electric guitar in churches and other small venues where no vocal amplification is available. Most of his repertoire is drawn from traditional gospel song, reworked to fit his style.*

"I don't write songs. They have to come to me. It's a feeling. I've got a thousand songs, different ones. You oughta hear me in church! You will never meet nobody else like me. I've got that little touch. God gave it to me. He takes care of me. I'm always somewhere to play. I've been to a lot of places. But I turn a lot of them down because they want something for nothing. You got to watch that. There was a fellow [a promoter], he called for me to send a [video]tape of me to the World's Fair in New Orleans. They came back, said, 'Oh, we ain't got room down there.' [at the New Orleans concert]. But they kept the tape. The next thing I know, a white friend of mine in Lexington, Mississippi, says to me, 'We looked at you on the television, listened to your music, for about an hour and a half. We paid six dollars apiece to go in there.' And they didn't give me a penny! That's a dirty trick. Five hundred people sitting up there, six dollars a head. Count it! And they send me nothing. Now this other fellow [he names another promoter], he's an honest man. He's fair. He says, 'You get this amount,' and that's what they give. I don't expect nothing else, 'cause I agreed to it. But this fellow got my tape down there and put the money in his pocket. I don't mind him making some money, but give me some, too. If we're in it together, you ain't getting all the hog. Give me a ham or something. He's been back at me again, wanting me to go somewhere. But I told him, 'Don't come at me no more. I ain't going nowhere.' I mean, singing God's praises with a crook?"

*Rivers made the transition from church performer to concert artist in the early 1970s, when he did some work for Worth Long, who also books Roma Wilson and Leon Pinson. He appeared several times at the Delta Blues Festival in Greenville, and one of those appearances led in 1980 to the recording of seven tracks—including "You Got to Take Sick and Die" in middle tone—for the German L+R label, which issued them in its eleven-album Living Country Blues series aimed at collectors worldwide.[5] In November 1986, came the highlight of his musical career—a trip to*

*France and Italy with blues singers Jessie Mae Hemphill and Hezekiah and the House Rockers, at the Mississippi Blues and Gospel Festival. In 1992, he was filmed at his home for a documentary shown on Japanese public television and seen by his son, who was stationed in Japan with the marines.[6] He has also made other thus far unissued recordings.*

*Rivers is not the only member of his family involved in gospel music. His uncle is Rev. Cleophus Robinson, a former Canton resident now based in St. Louis, Missouri. The gap between Robinson's urbane style and Rivers's hoarse-voiced shout is wide, and the more famous singer has had little detectable influence on his country nephew. But one song they have in common is Robinson's 1969 hit, "Wrapped Up, Tied Up, Tangled Up,"[7] which Rivers calls "I'm Wrapped Up."[8] Both performances have a blues-oriented backing, but Robinson's is a smooth studio performance in front of a skilled accompaniment by piano, organ, guitar, bass, and drums. Rivers's voice, recorded at his home, is backed only by his own guitar, playing phrases reminiscent of 1930s Mississippi bluesman Tommy McClennan.*

*Boyd Rivers's day-to-day life is a simple routine. It starts with a visit to JoJo's, where he meets friends and whiles away some time in conversation. "He's here every morning between eight and nine," said one worker at JoJo's. "Every morning."*

"Yes, I'll be over there. I go by there every morning. I ain't got nothing else to do. I just rise up, dress up, and go over there. I pray before I leave, because I don't know what I'm gonna meet. Amen. Don't nobody know. Then I might go to my sister's place. Or come back here. I'll be having a good time sitting here sometimes. On my own. I'll be singing . . . yeah. Get happy. He been good, ain't he? He's still good. 'Cause he woke us up this morning. We ain't got sense to wake up. See, some folk go round all day, enjoying God's health, God's strength, and God's life, then climb into bed without saying, 'Thank you Lord for another day's journey.' They'll do that. Sometimes he has to take his arms from round you to make you pray. Let a few trials and tribulations hit you. See, I lean, depend on God. I lean on him. I trust him. He'll take care of you. Give you water if you're thirsty, bread if you're hungry. Clothes if you're naked. If I call the Lord, he may not come when I want him to come. He come when he get ready. But he's always going to be on time. I love it. I get what I want. If it's wrong, I don't need it anyway. If you ask the Lord for something and he doesn't give it to you, it'll come to you later on that it's wrong.

"He will take care of you. I remember a lady told me—I didn't see it, but I believe it because she didn't have no right to sit up there in a building we call a church and lie—she said her house was burning down. She says, 'Oh, Lord, this is all I got. Please don't take it.' The blaze went out. It went out! Another lady was living in the Delta. Come a tornado one night, and her baby was two days old. God blowed the whole bed and all and put it up on a shed—and there wasn't a scratch on the little baby. God rides on every storm. You just can't do nothing away from him. I knew a man on the Delta, come a storm and blew his house away. Didn't hurt nobody. But he cursed God. He went and built another house and put a storm pit under it. Two or three years later, another tornado came through there and sucked them all up. Killed everybody!

"You know, the way some people act, they believe they ain't gonna die. But a man born of woman come here full of trouble, live here a few days, he'll be cut down. All of us live to hurt one another. Don't we do that? It's bad and it's sad. You can meet the ugliest person in the world and they can be so sweet. Then you meet the most beautiful person in the world, and they can be so nasty. You know, Jezebel was so bad they cut her up and threw her to the dogs. The dogs ran to her like they was going to eat, then walked away. You remember when Noah completed the ark? What he did? They celebrated with wine and got drunk. You know what he did with his daughters? People been getting drunk ever since, and people been fooling with their family ever since. Ain't nothing happening now that didn't happen in the Bible days."

*Rivers's accounts of the death of Jezebel and the misdeeds of Noah are, like his resurrection story, distortions of the Bible stories he believes he is quoting. Noah did get drunk, from the fruits of a vineyard he planted after the great flood (Genesis 9:20–22). But the incest of which Rivers accuses Noah was committed by Lot after he fled Sodom and Gomorrah to the mountains, leaving his wife as a pillar of salt—and it was his daughters who initiated the act, saying, "Come, let us make our father drink wine and we will lie with him, that we may preserve the seed of our father" (Genesis 19:32).*

*Although Rivers can read, his scriptural errors strongly suggest that religion is to him an oral tradition, and that he has absorbed most of his Bible knowledge from indirect sources. Much of it probably comes from sermons and church services; some of it may be from gospel songs. Ample precedent exists in gospel song to validate the existence of an oral tradition. When the Fairfield Four sang, "Just like a tree of level / I forever stand,"⁹ they were not using a metaphor for upright rectitude; "tree of level" is a mishearing of "tree of Lebanon," used as a symbol of virtue because King Solomon used Lebanese cedar to build the temple which housed the Ark of the Covenant (I Kings 6 and Chronicles 2–3), and, more directly, because of Psalm 92:12—"The righteous shall flourish like the palm tree; he shall grow like a cedar in Lebanon." Another popular gospel song may have been responsible for Rivers's mistelling of the story of Jezebel. The Golden Gate Quartet's 1941 recording of "Jezebel" tells that after the Queen of Israel died, "Nine days she lay in Jerusalem's streets / Her flesh was too filthy for the dogs to eat."¹⁰ This corresponds with Rivers's account. But II Kings 9:32–37 details how Jezebel—whose main offense was reintroducing worship of the fertility god Baal—was hurled from a window in Jezreel (not Jerusalem) on the orders of the new king, Jehu. When servants went to bury her, they found "no more of her than the skull, and the feet, and the palms of her hands." The rest had been eaten by dogs, fulfilling a curse placed on her by God through the prophet Elijah.*

*The study of misquotations and altered interpretations is of value in demonstrating how an oral tradition can unintentionally modify a message. A widespread example is the mispronunciation of the name of the third Hebrew cast on the orders of Nebuchadnezzar into the fiery furnace with Shadrach and Meshach (Daniel 3:13–26). In the Bible, he is Abednego; in gospel song he is almost universally Abendego. But such errors are of little significance in assessing a gospel performance. They make no difference to the musical proficiency on display or to the expression of faith. Boyd Rivers's biblical confusions take nothing from his ability as a gospel singer; nor do they detract from the sincerity of his belief, the depth of his passion, or the power of his impromptu preaching.*

"If you're dealing with a problem you're not able to wrestle with, ask the Lord to help you. You get so you can rassle with it. He'll make you able. If you're not able to bear your load, he'll make you able to bear it. Don't ever forget. Say, 'Lord, I failed today at something I was trying. I'm going to go back tomorrow and try it.'" [He moves into a half-sung, preaching-style chant.]

Will you make me able?
Then if I fail, Lord, give me the strength and courage to get up again.

If you do that for me,
I'll be able to do that. Yes, you'll be able
Able
To smile when you feel like crying
Able
Able to raise your head when you feel like hanging it, raise it anyhow
Able, able
He'll make you able this evening, he'll make you able right now.
Oh, just you call the Lord.
Said one verse say, if you call the Lord and he don't answer,
Just c-a-a-a-ll him again. Try it!
If you call the Lord and he don't answer-r-r-r-r
Oh, just c-a-a-a-a-l-l-l him aga-a-a-a-i-i-n.

[He drops suddenly back into conversational speech.]
"Ain't it all right. May God bless you, may God bless you. I love
   him so."

# 2 THE QUARTETS

*"They've got a following everywhere . . ."*

Quartets occupy a unique place in gospel music. Although they are an essential part of African-American religious music, few are directly affiliated with churches, and much of their singing is done outside the church environment. They are the best-known practitioners of gospel, rivaled in popularity only by a few of the top soloists, yet some church people, especially those of the "sanctified" pentecostalist faiths, regard them with suspicion because of their flamboyance and the worldly aspects of their craft. But throughout their history, the quartets have been the performers of gospel music who have had the closest links with their communities, and that continues to be true today. Their glory years may be a fading memory, but quartets still abound, especially throughout the South. Some consist of veterans who have been singing for forty or more years; others are composed of young people, influenced by those who have gone before and following a tradition that extends back to the nineteenth century. Some, in a development which augurs well for the future of the style, are transgenerational, with members in their fifties and sixties singing alongside more recent recruits in their twenties and thirties. While a few groups maintain the traditional a cappella style, most now use instruments, including drums and sophisticated electronic synthesizers. But all are singing "quartet."

The earliest written reference to African-American quartets appeared in 1851, when Frederika Bremer wrote of hearing Virginia slaves singing in "quartettes."[1] These ensembles were informal groups, without the element of organization and arrangement that characterizes a formally constituted quartet. But in a study suggesting that white "barbershop quartet" singing owes much more to black quartets than is generally acknowledged, Lynn Abbott says that by the end of the nineteenth century, quartet singing was so well established among African-American males that it was "the black national pastime."[2] Formal organization and arrangement were definitely part of the African-American university "jubilee" singing groups, pioneered by Nashville's Fisk University, which brought religious music into the quartet tradition. Fisk, founded in 1865 by the American Missionary Association, was short of money from the day its doors opened and by 1870 was facing bankruptcy. Treasurer and choirmaster George L. White had assembled a group of his best singers to perform locally and raise money; in 1871, the university decided to send the singers "on the road" to tour further afield as traveling fundraisers. The original group of 13—George White, a female chaperone, six female and five male singers—spent three months touring northern states, starting in Cincinnati, Ohio, and going on through New York, Connecticut, Massachusetts, Rhode Island and others, returning to Nashville with $20,000. In 1873, the singers went to England and Scotland; in 1875 they went back to Britain and to Germany and the Netherlands, returning to the US in 1878.[3] Subsequent Fisk groups went even further afield, traveling as far as to Australia and New Zealand. Between 1871 and 1878, the singers raised $150,000 for Fisk University, and provided the inspiration for a number of similar groups from other African-American learning centers. These troupes were usually large enough to be regarded as small choirs. However, by the 1890s, a separate tradition of university quartet singing was well established, and many of the larger jubilee singing groups included in their ranks male and male/female quartets. The Fisk Jubilee Singers apparently were using such groups as early as 1873.[4] The touring university groups also established entertainment as an element of gospel music. Doug Seroff says, "Though they had not intended to do so, the troupe from Fisk established a relationship between traditional plantation singing and the business of public performance."[5]

IN addition to the informal quartets and the university groups, the later years of the nineteenth century brought the heyday of "minstrel" shows. These were developed in the 1840s by white artists who caricatured southern black life, but, by the 1870s, when the genre was at its most popular, black casts were as common as white. Initially, the minstrel shows ignored religious music, but the success of groups like the Fisk Jubilee Singers sparked a demand for sacred material. By the end of the century, according to Joyce Jackson, "every minstrel company and every vaudeville troupe required a black jubilee singing group."[6] A side effect of the mix between minstrelsy and religion was the introduction of comedy and parody versions of spirituals, to the extent that some songs—"You Shall Be Free," for example, or "Oh, Dem Golden Slippers"—were eventually known only in burlesque versions.

Informal singing within the community, of the type noted by Lynn Abbott, was the spawning ground for the ancestors of today's gospel quartets. Groups were started by people who had something in common —belonging to the same church, working at the same place or simply living in the same area—and in the years following the turn of the twentieth century, they became an integral part of African-American community life. Already a part of the musical tradition which made use of hymn and spirituals, these groups were further influenced by the university groups and minstrel shows. Joyce Jackson writes, "The university quartets provided the model of close four-part harmony, a cappella singing style and sacred repertoire. The model for showmanship, humor and entertainment came from the minstrel tradition. The community-based quartets combined practices from both traditions, resulting in a set of aesthetic criteria which in many cases still applies to quartet singing today."[7]

In 1890 the New York-based Unique Quartette probably made the first African-American quartet recordings. Other early recording groups were the Standard Quartette and the Kentucky Jubilee Singers in the 1890s, the Dinwiddie Colored Quartet (1902), Polk Miller and His Old South Quartette (1909 and 1910)[8] and the Apollo Quartet (1912).[9] In December 1909, the Fisk University Jubilee Quartet recorded nineteen songs during a tour of the Northeast; in February 1911, it made another fourteen titles. Like most early quartets, the Fisk's repertoire was a mixture of sacred and secular, although records issued from its 1909 and 1911 sessions emphasized the religious side.

As has been discussed, recording of African-American religious artists began in earnest with the "race records" boom of the 1920s. The first quartet-style group recorded in this period was the Biddle University Quintet, five singers from Charlotte, North Carolina,[10] who recorded four songs in April 1920. In March 1921, the most prolific and popular of the early quartets made its first recordings. Initially, the group was called the Norfolk Jazz Quartet, and the first six tracks it made for the Okeh company—including "Jelly Roll Blues" and "Preacher Man Blues"—were secular. They must have sold well, as the group was back in July 1921, to make another eight, including two religious pieces, "I Hope That I May Join the Band" and "Who Built the Ark?," issued as by the Norfolk Jubilee Quartet. Another session, in September 1921, produced six more secular tracks. When the group next returned to the studio, in April 1923, with a new record company and new lead singer, it was poised to take a new direction. Its first session for the Paramount label was mainly secular, but included two religious songs, "Father Prepare Me" and "My Lord's Gonna Move This Wicked Race." Featuring the lead singing of Norman "Crip" Harris, "My Lord's Gonna Move" was so popular that it stayed in Paramount's catalog until the company's demise, in 1932. The quartet and the company were quick to take the hint. Of the ten tracks issued from the next session, in July 1924, eight were religious and only two secular.[11]

Regional styles also appeared. Norfolk, Virginia, was recognized as being a "quartet town."[12] In the 1920s it was home not only to the Norfolk Jazz/Jubilee Quartet but to the Silver Leaf Quartet of Norfolk and the Monarch Jazz/Jubilee Quartet, both popular recording groups. In Alabama, a strong a cappella gospel tradition developed in the industrial area of Jefferson County, around Birmingham, and continued into the 1990s.[13] The dominance of both areas is attributable to the rise of industry, which drew black workers in the first twenty years of this century. Later, northern cities—including Cleveland, New York, Chicago, and Detroit—would attract migrants seeking a better life, and would become gospel centers.

The Depression had a devastating effect on the recording industry, and gospel was one of the worst-hit facets. Total record sales in the United States slumped from 104 million in 1927 to six million in 1932,[14] and "race" recording virtually halted. It did not recover until 1934, and when it did, quartets were the leaders in the religious field. The singing preachers, top sellers between 1926 and 1931, all but vanished, as did the "guitar evangelists." But quartets retained their preslump popularity, and built on it. The two best-selling quartets on record during the 1930s were the Heavenly Gospel Singers, founded in Detroit but based in South Carolina from 1936 on, and Mitchell's Christian Singers, from Kinston, North Carolina. The Heavenly Gospel Singers made their first recordings in 1935, and by 1941 had recorded more than one hundred songs. They were a professional group, and traveled extensively, from Detroit to Florida. Mitchell's Christian Singers made more than eighty recordings between 1934 and 1940, but the group's four members retained their regular jobs, performing infrequently outside their local area. (One outing was to New York, in 1938, where they appeared on John Hammond's first *Spirituals to Swing* concert at Carnegie Hall.)

The group which had the largest impact on quartet singing from the late 1930s was another Norfolk lineup, the Golden Gate Quartet. The Gates borrowed freely from the style of the popular Mills Brothers; one of the devices they lifted from the secular group was vocal imitations of wind and reed instruments, a technique at which they were already adroit by the time of their first recording session in 1937. They also brought a new level of secular professionalism to gospel, paying careful attention to dress and presentation as well as to their intricate vocal arrangements. They toured widely, and were one of the first gospel acts since the era of the university jubilee groups to gain wide white acceptance.

In the 1940s, a number of factors contributed to the widening appeal of quartets. Foremost among these were recordings and radio broadcasts. After the war, a number of small independent record companies emerged, taking advantage of the end of shellac rationing (shellac was a vital ingredient of 78 rpm records) to challenge the market dominance of the major companies. As the majors had largely lost interest in anything but mainstream entertainment, gospel and blues recording became almost exclusively the preserve of these small record companies. At the same time, gospel broadcasting was increasing, with a number of stations selling on-air time, either directly to quartets or to sponsors who employed quartets to broadcast. The effect was to substantially widen the groups' potential audience and establish them as a form of entertainment as well as part of religious life. This made it easier for singers to contemplate making a living from their talent, and increasing numbers turned professional, working circuits that developed throughout the South, along the East Coast, into the Midwest and across to California. At the same time, the number of groups was increasing, and quartet singing was moving towards the dynamic and spectacular "hard" style.

The development of this style is sometimes credited to one or two influential singers. Anthony Heilbut cites Rebert Harris of the Soul Stirrers, crediting him with creating "the entire gospel tradition."[15] Doug

Seroff says Silas Steele of the Famous Blue Jay Singers "fathered" a new era in quartet singing by being the "first emotional gospel singer."[16] Harris and Steele are extremely important figures in the history and development of quartet singing. But a style closely related to "hard" quartet singing—without the formal arrangements that characterize the quartets—had been in existence at least since the 1920s in the "sanctified" pentecostalist churches. One example of it on record is in the singing of Bessie Johnson, whose shouted back-of-the-throat rasp anticipated the power and passion of the hard groups by twenty-five years.[17] Blind Willie Johnson employed a similar vocal technique on most of his recordings, as did many preachers.

Many of the groups that emerged with the development of the hard style were new, but among the leaders were several veterans. One of the best known was the Famous Blue Jay Singers of Birmingham, Alabama, whose lead singer until 1947 was Silas Steele, an influential and widely respected voice in quartet singing. When the Blue Jays made their first recordings, near the end of 1931, they began the session with "Sleep On Mother," performed in one of the most formalized styles of prewar quartet singing and known as "clanka-lanka" or "link-oh-link" from the rhythmic syllables chanted by the back-up singers behind the lead.[18] The ubiquity of the style is shown by the fact that the Blue Jays' version was issued as "Clanka A Lanka (Sleep On Mother)." The Blue Jays made no more recordings until 1947; when they returned to the studio, they had added Charlie Bridges—a quartet veteran who sang with the Birmingham Jubilee Singers in the 1920s—as another lead and were singing in the modern "hard" style.

Another prewar group which made the shift was the Dixie Humming-birds, from Greenville, South Carolina. They made their first recordings in 1939, and became a hard gospel powerhouse in the 1940s when they recruited lead singer Ira Tucker from his home in Spartanburg, South Carolina, and bass singer William Bobo from the Heavenly Gospel Singers. Tucker became one of the foremost figures in quartet singing, and his approach to his profession illustrates clearly the quartets' aware-ness of the need to entertain as well as to raise religious consciousness. "I'm a firm believer in giving people something for their money," he told Anthony Heilbut. "Talent. A variety—fast, slow, something sad, something with a lot of laughs."[19]

Not all groups performed in the frenetic hard style. The Harmonizing Four, formed in Richmond, Virginia, in 1927 and still recording in the 1990s with some prewar members, retained a soft melodic style, often featuring the bass singer as the lead voice. The Swan Silvertones featured the silken lead voice of founder Claude Jeter, whose main contribution to quartet singing was his astounding falsetto reach, which prompted many imitators and made the "high fifth" an accepted part above the tenor. The Silvertones were founded in 1938, and initially performed in the jubilee style. But after World War II, Jeter saw the changes coming and hired Solomon Womack (uncle of soul star Bobby Womack) to be a "hard" lead singer. When ill health put Womack out of the group, he was followed by a number of other singers, including some of the leading names in quartet singing—Rev. Robert Crenshaw, Percell Perkins, Paul Owens, Dewey Young—all of whom helped the Swans to shine in whatever style they used.

The 1950s were the great quartet days, when programs drew standing-room-only audiences in large auditoriums, and the top singers were gospel-household names. The Soul Stirrers, from Houston, Texas, had the inventive Rebert H. Harris as their lead until 1950, when he quit, disturbed by what he saw as increasing immorality in the relationship between the traveling groups and their female fans. His replacement was a twenty-year-old from the Highway QCs in Chicago, named Sam Cooke. Although Cooke subsequently made an international name for himself as a pop-soul singer, it is easy to argue that he never sang a secular note as fine as the best work of his seven years with the Soul Stirrers. The Blind Boys of Mississippi, formed at the Piney Woods School for the Blind in Mississippi and professional since 1944, were led in their greatest years by Archie Brownlee, revered as one of the hardest-shouting singers of all. Rivaling him was Rev. Julius "June" Cheeks of the Sensational Nightingales, who sang with a power that eventually shattered his voice, leaving him with all the passion and technique but only a splintered rasp with which to deliver it. From Alabama came the "other" Five Blind Boys, formed at the Talladega Institute for the Deaf and Blind and led by Clarence Fountain. In Memphis, the Spirit of Memphis played an important role in the development of quartet style, both through its singing and through its early promotion of professional programs.

The Pilgrim Travelers, formed in Houston in the early 1930s, moved to Los Angeles in 1942, and with Kylo Turner and Keith Barber as leads, recorded more than one hundred tracks for Specialty between 1947 and 1956. Under the tutelage of J. W. Alexander, who became manager and tenor in 1945, they mastered all the tricks of "housewrecking." Alexander said, "Turner and Barber just stood flat-footed. I told 'em you need a little more to pull the sisters up out of their seats. . . . We used to jump off stage, all of us, run up aisles."[20] The Bells of Joy, from Austin, Texas, had a hit in 1952 when their "Let's Talk About Jesus" reached the *Billboard* "race" pop chart. The Fairfield Four had its origins in a child quartet formed in Nashville in 1921. Among the members was seven-year-old Sam McCrary, who remained as the group's lead singer for forty years. The Fairfield Four were touring by the early 1930s, and were a popular recording group from 1946 until 1960, when McCrary became a full time pastor in Nashville. In 1980, an incarnation of the group featuring McCrary and 1940s members James Hill (baritone) and Isaac "Dicky" Freeman (bass), began appearing publicly again. McCrary died in March 1991, but the group continued singing, and an album was issued in 1992.[21]

To the gospel purist, the halcyon days of quartet singing ended around the mid-1950s as instrumental accompaniment became standard, moving gradually from a simple discreet guitar doing little more than stabilizing pitch and rhythm to fuller backings including organ and/or piano, bass and drums. The singers, not realizing the best was behind them, kept singing, and several new and powerful groups emerged during the late 1950s and 1960s, building on the style that had gone before. A few overdid the histrionics, collapsing the structure of their songs beneath the weight of unconvincing artifice. But the best were worthy successors to the masters who had gone before.

The Gospelaires of Dayton, Ohio, were formed in 1954, but did not become well known until the 1960s. The focal points of the group were the gravelly lead singing of Rev. Robert Washington, rendered even more distinctive by his ostentatiously guttural inhalations of breath—a technique more commonly used by preachers—and the ultrahigh tenor of Charles McLean. The Pilgrim Jubilee Singers were formed in Chicago in 1952 by brothers Cleve and Clay Graham, taking over from two other Graham brothers who had a Mississippi-based Pilgrim Jubilees in the mid-1940s. The group recorded without success for four different labels in the 1950s before succeeding in the 1960s with Peacock. Both Graham brothers are solid exponents of the "hard" style, and although their post-Peacock recordings often have a softened contemporary sound, their on-stage performances peak with a ferocious intensity. The Supreme Angels, later renamed Slim and the Supreme Angels to give more prominence to leader Howard "Slim" Hunt, have attracted little critical attention, but the stream of recordings they produced for the Nashville-based Nashboro label through the 1960s and 1970s attests to their popularity with the gospel audience.

Chief among the quartets of the 1960s were the Mighty Clouds of Joy, formed in Los Angeles in the late 1950s as the Sensational Wonders and featuring the lead singing of expatriate Alabaman Willie Joe Ligon. They adopted their present name early in their career, and their first recordings were issued, in a piece of nominative one-upmanship, as by the Mighty Mighty Clouds of Joy. The Clouds reached the top by being the hardest-driving, best-dressed, house-wreckingest group in the business. The formula worked into the 1990s, and the group is easily the best-known current quartet, with tours to Europe and Japan among its credits. Like the Pilgrim Jubilees, their later recordings have a smoother, less extravagant sound than their earlier Peacock releases, but their concert performances retain the high-powered extroversion for which they have always been known.

The 1970s brought a dilution of quartet music, as various developments from the previous decade coalesced. Whereas once the quartets had influenced soul music, now the secular influence rebounded. Rather than serving as accompaniment, the instrumental sound had by now virtually equal status with the singing, which had been adjusted to accommodate the change. Harmonies moved to a higher range and became less elaborate, with the bass singer all but ousted by the bass guitar. At the same time, the quartets' popularity was eclipsed by choirs and similar ensembles. But groups were still evolving. Formed in 1945, the Jackson Southernaires, from Mississippi, started recording in 1964; their 1968 recording of "Too Late" was a national gospel hit. In the early 1970s, the second generation of Southernaires, led by Frank Williams, incorporated aspects of choral style into their backup singing; today, the group is one of the most popular in the mid-south. The lead singer on the Southernaires' first recordings was Willie Banks, a baritone with a gospel pedigree going back to the 1940s. Banks left the Southernaires soon after "Too Late" and started his own group, Willie Banks and the Messengers, which contrasted his traditional lead singing with the more modern sound of his back-up singers. Banks died in 1993, aged sixty-four. Willie Neal Johnson and the Gospel Keynotes (called later " . . . and the New Keynotes") combine choral-styled backing with a "hard" lead and a frenetic concert performance style,[22] while the Canton Spirituals—originally from Canton, Mississippi, but now based in Jackson—enjoyed considerable Midsouth success with a concert recording made in Memphis in 1993.[23]

Regardless of the shadow that has fallen over quartets on the national gospel scene, hundreds of amateur groups exist all over the United States, singing at local programs, in churches, and at each other's anniversaries. Members of the backing band are usually counted as full members, so with four or five singers, a "quartet" can have a membership of eight, nine, or ten. Many groups, especially the older ones, are organized along quasicorporate lines, with office holders, formal rules, and a chain of command.[24] Posts include president, manager, secretary, treasurer and occasionally deputies; sometimes the group has enough positions for every member to have one. The president is in charge of the group's business affairs and chairs meetings and rehearsals. He is often the group spokesman, although sometimes the job is delegated. (In quartet interviews, it is common for the spokesman to do most of the talking, with the others looking on and responding only if directly asked a question.) The manager is in charge of performance-related matters, ranging from bookings, fees, and rehearsals to deciding what clothes the group will wear while singing. The secretary handles correspondence, minutes from the meetings and group membership records. Many groups also have a music director, or "minister of music," who selects and arranges repertoire. Most put any money they earn into a pool for expenses such as uniforms and travel. Anything left over—there often isn't—is distributed to members as earnings or kept as a reserve. The apparent on-stage hierarchy does not always reflect the group structure; the lead singer may be the most junior member.

For public appearances, most quartets wear matching clothes, known as "uniforms." These range from business suits with matching neckties to specially made stage clothes in bright colors. Portia Maultsby describes the wearing of costumes as "synonymous with Black musicians," and sees it as part of an on-stage flamboyance "providing another vehicle for expression that is a traditional African concept."[25] Certainly, African-American performers, secular and sacred, tend to reject the white rock music habit of "dressing down" to perform. The university quartets of the 1870s performed in suits or tuxedos; in the heyday of the blues, the touring entourages of top artists such as B. B. King, Bobby Bland and many others included valets to look after their wardrobes. Today, the Mighty Clouds of Joy boast that their uniforms are made by the tailor who makes clothes for the soul group the Temptations.[26] The rationale is simple—you have to be successful to have fine clothes, so if you have fine clothes, you must be successful.

The on-stage rules for quartets have changed little from the 1950s. Songs are mainly upbeat, with an occasional slow one for contrast. Many groups include at least one songwriter, so part of the repertoire is composed within the group, lending a distinctive style, and, through the songwriter royalties, an increased share of the proceeds from any recordings. Like many other aspects of gospel music, the area of songwriting has dimensions not present in its secular equivalent. One is the technique of using another song as the basis for a new composition—a practice which in the secular world usually leads to litigation. A significant difference between sacred and secular songwriting is that gospel writers generally believe they are merely conduits for words being handed to them by God.[27] Harvey Watkins, Jr., of the Canton Spirituals, explained his approach to songwriting: "When I get ready to write a song, I do it just like when I get ready to read the Bible. I feel like there's a time for all things, and when I get ready to read the Bible, I like to read it with spirit. I like to read it when I feel that feeling inside of me. Then I won't forget what I've read. When I get to feeling like that about a song, I don't have to write it down. It comes down from on high, and it don't go nowhere."[28] Jessie Mae Hemphill is a blues singer from Como, Mississippi, who also sings sacred songs, and has at times expressed a desire to "quit singing blues" and perform only "spirituals." She writes many of her own blues, and has also composed sacred songs, about which she says, "Those songs are given to me, just come to me. I don't know how, I guess God just. . . . I go to humming and going on, I'll be cleaning up and washing, or cooking or something and the Lord just puts something there. I start to sing one verse and I don't know what the next verse is going to be. But when I finish that verse, there'll be another one there waiting on me, just like somebody's writing them down. And I know it's God doing it."[29]

Gospel audiences also like to hear standards, songs that have been around since the beginning of quartet singing and before. Thomas A. Dorsey's material is still frequently found in quartet repertoires, along with arrangements of old spirituals and songs going back to Isaac Watts. Groups try to bring a different element to their arrangements of standards, something which puts their unique stamp on the song. The results can be interesting—in 1978, the Sensational Nightingales recorded the usually staid hymn "At the Cross" to a jaunty upbeat swing rhythm;[30] in the late 1960s, the Five Blind Boys of Alabama's lead singer, Clarence Fountain, recorded the usually flowing "Just a Closer Walk With Thee" in a rapid march time.[31] A number of songs—for example, "Too Close to Heaven," "Remember Me," "Jesus Is On the Main Line"— are staples which appear in the songlists of groups all over the United States. Other songs are identified with certain groups, usually after a recording success—the Mighty Clouds of Joy and "What a Friend," the Trumpeteers with "Milky White Way," the Swan Silvertones and Claude Jeter with "Oh, Mary Don't You Weep," the Spirit of Memphis with "Happy In the Service of the Lord," the Blind Boys of Mississippi with "Our Father" and "Leave You In the Hands of the Lord." Forty years after Archie Brownlee recorded them, people still want to hear the Blind Boys' old hits, says Sandy Foster, lead singer with the 1992 version of the group. "You do them, no matter what."[32] Since the late 1960s, the Pilgrim Jubilees have been performing a lachrymose "sermonette" called "A Child's Blood," which uses Thomas Dorsey's "Precious Lord" as its musical foundation. It first appeared as a double-sided Peacock single; when the group recorded it in 1994 in front of an audience in the Graham brothers' hometown of Houston, Mississippi, it had grown to a fourteen-minute hard-gospel epic.[33]

"Sermonettes" are a bridge between preaching and singing. They are not the exclusive property of quartets—Shirley Caesar is one soloist who makes frequent use of them—but they are popular with groups and their audiences. A sermonette is a morality tale, usually told by the lead singer while the rest of the singers hum or sing softly in the background. In most cases, the last line of the story is also the first line of the song it is introducing. In the early 1970s, the Mighty Clouds of Joy used a sermonette about a mother saying goodbye to her son as he leaves to fight in Vietnam to introduce their song "Pray for Me."[34] In 1992, the same song had a different story, about a young man who left the choir to sing rock 'n' roll, became hooked on drugs, was rescued by his mother, and after returning to the church, went back to "the club where he once sang" to perform one last song—"Pray For Me."[35] The Pilgrim Jubilees' "A Child's Blood" tells of a child whipped to death by her father for disobeying him and "finding Jesus." Most of the stories are simplistic and stereotyped, but all carry a strong moral point, and singers usually deliver them very much in the cadence of a preacher's sermon. (The cliché element was recognized in 1965 by the Drexall Singers, when they introduced the sermonette for their two-part "View the City" by proclaiming that "it's not about an old woman, it's not about an old gray-haired minister. . . ." However, they then reveal that "this is about a little girl who was blind and crippled from birth.")[36] Joe Ligon, of the Mighty Clouds, talked during a tour of Britain in 1993 about his "Pray For Me" sermonette, also offering an insight into one aspect of gospel music's appeal: "If I'm singing that song and there is a mother or father in the audience who has experienced this—and many of them have—and they finally got their child back, they can become emotional because they have lived it. Some people hear things [in gospel songs] that they have lived and experienced, and when it happens, they go, 'Oh, yeah. Ooooooh, I made it through there. Hallelujah! Praise the Lord.' "[37]

A quartet in performance has a dual task—to present a religious message and to be entertaining. The gospel group has an advantage over most of its secular counterparts, in that its audience is almost always predisposed to like the group and to respond positively to its music. A secular group has to win the audience to succeed; a gospel group has to lose the audience to fail. Gospel groups can be more passionate than their secular counterparts because they are singing about religious faith, a stronger emotion than the romantic love which is the staple of pop music. They are also singing about a communal experience. A secular singer can extol the virtues of his or her "baby"; the emotion may be one with which the audience is conversant, but the particular experience is the singer's alone. A gospel singer's message connects directly with the audience's firsthand experiences and beliefs, enabling a deeper rapport between singer and audience and fueling the intensity of the performance.

A group's success as entertainer and religious instructor is often measured by how effectively it can "shout" its audience—move it into a jubilant state of ecstasy, with some people "falling out." A "shouting" audience is taken as an indication of divine intervention, but groups have a number of earthly artifices with which to assist the Almighty. A heavy bass and drum rhythm will set the feet tapping. Various dynamics employed, especially by the lead singer as he builds to a climax or brings the pace down again, will influence the audience's mood, as will on-stage movement. Leaving the stage to go out into the audience is guaranteed to lift the excitement level, although microphone leads can tether a singer to a narrow strip along the front rows of seats. Sometimes the lead singer's microphone cord is much longer than the others; for the affluent group or venue, a radio transmitter microphone solves the problem. But when audience (and group) are deeply "in the spirit," a singer will often simply lay the microphone down and go into the audience, singing without amplification.

(The term "shout" is somewhat misleading, implying as it does a loud vocal expression. Any manifestation of religious delight, ranging from handclapping and rhythmic swaying to full-blown shrieks, is part of the shout. The term derives from the "ring shout," a now almost extinct African-based form of worship in which participants form a circle and move around, singing, praying, and stamping their feet until they achieve a state of religious ecstasy.)[38]

"In the spirit" is not a one-way street. Singing also affects group members, and lead singers often appear to be in a state of trance as a performance reaches its climax. This phenomenon is examined by Morton Marks in the book *Religious Movements in Contemporary America*.[39] He concludes that gospel music is "the repository of African-based performance rules in the United States," and that performances are intended to "shout" both lead singer and audience, sending them into a "trance." To a degree, this is true. Not only do gospel singers become "filled with the spirit" while singing, but, after a particularly intense performance, they can remain in a semihypnotic state for some minutes after leaving the stage. However, care must be taken in analyzing the depth of this state. No matter how "in the spirit" singers may become, they must remain aware of their surroundings and of the dynamics of the performance.[40] If they "fall out," entering the semiunconscious state of complete surrender to the Holy Spirit, they can no longer perform. This does happen, but only occasionally.

The specter of rock 'n' roll is constantly with gospel quartets. Soul music, in particular, has feasted off gospel, taking its moves, its singing styles, and some of its best singers. Sam Cooke from the Soul Stirrers, is the best-known quartet example, but there are many others—Wilson Pickett from the Violinaires, Lou Rawls from the Pilgrim Travelers, O. V. Wright and Joe Hinton from the Spirit of Memphis, Otis Clay from the Gospel Songbirds. Entire groups have defected. The Selah Jubilee Singers, gospel recording artists since 1939 (or 1931 if an unissued session for Columbia is regarded as the starting point) became R&B recording artists the Larks in the early 1950s. The Royal Sons, from North Carolina, became the Five Royales in 1951. In Memphis, the Dixie Nightingales became Ollie and the Nightingales in the early 1960s; lead singer Ollie Hoskins later went solo as Ollie Nightingale, and was still performing soul music in Memphis clubs in the 1990s. Occasionally, groups tried to work both sides of the street—a ploy which had embarrassing results for the New Orleans Humming Four, who, after recording gospel numbers for the Imperial label, were persuaded to "switch over to rock 'n' roll." Two of the five members didn't want to change and were replaced; the revamped group took the name the Hawks. "We were two groups in one," lead singer Joseph Gaines told Lynn Abbott. "When we went for the saints we were the Humming Four, and when we went for the sinners we were the Hawks."[41] Soon after making the change, the group was booked to appear on a show split between gospel and R&B. Before an audience of ten thousand people, the New Orleans Humming Four appeared in the first half and the Hawks in the second. The juxtaposition had immediate repercussions, with many churches closing their doors to the turncoats.

But for every quartet singer who "crosses over," many more stay resolutely with gospel. James Payne, baritone singer for the Soproco Singers (also known as the New Orleans Chosen Five), recalls rejecting a nightclub owner's urging in the early 1940s to "sing Inkspots stuff" and make more money, saying, "I'd rather sing gospel if I have to sing it in overalls!"[42] Clarence Fountain rebukes audiences which he feels are not showing enough enthusiasm by contrasting the program with a secular show. "If James Brown was here tonight, you couldn't get near the place. People would be screaming for blocks away, serving the god they want to serve. In rock 'n' roll, folk don't mind letting the world know what side they're on. We say we're Christians, but we sure oughta show some sign."[43] Many groups and artists tell of rejecting offers to sing secular music; in 1965, the veteran Dixie Hummingbirds sang of their devotion to gospel, echoing James Payne's rebuff of nearly twenty-five years earlier:

> We would make more money,
> If we would sing rock 'n' roll.
> But I'm gonna sing for Jesus.
> If I don't have change of clothes.[44]

# MELVIN MOSLEY AND THE SPIRIT OF MEMPHIS

*"If the Spirit hits you, you're gonna move!"*

*The Spirit of Memphis in performance (from left): Melvin Mosley, Robert Stewart (partly obscured, in white shirt), Brown Berry, Willie Wilson, Lee Thompson (with guitar), Jimmy Allen, Jesse Allen, Percy Cole, Huebert Crawford. (In the background is the pastor of the church at which the group is singing.)*

The small boy sits in the front pew. He's tried a few other seats, but this one has the best view. He's so close to the singers that he has to lean his head back to watch their faces; if he looks straight ahead, all he sees are tailored jackets, white shirts and rhythmically moving hands. One member of the group he's watching is tucked off to one side behind a drum kit. The other eight, wearing identical charcoal-gray suits, are lined across the narrow space between the front pew and the altar table. Two play guitars, one a bass guitar. They are singing:

> We are the Spirit of Memphis Quartet
> Been singing sixty-two years, haven't got tired yet.[1]

The group *is* the Spirit of Memphis. And it *has* been singing for sixty-two years, although none of the men performing before the small boy's solemn gaze was born when the original Spirit of Memphis started singing in 1930. It doesn't matter. The group is an institution, a legend that transcends individuals.

Today, its manager and lead singer is Melvin Mosley, a solidly built, athletic-looking man, soft-spoken, with a formal cast to his speech so that he sometimes sounds as though he plans complete sentences in his mind before uttering them. He is affable, but with an underlying air of detached reserve. He's forty-one, a family man with a wife and four children, who was born and raised in Memphis. A church-goer all his life, he was brought up in the Mt. Zion Baptist Church and was a member of it until "the second Sunday in December 1991," when he moved his membership to the Bethlehem Baptist Church to be where his wife and children were. He's a supervisor in the clothing department of the Shelby County Correctional Center, the county prison on the eastern outskirts of Memphis. He became manager of the Spirit of Memphis in 1988, on the death of Spirit pioneer Earl Malone. That was ten years after he joined the group, when he faced the daunting task of taking over as lead singer from Jethroe "Jet" Bledsoe, one of gospel's great voices, who was retiring after a forty-four-year career with the Spirit.

"I've been with the group since 1978. When I came into it, some of the original singers were still here. Earl Malone was here, Robert Reed was here, Fred Howard was here. He was a baritone singer, and he was the one that brought me to the group. He and I were working at the same place at that time and Jet Bledsoe was retiring, so they needed another lead singer, and I replaced him. Those were some big shoes to fill, I'll tell you. He was powerful. At the time, I was singing with my choir, in the male chorus at church. I've been in church all my life, and I've been in music since I was about eleven years old. I recorded a gospel record in 1973, 'The Day I Was Converted.' The flipside was 'It is Real.' It did pretty good. I had a thousand pressed and I sold a thousand, so I was proud of that. But I had never sung with a quartet before I started singing with the Spirit of Memphis. They just liked my talent, and after I got into the group, they molded me into the sound they needed me to produce. It wasn't too much of a . . . well, it was a lot of change, but it was more of a challenge than anything else. It wasn't a strain. Because I'd always liked quartet singing, and in my spare time I would sometimes practice by myself, singing with some record I might hear. Sometimes it was the Spirit of Memphis. So when the opportunity presented itself, it was a real smooth transition because it was something I had always wanted to do. And it just worked out real good. Earl Malone was a great voice instructor, he was a great teacher of singing. Although he was the bass singer, he could master each voice, including tenor, so I really had it made. I think he was 'bout one of the greatest singers I've heard."

*Malone, Reed, Howard, Bledsoe—add in Silas Steele and Willmer "Little Axe" Broadnax, and it's the greatest of all Spirit of Memphis lineups, from its finest era, in the late 1940s and early 1950s. This was a time when every "name" group had its powerhouse lead singer, someone who could "rock the church" until the rafters cracked. The Spirit of Memphis was different. It had three, which meant that Jet Bledsoe could start a song like "Every Time I Feel the Spirit" in his baritone range, work it until he peaked, then pass it on to the higher voices. Silas Steele would ratchet up the tension and the pressure, then hand it off to Little Axe for the catapult into high tenor and the hard-edged coruscating brilliance of molten metal being poured from a blast furnace.*

*Melvin Mosley and the Spirit of Memphis are very aware of the legacy they have inherited. They do a lot of vintage Spirit material, and the group is still organized "in the old way" with businesslike formality. Responsibilities are divided among the nine members, and only guitarist/singer Rev. Percy Cole, forty-six, second lead Willie Wilson, forty-five, and drummer Robert Stewart, thirty, do not have titles. Membership records are kept, and it is to these that "minister of music" Huebert Crawford turns, unfastening a small suitcase and taking out a hard-covered notebook. "Brown Berry, joined January 3, 1965," he says flicking through the pages. "Huebert Crawford, joined December 3, 1977. Melvin Mosley, June 10, 1978." Every member, including those who have been and gone, has a page.*

 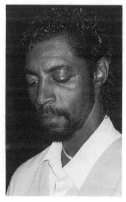 

*Melvin Mosley, manager, lead singer.*

*Rev. Percy Cole, high tenor vocals, guitar.*

*Willie Wilson, second lead and tenor vocals.*

*"Jimmie Allen, September 4, 1982. Jesse Allen, November 2, 1985. Lee Thompson, February 21, 1989. Willie Wilson, March 1, 1991. Percy Cole, now he joined in 1976, but he was out for a while. He stayed as a member and rejoined on July 25, 1991." The distinction is important. Anyone who leaves the Spirit of Memphis and relinquishes his membership is not allowed to rejoin. While Percy Cole stopped singing, he retained his membership, and so was able to come back. "And Robert Stewart, he joined officially on February 6, 1992, but he's been playing with us for about two and a half years." As well as being musical director, Crawford, fifty-four, sings and plays guitar and keyboards. Jesse Allen, fifty, is the bass singer and the assistant manager; his brother, Jimmie Allen, forty-three, is the baritone singer and the secretary-treasurer; Lee Thompson, fifty, plays guitar and is the vice president; Brown Berry, fifty-six, the longest-serving member of this Spirit incarnation, plays bass guitar and is the group president.*

"THE group originated in 1930 as the Spirit of Memphis. In 1928, they were singing as the TM&S Singers. They assembled from different churches, and called themselves the TM&S Singers. [The initials derive from the Baptist churches attended by the founding members—Tree of Life, Mount Olive and St. Matthew's.] But in 1930, those singers decided under the leadership of Mr. James Darling to change the name to the Spirit of Memphis Quartet [derived from the *Spirit of St. Louis*, the aircraft in which Charles Lindbergh flew the Atlantic in 1927]. So when

*Robert Stewart, drums.*

*Huebert Crawford, minister of music, guitar, keyboards, tenor vocals.*

*Jimmy Allen, secretary/treasurer, baritone vocals.*

we celebrate our annual anniversary date, we relate with 1930 being the year of the group starting. We try to keep the original sound, as close to it as we can. With the new personnel, we have to constantly branch out and do new material. But we still have the traditional sound of the group, so the older people can still perceive us as the original group.

"Off the top of my head, I would say we have about thirty-five or forty songs in the group's repertoire. We're in the process of learning new material now. Well, it's not so much new material—we don't do a lot of original tunes. The only people who really bring original tunes are Crawford and myself—songs that he's written or I've written. Most of the songs we do are PDs [public domain]. We take them and rearrange them, put the Spirit of Memphis style to 'em. Crawford and I take care of most of the arranging. Everybody can just about master their voice [vocal parts], but if there's a certain role we want a voice to make, then usually he or I will do that."

*The group's 1930 name was the Spirit of Memphis Quartet. The group has long had more than four members, so the "quartet" was dropped years ago—a 1936 photograph is captioned "Spirit of Memphis gospel singers." Recordings for King between 1949 and 1952 were credited to the Spirit of Memphis Quartet, but when the group moved to Peacock in 1953, "quartet" did not go with it. Old habits die hard, however, and some people still refer to the "Spirit of Memphis Quartet."*

Jesse Allen, assistant manager, bass vocals

Lee Thompson, vice president, guitar.

Brown Berry, president, bass guitar.

"I try to portray it as the Spirit of Memphis, because we have nine members. But some of the disc jockeys that have been following the group down through the years, they still use Spirit of Memphis Quartet. I think the reason they say this is because a lot of times in our repertoire, we just cut all the music [instruments] off and cut the extra singer, the top voice, off and just do bass, baritone and tenor songs. We do four-part harmony stuff, so I guess they still relate to us as the Spirit of Memphis Quartet. Because quartet is more of a style than a number. Basically, the definition is four, of course—bass, baritone, tenor, and lead. Later it became just a style. When I talk to people to book programs, I usually say 'the Spirit of Memphis.' But a lot of the people who have been in this a lot longer than I have will say 'the Spirit of Memphis Quartet,' 'cause that's what it was called down through the years. So we won't argue with that.

"Memphis is a real gospel center. We have a lot of gospel singers that have originated here in Memphis, then moved out. And there's a lot of groups—I couldn't give a number, but there's a lot. And I would like to think this group had a lot of the bearing on this, because it was the first professional group in Memphis. And a lot of groups respected the Spirit of Memphis for a long time; a lot of the groups that started singing here in Memphis came out trying to pattern themselves after the Spirit of Memphis. I like to think of my group as the father of all those ones, because this group was the first group that brought other professional groups in. Like Sam Cooke and the Soul Stirrers, the Golden Gates, the Trumpeteers, the Swan Silvertones, Dixie Hummingbirds— this group, the Spirit of Memphis, was the first group that booked all those professional groups into Memphis. Groups now are booking in the Mighty Clouds of Joy, the Jackson Southernaires, the Gospel Keynotes and so on. But it all originated with this group. So we have a good feeling. If they had another hundred groups here, it would make us feel good, because it's something that came after this group started the ball rolling."

*Mosley's reference to the "bringing in" of other groups reaches back to the late 1930s, when the Spirit of Memphis booked the Famous Blue Jay Singers, from Birmingham, Alabama, to perform at a local program.[2] Other local groups copied the idea of booking out-of-town headliners, but the programs presented by the Spirit of Memphis, often in the Church of God in Christ's seven thousand-seat Mason Temple in south Memphis, were always among the biggest and best. The Spirit became Memphis's first full-time professional group in 1949, its members pushed into abandoning their day jobs by the success of their broadcasts over radio station WDIA and of their first nationally distributed commercial recording, "Happy in the Service of the Lord/My Life Is in His Hands,"[3] made soon after Silas Steele joined the group. Within a short time, they were earning enough to pay each member two hundred dollars a week. The quartet boom faded in the early 1960s, and the Spirit of Memphis "came off the road" in 1962, reverting to semiprofessional status. It was still a top gospel quartet, and continued recording for the Peacock label until 1968—the most senior member of the current group, Brown Berry, played on the last two Peacock sessions—then for a succession of smaller regional labels. In 1987, it had a local hit with a remake of "Happy in the Service of the Lord," and the number is now one of the most frequently requested in its repertoire.[4] Today, all members work at regular jobs, except for Huebert Crawford, who retired after being injured in his job as a truck driver. But the Spirit still does better than most other Memphis groups.*

"We have been blessed to make enough to not only buy clothes [uniforms], but we own our van, and one of our members [Crawford] has invested in a Greyhound bus. So we're fortunate as far as the finances are concerned. We'd be one of the more successful groups in this city. We try to get a new uniform at least three or four times a year. And we try to have the treasury in such a shape that we can use it to purchase the uniforms. The rate we charge for performances is usually just an agreement between myself and whoever the promoter is. We usually charge based on the distance of the concert from where we are. Local churches are cheaper than out of town because we don't have as far to go—we're right here at home. We draw enough people to sometimes have open door programs where you don't charge a fee, you just have a collection. But my main thing since I've been manager is not to harp so much on the finance. My main concern is that we be as spiritual as possible in our singing, and the only finance I ask is to make sure that my fellows are not out anything, that we're not spending out of our pockets to go sing. As long as we're compensated for our efforts, I'm satisfied. We don't have any trouble making out-of-town trips if the distance isn't more than five hundred or six hundred miles. Anything over six hundred or seven hundred miles, it can be kinda strenuous to try to get back before work on Monday morning. But we have done it. We've been as far as Detroit, and that's seven hundred and fifty or eight hundred miles. Once we've done the program, we have to hit the highway. Now this is not often. More often it's something like from here to St. Louis or Little Rock. That's not bad. You're talking about two hundred or three hundred miles. But when you start talking about seven hundred or eight hundred miles, that's hard work."

*The Spirit of Memphis will sing wherever gospel music is wanted— auditoriums, schools, colleges, churches large or small. The only restriction is that Sunday programs don't start too early. "We all go to different churches," Mosley explains. "So our afternoon concerts are usually booked at 3:30 to give us time to come from our churches, get into the uniform we are going to wear and get to the program." Aside from his family and church, gospel music is the hub of Melvin Mosley's life. He enjoys his singing, he's proud of his group and its history, and he enjoys talking about it to anyone who is interested. He also has clear ideas on what a gospel singer's character should be, the nature of the music, and what it can do.*

"A person has to have that inner spirit to appreciate gospel music. If you are a spiritually inclined person, you can relate to the emotion of getting caught up, and to words that relate to the awareness of God. And as you sing inspirationally, you become inspirational. And as you become inspirational, you can reach someone else that has that same inner Christianity. The more energetic you become, the more in the spirit you become, the more the person who can relate to it in the same way as you will get something from what you are singing. The biggest thing to me is to reach someone. If there's someone in the audience that's bewildered or dismayed and you can reach that person—that's an inspiration to me. And I know this group is not singing in vain because we have helped someone spiritually.[5] That's the biggest thing for me.

"I sang a little rhythm and blues in the late '60s, 1967, '68, '69. It's not that much different from gospel—it's just the awareness of God in gospel, the awareness that he is alive and you're gonna praise him. In blues, it's . . . 'Well, I'm having a bad day, my girlfriend left me, everything's gone wrong. . . .' They say gospel basically does stem from blues. I agree with that, because in traditional gospel, the musical changes, the patterns are the same as blues. But like I say, with a blues you like to say you're sad and your girlfriend has left you or your wife has left you—you're having a hard time. The gospel is more like, regardless of how bad my times is, I can always look to the Lord, and I have a good day because he inspires me. The musical changes, like from C, F to G, are basically the same, but you're singing different words.

"The thing I really like about gospel is that it enlightens you. If you sit and listen to the blues and it's a good blues song, the first thing a person will probably want to do is, 'Well, I can relate with this song, so I think I'll take me a drink.' But with the gospel, when it is sung traditionalist like we do and with the feeling that we put into it, it lets you know, 'Well, hey! The Lord is really good, and it's not as bad as I thought it was. And I think I'm going to have me a real good week this week that's going to last until next Sunday. And I can't wait until next Sunday gets here.' Gospel gives you that inner glow about yourself that makes it so it's not so bad."

*The church is a small wooden building, tucked back under trees on Warford Street in north Memphis. The front door is unpainted plywood; the few windows are screened or boarded over. The homemade sign in front says in black letters on bare wood that it is The Temple of Truth and Love, of "no denomonation" (with the second "n" reversed). The pastor is Elder Toney; service is 11 a.m. Sunday. But now it's 3 p.m. Sunday, and the temple is hosting a Spirit of Memphis program. The temple's interior is more sumptuous than the outside suggests. The walls are paneled in wood veneer; the ceiling is white and low. The choir stalls, pulpit and altar occupy half the room, leaving space for only about half a dozen white-painted pews. With fifty people in it, this temple would be crowded.*

*The program is virtually an extension of the Sunday service, and the opening set is done by the church choir, about a dozen of them, with guitar, bass guitar, and drums. "We don't get in the spirit like we used to," they sing: if it's true, they must have been awesome in the days when they did get in the spirit. By the time the choir has done its three songs, two of its lead singers have "fallen out," overcome by the Holy Spirit, and the congregation is on its feet swaying, clapping, and shouting. The Spirit of Memphis keeps up the excitement. The members line up across the narrow space between the altar and the front pew, singers in front, musicians behind. Huebert Crawford stands at one end of the line, Melvin Mosley at the other. They swing into "We Are the Spirit of Memphis," and the professionalism and tradition are immediately apparent. With no "foldback" monitor system— the temple is too small to accommodate it—the singers cannot hear each other clearly, but the parts are still crisply defined and on key. At the bottom end, Jesse Allen sings the percussive "pumping" bass style he inherited from Earl Malone. It hasn't been fashionable for thirty years, but it provides a sure foundation for the other singers, particularly in the high-powered songs, such as "He Never Let Go My Hand"—a Spirit staple since 1951— as they gain momentum like a wall of water rushing down a dry river bed. The Spirit has newer songs, mostly written by Mosley or Crawford, but today the focus is on the old ones, and they're going well. By the time Percy Cole's tenor swings into "This Is a Mean Old World," underpinned by Jesse Allen's resonant bass, the church is alight. Three young women stand, clapping and swaying in unison. In the pew ahead of them, an elderly woman wearing a light-blue Sunday best dress and a formidable black hat does her holy dance. She hasn't got much room, so she moves in the space between the pews. Four steps towards the aisle, four steps back; four steps forward, four back. Out front, Percy Cole is singing "I shout when I get happy, that's the way we Christians do."*

"It's very seldom we perform where they're not shouting and running down the aisle. And the thing I feel when all this is going on . . . I'm just grateful. I'll be feeling thankful at that particular time to the Lord himself. This is why I'm here. I'm trying to inspire somebody, trying to make them feel spiritually good today. If there's someone here that hasn't felt this before and feels it today, then my singing is not in vain. And it gives me a feeling just to be more in awe of the presence of God's spirit. By being the lead singer, I move a lot when I'm singing. The background singers don't move that much. They'll show expressions . . . it's mostly face or hands. But if I just stand here and sing my lyrics, well, I may just bob my head, then you'll bob your head. But if I move, before you know it, you'll move. It's a spiritual relationship with the audience that never fails. When someone is caught up in the Spirit, they wanna move. Even if they don't normally move. They wanna move. Once the Spirit hits you, you're gonna move. I don't care who you are, how calm you try to be, how stiff-necked you try to be, if the Spirit hits you, you're gonna move!"

*The group rehearses once a week at the First Pleasant Hill Missionary Baptist Church in the suburb of Binghampton. Mosley says, "We meet every week, whether we rehearse or not. Sometimes we just have a meeting and discuss business and what we have to do, engagements and things." In rehearsal, the group lines up as it does on stage, only with Mosley and*

*Crawford standing off to one side to direct the singing and playing. They maintain a busy pace, working through the songs, and are quick to rebuke any lapses in attention. At the end of the evening, everyone stands in a circle and joins hands while a prayer is said. Equipment is loaded into vans; the church door is locked. But the members of the group are in no hurry to leave, and stand in the small parking lot talking and laughing. Melvin Mosley, looking on, speaks quietly and reflectively, almost to himself.*

"This is what makes the group. Everything is all over. We've had the rehearsal, we know what we're going to wear [at the next program], but everyone is still standing around together. That's the fellowship. That's what makes the group. Talent isn't everything. You can have a fellow that has the talent, but he's got to be able to get along. It's the fellowship that makes the group."

# ODELL HAMPTON AND THE TRUE LOVING FIVE

*"Just holding on to our same style . . ."*

*The True Loving Five in rehearsal (from left): Atlean Harris, M. H. Hampton, Goodlow Kilpatrick, Odell Hampton. Absent: Shone Hampton, Curly Hampton.*

Odell Hampton talks quickly, even when he's relaxed. When he's excited, he leans forward and the words come rushing out, tumbling over each other in their haste to be heard. He is a tall slender man, sixty-six years old, with short graying hair and a close-cropped mustache. The gold in several of his top teeth glints as he talks, and his posture seems slightly stooped, as though his spine has permanently adapted to years of his leaning forward eagerly to talk or listen. He's manager and second lead singer for the True Loving Five, a family-based a cappella gospel singing group from the small town of Lamar in Benton County, Mississippi, near the Tennessee border. Twelve miles south is Holly Springs, the nearest town big enough to have a shopping mall of sorts; when the True Loving Five are away from home, they are often billed as being from Holly Springs.

The group has been singing since 1950—although members of the Hampton family started singing together as children well before then—and still cites as its main influence the Golden Gate Quartet, the silken-voiced Virginians who dominated jubilee gospel singing from the late 1930s through to the style's decline in the 1950s. The True Loving Five don't sound much like their mentors; whereas the Gates had an easy mellow style, the Five have a much harder rural edge. And the Gates sang in smooth elaborate harmonies, while the True Loving Five use almost no arranged harmonies at all. Instead they use the different textures of their voices to create a style virtually unique in quartet singing; the closest comparison is with work songs in which a number of men sing together to synchronize group labor such as wood chopping or laying railroad tracks. The True Loving Five have the same precision in their singing, and create the same crisp, jaggedly clear sound. They may set up disciplined rhythmic vocal patterns behind the lead singer—as with the interplay between lead and backing used in parts of "I'll Be Home When the Roll Is Called"—but it is all done in unison, with only the lead taking a part that sometimes differs from the backing.

*Odell Hampton, second lead singer and manager of the True Loving Five.*

Although they do not sing harmonies, the members identify their roles in the group by the traditional names used in quartet singing. The lead singer is sixty-eight-year-old Eugene "Curly" Hampton; Odell is second lead and manager; fifty-three-year-old M. H. Hampton—M. H. is his name, the initials don't stand for anything—is the high "fifth" singer. These three are brothers. Their sister, Atlean Harris—short, a little on the rotund side and looking a decade younger than her sixty-four years—is the tenor singer. Odell's son Shone, an eighteen-year-old college student, sings bass, and the baritone singer, the group's only non-Hampton, is thirty-nine-year-old Goodlow Kilpatrick. Count the names. Curley, Odell, M. H., Atlean, Shone, Goodlow . . . it's the True Loving Six. But there's plenty of precedent allowing gospel groups to have more members than the name suggests. The True Loving Five has had its name from the start, and a slight numerical disparity isn't going to force a change.

"We got that name and we've been having it ever since. Ain't never changed it. A lot of these gospel singers change their names, you know.

Get up and want to change. But that don't help none. That don't help a bit. The True Loving Five ain't *never* changed! It started as a family group. Me, I'm original. M. H. is original, and Curley—we're the ones that started the group. Our sister, she's one of the older ones in there, too. There's several others that have died or left the group, but now the young ones are coming along, like my son. The way we got it going, we used to have a quartet they called the Golden Gate Quartet. That was many years ago. And we used to listen at them when we were little children. We had those old battery radios, and that group would come on and sing, and we'd sit there at that radio. We decided we wanted to sing, too. And we used to copy them. So that's the way we got started. We used to have a boy that bassed [sang bass] for us, his name was Frankie Lee Stepson. He passed about five years ago. He wasn't kin to us, but he seemed just like a brother. And we used to have two boys sang with us; both of them have passed. We had one more boy, but he left away from here. He went to . . . I don't know where . . . New York or somewhere. And I say God's been good to us. He's still leaving some of the old True Loving Five back here. It's a blessing. Then my son, Shone, he took over the bass part since Frankie Lee died. We were practicing and he came to the door and listened. Then he said, 'Daddy, I believe I'm gonna practise with y'all.' I said, 'Do you know how to sing it?' 'Yes, sir.' I said, 'You asked for the job, you've got to mean it, you've got to go on.' He says, 'Yes, sir, I want to do it.' So then I talked to the rest of the group and they agreed. And he fell right in there. He was twelve years old. He wasn't singing bass then. He just took that over when he got able.

"We usually rehearse here [at Odell's home] or sometimes at Atlean's house, about a mile and a half on down the road. Every week, every Tuesday night if the Lord says so, we rehearse. There's got to be something happen mighty serious for us not to get together. We'll rehearse for, oh, about an hour or so. Sometimes, when we get on something we want to learn, we don't rehearse but one or two songs. We keep going back over it until we get it right that night. We'll try it again next rehearsal, then we'll say, 'How's it sound?' Say, 'It sounds good.' I say, 'Well, it's ready for the road then.' That's the test. We're ready to go out and sing it then. Curley is the main one who brings the songs into the group. He's the main arranger. Nobody in the group writes songs; we just pick 'em up. Sometimes we'll practice half a night on one song, trying to get it 'ranged up right. If it sounds right and fits in there right, we go on with it. If it doesn't, we come back and arrange it again. Work it around until every word fits in its place. That's the way we do it."

*It's uncertain how many songs the True Loving Five knows. "It's a gang of songs" is Odell Hampton's best estimate; Atlean Harris thinks it is "about two hundred, it could be more." Songs and arrangements are not written down. "We can just stand up, reach back and get 'em," says Odell. Their songs are firmly traditional, many of them drawn from the jubilee era that had such an impact on the Hampton family. The Five have never used instrumental accompaniment—referred to as "music" by gospel veterans—which Odell believes now works in their favor, although it also makes learning songs more difficult and calls for a high degree of cooperation among group members.*

"When a fellow wants to do something and you can't tell him, then you don't need him there. The one that can't stand being talked to, you don't need him. If the others can't talk to me and tell me to sing a little lower or whatever without me jumping off the handle and getting mad, then they don't need me. But when we want to do something and all of us get together . . . we'll agree and we'll finally get the song right. When you sing without music [instrumental accompaniment], it's a little harder. You've got to *sing* without that music. Nothing to hide behind, you see. It's that old style. It's coming back now. I have people call me up, say, 'Y'all the group that does the a cappella singing?' I tell him, 'That's the only thing we know how to do.' He says, 'That's what we want.' So then we talk and they tell me where we have to come to, and the next thing we'll be going somewhere we ain't never been before.

"We go everywhere. Wherever people want us to come, we go there. We work all round the [Lamar-Holly Springs] area, over to Memphis, to Jackson. We've been to New Orleans—that's the furthest we've been. We were on that World Fair down there in 1986.[1] Around here, we sing at churches. And we go to schools, fairs—we go to anywhere. Sometimes we'll go out during the week, like we've been to Ole Miss [University of Mississippi at Oxford, about forty miles from Lamar] during the week. Then we'll come back and on Saturday night we'll go somewhere, then on Sunday we'll be at another church. Sometimes we'll go to one church in the day, then at night we'll be in another town. They pay us. When the churches around here ask us how much we want, we tell 'em fifty-fifty. Half-and-half of whatever they raise. That's just to help the church. So if there ain't but two dollars raised, we take one and leave one for the church. But when we're going to these festivals and we're going off a good distance, they've got to write me a contract. Tell me when we get together, what they're going to give us to come.

"You don't find many groups now singing without music. Maybe that's where we're so lucky and get around so much. We've never used music. When we started out, there wasn't any music. We started out a cappella and we're still just holding on to our same style. We never used no guitar, nothing. One time we got a whole lot of amps and guitars and things, but we never used them. Just sent them back and kept on in our style. No music. And by the help of the good Lord, it looks as though we're having success with our style. It's hard to part from your raising, and we came up without music. And I'm glad we did. I've got nothing against music, but I'm glad we held on to our a cappella. We sing jubilee, we sing spiritual, and we sing bassing songs. We just try to sing 'em all, as long as it's gospel singing. The bassing song is one where the bass takes over. Then a jubilee, it's spiritual, but it's a fast song. Then we sing a spiritual song, that's sorta slow and you can feel the Spirit pretty good."

*Members of the True Loving Five attend three different churches. Atlean Harris belongs to the Church of God in Christ, and goes to services in Holly Springs. Goodlow Kilpatrick also belongs to a Holly Springs church, St. Mark's Baptist. Odell, Shone, Curley and M. H. Hampton are members of the Sand Hill Missionary Baptist Church on the outskirts of Lamar, just across the railroad line on the turnoff from Highway 7. It's been the family church all their lives—Odell and Curley are on the board of deacons—and it was where fourteen-year-old Odell Hampton saw his idols, the Golden Gate Quartet.*

"The Golden Gates were the first group I ever heard singing that song 'Jonah.'[2] It was a jubilee song. And when I heard that, I was like'n' to have a fit. 'Cause I didn't figure nobody could make their mouth do like the way those boys were singing. And finally, our old pastor got them to sing down here. We were standing outside the church, 'cause we didn't have the money. They weren't charging but fifteen cents at the door, but we didn't have it. So we were all round, trying to peep in. And my granddaddy said, 'It ain't nice, all you standing around out here. Do you want to go in?' And he paid for about ten of us to go in there. Said, 'Go on in and enjoy yourselves.' And I'm telling you the truth, when those boys got to singing, if my granddaddy hadn't paid our way in, I'da broke in there somehow. I never heard anybody sing that way. People jumping up and down, man, weren't those people jumping up and down! Those Golden Gates. And they were dressed fine, oh, man, they were dressed fine. I remember it like it was last night.

"The Golden Gates were the first group we ever listened to. That was where we started. After the war another group came on, that was the Fairfield Four. Then the next one we heard singing nothing but jubilee was the Trumpeteers, from Baltimore, Maryland. Man, they were rough! [i.e., very good]. We heard them singing that 'Milky White Way.'[3] And we just kept on listening to all those good singers. The Five Blind Boys [of Mississippi]. Man! We heard the Five Blind Boys, then we heard the Five Blind Boys from Alabama. We saw all of them. They've been to Holly Springs, right here, in my time."

*Then came the days of the big programs in Memphis. They started around 1937 or 1938 when the Spirit of Memphis Quartet brought the Blue Jay Singers from Birmingham, Alabama, to town for a special program. Soon, other groups such as the Pilgrim Travelers and the Golden Gates were regular visitors; it may have been on one of these trips that the Gates traveled the extra forty or so miles to Lamar to start the Hamptons on their singing career. As quartet singing boomed in the 1940s and 1950s, more groups went on the road, and more visited Memphis. Mason Temple in southwest Memphis was a popular venue for the big programs, and that's where Odell and the other Hamptons went to see the finest gospel singers in the land—the Spirit of Memphis, the Fairfield Four, the Pilgrim Travelers, the Five Blind Boys (of Alabama and Mississippi), and many more—"we saw 'em all."*

"We used to hear tell of them coming. The Spirit of Memphis used to bring 'em. They used to come to Memphis once a year. And Lord, Mason's Temple couldn't hold the folk. Couldn't hold 'em. And that's a big building. But every time they put out that the Fairfield Four or the Spirit of Memphis or the Five Blind Boys were going to be there—man, a month before time, those boys would have sold so many tickets. So we would go there and get the tickets away ahead. And that's the way we got to see and hear them. They were all there, man, and I'm sitting there hollering and whistling at them. Yes, sir! I hollered at those boys. They could sing!

"Now you take the Trumpeteers, Pilgrim Travelers, Spirit of Memphis, Five Blind Boys and them all, they've been here in Lamar. They would go to churches, but they would also go to big places where there's more room. One time here, they had the Spirit of Memphis, the Five Blind Boys [of Mississippi] and the Pilgrim Travelers from Los Angeles, California. And man, it was packed. Folks couldn't even get in the building. They were upstairs, downstairs, all in the door. And as many on the outside trying to peep in the windows. And I thought that was the biggest crowd there was. But I was talking to the Spirit of Memphis. I said, 'Boy, y'all got a crowd in here today.' And they said, 'Ain't nobody here, Mr. Hampton. You wait until tonight. You come on, go back with us tonight to Mason Temple.' And he was telling the truth! That night, they had folks falling out in all different directions. Towing folks out like they was dead."

*The mass excitement generated at a gospel program can render people unconscious under the power of the Holy Spirit. Churches and programs usually have ushers, often clad nurse-like in white, to make sure no one comes to harm. The performers also get "happy" in the Spirit, although it is rare for them to become so overcome that they fall out. Odell Hampton knows the phenomenon well, from both sides of the footlights.*

"The Spirit hits 'em. You've sung something or said something in your singing to make 'em turn over. They get happy. And you hear folk hollering, 'Sing it boy, woh, sing it boy, sing it!' They're feeling good then. And sometimes when you get to singing, before you've sung that song too far, you'll get to feeling good. You'll say one word and God's spirit will hit there, and you'll go further than you was aiming to go. Sometimes we start practicing on a song and we say, 'We're gonna sing a verse or two.' Then when we get to singing it, we go so far and get to feeling good with one another, and we go on out to the end with it. You never know. You know when you start, but you don't ever know how it will end. That's the way the good Lord works. He works in mysterious ways, you can't understand his ways.

"Singing gospel, to me, it just gives me more strength. See, when I'm singing gospel, I say I'm working for the Lord. And I get a good feeling all down in my soul. And it seems to me that I can come in at night and rest at night much better when I've been and sung and felt

God's spirit. Now I wouldn't get that feeling out of blues . . . well, I don't know, because I don't do blues, but I get something out of the gospel. Going to church, singing and praying, hearing the gospel preached, I get something out of it, I sure do. I sure do. I don't sing blues, and I hope none of my members sing it. I listen to it, but I'm not learning from it, I'll tell you that. Listening to it doesn't make you do it. A lot of people say there's no difference [between blues and gospel], but I say it's different to me. When I'm singing gospel, I'm calling on the Lord's name. And I get a feeling out of it. Now get me right. I like seeing 'em play the blues. I enjoy 'em, but I ain't doing it. I ain't got nothing against the blues singers, I ain't got nothing against their music. 'Cause everybody ain't our type. We came up singing gospel, and we just like the gospel. And what I'm doing when I'm singing that gospel, I'm getting a good feeling out of it. And the further I go, the further I want to go. So now, I don't know, the blues singer may be the same way. The further he sings blues, maybe . . . [he laughs] he may be getting the same feeling. He's got to be getting something from 'em."

*The area of Benton and Marshall counties, around Lamar and Holly Springs, is rich in gospel singing. None of the True Loving Five knows for sure how many groups are in the area. Odell names the Golden Stars, the Stars of Faith, the Mighty Inspirations, the Gospel Tones, and the Gospel Travelers, and that's only a few of them. Around the area, the early evening sight of half a dozen or so neatly dressed men in a van towing a trailer bearing the name of a gospel group is a common one. But the True Loving Five is a senior group, in longevity and in professionalism. On stage, the lead singer, Curley or Odell, uses a handheld microphone and paces back and forth across the stage in front of the other singers. Sometimes, Odell will step up and rest one foot on a monitor speaker as he leans forward over the edge of the stage to deliver his message. The other members, unlike the backing singers in many groups, also hold their microphones, rather than using stands. They stand in a line, swaying and moving their arms and hands to the music. Some songs have coordinated movements, as in "Tone the Bell Easy," where on the "bong" of the bell everyone dips left and forward, left arms extended. But most of the movements are unrehearsed.*

"We don't say what we're going to do. The first one who starts it is the lead singer. He may walk out. Then the background guys start. That's the way it goes. 'Cause when you get in the movement, then it's a little better. It looks a little better. May not do no good [a chuckle]. But when everybody's moving like that, it looks as if you are going on a bit further. I think if you stand tight, you ain't got no lift to it. Everything you do, you've got to have a swing to it. And if you haven't got a swing to it, it's a strain to you. So when we do all that [moving], it gives us a lift.

"There's several other groups around here, but we, the True Loving Five, are the only ones that do that a cappella singing. Well, there is one other, that's the Golden Stars. But most of the other groups, they go pretty good, but—and this might sound kinda down on them, but I'm just telling the truth about it—the biggest town they'll be at is Holly Springs, and the biggest thing they do is around these churches here. But we're at Rust [Rust College's Northeast Mississippi Blues and Gospel Festival] once every year, and the rest of the year we go some of everywhere—over at Memphis, or at other places."

*Extended trips have never been possible for the True Loving Five, since, for most of their career, the members have had jobs. Fortunately, those who still work have understanding employers. "They know we sing gospel," says Odell. "So we tell them away ahead that we want to be off for four or five days at such-and-such a time. And they let us off, no problems." Odell is a retired brick and tile worker; Curley, although the oldest, still works at the Chickasaw Flower Center in Memphis. M. H. announces firmly that he is "retired" without specifying what from; Goodlow Kilpatrick drives a concrete delivery truck. Atlean Harris has had a busy career as a mother— "I've got thirteen children still living." But at an average age when most people are thinking of slowing down and taking it easy, the True Loving Five are still looking to the future. They've never recorded, but it could happen. "We've been putting it off and putting it off," says Odell. "But we've been thinking about it. We're thinking about making a record." So what keeps them going?*

"It ain't our goodness, but it must be God's goodness. He opened ways for us, ways for someone to always want us to go somewhere, to always be on some stage. It's his goodness, that's what it is. You know, your reward is at the end. I don't care how far you go, if you turn round you won't ever get to the end. You've got to go to the end. You can make a start and turn around, but that's work you throwed away for nothing. So we just started out when we were young, and we haven't stopped yet. We want to see what the end gonna be."[4]

# The Watson Family Singers

*"The gospel's my best friend."*

The Watson Family Singers in Handy Park (from left) Karen, Rita, Regina, W. C., Angela, Ron, Tyrone (obscured, behind).

Beale Street is "home of the blues." After years of neglect, it has staged a comeback, and the bands once more play in its bars and clubs, even if the target audience today is tourists, and much of the music they hear owes as much to hard rock as it does to the style it purports to venerate. But every Sunday afternoon from May through October, gospel music comes to Beale Street.

Handy Park, named for "father of the blues" William C. Handy, is an open space in the center of Beale Street's tourist area. A statue of Handy holding his trumpet looks over the street; behind him, much of the park is paved and given over to an amphitheater for outdoor performances. Each Sunday afternoon during summer, the Watson Singers set up their sound system there to sing gospel music for the tourists, the curious and a smattering of the faithful who venture on to Beale Street for the occasion.

They are a family group, and their full name is the Watson Family Singers. Of the nine people on stage, seven, sometimes eight, are

Watsons. With one exception, their ages range from mid-twenties to early thirties. The exception is the forty-nine-year-old patriarch of the group, W. C. Watson. Most of the others are his children— Tyrone, thirty-one, who plays the bass guitar and does some occasional singing "just to help out," and the full-time singers, Regina, twenty-nine, Angela, twenty-seven, Rita, twenty-six, Ronald, twenty-five and Karen, twenty-three. The non-Watsons are guitarist Greg Walker and drummer Jesse Willis, both in their early thirties. The rest of W. C.'s ten children take no direct role in the group, but help behind the scenes.

*W. C. Watson.*

W. C. Watson is tall and lean, with the slightly worried, watchful look of an organizer. In addition to being manager and booking agent for the family group, he's had a long involvement in a range of community activity and activism. He works night shift as a Shelby County prison warden in the city-center Memphis jail. He's the driving force behind the group, the vocal trainer, and author of some of the songs. But the group wasn't his idea.

**Angela:** I was probably around eight or nine. My dad sang in a gospel quartet, and we followed him around and watched how they performed and how they were singing. And it was just something we kinda started one day. We had no knowledge of what we were doing, or of the meaning behind it, but we figured Daddy was doing it, and that was good enough for us.

**Rita:** I was seven years old. I would go with my father to church, and it just did something to me to see these people up in front of this big congregation singing.

*Angela Watson.*

And I thought, "Uh huh. I can sing like that." I started playing records and copying what they were singing. I would say, "Daddy, listen to this," and he would listen to me, say, "It sounds good." He would encourage me, and that's what really did it, his encouragement. So I got with Angela, and I said, "I think we should get a group like Daddy's." So it was Angela and I at the beginning. Then we got with Regina, then Ronald, then Karen.

**W. C. Watson:** W. C. is my name. Initials only. People say to me, "You need a name." I say, "I have a name—W. C. Watson." My father didn't get a chance to go to school as much as some people did, and when I was born, he said he had to have something he could recognize in writing. So he didn't name me nothing but W. C. I was born in 1943, March 1, in Fayette County, Tennessee. We stayed in Fayette County until I was sixteen, when I left and came to Shelby County [Memphis]. I wasn't involved in church and singing in the early days. I always wanted to sing, but we lived a long way from the church, and we didn't get a car until I was about fourteen. Then I did get a chance to sing with the choir at church. That was the Philadelphia Missionary Baptist Church in Rossville, Tennessee. I think that's how I really got tuned into it, from being in the church, singing with the choir and the congregation. And my mother steered us heavily to go to Sunday school and be brought up in church.

*Rita Watson.*

I came to Memphis and got a job. After I got the job, I got married [to Janet, also from Fayette County]. We had one child at the time we got married, and down through the years, the other nine just came on. I started work at the hospital, then I worked at a lot of different places. Finally, I worked at the tile company. I used to go all over the country and do ceramic tiles. I stayed with them a long time, until we had about five or six children. Then my wife wanted me to get a job where I could be home at night. That was in 1966. So I said, "OK, I'll quit the job I've got and find another one." I found a job at Sears Roebuck in Memphis, in the mail order division. I started in the janitorial department, then I moved into maintenance and stayed there from about 1967 through 1987. I worked for the company twenty-one years. I left in 1987 because they closed the mail order division. I went and applied at the sheriff's department for maintenance there. But a young man that was ahead of me, they hired him for the opening. So they said to me, "Since your record stands as good as it is, and since you've been recommended, we want you to come aboard in the system, and you can change over when there's some more openings that you like." So I've been there since 1987, and I'm still in security. I changed from day shift to night shift so I could be in the music. I can arrange programs and take care of the necessary business for the Watson Singers during the day. I work at night on the midnight shift, and I sleep when I can. Some days I just take off and sleep all day.

Once I was at home, I started singing with a group called the Jordan Wonders. They were older fellows. They were a real business group, they were a real technical group, and they were thought of in the community as a very spiritual group, which I liked.[1] And they were good. They sang around Memphis and out of town. We didn't take any long trips, like to New York or California, because most all the people in the group worked. But we would go three or four hundred miles—Arkansas, Georgia, Alabama, Nashville, places like that. I was singing tenor and sometimes fifth, that's the high part, right at the top. But as the children got to be six and seven years old, they took a liking to the character and personality of the group, and they wanted to follow us. So I started taking them with us on some programs. And they decided, by going to church and singing in the junior choir as well as going with the group, that they wanted to sing, they wanted to portray the image of [imitate] the group I sang with—the numbers and the way we would act and do. So they started singing at home. And when they went to a program, they would come back and talk about it. And that's how it got started.

**Regina:** We would come back home after hearing my father's group, and we would just repeat what we heard them do at church. And daddy would come in and say, "Well, that was OK, but you need to sing this and you need to sing that." He was teaching us to harmonize. We were just singing the same thing at the same time [in unison], and he started working with us, teaching us to harmonize. And once we got that down a little, he taught

*Regina Watson.*

us to understand what we were singing. Being young, we were just singing songs because that was what we had heard. But he let us know that people won't feel it, can't feel it, if you're just singing words. So part of our practice is to sing something we feel. You can't please everybody all the time, but if you sing it from your heart, and there is a true message, it'll reach somebody. So we had to learn to harmonize, but we also had to learn to understand what we were singing about.

*Knowing what you are singing about is important to W. C. Watson— more important than having a good voice and certainly more important than a polished stage act or stylish uniforms. In fact, singing ability, presentation, and dress do not feature at all in his recipe of "what makes a gospel singer."*

**W. C. Watson:** To be a gospel singer, you've got to be able to understand so you can be able to accept, to be able to yield so you can later receive. You've got to have Christ in your life, you've got to know some of the things that he left as instructions in the Book for us to do, to live by. You've got to be able to choose between right and wrong and make a good decision. You might not make the right decision all the time, but it's got to be based strong enough that you can live with it. To be a gospel singer, you've got to be able to listen, observe, wait—and put it all together to make it come out. If you listen, you can learn; if you observe, you can learn. If you have the talent to put the listening and the observing together in gospel music, you have a unique service, along with being a Christian, that will come out of you and touch and reach other people. And I teach my children that. I tell them that when we're doing a concert or a service, make sure the things you do are done by the innermost part, and not as a show for the public. Because I believe that when we take on the honor of singing gospel music, it's to help. And once you've groomed yourself and got yourself conditioned, then you can help somebody else because you know what their feelings are like, you know what their needs are to some degree.

*Not surprisingly, given the group's beginnings, its sound is influenced by male quartets. Its singing leans towards the modern style, with no bass singer and without the precisely separated harmonies of the old-style quartets. Broadly, Rita is the hard lead, Angela is the second lead, Karen sings the "high fifth," Ron the baritone and Regina—whose lead-singing*

*voice is reminiscent of that of a young Mavis Staples—is a "utility," fitting in
around the leads. W. C. Watson does not sing on every song; when he does,
he either takes the lead or fits in as a lower-end utility. The group's main
forum is the summer Sunday afternoon programs in Handy Park, but it also
sings at churches and on other programs, including some with gospel music's
big names—appearances which W. C. Watson turns into object lessons for
his children. Their first exposure to the upper echelons of the gospel world
came in 1981, five years after their first public appearance, when they sang
in a program with the Mighty Clouds of Joy, Chicago soloist Inez Andrews
and the Five Blind Boys of Mississippi. The two groups that have had the
greatest influence on them are both long-established "hard" quartets, the
Pilgrim Jubilee Singers and the Mighty Clouds of Joy. One of the Watsons'
songs, "We're Gonna Ride That Freedom Train," was written for them by
the Pilgrim Jubilees, and they have made a number of appearances with
the Mighty Clouds.*

**W. C. Watson:** I have tried to work with some of the greatest stars to
let the children see what the benefits are, how much work is entailed,
what kind of character and personality you have to have, and all the other
things that go along with it—just to make certain they want to stay in this
field. The Mighty Clouds of Joy have inspired the group a whole lot, and
have taken up time with them. I don't feel it's only because I have four
young ladies, but I think it's because of their character and their personality. The Mighty Clouds of Joy have played a great part in the Watson
Singers being together and staying together, because they sit down with
us, talk to us, explain what we'll run into, what to expect on the road,
and what to expect from other people right in your own neighborhood.
See, if my group tries to get this knowledge, this feeling, from another
women's group, seems like there's kinda almost an envious thing between
them. But when a mostly women's group sits down and listens to a male
group talking about the problems that you run into, it takes better.

*Exposure to top-name touring groups brought pressure on the school-
age Watsons to turn professional and join their mentors "on the road." The
idea was attractive, but W. C. Watson rejected it. Today, his children have
differing views on making gospel music a full-time occupation.*

**Regina:** They would say, "You need to come on with us," and, "Why
don't you try to make it a career?" There were plenty of offers when

we were younger, and it was tempting. At one point, we said to Daddy, "Why not?" He said, "Well, you're only young and in school." Today, I'm glad he said, "no." We didn't understand then. Now we've gone through the ropes, step by step. We've done the TV shows, the concerts and a lot of things, and now I think we're in a frame of mind that if we had the opportunity, I think we could handle it. Now that things have progressed, I think it would be nice. But I'm glad now that it didn't happen to us years back when we were younger.

**Angela:** We've had opportunities to make this a road-type thing, but I really don't want to sing professionally. I don't want to be a road group-type person because I don't like traveling. But don't get me wrong. I love what we're doing, and whatever comes we will challenge it. We can do an inner-city thing, or maybe just go to a couple of states here and there each year. But the little time that we have traveled, I just found it boring.

*W. C. Watson's influence is heavy on the Watson Family Singers. As well as being father to most of them, he is the group "trainer"—the person who supervises the group's repertoire and arrangements[2]—and takes care of most administrative matters, ranging from organizing performances to supervising dress standards.*

**Regina:** He has to have total control for things to work. There's a lot of business that goes on with singing, and rather than us trying to handle it all, we like Daddy doing it. We think he does a good job. But it means we have to look at him and understand him as Daddy, as a booking agent and as a businessman.

**Ron:** I remember once I came down [to Handy Park] with a pair of jeans on. They were in style, but they were the kind that have a tear here and a tear there. They weren't showing my legs or anything, but that was the style. Daddy told me, "Son, you might get by with that today. But I don't like it." And he was right. When you're doing the kind of singing that we do, you have to be careful. We are well

*Ron Watson.*

known in the city, so you have to be careful in the things that you do and say when you're out in public.

**W. C. Watson:** Right now, I'm seeing the results. After all those years of pushing, I'm beginning to see the results of my teaching and my pushing and explaining. They're displaying some of these traits, and I'm glad I can see it coming back before I get too old. They have the sense of workmanship among 'em, they have a sense of courtesy among 'em, a supportiveness among 'em, and they have a sense of unity. Now, it hasn't been easy, and it hasn't always been joyous. But it's like buying a house or a car. You pay a large sum down on it, then you start making the payments. And if after a while something doesn't go right, you don't quit paying it, because you've got too much in it. I've got too much in it to quit.

I would like to see the children develop a more business working relationship between themselves in the gospel music. I would like to see them go out, go on tours across the country or the world, and at the same time, maybe form some business of their own from the resources they get from the tours so they will have this to fall back on when they get to the point that they can't sing or want to retire from singing. And they'll be able to give it to their children and show their children that they can take the talent they got and make it and keep it going.

*Between them, Tyrone, Regina, Rita, Angela, Karen, Ron and group guitarist Greg Walker have ten children, aged between nine months and ten years. Eight of these—all but the two youngest—are following their parents' musical example. A feature of most Watson Family appearances in Handy Park is a short set by the Little Parrots, backed by Greg and Tyrone, but with Angela's son, Keelyn, on drums. He's too small to work the bass drum and play the cymbals at the same time, but when regular drummer Jesse Willis is unable to play with the group, Keelyn is the stand-in.*

**Angela:** He's been playing about four years, since he was little. He's seven now. I guess he was about three years old when he started pecking on stuff. I think he keeps time real good now.

**W. C. Watson:** He's in the learning stage, but he's doing real well. He's just not heavy enough to crash [the cymbals] as I would like him to crash. But I would rather use him [than another fill-in drummer] because he's in training, and I know he's going to grow into it. And he'll be right there for me when I need him.

**Tyrone:** They want to sing, they want to learn how to play instruments. It's nothing that we try to influence them, they just see their mothers and fathers doing these things and, "I wanna try, too."

**Regina:** I am their overseer for now and . . . I didn't realize it at first, but now I realize that I'm upbringing them the same way Daddy did us, and I'm really conscious of it. Teaching them, "I want you all to believe in what you're doing. And I want you to understand what you're singing." I'm against them singing any old song. To me, that takes from them being little children. I want them to sing things they can relate to. They sing the song "God Is Alive." And I say to them, "Who do you think woke you up this morning?" Or, "You once were ill, but you got well." I talk to them, make sure they truly believe and understand before I let them sing anything.

*Ron (left) and Tyrone Watson.*

**W. C. Watson:** I'm trying to give them all the opportunity, the opportunity that the Watson Singers get. Hopefully, the Watson Singers will keep on going and going and be great stars or great artists. And since I'm the grandfather, I want to see that the little ones, if they want to be . . . I want to give them the same opportunity—start them, and then maybe their parents will take 'em up and carry them further than I can take them.

*At thirty-one, bass guitarist Tyrone Watson is the eldest son in the family (the eldest child is Kathy, thirty-four, who does not sing), but he was the last to join the group, in 1979. Greg Walker, a family friend, was the original bass player; his first cousin, Reginald Walker, was the guitarist. When Reginald left to join his family group, Greg took up the guitar, filling one vacancy but creating another.*

**Tyrone:** I wanted to join just to help out, because I didn't want to see my brother and sisters get disgusted and quit. Greg took the time out to teach me, and I worked pretty hard at it. Between Greg and my dad, my sisters and my brother and my ma, I got it. Gospel is something that I like playing. It's a message, if you only take time to listen to it. If you take the time out to sit down and listen, you can get something from it. I enjoy it, I really do. And from time to time I have people come to me wanting me to go and play with them in a club or something like that. But I don't choose to play jazz or blues. Since I've been with this group, I've only played once or twice [outside the group] to help another gospel group out. And I've often been asked, if my group ever decided they don't want to sing any more, would I join this group or that group. But I don't feel like I'd want to play for anybody else. I get my most enjoyment playing for my family and trying to get something to go for my family. I could go out into the clubs, but I just don't choose to. We have an appearance to try and uphold because we sing gospel and we try to sing about the life that we live, the life we want to live. So if somebody can say, "Well hey, Tyrone, I saw you on Sunday, you was at the church singing so well about God and Jesus. Now you're over here in the nightclub tonight, you've taken in two or three drinks and you're acting up." Well, that's not good. That's not a good appearance.

**Regina:** People have said to us, "You're not doing the right thing." And they present things like the money, the contract, this whole new lifestyle. But if it's not truly what you want to do, you become spirit-sick. I don't think I would last on that side of it, I really don't. I think if I left gospel music totally, I would be killing a part of me.

**Angela:** The thought has crossed my mind several times, and the opportunity has presented itself on several occasions. But being from the type of family I'm with, even though gospel has not been easy and doesn't pay a lot of money. . . . I guess because this is where I come from it weighs a little heavier, so I'll stay. But I look at the R&B, pop and soul singers and how their field is so vast, and how producers are out there every day looking for new voices, new faces, and new talents. So if the opportunity presented itself again with a more promising future . . . I mean, I may eventually do this, but I don't foresee it as a realistic option right now.[3]

**Ron:** I've always been the versatile type, even in school. In junior high, I used to dance with a dance group, and then I sang with a band at one time. It was rhythm and blues. And it was fine. I guess I have this thing about music—I don't really care what kind it is. If it's music, I love it. I like it all. But it's obvious where I belong, where the heart is. And I'm here.

**W. C. Watson:** Blues comes to some degree from gospel. That's the way I see it. It comes out of gospel. Blues is good. I listen to blues. I like blues. But when it comes to what's going to be with you the longest, what's gonna be the strongest, what's gonna support you when you're going the last mile of the way at your life's end, the blues is not going to give you that sustaining support. You're gonna need more. And we find it in doing gospel and reading the Bible and going to church. That's what you've got to have to make it. I don't push blues down, I don't condemn it, or make like it's bad. It's music. And if you can listen to it and get something out of it to uplift you, fine. But at the same time, I have never been around blues singers—or people in general—on their dying bed and heard them say, "Oh, Devil, come on and get me." If you've got cancer, or you've got AIDS, or you've had a car wreck and your breath is running out of you, you always say, "Lord, have mercy."

**Karen:** I've been asked by a singer down on Beale Street if I'd go during the week to see what affairs are going on there [in Beale Street's clubs]. Like, "Will you come and help us." Oh, no! I would not trade my gospel for anything. Not even for a million bucks. Because my belief is that Jesus died, and he died for me. He set me free. God gave us his only begotten son. And I want to give everything I can back to him, because we owe it to him. And I would not ever stop singing gospel. I will always do it. I cannot see myself going to R&B or blues or jazz or rock—I cannot see myself doing that. Gospel fills me, gospel makes me feel good. The gospel's my friend. The spirit just leads me, it teaches me, and I understand it.

*Karen Watson.*

Getting the message across, that's what the music means to me. That's the main thing—getting across what the song really means. When you sing it, you have to feel it, and you have to understand what you're singing. And it means a whole lot. It is my life. It's very emotional. You get up there and sing those gospel songs and the spirit's just pulling you, pulling you, "Talk to me, talk to me." And you get to crying and you wanna run, you wanna go and hug somebody . . . you're just getting full like you were getting choked, and you just want to let it out just to let everybody know how good you feel. The tears you shed, with the voice you're just screamin' and a-hollering. You go and shake somebody's hand, hug somebody. It feels just . . . just . . . power! Giving you so much strength. Like, where did I get this power and strength from? It feels good. Then when you finish and you try to relax . . . I need to walk a little bit to walk it off. And you'll be tired. It pulls all the energy out. But it's wonderful.

**Regina:** It's a feeling of . . . like somebody said, "You just won the lottery." It's this rushing feeling. You're singing, and when you mean what you are doing, once you get into it, the feeling is just a rush. And you want to show everybody, you just want everybody to see, and hopefully they can feel something. It's a good feeling. A lot of what we sing reflects back to something that has happened in our lives and how we came out of it. . . . I mean, you go through trials and tribulations in life, and we relate songs to our situation in life. Say I didn't have food last week. Then when we get up and sing, "He's food when you get hungry," I can feel it. I *was* hungry last week. Or maybe you're down and your friends or family don't understand. No matter what you say and do, nobody seems to understand. So if you sing, "when your friends don't understand," well, you *feel* it because you just dealt with that. And I bet you that the majority of people listening to us, if it didn't happen to them last week, it happened to them at some time. So they can feel it, too.

*Regina's view on the sharing of experience through song is very similar to statements made by many blues singers about the content of their songs, a philosophy encapsulated by veteran singer Brownie McGhee in the slogan on his business card—"Blues is Truth" (he has also used it as a song title and an album title). In his study of tradition and creativity in folk blues,* Big Road Blues, *David Evans quotes a number of blues singers on this aspect of their craft: "Henry Townsend feels that the heart of the blues is 'the true feeling.' Furry Lewis says, 'All the blues, you can say, is true.' And J. D. Short says, 'There are so many true words in the blues, of things that have happened to so many people. . . .' Memphis Willie Borum states, 'A blues is about something that is real.' "[4]*

*The messages in their songs may be markedly different, but, effectively, Regina and the blues singers are saying the same thing—their songs succeed because they unite singer and audience in a bond of shared experience. Blues generally states the experience, leaving listeners to take from it what they will. Gospel takes a more assertive approach, offering a way to resolve difficulties—invariably, by turning to God.*

**Angela:** When you get in the spirit, you feel joy, much joy. You feel a sense of relief, you feel strength—you get strength in what you are doing. A lot of times when you start singing, you are just getting kicked off, getting yourself together. But once you get up into it and the spirit begins to dwell, you begin to minister to the people through your mouth, saying things that will possibly help someone in the crowd. You begin to tell or testify about things that have happened to you, and probably someone in the crowd is going through similar problems. It's a thing you just have to grasp—once you know the difference between when the spirit is dwelling and when it's not, I mean, hey, you got it all. They call it your "help," and once you feel your help dwelling, you can go forward to higher ground. It's not like you're just standing up there reciting something off paper, you're really singing and living this inner you. It's not like we're just out there hollerin' words and saying things we've heard other people say. A lot of the things we're singing about are things that we've actually had . . . personal experiences. And I love what I'm doing. I put everything I have into my singing. I don't do it for a show. It's real. I try to live the life that I sing about.[5]

**W. C. Watson:** We portray a spiritual sense of human feeling within ourselves that we hope will go out and touch other people. Let them know we're doing it because we enjoy what we're doing. We're there because we were born and raised up into the gospel circle, and we've been in it for as long as we have been trying to do as the Book say—"Do unto others as you would have them do unto you." I've been working in the community for more than twenty-five years. Just making sure that people who are perhaps less fortunate have different things—things in the school system, things in the community such as lights at crossings, such as food stamp offices staying open . . . I went to the light company here to get it to stay open longer in the afternoons so that people who were working until five o'clock could get in and pay that light bill. See, people were worried because by the time they got paid on Friday and rode a bus from 'way out to the office downtown, it was too late. But we got that extended until six o'clock in the afternoon.

*From the early 1970s, W. C. was involved with the multistate community action group ACORN—A Community ORganizatioN. From 1974 until 1981, he was "territory representative," or president, of all the chapters in Tennessee; Memphis alone had sixteen. He also founded the Memphis Friendship Train, a loose confederation of gospel performers, churches and ministers. The family's Handy Park concerts, although covered by a contract between W. C. and the city of Memphis, are an activity of the Friendship Train, and other groups often join them.*

**W. C. Watson:** The Memphis Friendship Train is dedicated to the preservation of gospel music in its finest forms. It's a shelter for gospel artists to work from. It gives them a cover, an umbrella, some kind of identification. I named it the Friendship Train because I felt that the Watson Singers would be one car, another group would be another car, and so on with boxcars right on down the line. And the unity that we have, that makes up a train. Right now, we have about sixty groups involved. There's choirs, solo singers and groups.

*Religion is one of the strands that binds the Watsons together. Equally strong is the tie of kinship. "The family" is a fundamental ingredient in W. C. Watson's recipe for life; in turn, his children laud the influence their parents have had on them. All now live away from their parents' home (although none is married), but family gatherings are frequent, and all stay in close contact.*

**Tyrone:** We are an extremely close family. I mean . . . if one of us stubs a toe, the rest know about it within an hour. I am the oldest son, so if there's a problem in the family and Dad's not around, the family looks me up. I'm supposed to have the answers. But I like to just sit around and talk to my dad—we talk two, three four hours at a time.

**Regina:** We've been through a lot, because being a family group is not as easy as people may think it is. But Daddy always told us, "If you don't all stick together as a family, you're not going to make it. So you need to learn to love and treat your sister and brother the best that you can." So from way back when, we've been thriving on that.

**Karen:** We're very close. Sure, we argue. A lot of the time it's about the music—"I didn't want you to sing that song. I asked you to sing this song." Yeah, we argue about little things, but we never have fights, we never shoot each other, nothing like that. Just little bitty things.

**Ron:** When we were coming up, Daddy and Mommy taught us well. I wonder to myself sometimes, do my brothers and sisters think about how blessed we really are? Because this is a great thing. It hasn't been easy. A lot of people see us singing in churches or on Beale Street—they look up there and see one big pretty picture. But if they only knew what it takes to keep that beautiful picture standing there, they'd be really surprised.

*W. C. and most of his children stress the egalitarian nature of their group. Everyone can take the lead, and no one is a star. But when the Watsons perform, Rita is the focal point of the group. She sings many of the leads, her performances—especially once her "help comes down"—are the most uninhibited and flamboyant of any of the singers, and she seems to be the group member most aware of the dynamics of performing, working the audience and wringing every drop of emotion from her songs. She's also the only family member who talks freely of conflict within the group.*

**W. C. Watson:** I worked tremendously hard to form a unit that could be versatile. All the vocalists are interchangeable. All of them can lead, and all of them can sing two or three parts in the background. Sometimes we sing two, two and a half hours without stopping. With only one lead singer, that would be impossible. But when all of them can lead and give each other a rest, that makes it easier. We've got five singers, and most times we use three in the background and one lead. So that fifth one can give someone a break. . . . Rita enjoys it [singing lead] so much that she don't ever want to quit. So I go and take her back out of it and let some of the rest of them get into it, because she will sing herself to death.

**Ron:** Rita is the lead singer, and she carries a lot of weight in the group. Don't get me wrong. Everybody in the group can lead. But the way gospel is, there is *a* lead singer, and Rita is classified as the lead singer. So she's put in the position as the star. But everybody's happy with that. No problem at all. Because everybody gets a chance. Daddy lets everybody sing. He treats everybody equal. And he makes sure that we kept in our minds that we're not stars. It's just like a football team or a baseball team. One person can't do it alone. So we work as a team.

**Rita:** It gets hard now, it gets rough, because I am the lead singer. At one stage it was Angela and I together all the time, but now it's basically just me. Every now and again Daddy may ask one of the others to sing a song, but it all falls on me. I don't know if you would call me a star, but everything falls on me. And I like it. But there are some things going on right now in my group that are not very pleasing to me. I'm not completely happy, I must be honest. It's the music and the management. I'm the lead vocalist, and I just feel like I should have what I need if I'm

gonna be out front all the time. And I don't have that. . . . I just want
the music [accompaniment] to be right. And we have one musician that
will tell you . . . if I want it a certain way, then just play it myself. I want
us all to be on one accord. But if my music is not right, I don't like it.
I don't like to go to rehearsal on Wednesday nights, I don't like to go
to Beale Street, I don't like to go to other programs if the music is not
going to be right. And I asked the Lord, "Are we going to continue to
quarrel like this, are we going to continue to be on bad terms or what
is going to happen?" He hasn't showed me yet. And I asked him, "Am
I going to continue to sing with my family, or am I gonna want to do
something else?" I don't think I could make it by myself. I would go
solo if I could try it, if somebody could discover me. But I don't believe
I'd make it. In my heart, I need my brothers and sisters.

Sometimes I feel like I've been picked out to be picked on.[6] Because
sometimes, I don't know what my daddy wants. I don't know what my
sisters and brothers want! All I'm going to do is what I know to do, but
sometimes they make me feel like . . . sometimes I can be singing and
I hear certain remarks in the background. "Rita, hold the microphone
up." Or, "Rita, don't testify right now." I don't like to be put on the spot,
and I don't like to be caught off guard. But that happens very often, and
I've told them that if it continues, I'm going to do something different.
And I am!

*Much of the Watsons' repertoire is written by group members, mainly
W. C., Regina, and Rita. Other local songwriters also contribute, and
the group learns some songs from recordings, generally those of more
modern groups—although older songs, such as "He Is the Light of the
World" or "Prayer Changes Things" are also on the songlist. Like the Spirit
of Memphis, the Watsons have a self-composed song which they use to
introduce the group; lines about each member are linked by the chorus:*

> We are the Watson Singers,
> Traveling on by grace.

**W. C. Watson:** Some of the songs that we sing I write, some my
daughters write, and some we get from other people that write music
and want us to sing their songs. They come to us, and we pick out
the ones that we feel fit us. We sing some songs off records sometimes. But it's not a thing where we can't sing unless we sing some-

body else's material. We can do a whole concert and not sing anybody else's music.

**Angela:** Like tonight on my way home from work, I was thinking of a song. It's an old spiritual, but I want to take it and rearrange it so it would be able to accommodate my family, in a different style that we can sing it in. And sometimes you just sit down and jot a few words. Then we all come together and I say, "Hey, I got a new song I want to try out tonight." And we all put our little two cents worth in and come out with something whole. It'll take us a couple of rehearsals to get it right. We'll get all the words, and we'll get the melody. Then we get the beat of it, then we'll just go step by step until we have the whole song formed. Then we have to put the music in—the introduction and all the little breaks. So it's a job.

**Ron:** The songs that we have done, like on our album, we all put our heads together and wrote. But I also write songs alone. I'll sketch one, then go back to it over the next couple of days. And I enjoy it. My job keeps me on a busy schedule [he's assistant manager of an insurance company's mailroom], so I don't have a lot of time. But every chance I get, I'm in there with my pencil.

*"Our album" is one of two Watson Family attempts to get a record on the market. Like most local gospel groups, the Watsons cannot look to a major record company for a contract. In his first effort to get the family on record, W. C. struck a deal with an independent Memphis label; for his second, he financed the recording sessions himself, then tried to get a label and distribution deal. Both attempts failed, although pressings of the second album went to Memphis gospel radio stations and received some airplay. W. C. is now planning a third attempt.*

**W. C. Watson:** Our first recording was done around 1984. But the company that we did it with did not put it out. We got kinda messed with it. We never got off the ground. We got in the studio and recorded it. They paid for everything—we were only the voices—and today, I don't even know what happened to it. So after that, I decided, well, from now on I'm going to do all my stuff myself. So the second album, I paid for it. But I didn't have my own record company and I didn't have my own label, so I got messed again on that deal. The guy got my master, and he doesn't want to turn the master loose because I won't give him the rights that he wants. He wants all of it! But rather than take him to court and spend a lot of money . . . I mean, I just don't make that kind of money. So what we decided to do, we're going to rerecord that album. We're gonna go right round him. Because that album is ours. We signed a contract, but we didn't sign a contract with anybody for rights or songs or songwriters' rights. So he can't make no money off it.

We've got the group, and we've got some material we think is great, but I don't want to put it out and get into the same situations I just got out of. I didn't do a lot of research at first, and I wasn't able to hire the attorneys I needed to put their arms around me and keep me going straight. That stuff I didn't understand and know. I'm really just now beginning to learn what I can do to protect the group.

# 3   WOMEN'S VOICES

*"All the churches enjoy that sweet melody . . ."*

"The first time I ever heard a boogie-woogie piano was the first time I ever went to church. That was the Holy Ghost Church in Dallas, Texas," Texas blues guitarist Aaron "T-Bone" Walker told an interviewer in 1955.[1] He didn't say who the pianist was, but blues and gospel historian Paul Oliver suggests it might have been Arizona Dranes.[2] On the face of it, his comment is little more than wishful thinking, except that Arizona Juanita Dranes, a teenaged blind pianist from Fort Worth, was playing her up-tempo—albeit non-boogie-woogie—piano style for prayer meetings around Fort Worth and Dallas in the years after World War I, the years to which Walker referred. It would be a nice touch— one of the pioneers of gospel music influencing one of the pioneers of blues. But Arizona Dranes's place in African-American musical history does not depend on the possibility that her music pointed a direction for a single blues player. She epitomizes the Church of God in Christ's approach to religious music, playing in a style designed to appeal to sinners as well as saints. She was instrumental in getting Rev. F. W. McGee, one of the most influential of the "singing preachers," recorded. She influenced several other leading Church of God in Christ gospel musicians and singers. And she was the first female religious soloist to record extensively on "race records" in the 1920s.

She was not the first African-American woman to record religious music. In September 1921, the Virginia Female Jubilee Singers went to New York to record ten songs for the Okeh company. Their style was based closely on the male quartet style of the time, with a strong bass line, and all ten tracks were issued. But the group did not return to record again. In 1924, Madame Magdalene Tartt Lawrence recorded two songs which have become gospel standards, "His Eye Is On the Sparrow" by Charles Gabriel, and the even better-known "Stand By Me," by Charles A. Tindley. In 1926, she recorded four more songs, including another Tindley classic, "What Are They Doing In Heaven?" Other female soloists were also recorded, and women were members of early recording groups, including the Paramount Jubilee Singers, the Elkins-Payne Jubilee Singers, and the Pace Jubilee Singers. But none of these appears to have had the impact and influence of Arizona Dranes.

The story of women in the church and in gospel music starts long before the days of "on record." As far back as the seventeenth century, slaves of both sexes were allowed to attend white services, although they were segregated, sometimes in seating marked BM (Black Men) and BW (Black Women).[3] In 1794, Hannah Bryan, Kate Hogg, and Hagar Simpson were among the four people who founded the First African Baptist Church in Savannah, Georgia.[4] The fourth was Hannah Bryan's husband, Andrew, who became the church's pastor—then, as now, the Baptists did not allow women to preach. Although pentecostal churches, including the Church of God in Christ, do not bar women from the pulpit, most ministers are male. But any pastor will freely concede that women are the backbone of his congregation. They are almost always in the majority at services, they do much of the organizational work which keeps the church going, and they play a leading role in church music as choir members, lead singers and choir directors. So it is not surprising that they have also played a major role in the development of gospel music. Many of the best-known stars, especially those who have found audiences beyond the church, have been women: Mahalia Jackson, Marion Williams, Clara Ward, Rosetta Tharpe. And many of the northern singers who were among the first to adopt the new sound of Thomas A. Dorsey were women.

By the time Arizona Dranes started playing in church, the Church of God in Christ's musical style was well defined. Its founder, Bishop Charles H. Mason, wanted the church's music to be lively and appealing, and Arizona Dranes's "mixture of ragtime and barrelhouse techniques, with considerable rhythmic drive"[5] fitted his recipe. By early 1926, she was well known around Dallas and Fort Worth, and Rev. Samuel Crouch, pastor of a Church of God in Christ temple in Fort Worth (and a forefather of modern gospel star Andrae Crouch), wrote a letter commending her to the Okeh recording company. "Since she is deprived of her natural sight, the Lord has given her a Spiritual sight, that all the churches enjoy that sweet melody made from the instrument," he wrote.[6] Jazz and blues pianist Richard M. Jones, also a talent scout for Okeh, heard her play in Rev. Crouch's church, and on Thursday, June 17, 1926, she sat at a piano in a Chicago studio and recorded four songs and two piano solos. Her driving instrumental style provided a solid foundation for her sharp clipped singing, and she was an immediate recording success. Her records served to promote her abilities beyond her native Texas, and she started traveling, playing and singing for COGIC churches in places as diverse as Tennessee, Oklahoma, and Missouri. She returned to the Okeh studio in November 1926 and July 1928—she was also supposed to record in 1927, but Okeh could not trace her—recording sixteen tracks in all before the Depression ended her recording career.

The peripatetic Dranes had a significant impact on COGIC music. She continued playing at least into the 1950s, often appearing at COGIC conventions and traveling with Bishop Mason. Many musicians saw and heard her, and she had a direct influence on two other major female singers from the church, Ernestine Washington and Rosetta Tharpe. Washington moved from Arkansas to New York, and married Bishop Frederick D. Washington, pastor of the Washington Temple Church of God in Christ. Although she was also influenced by the Roberta Martin Singers,[7] her singing style bears a marked resemblance to that of Dranes. She made her first recordings in January 1943, and the following year made two tracks with the Dixie Hummingbirds. In 1946, she joined veteran New Orleans trumpeter Bunk Johnson and his band to record four gospel standards with jazz band backing. She did most of her performance singing in her husband's church, and her later recordings, in the 1950s, were made with the Temple choir—including a "live" recording made in 1958.[8]

Rosetta Tharpe heard Arizona Dranes in St. Louis, and was particularly influenced by the fervor with which she approached her songs. Tharpe carried this zeal into her own approach, equaling her vocal attack with a fiery and skillful guitar style. She started singing as a child with her mother, evangelist Katie Bell Nubin, at church functions, and later performed in a trio with her mother playing banjo and her first husband, Rev. Thorp (she modified the spelling of the name after the marriage ended), on ukulele. By 1938, she was recording for Decca and entertaining audiences at New York's Cotton Club with up-tempo pop-gospel songs such as "Rock Daniel" and "Down By the Riverside," turning her bouncy melodies, aggressive guitar playing and ebullient stage presentation into a stardom that reached beyond gospel. In her early years, she sang with bandleaders Cab Calloway and Lucky Millinder, and, in 1944, she started using blues, jazz and boogie pianist Sammy Price and his trio to accompany her on recordings. Their first record, "Strange Things Happening Every Day," reached the "race records" top ten; between 1944 and 1950, they recorded nearly fifty titles.

She brought to her gospel music a worldly ostentation and showmanship probably exceeded only by Gertrude and Clara Ward in their later years. In 1951, about twenty-five thousand people paid between ninety cents and $2.50 each to see her marry her manager, Russell Morrison, at the open-air Griffith Stadium in Washington, D.C. The service included music from the Sunset Four, the Harmonizing Four and the bride with her Rosette Gospel Singers, and was conducted by the flamboyant Rev. (later Bishop) Samuel D. Kelsey of the Temple Church of God in Christ in Washington, who interspersed the marriage service with ad libs and asides as he worked the audience for laughs—"I know how to marry people, I know how to put 'em together. If they don't stay together, it's not my fault!"[10]

But for all her glitter, Rosetta Tharpe was a gospel singer, welcomed at churches and by the black religious community—until she and her regular pianist and singing partner Marie Knight recorded blues in 1953. It wasn't Tharpe's first flirtation with secular music. In 1942, she recorded "Tall Skinny Papa," and, in 1946, the blues standard "Trouble In Mind." These falls from grace did not affect her gospel career, probably because she was still in the process of building her reputation. But by November 1953, when she recorded blues with Leroy Kirkland's orchestra, she was an established gospel star. And when a star figure "crosses over," church members tend to forget Christ's teachings on forgiveness. The result was that Tharpe's church base disappeared, and while she retained her international popularity—especially in France—she never regained her standing in gospel music circles. In 1970, she suffered a stroke which limited her abilities; a second one in 1973 caused her death at the age of fifty-eight.

Some of gospel's greatest female talent came out of Chicago as Thomas A. Dorsey developed and marketed his brand of gospel music. Two of the most influential were Roberta Martin, who was extensively recorded, and Willie Mae Ford Smith, who recorded only six tracks in her prime. Much of Roberta Martin's legacy lies in the number of artists she influenced and her role in writing songs and distributing them through her publishing business. Willie Mae Ford Smith met Dorsey in 1932, and was among the first singers to feature his songs. Her bluesy style wasn't always admired by the more conservative of Chicago's churches. "They said I was bringing blues into the church," she said. "[They said] 'You might as well be Mamie Smith, Bessie Smith. . . .' I kept going because that's what the Lord wanted."[11] Smith was not particularly interested in performing widely or in recording—although when she did, in 1950, a recording engineer said her vocal power was such that the studio had to be set up as though a five-piece chamber group were playing.[12] Among her disciples were "The Thunderbolt of the Middle West" Brother Joe May and Edna Gallmon Cooke, both prolific recording and performing artists of the 1950s and 1960s. Gallmon Cooke never had the vocal power to fully imitate "Mother Smith," and is today better known for her softly spoken sermonettes. But it was Smith who influenced her choice of career: "The woman sang with such finesse until I knew I had to be a gospel singer."[13]

Ironically, the best known of Mother Smith's protégés *was* influenced by Bessie Smith. Mahalia Jackson was born and raised in New Orleans, and recalled listening as a child to records by the great blues singer. "When the old people weren't home, I'd turn on a Bessie Smith record. And I'd play it over and over . . . Bessie was my favorite, but I never let people know I listened to her."[14] She moved to Chicago in 1927, and sang in a church choir, as well as with brothers Prince, Robert and Wilbur Johnson in the Johnson Gospel Singers. She made four recordings for Decca in 1937, but although they sold reasonably well, she made no more at the time, instead joining Thomas Dorsey to travel with him and demonstrate his songs. The two had known each other since 1928, and Dorsey biographer Michael Harris says Jackson's singing style showed Dorsey "how he could find the blend of blues presence and spirituality that would convey the sentiment of his new, more emotive gospels."[15] In return, the partnership gave Jackson excellent material—Dorsey wrote "Peace In the Valley" to showcase her voice—and wide exposure. By the mid-1940s, she was easily Chicago's "gospel queen."

Her recording career resumed in 1946, when she made four tracks for the New York label Apollo. Initial sales were low, and a dispirited Jackson told label owner Bess Berman she didn't want to make any more records.[16] The two eventually agreed to try one more time, and Mahalia returned to record again on Friday September 12, 1947. All the tracks were superb—"What Could I Do," "I Have a Friend" and the vocal tour de force "Even Me." But the big success was "Move On Up a Little Higher," written by Memphis preacher and composer Rev. W. Herbert Brewster, which Jackson recorded in a two-part version backed by the stately piano of James Lee and the organ interjections of Herbert Francis.[17] The record produced royalties of more than three hundred thousand dollars for Jackson in its first year of release, and many other artists recorded their own versions of it. It also featured an innovation which has become a staple element of gospel music—the "vamp," a repeated phrase or series of chords over which the singer can improvise for as long as he or she desires.

Jackson's transformation into international gospel figurehead started with a tour to Europe in 1952 after her 1949 Apollo recording of "I Can Put My Trust In Jesus" won a French music award. In 1954, she appeared in her own program on a CBS-owned Chicago television station. In the same year, she left Apollo Records to join Columbia. As a career move, it was an excellent step. With Columbia's distribution and promotion behind her, she came to epitomize gospel music all over the world. Musically, it wasn't such a good move. Columbia replaced the sympathetic starkness of longtime accompanist Mildred Falls's piano with increasingly lush arrangements and, by 1960, she was being recorded with full orchestras. The choice of material also often left much to be desired. "Rusty Old Halo" is usually cited as the nadir of her Columbia days, but items such as "Danny Boy" and a 1963 version of "Guardian Angels" with comedian Harpo Marx playing harp are also a long step from "Move On Up a Little Higher."

Roberta Martin, Willie Mae Ford Smith, and Mahalia Jackson are among the leaders of what might be called "classical" gospel. Although their music has the gospel swing, it is altogether more stately and controlled than that of more fiery soloists like Rosetta Tharpe and Arizona Dranes. And it is a world away from the sound of the quartets. Gender is part of the division; quartets are generally male. But some quartet-style groups have mixed membership, a few female groups perform in a straight four-part quartet style, and other female and mixed-voice groups perform in a style that bridges the "classical" and quartet styles.

If the recording industry is an accurate indicator, it seems that few women were involved in quartet-style gospel music between the 1920s and the 1940s. But given the number of small groups that were active thereafter, it seems at least possible that women were victims of their times when it came to recording. This changed after World War II. Male quartets flourished, and with them, so did female groups. From Chicago came the Davis Sisters and the Caravans, from Philadelphia the Angelic Gospel Singers and the mother-and-daughter team of Gertrude and Clara Ward and their various groups. From Birmingham, Alabama, a bastion of male quartets, came the Gospel Harmonettes, led for most of their career by Dorothy Love Coates. The Davis Sisters, the Wards, the Angelics and the Harmonettes all started establishing themselves during the mid and late 1940s; all made their first recordings in 1949. The best known were the Ward Singers, organized by Gertrude Ward but with Clara as the focal point. Clara first made her presence felt with a dramatic performance at the 1943 National Baptist Convention, and developed a style that influenced, among others, the young Aretha Franklin. In 1947, the Wards hired Marion Williams, a young singer from Miami, Florida, who quickly became the vocal mainstay of the group. Her range was impressive, from contralto to the piercingly high soprano which is a hallmark of the female groups, soaring above the other voices on a trajectory of its own. The group also began drawing on the songwriting of Rev. W. Herbert Brewster, and, in 1950, made his "Surely God Is Able" into their biggest hit, with Marion Williams and Clara Ward sharing the lead. For most of the 1950s, Clara Ward and the Ward Singers were gospel music leaders.

They didn't rely solely on their vocal ability to attract attention. As their fame grew, so did the ostentation and eccentricity of their costumes and hairstyles. Singer Jessy Dixon recalls: "They wore fabulous gowns, and they traveled in this long limousine with a trailer on the back that carried their costumes. They would go to different churches on Sunday mornings and sing just one song and then announce that they would be back that evening. At night, you wouldn't be able to get near the place. . . ."[18] But in 1958, Marion Williams, Kitty Parham, Henrietta Waddy and Frances Steadman wearied of working for low wages as Ward Singers while Clara and Gertrude were among gospel's biggest earners. They quit en masse to form the Stars of Faith, and the defection was the end of the Wards as a force in gospel. They found new singers, but started working in nightclubs, offering performances that were a burlesque of what they had been doing in their prime. After a slow start, the Stars of Faith made their own reputation, built mainly around the talents of Marion Williams. In the early 1960s, Williams starred with Alex Bradford in the gospel-based musical *Black Nativity*; when she died in 1994 at the age of sixty-six, she was an international star who had made major label recordings and a number of overseas tours.

The Caravans, from Chicago, were another aggregation of first-class voices. Led by Albertina Walker, they were formed in 1952 as a backing ensemble for Robert Anderson, who had sung with Roberta Martin. Their first recordings, made in April 1952, were part of a session with Anderson, but the Caravans quickly established their own identity, especially once Bessie Griffin came from New Orleans to join the group in 1953. Griffin didn't stay long, but the Caravans never had trouble attracting singers. Cassietta Baker, Inez Andrews, Shirley Caesar, Dorothy Norwood, Julia Price, and Imogene Green were all members at various times, and James Cleveland was pianist, arranger and singer with the group during the mid-1950s.

The Gospel Harmonettes were from Birmingham, Alabama, but their influences came from the Chicago pioneers, including Mahalia Jackson and Roberta Martin. These were transmitted by the group's founder, Evelyn Starks Hardy, who spent time in Chicago in the mid-1940s. The group, known then as the Harmoneers, toured in its early days with a Cleveland evangelist, Bishop Williams. Another artist on the tour was Arizona Dranes, of whose style Hardy also took careful note.[19] Renamed the Gospel Harmonettes, the group appeared on the *Talent Scouts* radio program run by Arthur Godfrey, and was signed to a recording contract with RCA Victor. It made four 78 rpm records as the Original Gospel Harmonettes (including "In the Upper Room," later a success for Mahalia Jackson), but sales did not justify further sessions. In 1947, Birmingham singer Dorothy Love joined the group, but was forced to leave again when her daughter became ill. She rejoined in 1951, and took part in the Harmonettes' first recordings for Specialty. Born Dorothy McGriff, she married Willie Love of the Fairfield Four in 1946. The marriage did not last, and about 1960 she wed bass singer Carl Coates of the Sensational Nightingales (and, before that, the Sunset Harmonizers, who sang at Rosetta Tharpe's Griffith Park wedding spectacle). Evelyn Hardy stopped traveling with the Harmonettes in 1953; Dorothy Love Coates kept the group going until 1959, when she too quit the road. But three years later, she was back, to keep various Harmonette permutations going into the 1990s. As well as leading the group, she has written many of its most successful songs, including "Right On Time," "I Wouldn't Mind Dying" and "Come On In the House."

Most of the female groups used a three-part harmony, with the group backing a strong lead singer. A high soprano singer, like Marion Williams or Inez Andrews, was an advantage, but the bass line was usually taken by the accompanying instruments. However, a few female groups structured themselves along traditional male quartet lines, using four-part harmony. One was the Jackson Gospel Singers, named for lead singer Alma Jackson, who were active in New Orleans after World War II. Others included the Songbirds of the South and the Harps of Melody, both from Memphis. Among the Songbirds' members was Cassietta George, who later sang with the Caravans under her married name, Cassietta Baker. The group was run by Elizabeth Darling (wife of Spirit of Memphis founding member James Darling), who sang the bass part; female quartets did not use the descriptions of contralto, alto and soprano, but instead defined themselves in the tenor, baritone, and bass terms of the male quartets.[20]

Georgia produced two popular female soloists of the 1960s and '70s, Maggie Ingram and Sister Lucille Pope. Ingram was born in Mulholland, Georgia, and was married by the age of sixteen, raising a family of five children. Her first recordings, made in 1961 while she was living in Florida, were accompanied by the Six Trumpets male vocal group; later, she moved to Richmond, Virginia, and teamed with the Silver Stars Quartet. Since 1964, she has been accompanied vocally and instrumentally by the Ingramettes, made up mainly of her children.[21] Her singing is strong but relaxed and clear, and her songs are firmly in the traditional vein. Her 1960s recordings were mainly for the Nashboro label; since 1985, she has been with Atlanta International Records. Lucille Pope also made most of her early recordings for Nashboro and later joined Air. She came from Concord, Georgia, and had her first successes in 1964 with "Almighty God" and "Jesus Tore My Heart to Pieces." The two songs were recorded in a private session; "Almighty God" was issued on Vee Jay, and "Jesus Tore My Heart to Pieces" on Checker—and later on Nashboro, which licensed the track after Pope joined the label in 1975.[22] Lucille Pope has a more urgent and driving style than Maggie Ingram, and her Pearly Gates backing group makes use of 1970s stylings, including ultra-high tenor singing and a prominent bass guitar line.

In the 1970s and 1980s, women figured strongly in the choirs that took over from the groups and the quartets. Older styles—and performers—also retained their followings. Today, Shirley Caesar remains a popular recording and performing artist; the Angelic Gospel Singers are now a

mixed voice quintet still led by founder Margaret Allison. But new voices
are also being heard. Shun Pace Rhodes, who made her first solo album
in 1991,[23] cites as her influences Mahalia Jackson ("my number one
favorite"), Clara Ward, the Dixie Hummingbirds, and Julius Cheeks of
the Sensational Nightingales. But her style is jazzy and modern, and her
aim is "to take it [gospel music] beyond" the sound of her role models.[24]
Vanessa Bell Armstrong, of Detroit, raised five children before making
her first album, in 1964; her 1990 album *The Truth About Christmas*
(Jive 1372–1-J; U.S.; vinyl) has a cover picture of her bedecked in furs
and jewelry, and features a gospel rap by her son, Terence Armstrong.
Also from Detroit and a leader in contemporary gospel is the Winans
family, which includes among its eight separate acts the soloist Vicki
Winans, Angie and Debbie Winans, and the family stars, brother and
sister BeBe and CeCe Winans.

# RITA WATSON

*"I* am *an actress, I just am . . ."*

At twenty-six, Rita Watson is a veteran of gospel singing; she has been at it for nineteen years, all with the Watson Family Singers. While the Watsons are ostensibly egalitarian under the direction of W. C. Watson, Rita's role has expanded so that she is clearly the focal point at any appearance by the group. She sings with the impassioned urgency—and sometimes ferocity—of a young Tina Turner, frequently moving away from the rest of the group and advancing on the audience as though being closer to her listeners will help drive the message home. Towards the end of performances, she is often so

*Rita Watson singing in Handy Park (Tyrone Watson, rear).*

deeply "in the spirit" that she is apparently unaware of her surroundings, and other family members have to look after her microphone cable to make sure she doesn't lose her footing.

The ambivalence of her role as the star of a group that doesn't have stars is reflected in her relationship with her family. She extols the family's togetherness, but also cites failings in the Watsons' management—meaning her father—that she believes are forcing her towards quitting the group. Her approach to religion is equally dichotomous. She is a devout Christian, but has left her family's Baptist faith to join a "nondenominational" congregation in which she and her eight-year-old son, Larandus, are the only African-American members. She pictures God as a benevolent being sitting on a throne, but also believes he took away the top end of her singing register as a punishment for her having had a child out of wedlock. Even the influences on her singing offer a contrast, with top billing shared by a secular soul/R&B singer and a hardcore gospel matriarch.

"PATTI LaBelle and Shirley Caesar. I can't explain it, it's just something about these two. I used to tell Daddy that I wanted to sound like Patti LaBelle. And I asked him was it a sin for me to pray to God to bless me with a voice that sounds just like hers. He said he didn't think it was a sin, but that I should pray to the Lord that he would strengthen the voice I already have and that it would be as good as Patti LaBelle's. So that's what I started doing, and I think the Lord has really blessed me with a wonderful voice. I get hoarse sometimes, my voice gets tired. But the best remedy for that is to rest it. Don't sing for two, three, four days. Because sometimes, it's a bit much. Like last Sunday, I went to church, then we had an engagement at 1:45, then we left there and went to Beale Street. Then we had another engagement Sunday night, so that's actually three different . . . four different times, because I sing at my church too. But it's great—I like it.

"I belong to the First Christian Assembly Church. It's a nondenominational church. I got involved three years ago. My son was attending the First Christian Assembly private school, and the principal was the pastor of the church. He asked me to come, please come, but it took me maybe three months before I even went to visit with them. I've been going back ever since. I love it and they're beautiful people and I wouldn't trade them. We're the only black people there, me and my son—and all my nephews, because I take them with me every Sunday. I pick them up and I take them to Sunday school, and I make sure they're there on time. That's very important. Because my father and mother made us get up early on Sunday mornings to go, even when we had to walk. You get up and go to church. I tell these children when we're in the car together: 'You are no better than we were when we were young. You have to go to church. You have to. Because when you grow up, you'll be better people.' So this is where it all comes from. It comes from my mother and father raising us up in the church, and I think it's really done a lot for us.

"One thing about my church, I'll tell you . . . black churches, they start late on Sunday mornings, and they get out late. But at our church, we go early and we get out early. When we get out, my sisters are just going. Black churches start their service at 11:30 or 12 o'clock, and they don't get out until 1:30 and sometimes 2. To me, it's just too long. I go at 9:45 in the morning for Sunday school; that gets out at 10:30. At 10:45 we have morning service. And at 11:45, we're through. And I learn so much. In Sunday School, they're teaching us things that I don't understand in that book [the Bible]. It's just so powerful! And you don't have to be there all day to learn the way that God wants you to live.

"I read my Bible all day when I'm at home, because I feel it's wrong for me to sing songs that have such a wonderful message and then not be able to explain it if somebody comes up to me and asks, 'What does it mean when you say this or that?' So I read my Bible all the time, and I try to get the meaning of my singing. And I try to live by what I read and what I sing. Gospel music is a very soothing sensation for your soul. To me, it doesn't come better than gospel music—I don't care what type of gospel music. It consoles you. It consoles me. It does more for me than anything. It's great. It does a lot for you if you just sit and listen."

*Rita has written a number of songs in the Watson Family repertoire, and has brought to the group a number of songs which she heard on recordings by other artists. She has also indulged in a fairly common gospel practice by taking "blues songs" and reshaping them into gospel songs for the Watsons.*

"I say a lot of times, 'I'm gonna take this blues song and I'll change it around and make it into a gospel song.' I've done it. There was a blues song called 'I Forgot to Remember to Forget About You.'[1] And I changed it to 'I Forgot to Remember to Say Anything Against You.' Another one was 'God's Love Is Like a Quiet Storm.' The original song was, 'Your love is like a quiet storm, and I love it when it's raging.' But I rewrote it and changed the words, and it sounds good. I changed it to, 'God's love is like a quiet storm and I love it when it's raging.' It's pretty.

"When I first started singing, I would play records and copy what they were singing. . . . 'Almighty God,' that was one. It was by Mrs. Lula Collins, they call her the Delta Queen of Memphis. Then there was 'Lord, I Want to Feel Your Holy Spirit One More Time.' That was done by the Bogard Brothers. They still sing here in Memphis. I would just play it over and over, and Daddy, he would never tell me, 'Do something else.' I was in the bathroom humming once, and Daddy said, 'Was that you?' I said, 'Yes, I was just humming.' And he said, 'Well, I want you to know it sounds good. Don't ever stop.'

"We really are a very close family, and we've always been that way. And it's a blessing, because there are so many families that are so distant. We talk every day. We've always prayed together, and we went through hard times together. We just hung in there all together. We do argue, but we always come to an agreement. A long time ago, when we first started

singing, I had . . . I don't know . . . I had a bad attitude. I always wanted
to sing certain songs the way I wanted to do it, and if you were going
to help me, just do it the way I want it done. And the squabbles always
came when they would tell Daddy on me, and he would get on my
case and tell me to stop being so selfish, to let's cooperate here. But we
would always work it out. I think it was just that I was selfish, but I'm
better now.

"I listen to the blues. On Saturday we have what they call the All-
Blues Saturday [on WDIA], and I hear that, and a lot of it I understand
and some of it I don't. A lot of modern blues and stuff like that, I
don't understand it. But the older blues I do, and I like it. But I don't
think I could sing it. Seriously, from my heart, I don't think I could.
I hear it, but I don't think I could sing it. I listen to a lot of country-
western singing, because I understand it. But this other singing, pop,
rock, whatever, I just don't understand it. So I don't believe I could do
it. My heart wouldn't be in it. You could give me the words and I could
hum it, I could let you hear how it sounds. But I don't believe I could
hold the tune long enough to say whatever it is if it's not gospel. I love
my gospel singing, and I just would not take anything for it."

*The world of pop music may have no appeal for Rita, but another branch
of show business has a very strong allure. In 1987, a television crew from
New Zealand filmed the Watsons as part of a documentary series,* American
Pie, *which focused on the parts of American life that have traditionally
fascinated foreigners—other segments in the series examined American
attitudes to firearms and aspects of the U. S. justice system. The series
was shown in New Zealand and sold to other countries around the world.
Rita was interviewed in the program, and was prominent in several of the
singing segments; she saw it as her big break.*

"These people came to our home, and they were videoing everything
we did. I felt just like a movie star. I was thinking, it's happening!
Somebody's gonna see this and I'm gonna be discovered. I'm gonna be
in the movies, I'm gonna be on TV. And ooohh, it was great! I enjoyed it.
I just thought I was a star. I've always wanted to be an actress, and I still
do. I want to be a movie star! I *am* an actress, I am. I just am. I went and
auditioned with some people from New York. I heard about it on WDIA
radio station; they were saying that if you want to be discovered, if you
want to be on TV, come to this audition. So I went, and they had me on

camera. I had to read some lines, and I read very well. They contacted me about a week later and told me I did well, and they wanted me to come and do some things with them. But the man told me I would have to go to school for about six months, and it would cost six hundred dollars. I told my family, and they disagreed totally—about the money part of it. They know I can do it, because I can. I was born with this gift. I am an actress, I just am. And I wanted to go to school, but I didn't have the money. And they said, 'Well, if they want you and you're as good as they say you are, then they should help you.'

"But I still want to be a movie star. I may not make it, but I'll always want to be a movie star. The only thing is that my gospel singing, programs or whatever would have to be scheduled. Because if I could not sing gospel music, if there was to be no more gospel singing in my life, I would just have to let it go. Because I'm not going to stop singing gospel. I would hate to lose an opportunity, but the Lord will send other opportunities. I must have gospel in my life. But I think we could work out some kind of deal [if she became an actress]. I believe that if I had continued with my rehearsals with those people from New York, I would've made it. They called me three times after I didn't show up for rehearsals. They wanted me, and I know that if I had gone I may have . . . by now, who knows? At first I wanted to be on the soap operas, but then I told them that it doesn't matter. I'm not pretty enough to be on the cover of a magazine, so I never talked about that. Just get me on TV! I like that. And you know, gospel singing doesn't make a lot of money."

*"I wanted to be on the soap operas" is another strand in the web of complexities that make up Rita Watson. The would-be movie star is a "very private person" who doesn't like crowds and doesn't like to "communicate with lots and lots of people." Point out to her that this is exactly what she does with her singing, and she replies, "Yes. That's just part of my gift from God. But I don't like being approached by a lot of people. I'm not a people person."*

"I just cannot go out and do anything and everything. When I was a teenager, I wanted to do everything that everyone else was doing. I was a cheerleader and a majorette, and I just wanted to hang out. But I never did. And now, I can't go to these different places and drink. People say, 'Well, there's wine. I know this really light wine you could try.' I can't do it. And they say, 'Why not? How about a cooler. It has hardly any alcohol in it, it does nothing to you.' 'Well, why do you want me to drink it? You drink it, buy me a soda or something.' I won't try it because I'm scared I'm gonna get drunk. I can't drink beer and wine, just can't do that. I don't smoke. I don't dance because I don't know how. I've never been in a club. People tell me all the time that I'm a square. I say, 'Yes, I am. And I will continue to be a square.' I used to think I was missing out on something by not going to parties and so on, but I don't any more because I know it's worthless.

"I believe in prayer. I pray all the time. And when I'm on my knees in prayer—I don't pray any other way than on my knees—there have been many times as I've kneeled with my eyes closed, praying to God, and there was someone else there beside me. I've never opened my eyes to see this person, but I felt this person kneeling right beside me—just like I could reach and touch them."

*In performance, Rita Watson's passionate Christianity and the power of her message frequently combine to push her "into the spirit." As her "help comes down," her body tenses, her eyes close, and her left arm is stretched out behind her, the fingers extended and fluttering.*

"We have videos that I look at, and I see myself doing things that I cannot believe. Sometimes it is embarrassing. But I can't control it. When the Spirit begins to come into my body and dwell in me, I can't stop, I can't control it. I just ask the Lord every time I get ready to leave home [to sing] to speak through me and give me everything that I should say. Just make sure it's right and in order. I do this all the time and he speaks through me—and it works.

"I had a person ask me about two weeks ago, 'Why do you sing with your eyes closed?' When I'm in front of the audience, I'm just a whole different person. I move myself out of the way. I just take myself out of my body and . . . it's just different. And when my eyes are closed, there's a vision of God sitting on the throne with a very pleasing expression on his face. And when I'm singing, I'm singing to him. Ever since I was about six years old and my momma used to kneel me down beside my bed and help me with my prayers—'Now I lay me down to sleep, I pray the Lord my soul to keep'—there has been a vision in my mind, and it's just God. So when I'm singing with my eyes closed, I'm singing to him. For the audience's enjoyment too, of course, but I'm singing to God.

My eyes are closed and I don't know what I'll be doing. I don't know. All I know is that I'm crying before the Lord to please hear the words of this song, because this song is for you. Asking him to please accept me as I am, and to continue to make me strong and to make me better. He is my secret witness, and he knows. I'm crying to him, asking him, 'Please don't ever leave me, don't turn your back on me, because I can't make it if you do. So please accept me as I am to save my soul from sin and shame. Don't let me live in sin.' I'm not perfect. But I do try to be. I do. I try.

"You know, other young artists like us, they have what we call a show. They know what they're gonna say, they know what they're gonna do, they know how they're gonna stand—they practice their shouts. They practice their shouts! To me, it's wrong. You don't practice that. If you practice it, it's not real. I'm scared that if I ever did anything like that, God would take my voice away from me.

"When I got pregnant, I was not married, and I was wrong. I got pregnant and I had a son out of wedlock—and the Lord took my voice then. I have a couple of tapes, and you would not believe it! My voice used to sound just like Patti LaBelle. I could sing so high you would have to close your ears. Now I can't get that high. It's not because of my age, and I don't strain my voice. The Lord took part of my voice. He just did! And I know that. Because I prayed, prayed, prayed, fasted—I've just done everything I could to ask, 'Oh please, Lord, give it back.' But there is still something I am doing that the Lord is not pleased with. That's why he has not given it back. But I know that when I do whatever it is that the Lord is telling me that I should do, he's gonna give it back.

"I wanted to be married at one time, very very strongly. But the Lord told me, 'not now.' Because when I'm confused, I ask the Lord for an answer. I don't ask him to come down and sit beside me on the bed, I ask him to give me all my answers in a dream. And he does that. And I follow the response I get from him. I have been shown in a dream that I am to . . . I don't know if it's 'preach' or 'teach' the word of God. But I'm scared. It's the same dream, over and over. It doesn't change. He's telling me to go out into the world. Just go! And teach and preach his word. I'm telling myself that I can't do it because I don't know enough. But he's constantly telling me that 'if you will step out on faith and don't worry about what's going to happen—just do it—I'll be there for you. Just as I speak through you when you sing, I'll speak through you when you preach, when you teach.' But I'm still scared. I want to say, 'Yes,

Lord, I'm gonna do it.' But I don't know how to say, 'Yes.' I just feel like I don't know enough. But he wants me to help as many people as I can to be saved.

"I try to live a Christian life. This man said to me once, 'When you find out what living right is, you be sure you call me and let me know.' I said, 'Well, it's in the word, it's in that book.' That's why I sing the song, 'Look in the book and you'll find the answer to all your problems. . . .' And I just try to live by the word of God."

# LEOMIA BOYD

*"You pay for your learning . . ."*

Aberdeen, Mississippi, a town of about eight thousand people, is at the lower end of the northeast region of the state, approximately thirty-five miles south of Tupelo. Much of its business life is concentrated on the main street, appropriately named Commerce Street. At one end is Leomia's Fashions. Outside, it looks like other small-town stores; the inside has been remodeled, with brick walls and a tiled floor at the front and a raised second stage towards the rear. It is crowded with displays of women's clothing, from fashionable wear to everyday garments. On the small counter is a display of $4.99

*Leomia Boyd at her fashion shop in Aberdeen, Mississippi.*

cassette tapes. Most are by blues or soul artists, including Roosevelt Sykes, Percy Sledge and Howlin' Wolf; the exception is one by Mahalia Jackson. The shop is owned by Leomia Boyd, a statuesque woman of about forty, elegant in a scarlet trouser suit and coiffeured wig. Today, she's serving customers; sometimes, the doors are shut while she's away working at her other "job." Leomia Boyd is a solo gospel singer, with eight record albums, a busy tour schedule and a permanent spot on a television gospel program in Nashville, Tennessee. But despite her success, the shop is her backstop, her way of ensuring that the bills are paid.

"You won't get rich singing gospel. You get rich in the spirit of the Lord, but. . . . That's one reason I decided to open my own business. I realized that working on a job, there'd come a time when I needed to go and I couldn't go or I'd lose my job. I was working in a garment plant here in Aberdeen, making men's pants. But I felt that if I had something of my own, it wouldn't be a question of asking, 'Can I go?' I can go, because I can close my business when I get ready and sing when I need to. And my husband has been real supportive, especially in the first four or five years, when I put him in such a bad financial state. Like, I'd be going away and then he'd have to send me money to get me home, and take money that needed to be spent in the home just to keep me going. And that's another reason I decided to start my business. I just woke up one morning and said, 'My God, I got this man in this position, and it's my place to do something to bring him out of this.' I've had the business for four years. And a lot of times, I've left the business to go singing and the singing doesn't pay for the trip. So I'm just grateful to the Lord that by having this business, I've still got something to keep the bills paid and keep everybody going.

"I was born here in Monroe County, in Aberdeen, and I've lived here all my life. I grew up in church—Daniel Baptist Church, here in Aberdeen—and I started singing in church. I always liked singing, doing solos in church. About fifteen years ago, I was in Nashville and met a man named Jimmy Lancaster. At that time, he had One-Stop Records, and he asked me if I would be interested in recording—he was starting a label at the time. Which I did. But then his label folded, and he transferred all his artists to the Jewel label out of Shreveport, Louisiana. I was with Jewel for about two years. Then I had three albums on the Big D label out of Anderson, Alabama, then I went to Atlanta International, Air Records, out of Atlanta. I was there for five years, then for three years, I was with Malendo Records, out of Jackson, Mississippi. Most people would know Malendo Records by [the modern gospel group] the Williams Brothers. One of the brothers, Leonard, started their own label. He had been producing me for Jewel and Air, so when he started his own label, I transferred to it.

"I've made eight albums. Two of them have done better than the others. One was the first one, the *I'm Depending on You, Lord* album, with the song 'Stranger In the City.'[1] Then the other big one was in '89, *That's the Way the Lord Works.*[2] That got a Grammy nomination. I guess that's been the highlight for me. It was the most overwhelming thing. It's what every artist would dream of. Even by not winning, just being one of them—it was great. Just fantastic. I just hope the one we're working on now will have the same prestige. We hadn't made an album in two years—we were gonna take our time. Leonard had been producing me all these years, so this time I decided I wanted to produce myself and see what I can come up with. Because I figure, nobody knows me like I do, and it's a new adventure. Trying to produce myself is something I've never done before."

*The new record will not be on the Malendo label. As well as producing
it, Boyd is recording it without the backing of a record company, planning
instead to place it with the company which offers her the best deal.*[3]
*Malendo, she says, is a small company, "and in order to do bigger things,
you've got to deal with bigger labels." She regards the album as a return
to her roots. Her collaborations with Leonard Williams show very clearly
the producer's modern leanings, with prominent synthesizers and electronic
percussion. But on stage, Leomia Boyd performs in a more old-fashioned
style, with a small band and a couple of backing singers underpinning
her powerful open-throated delivery. That's the way she prefers it. She's
unequivocal about her style.*

"Traditional! When you come to style, a lot of singers want to . . .
they idolize Shirley [Caesar], Mahalia [Jackson] and so on. And the
average person, when they idolize people, they have a tendency to
sound like those people. But I've never been one of those people. I
like my own style of music. Shirley, Mahalia, they're great people, but
I want to be known for Leomia. When people hear me, they know
that's Leomia. The sound on the records, that comes from the producer.
That's one reason I wanted to produce myself. Leonard's got the thing
where he wants some contemporary and very little traditional. But I'm
basically traditional, and when I'm on stage, I'm just traditional because
that's where I'm comfortable at. So I want this album to be just me,
traditional. Therefore I had to keep Leonard out of it. I just want a
traditional album. Traditional is our roots, it's our heritage. There's so
much feeling in traditional. Contemporary's good, but most times when
people are listening to contemporary, they're into the beat. Traditional
is somewhere like the blues—it's soul stirring. And that's me. I like to
sing what I feel, and I just don't have the feel for contemporary music.

"I have had several offers, record offers, to sing blues, but I've never
had any desire to do it. I don't think there's anything wrong with the
blues but . . . I guess it all depends on the lifestyle of a person. I'm not
the party person who hangs out in the loud places and with the wild
bunch. If I was a blues singer, I would have to deal with these people.
And I've never had any desire for it, because it's just not my style of
living. I have opened some shows for the big blues artists. People like
Little Milton, Bobby Bland, Bobby Rush, and Lynn White. They get into
the thing where they now want three or four gospel songs before they
open their act. So I am singing strictly gospel. And it's sad to say, but
when you do these openings, you see the same people at these things as

you see at church. So it's not singing to a different audience at all—it's singing to the same people. These are events at outside parks, where a radio station puts on a big blues show but they get a gospel act to open the show. I don't mind doing the outside things, but I don't know about going into the clubs and opening. I don't think I would like that idea.

"But gospel is gospel, and as long as I can sing gospel, I will consider going wherever you ask me to go. But I'm definitely not a blues singer. A lot of times, people have tried to get me to sing blues. I have been told a lot of times I could be a blues singer, but it doesn't tempt me at all. I love singing, but I just don't think I would enjoy singing blues. It's hard enough singing gospel—I don't know what kind of trials and tribulations I would have singing the blues. The money would probably be better, I'm pretty sure it would. But money's not everything. And I've got to say that the Lord always some way and somehow supplies my needs and brings me round and brings me out. I never had to sing blues to get the bills paid. Don't get me wrong. I don't consider blues people to be bad people. Because singing is singing. And when people are blues singers, it doesn't mean they're not saved. A lot of the time, people just look on it as a job. It's what's within your heart that counts. I don't consider them as bad people. No, no! They could be just as saved as I am. The way I look at it is, who are we to judge people?"

*Leomia is married to James Boyd, production manager at a local cement company. "I'm one of those people who decided to sing after high school," she says, "and he's one of the people who decided to get a master's degree in chemistry." They have four daughters—Alesher, twenty, college student Danielle, eighteen, and fourteen-year-old twins Christy and Misty. But in addition to being a wife and mother, Leomia Boyd has sung all over the United States, sharing stages with some of gospel's biggest names.*

"I've sung on concerts with all the major artists—James Cleveland, the Pilgrim Jubilees, the Mighty Clouds, Inez [Andrews], Albertina [Walker]. And with some of them, I've established a great relationship. Like, for example, Albertina Walker, she's one of my best friends. And I'm grateful for some of the people I've known and learned to love and have a friendly relationship with. When you think about it . . . I'm a person here in a little town, and you think about all the people that are out struggling in the larger cities and their words and songs can't get out. We've got people in the larger cities that have just as much or more talent than I've got. I just count it as a blessing from God. I think of it this way—the Lord picks some people out to do certain things. And I feel like I was one of those people. It's not that I do anything more special than any of the singers in the larger cities. But when the Lord decides he's gonna do something for you, it doesn't matter where you come from, he's got his way of doing it.

"Besides my family, I think gospel music is one of the most important things to me. There have been times when I tried to stop. I decided I wanted to stay home with the kids and my husband and just be a family person. But it's a part of me. If I'm not involved in gospel singing, my life is not complete. So it takes all of that—the family, the husband and the singing—to make me feel like a whole person. Singing is just as important as the other. Because I love doing it. A lot of time people think it's the money. But often with gospel, the money's not there. There's gotta be something that comes from within the heart."

*As would be expected of a traditional singer, Boyd's repertoire includes a number of standards, sometimes extensively rearranged. But she also writes many of her own songs. Some, such as "I'm a Country Girl" ("I was born and raised in the country, y'all/I didn't have much money to spend/But I had the love of Jesus . . .")[4] are unlikely to occupy much space in the annals of great gospel songwriting. But others show clearly her leaning towards gospel's traditional side. "Holy Ghost Fire" overcomes the wooden "thud" of electronic percussion to deliver its pentecostalist message with sanctified passion and zeal.[5] "I've Been Dipped in the Water," although label-credited to Leomia Boyd, reworks a song recorded around 1966 by the Hardeman Singers and in 1967 by Brother Joe May and Rev. James Cleveland.[6] Up tempo celebrations of the joys of salvation provide the theme for a number of her songs, including "Walking in the Light," which Boyd sees as one of the highlights of her new album. She also hopes the album will help her twin daughters in their singing careers.*

"When I write songs, they are dealing with things that I experience. Sometimes things happen to you and they kinda stay with you. Sometimes they're good things, and sometimes they're bad or depressing things. It's just like writing a poem. It's how you feel about it. And when you get to the point where you're going to put it in lyrics for songs, you have to do a little changing around. But basically, the songs I write are about things that I deal with in life. I don't write the music. There's a guy that's been with me for about ten years, Issac Gillespie. I tell Issac what I've got in mind, and he puts the music to it. I tell him if I want it as a ballad, which is slower, or whether I want it up-tempo, and he's been with me long enough to know how I want it to go.

"The twins are now singing with me. They do the backup on the new album, and they travel with me. We had to hire them a tutor so that when they miss days at school, they can catch up on their work. They've been singing backup now for me for about a year. Since I realized the girls are going to be singers, I hope that in my lifetime I can do something well enough to help them get ahead. Gospel is such a hard struggle when you try to start and nobody knows who you are. And I just hope that my singing and my life would be such an inspiration that it would give them an advantage. Because it is really hard to get started. The expense of making a new artist is so great now, that even a lot of the major record companies are running into financial problems and don't have the money to invest in new artists. So it's rough. And now is worse than it's ever been.

"But I'm against people making [financing and distributing] their own albums. Because if you make your own album and you can't send it any further than Mississippi or Tennessee, you're not doing yourself any good if you want to become a national artist. And that's where the record company has such a big advantage, because when it makes an album, it's going to distribute it—send to every radio station all around the United States. And once one state picks it up and plays it enough, it's gonna go on to the next state. But when you make your own album, you can't send it no further than Mississippi. You're helping yourself for traveling in Mississippi, but you're not helping yourself for traveling in Chicago. If you deal with a company, they're gonna make sure that album is all around, that it's got the distribution. Making your own album can become real expensive. Most of the people that try to do it are working people, and they end up with a lot of their money tied up in an album. It can hurt. And a lot of time, people ask me about it. I don't say anything to discourage them, but I try to be fair about it. Because I've been there. The first album I did, I paid for. I did it in Memphis, Tennessee, for Messenger Records. I had to pay them for it. But it gave me a start. The album was pretty good, and they liked it, so they distributed it a little further. That's one reason why when Jimmy Lancaster saw me in Nashville, he already knew me because he had the One-Stop [record shop], and he was connected with Messenger Records distributing their records there. So yes, it did work for me. It's just that . . . I know gospel is hard."

*Leomia Boyd has been in gospel music long enough to experience all the vicissitudes of the business—the euphoria of a Grammy nomination, the disappointment of traveling a long way from home and not making enough money to get back without running up credit card bills. And being a female soloist on the road has never been easy. Even after she became a recording star, Mahalia Jackson protected her interests by demanding payment in cash for each performance.7 Ask Leomia Boyd if being a female makes her life as a soloist more difficult, and the answer is emphatic.*

"Yes! Yes! Because the majority of church people are women. All over the world, 90 percent of the church is made up of women. And women have the tendency of . . . they like dealing with the men better than they do women. It's sad, but it's honest. I tell my husband all the time, I say, 'I hate women!' He says, 'Why?' I say, 'They make me sick about these men.' But it's just a natural thing, I know. Male and female. Like I said, 90 percent of the churches are made up of women. And most of them—I would say 60 percent of them—are unmarried women. So they're automatically going to have a tendency to rather deal with the men. But there are some ladies, it doesn't matter to them if you're male or female. Long as you sing. There've been a bunch of times where I've felt people withdraw because I'm female. But there are some places and some audiences I had where it didn't make any difference. It's just one of those things.

"With gospel, you run into a lot of not being paid. You send contracts out. And the contract might be for twenty-five hundred dollars; you get there you might get fifteen hundred dollars, you might get one thousand dollars. I learned this, and I feel better when a man books me. Because most men will be more partial towards a female than they would be to a male. When you don't get paid, in some cases the money's not there. The program or the concert didn't draw the people. Like, say, if I go to New York City and I got a contract for thirty-five hundred dollars and I don't draw the audience, the nicest and the best thing to do is just work with what you got. But there's a lot of cases where you've got the audience . . . it just depends on the promoter. Some just pocket the money. And there have been cases where the artists know the money's there but the promoter refuses to pay 'em, so they won't sing. Then the promoter gets up and makes the audience think, 'Hey, they're the bad guys. They won't sing.'

"It's not an easy job. So much stress. Say you leave home with five or six people [her band and backing singers], you're responsible for these people. If you get to where you're going and they won't pay you, you gotta sleep 'em, you gotta food 'em. It can really make you an old person way before your time. There's a lot of stress in trying to travel and sing. And then there's some good times, where you just enjoy going. I got some promoters, they could tell me to get on a plane and go to Italy, don't worry about it, when you get there your money'll be there, I would do it. Because I've been working with them and I know they're gonna be fair. You learn who to work with and who not to work with—but you pay for your learning, believe me. I don't believe you ever get through paying your dues in this thing.

"I've got to the stage where . . . there was a time when people would call and book me. I'd send 'em a contract and they'd send a small deposit. Now, I still send a contract, but they have to send me more than a small deposit. So I can feel that if I'm going, whether you pay me the balance or not, I still got money to eat and sleep the kids and come back home, where I won't have to call home for somebody to send money that needs to be paid on bills at home."

*Musical fashion presents another difficulty for gospel performers. Different forms of gospel—traditional, contemporary, quartets, soloists, choirs— do coexist, develop, and continue to find work. But fortunes fluctuate according to what's in vogue.*

"Right now, choirs are the biggest thing there is. But that makes it easier for me as a soloist. Because choirs will accept a soloist before they will a quartet. I don't think it's fair, because gospel is gospel. But choirs have this hang-up about quartet singers. I don't know why, but they have. Some churches won't have a quartet in their church. They use the choir. Then you've got some people, they wouldn't dare bring a choir to their city. They bring the quartets. But by me being a soloist, it's better in a sense, because I can sing with either one. It doesn't matter. If a person wants a soloist and a quartet, there's no problem with them bringing me. And if a person wants a soloist with a choir and the choir backs me up, then that's no problem either."

*A boost for Leomia Boyd's career has been her inclusion on the Bobby Jones Gospel Explosion, a television program broadcast four times a week from Nashville, Tennessee. She made twice-yearly appearances for two years, then became a staff singer, which gave her the opportunity for more frequent appearances. She believes much of the recent demand for her services is attributable to her TV appearances, but she is also optimistic about the future of gospel music—and pessimistic about the reasons for its resurgence.*

"I think gospel music is on an uprise. I don't know if it's because of the hard times, this recession, but people have a tendency to think of the Lord when they're in need. And now we're in this time where everything is going downhill for people, and they feel like they're relying on the Lord to bring them out. And I don't know . . . does that have anything to do with it? I really can't say. But so many people have personal problems and they're following gospel singers and ministers because they're looking for an answer. It's just the times we are living in. We're in troubled times. A lot of people never thought anything of the Lord, of singing in churches. But now, when you turn your TV on, there's a minister or gospel singing. People are at the stage where they feel like they need the Lord in their life now more than ever. Because all of our problems, all our everyday needs—I just feel within myself that he is the answer. We've got so much drugs and everything on the street. In the cities and states where I go, if a person didn't have the Lord on their side, I'll tell you, I'd be afraid to lay down in my bed at night and go to sleep. Because we got to have someone to watch over us, because there's so many things that are ugly all around us. So if the Lord doesn't guide us, have an angel to watch over us, we might not get up out of our bed the next morning."

# KATIE DAVIS WATSON AND THE GOLDEN STARS

*"We're the old cottonfield-type singing."*

*Matriarchs of the Golden Stars (from left): Katie Davis Watson, Viola Watson, Mary Brown.*

Sitting together on a slightly-too-small bench shaded from the late-summer Mississippi sun, the three women radiate an aura of matriarchal solidarity. Pillars of the community, and of the church, they are also the front line of the Golden Stars gospel singing group of Holly Springs, Mississippi. On the left is Katie Davis Watson, fifty-eight, an institution around Holly Springs. She emcees gospel programs, and led the Golden Stars in a long-running weekly local radio show for which she also sold the advertising. She is the group's "booking agent." It doesn't matter that five years ago she remarried and moved to Tyro, thirty-odd miles from Holly Springs. She still drives back to rehearse and perform with the Stars, and the locals still regard her as one of their own, ignoring her "new" name and referring to her as "Sister Davis."* (Her second husband died in August 1992.)

---

*Katie Davis Watson died in December 1993 at age fifty-nine.

In the middle is Viola Watson, sixty-one (no relation to Katie), mother of ten children—seven boys and three girls—and a leading light in the choir of the rural Mt. Newell Missionary Baptist Church near Holly Springs. On the right is Mary Brown, sixty-five, president of the Golden Stars and a mainstay in the choir of the Strawberry MB Church in Holly Springs. Although Katie Davis Watson is the group spokeswoman, Mary Brown is the Golden Stars' leader, and the others quickly defer to her when she enters a conversation.

The other two group members are men. John Wesley Watson, fifty-three, is Viola Watson's first cousin and takes the highest vocal line in the Stars' harmony, a part usually called "fifth" or "high tenor"; the Stars call it "high soprano." Roosevelt Jack Boxley, seventy, is the bass singer. A big man with a stately, almost monolithic presence and a face that looks as though it were ripped from granite by a sculptor in a hurry, he is a second cousin to Katie Davis Watson.

The Golden Stars officially started in 1960. But they evolved from an earlier group, the New Hope Specials, of which Mary Brown was a long-standing member. New Hope, named after a local Christian Methodist Episcopal Church to which most of its original members belonged, started in 1949 and lasted until 1960, changing personnel as two older members died and younger ones drifted away. When the group became the Golden Stars, Mary Brown, Jack Boxley, and Katie Davis Watson were members. Viola Watson joined in 1976 and John Watson in 1978.

**Katie Davis Watson:** I went to Sunday school and catechism and on up ever since I was a little bitty child. And I was singing. I was a kid, trying to sing solo. I sung my first solo in church when I was eleven. And when I was about twelve, we formed a little group. But I was just so crazy about the New Hope Specials! I just wanted to be in that choir. I loved their singing. I remember going to their first anniversary, in October 1950. It went for three days and three nights. Eventually, I did join the group—I was the baby of New Hope. Soon after, we had to change the group name because we couldn't go from that church [New Hope] no more. They were CME, and we're Baptists. But when I joined, it was still New Hope. I was in New Hope.

**Mary Brown:** How did we come about that [name] Golden Stars?

**Katie Davis Watson:** We were over at your house one night and we got to thinking about it. You remember we had bought those robes with the gold collars? Beige-looking robes, with gold collars. And we had some gold shoes. Those shoes hurt my feet so bad! So we just took the gold collars and the gold shoes, and we started out as the Golden Stars. Been going ever since. Our style is an old one. We're the old what-you-call cottonfield-type singing. We sing the songs the way they did back in the cottonfields. We don't use music most of the time, but even when we have music, it's some of the first type of singing. It comes from way back, when people had slaves. And if someone told them somebody was coming to get them [to help them escape], they couldn't say nothing. So they would start to singing in the field. "Swing low, sweet chariot." That would let you know, come on, somebody's going to be around to pick you up, or that you can catch on with.

*The Golden Stars' songs are designed to be sung without accompaniment. The group sings in defined parts, but the overall sound is loosely structured so that each member has room to move—the arrangements do not demand that each person always be right on a certain note at a certain time, and many of the songs have an easy lope reminiscent of the Staple Singers in their early years. A disadvantage of the style is that when the Stars do use backing musicians, the performance can falter as the group wavers between its own rhythm and the stricter tempo and timing of the band. Katie Davis Watson acknowledges this when she says she doesn't like drums behind the Stars because they interfere with the vocal rhythms. Stylistically, they fit into a quartet mold; they are unusual in that there is a mix of males and females in the lineup, the women take all the leads, and a male sings the highest part. Another idiosyncrasy is that the Stars pitch themselves lower than most groups—when they learn a new song from a record, one of their first moves is to repitch it in a lower key—so John Watson's "high soprano" is not particularly high, while Jack Boxley's bass is subterranean. Viola Watson sings the baritone, Mary Brown is the main lead, and Katie Davis Watson is the second lead, singing with Mary Brown or leading the chorus—a role she describes as "repeat singer." If Mary Brown is unable to make it to a performance, Katie will take over as lead singer. She also serves as a memory aid for Mary Brown.*

**Mary Brown:** Well, I'll tell you. I'm the person that forgets my songs. They call me up on stage to sing, and I know what I'm going to sing when I get up out of my seat. But then I kinda forget. And I always back up to her [Katie Davis Watson] and she'll start singing and it'll come back.

**Katie Davis Watson:** Over the past five years [since her remarriage] I haven't done a whole lot with the Golden Stars, although I've been with them at different times. So we haven't been rehearsing regularly. But we're starting to get back into it. Once a week. We go to Sister Brown's. First we'll have devotion. We'll have the opening psalm, then we have scripture, then prayer. Then we begin to rehearse. And if we've got a new song, we'll practice on that. We just sing some of our old songs too. I couldn't remember how many songs we've got unless we sit down and start writing them out. It'd take me a long time to write out the songs that I know.

**Mary Brown:** I'd be afraid to count it! It wouldn't be a hundred, but it'd be lots of them. When we rehearse, if Sister Davis is the one that's heard the song, she knows how to tell us what part to hit on. If she's gonna lead, she knows where to tell us to come in. And I can do the same thing. When we get ready to rehearse that song, we begin it as though you're saying a poem. We recite it first, and we can tell where the background's supposed to come in. Then we start singing it. Sometimes we have to stop and tell the others where to come in. We don't ever get a song the first time we try it. We have to work on it awhile—a couple of rehearsals.

**Katie Davis Watson:** We have to rearrange it to our way. You have to do it to your way of doing it—your voice. You have to rearrange it. Maybe it's too high; we can bring it down to our level. To me the big difference between us and some of those other [more modern] groups is that they have more of the know-how. They know all the modern way of doing music [accompaniment]. See, we don't have any music. We just take a song and go for it.

*None of the Golden Stars' songs is written down; they perform everything from memory, a process aided by Katie Davis Watson's nearly photographic recall.*

**Katie Davis Watson:** I'm getting old now, and I sometimes have to jot just a few words down. But I used to be able to . . . you could go over a song once and I could bring it on back to the group and tell 'em. When I was on the radio, at one time you could tell me something on Monday and I could think of it next Sunday morning and tell it over the radio. When I was on the radio, I was presenting this group [the Golden Stars]. We used to sing every Sunday morning over WKRA here in Holly

Springs. We did that for twenty years, singing there in the studio—we didn't have no recorders. But we stopped about five years ago. They had a new owner of the station, and we were on the FM. You couldn't hear us as far on the AM. One Sunday morning, we got there and he said the white peoples wanted the FM and he just put us back on the AM without conferring with us. And we all just quit.

We used to pay for the time . . . well, our sponsors did. I would go and see the sponsors. One would hear me talking on the radio and they would tell somebody else, and that person would call me to come by there. I didn't charge them a whole lot for it. When we first started, we had fifteen minutes, but that wasn't long enough for me to run my mouth, so we got to thirty minutes. It used to be ten dollars for the fifteen minutes, and seventeen-fifty for the thirty minutes. Then it went up to twenty-five dollars for the thirty minutes. It'd be Katie Davis and the Golden Stars. I'd talk about all the sponsors, tell about everything happening in church, who had a new baby, who got married, anything.

*"Run my mouth" is Katie Davis Watson's self-effacing description of a loose informal style which communicates its message without artifice, as one member of the Holly Springs religious community speaks unself-consciously to others about matters of interest to all. She carries the same ingenuous style on stage, whether introducing the Stars' own songs or acting as announcer. "I keep looking at my watch," she told the audience at an outdoor program. "When Sister Gibson [another singer on the program] was up here, time sure was running fast. Now I'm here with the sun burning my face and my feet and all, I'm thinking time sure done stopped." As she waited for another group to get ready, she filled the time by explaining how she had to have the microphone lowered because her shoes were "hurting my feet so bad 'til I had to take them off." With or without shoes, she is an effective and popular emcee, in demand for programs and other church events.*

*The Golden Stars generally perform around Holly Springs, usually at church-related functions. Occasionally they will go further afield; a group highlight was three trips to Wisconsin in the late 1970s as part of what they describe as a "self-help" program under which southern blacks spent time with northern whites and vice versa. They are vague about the details—it appears to have been a scheme devised by a federal government agency to improve race relations—but they have fond memories of the experience.*

**Katie Davis Watson:** They had us there, and the white kids had never seen black people. One of them, she was twelve, she thought everyone was [white] like she was. We went to one town, and there wasn't but one black man there. And when we got up to sing, well, we always had this rhythm. We'd clap and they'd clap, but they couldn't quite get the rhythm right.

**Viola Watson:** They were crazy about our singing, though.

**Katie Davis Watson:** We go out [to sing] on the first Sunday, second Sunday, third Sunday. The fourth Sunday is choir day at our church. We sing at churches, schools, out in the park if you need us. We got three or four anniversaries coming up right now.

*Like other gospel groups, the Golden Stars take pride in their on-stage appearance, performing always in matching dresses and shoes for the women, and suits, shirts and ties for the men. The money they spend on their uniforms far exceeds any they make from their singing.*

**Katie Davis Watson:** We don't get paid when we sing, but we have an anniversary. Every year, every group has an anniversary. We sell tickets, and we give away prizes. And when we get through the expenses, there may be a few dollars left for us. But when we go to the different churches and they get you on the program, then they give you expenses for the car. That's as big as you get, the expenses for the car. So when we're wearing these clothes, we done worked a hard month or so to pay for those dresses and shoes. It costs a pretty penny! I know we've got five [uniforms] ready to hand that we can put on. And we've got five more back there we ain't worn in over five years. The menfolk are the same about the suits. But it's a trend. It's like when one kid starts doing something and then all the others wanna do it. Your group comes out looking good, so mine will have to look good. Then everybody starts doing it. But at least we're not like some of the groups. It's like they say: "Here they come in their summer suits," and it'll be winter. But it doesn't mean "summer." It means "some're theirs and some're Berts" [a menswear chain]. We've been and paid for ours, but some of them have gone and bought them on credit and ain't paid for them.

*To the Golden Stars, gospel singing is inextricably linked with church, and all are involved in church affairs. Mary Brown belongs to the Straw-*

*berry Baptist church in Holly Springs; Viola Watson, John Watson, and Jack Boxley are all members at Mt. Newell. Katie Davis Watson joined the Ebenezer Baptist Church at Tyro when she moved there, and sings in its choir. But during her years at Holly Springs she was a member at Mt. Newell, and when she speaks of "our pastor," she is referring to the pastor of Mt. Newell. The church is among the more traditional Baptist congregations; only in 1990 did its choir accompaniment expand beyond a basic piano (these days, a guitar and drums join the backing), and it is one of the few churches still to hold its baptisms outdoors—once a year, usually on the second Sunday in September, at a nearby shallow lake. It's a highlight of the church year and a custom of which the Stars wholeheartedly approve—although they think it may be under threat from the church's new pastor.*

**Katie Davis Watson:** Our pastor's afraid of snakes. He wants a [baptismal] pool in the church so bad! There are snakes out there in the lake. But they don't bother us, not while we're baptizing. I think the Lord takes care of it. He will take care of us while we're out there. 'Cause our old pastor, that's the only way he wanted to do baptizing, and he'd get out there and preach in that water.

**Mary Brown:** That's the way baptizing oughta be. My church has got it inside, but I don't like it. You got to be out there in that old muddy Jordan. That's the way I like it to be; that's the way I was ducked under the water. We have a pool in the church now. So if you join the church and want to be baptized, we can baptize you that same day.

**Katie Davis Watson:** There's some funny things happen in church, Lord have mercy. One year, we had about thirty people being baptized, and I think poor preacher got tired. He had some great big ones—he like to lost one when he went down. Somebody had to be in the back to push him back up. When the preacher ducked him and he couldn't hardly get back up [she is laughing], well, I threw my hands over my eyes.

*The Golden Stars are vague about their gospel influences. They draw their material from recordings and other artists—nobody in the group writes songs—but the choice of material is all traditional. "They're originally songs that the old people used to sing," says Katie Davis Watson. None of the Stars acknowledges any direct outside influence on their singing. Viola Watson cites Mary Brown as her inspiration; Katie Davis Watson says,*

*"I just modeled myself on the New Hope Specials." The others murmur vague negatives when asked about gospel stars who may have influenced them. Jack Boxley sang with a local male quartet called the Pleasant Grove Specials before joining the New Hope Specials/Golden Stars; the others have only ever sung outside church with New Hope and/or the Stars. But although they have not played the big emotion-charged programs at which top names generate "house-wrecking" fervor, the Stars recognize the power of gospel. It's something they link directly to church experience and the African-American style of worship.*

**John Watson:** Well, what I think about it is . . . if you don't put nothing into it, you're not gonna get anything out. It's just like making up some bread. If you don't put it in the stove, it's never gonna get done, is it? But if you make up that bread and put it in the stove, you gonna get it done. So that's the way it is when you go to church. If you get into the service, you're gonna get something out of it.

**Viola Watson:** People at our churches praise the Lord a different way to the way white people do. Some of them do it physically.

**Katie Davis Watson:** You see, the old folks used to have to get up under the pot, put their head under a pot and shout.[1] They weren't allowed to holler out loud. I guess that's one of the main reasons they holler loud now—you have freedom, so you can do it.

*The only one of the Golden Stars who has not always been involved with the church is Jack Boxley. He was raised in a religious home, but in his younger days let his church membership slip. A tractor driver on a plantation, he would sing blues to himself as he worked, to help pass the time. His recollection of those days sparks a lively reminiscence among the Golden Stars.*

**Jack Boxley:** Oh, I used to sing a lot of 'em. Get on that tractor . . . I used to drive all day and half the night. All night, you could hear the sound of the tractor and my voice. I used to sing that one about the crawling kingsnake going all round the door. . . .[2]

**Katie Davis Watson:** I came up when I was young with the blues. I like blues. I don't mean some of this modern stuff; I don't hardly know what they're saying. But when they're singing the blues like B. B. King— that "Three O'Clock In the Morning" and things like that—I can relate to that. That's something. I don't think church people have any right to condemn the fellow that's doing the blues. It's in your mind how you feel about it. Now I can be upset and I can be singing spirituals but thinking sinful and doing just as bad. . . .

**Mary Brown:** Well, I used to sing blues myself. [This statement comes as a surprise to the group; she pauses straight-faced for a moment to appreciate the effect of it, then giggles.] Now I didn't go out on no stage singing or nothing like that. But I was young, and I sure did sing 'em, Lord, Lord. Just as well as I do the church songs. "Little Schoolgirl," "Sugar Mama" and all them. . . .

**Katie Davis Watson:** Don't miss "Baby Please Don't Go." [Everyone laughs.]

**Mary Brown:** Lord, have mercy! That's one I used to sing. I'd be out there at church seeking my soul's salvation, then I'd get back home and get right out there and start to singing, "Baby please don't go. . . ."

**Viola Watson:** (completing the line): " . . . down to New Orleans 'cause I love you so."

**Katie Davis Watson:** Then there was "Mama killed a chicken and she thought it was a duck. . . ."

**All group members:** (amid laughter): " . . . put it on the table with its legs sticking up."

**Katie Davis Watson:** Lord have mercy! We all did some.³

**Viola Watson:** I always remember our former pastor, Rev. Houston—he's dead now—he used to say he'd never turn his car radio off when he was riding along. Whatever came on that radio, he'd listen to it. But a lot of people, as long as the church songs are on, they listen to it. Then if something else comes along, they turn it off. But Rev. Houston didn't turn his radio off. He said that every song you heard had a meaning.

**Jack Boxley:** Well, I quit singing the blues. I was out there in the field one day with the blues, and something came to me and told me, "leave those blues alone." And I went back in the church.

**Katie Davis Watson:** Instead of singing the blues, we go to the church and sing. That's what we have. It's our main thing is the gospel. We go to the church and we have to have something. And gospel, that belongs to the church. When you pray, you're asking God for something. But when you sing gospel music, you're praising God. And I guess it's love keeps us doing it. It was love that kept Jesus hanging on the cross. So it's love. Just love singing that gospel.

# 4  ON THE AIR

*"You've got to talk to the disc jockey . . ."*

Radio has played—and still plays—an important role in the gospel music story. Since the 1920s, preachers, choirs, soloists, and quartets have made broadcasts with the dual purpose of spreading the message and promoting "in person" appearances. The development in the 1960s of tightly focused radio stations aiming for specific audiences led to the establishment of gospel broadcasting, and, today, virtually every city with a significant African-American population has at least one gospel station. Memphis, in the heart of the "Bible belt," has five for a population of about nine hundred thousand (other city stations also have occasional gospel programming, especially on Sundays). Gospel broadcasting is particularly well established in the South, and it is possible to drive from Memphis to New Orleans without ever being out of range of a religious station. Some are powerful, transmitting at up to fifty thousand watts and covering multistate areas; many more transmit at much lower power, covering as little as a twenty-mile radius around the transmitter. Some transmit twenty-four hours a day, while others run only during daylight hours. Though an increasing number are using the FM band, most of the major ones are on AM. All are vital links in the gospel community.

Programming is basic and is similar on all stations. A mixture of music and church services, with advertisements usually running at a lower ratio than on secular stations, is the staple diet of the gospel radio listener. The music covers a wide spectrum, from recordings by the great quartets and soloists of the 1950s to the latest choir offerings. Since the aim is to reflect public taste, in the 1990s, choir recordings dominate. But programmers know that all types of gospel music have their devotees, and all tastes must be satisfied. "Maybe I'll play one record that you don't like, but then the next one you'll like," sums up veteran gospel DJ Early Wright of WROX in Clarksdale, Mississippi. Interspersed with the music are church services, sermons, in-studio speakers and other features related to religion. Some church broadcasts are syndicated, so that, for instance, listeners in rural Tennessee can be listening to a recording of a service in Chicago, but many come from local churches. Some are broadcast "live"; more often, they are taped and played later, often during time paid for by the church. Editing tends to be minimal, and when the time allocated for a service comes to an end, so does the broadcast, even if the preacher is in mid-sermon.

The most distinctive characteristic of gospel radio is its ties with the community that listens to it. Disk jockeys appear as emcees on local programs and anniversaries. Stations run "community noticeboards" to publicize local church and religious events. DJs dedicate songs to regular listeners. And gospel artists can get their music played on their local stations. Many of these recordings are self-financed and produced by the artists, and an airing over the local station is the only broadcast exposure they will get. Sometimes a hometown record will catch the ears of listeners and produce a local hit. It happened to the Spirit of Memphis with its 1987 recording of "Happy in the Service of the Lord";[1] in 1992, the Brown Singers of Memphis had a success with their version of the standard "Jesus Is on the Main Line."[2]

The use of local talent has been a hallmark of gospel radio since its beginnings. In the early days of broadcasting, much of the music trans-mitted was performed "live" in the studio, and radio stations provided an outlet for a wide range of community talent, including dance bands, comedians, and "hillbilly" musicians (especially in the South). The exact date of the first gospel broadcast has not been pinpointed, but, by 1926, the Eva Jessye Choir, a professional choral group from New York, was appearing on syndicated radio shows singing its formal arrangements of spirituals.[3] One of the first quartets to appear on air—certainly the first on a nationally syndicated program—was the university-based Utica Jubilee Quartet, from Mississippi. The group moved to New York in 1926, and in 1927 secured a regular half-hour program over the NBC network based on WJZ-New York, performing spirituals, jubilee songs, and hymns, as well as some secular material.[4] Gospel historian Kip Lornell points to the parallel rise of gospel quartet broadcasting and recording, noting that "quartets began performing 'live' broadcasts at about the same time as they began recording in large numbers for the commercial record companies."[5] Among the early broadcasting groups he identifies are the N&W Imperial Quartet, which made no recordings but appeared on WDBJ-Roanoke, Virginia, in 1928, and the popular Norfolk, Virginia, groups the Golden Crown Quartet and the Silver Leaf Quartet, which began their radio careers around the same time. In Memphis, the I. C. Glee Club broadcast over WREC in 1928, the same year in which it first recorded.[6] In Alabama, the Birmingham Jubilee Singers broadcast over local stations WAPI, WWRC and WJLD.[7] Veteran Alabama singers James and Rufus Williams first performed on radio in 1929 with their Williams Brothers Quartet, then in the early 1930s with the Ensley Jubilee Singers.[8] (The Ensleys later had a regular program in Jefferson County, Alabama, which ran from 1942 until 1980.) New York gospel researcher Ray Allen found ample evidence of early gospel broadcasting activity in that city: "[A] review of the Radio Features section of [New York's main African-American newspaper] the *Amsterdam News*, during the late 1920s and early 1930s reveals that 'quartets' and 'jubilee singers' received a good deal of air time. . . . Radio listings during this period include not only programs by the nationally-known Fisk Jubilee Singers and the Southernaires, but also performances by the Wandering Boys Spiritual Quartet, the Slow River Negro Quartet, the Metropolitan Four, the Eveready Jubilee Singers, the Excell Jubilee Singers, the Eastern Star Quartet and the Grand Central Red Caps Quartet. It is presumed these latter groups consisted of local New York singers."[9]

The 1930s brought a proliferation of gospel—mainly quartets—on radio. Lornell summarizes the impact the music had on a nation hard hit by the 1929 Wall Street crash: "Grassroots gospel quartets had grabbed the musical imagination of America by the time the Great Depression settled over the country. Although the record industry was decimated by the depression, Columbia and Okeh continued to distribute recordings by a few select groups. Meanwhile, the radio broadcasts of other quartets continued to reach hundreds of thousands of listeners, no doubt including a significant number of white Americans. Thus black gospel quartet singing began its rapid transformation from a religious regional genre to a form of popular entertainment that was being heard across the United States."[10]

The airwaves were one area where Jim Crow's grip could be weakened. African-Americans could be denied access to America's democratic process and segregated as second-class citizens, but their music could be heard by anybody with a radio. This erosion of the color bar sometimes spread into the studio. The Soul Stirrers, who started broadcasting in their hometown of Houston, Texas, in the early 1930s, went on to Philadelphia, where they broadcast every day for eight months during 1939.[11] During that time, they shared a program with the white Stamps-Baxter Quartet.[12] In the early 1940s, the Fairfield Four would co-opt a white announcer to sing bass if the full group did not turn up for its daily 6:45 a.m. broadcast over WLAC-Nashville.[13] In 1944, the Five Blind Boys of Alabama—then still known as the Happyland Singers—left Talladega School for the Blind and went to Birmingham. Their first broadcasts were on WSGN, but, soon afterwards, an appearance at a white church led to a fifteen-minute daily show on the white gospel station WKAX.[14] For nearly forty years, starting in 1950, the Zion Travelers broadcast over WBIR-Baton Rouge, Louisiana, every Sunday morning. Historian Joyce Jackson noted: "As this radio station is owned and operated by whites, and its programming is basically targeted towards country and western fans, one may safely assume the Travelers have a white audience as well as a black, especially on Sunday mornings."[15]

The most successful early "crossover" group was the Golden Gate Quartet, which started its radio career on WIS in Columbia, South Carolina, in June 1936. By the end of the year, it had a regular program on the fifty thousand-watt WBT in Charlotte, North Carolina, which could be heard over most of the East Coast and as far west as Nashville. It provided the Gates with a platform which they used for three years to spread their music before going on to New York, where they won a five-day-a-week program on the CBS network. In the early 1940s, they appeared on a wide range of mainstream radio programs, including a coast-to-coast broadcast of the gala held to mark the 1941 inauguration of President Franklin D. Roosevelt.[16]

Other groups also used the radio to advantage, albeit on a lesser scale than the Golden Gate Quartet. One of their closest rivals was the Southernaires, whose NBC network show, *The Little Weatherbeaten Church of the Air*, ran from 1933 until 1944. The Soul Stirrers moved from Philadelphia to Chicago, which became their permanent base, and, in 1940, gained a Sunday morning show that ran for more than ten years on WIND. The Selah Jubilee Singers, from New York, made their first broadcasts over Brooklyn radio stations around the late 1920s in programs presented by their home church. After the group turned professional, in the early 1940s, its popularity was boosted by daily broadcasts over WPTF in Raleigh, North Carolina.[17] The Fairfield Four started broadcasting on WSIX, a small Nashville station with only local coverage. In 1942, they won a promotional contest, which had as first prize a program on WLAC, a fifty thousand-watt station audible over most of the South.[18] The program was initially sponsored by the Colonial Coffee Company, which ran the contest; it was later taken over by the Sunway Vitamin Company, and continued until about 1955. Other stations also took the broadcasts on transcription discs, twelve- or sixteen-inch acetates which held a complete fifteen-minute program. "We had to come in every Tuesday and work all day to supply those other stations," recalled group leader Sam McCrary. "We did them all live at WLAC, and they would ship them to other stations [in] Salt Lake City, Utah, Chicago, New Orleans, Birmingham, Philadelphia. . . . We were heard all over the country."[19] A total of thirty-seven stations took the Fairfield Four transcriptions, and McCrary's claim of being heard "all over the country" was not far wrong. The broadcasts made the Four one of the South's most popular gospel acts, and created a continuing demand for personal appearances.

For the quartets in particular, this exposure was one of the main reasons for performing on radio. The work was not rewarding in itself—only a few acts were paid by their sponsors, and most performed for little or no financial recompense. Many paid the radio stations, buying a fifteen- or thirty-minute block of time. Some then found sponsors to buy advertising and indirectly pay for the broadcasts; others simply carried the cost. (In the early 1950s, says Kip Lornell, a fifteen-minute segment on KWAM-Memphis cost about twelve dollars.)[20] The payoff was the amount of "live" work the broadcasts generated and the increased standing accorded to radio stars. Lornell quotes "Cousin" Eugene Walton, a member of the Gospel Travelers and a gospel DJ for KWAM from 1953 until 1982: "That was their way of getting heard . . . getting on the air so people could hear them. And by the same token, the people listened to them on the air. That's how they got established. If you weren't on the air, you had a pretty rough go with trying to get programs. That's why it was vitally important to be on the air."[21]

Another popular and long-lasting group changed its name twice to accommodate radio broadcasts. In 1938, twenty-four-year-old West Virginia coal miner Claude Jeter organized a group which he called the Four Harmony Kings. In the early 1940s, the Kings started a weekly Sunday morning broadcast on WBIR in Knoxville, Tennessee, and changed their name to the Silvertones to avoid confusion with another broadcasting group, the Kings of Harmony. (In the late 1930s, the Kings of Harmony had a Houston, Texas, program which was broadcast at 2 a.m. A wide audience of loyal listeners set alarm clocks so they could wake up and hear it.)[22] The Silvertones received no payment for their broadcasting until 1942, when the local Swan Bakery began sponsoring the program and paying the group, which then became the Swan Silvertone Singers—the name it carried for the rest of its career, more than forty years. In a 1950 letter to Specialty recording company owner Art Rupe, the group's manager and baritone singer, John Myles, wrote: "For six years we worked for the bakery and did personal appearances, which brought us pretty good dough."[23] (History does not record whether the pun was intentional.)

The Swans started recording for King in 1946, but in 1952 switched to Rupe's label, making their first Specialty recordings at station WPGH in Pittsburgh, Pennsylvania. This was not unusual in the early days of post–World War II gospel recording. Many small labels did not have facilities for recording, or could not afford to bring artists long distances to record. But any reasonably equipped radio station had recording gear and trained staff to operate it. The Radio Four—a name which indicated the group's awareness of the importance of broadcasting—started their recording career near April/May 1952, with a six-track session recorded at station WBDL in the group's hometown of Bowling Green, Kentucky. The Spirit of Memphis also made its first recordings in a radio studio, WJLD in Birmingham, Alabama, during a 1948 visit to sing at a program in the city. "We sang this song, 'Happy in the Service of the Lord,'" said group member Robert Reed. "And the audience . . . they acted like they hadn't heard a song like that before. It just went over big! So this guy, this nice white guy, said, 'How would you guys like to record that song for me?' We said, 'Okay'. He was the director of this radio station. . . ."[24]

It may appear that quartets were the only religious performers to make radio broadcasts in the pioneering days. Certainly they seem to have dominated the gospel airwaves, for very good reasons. Their relatively small size and limited instrumentation made them easier to broadcast than larger ensembles, and their performing style was aimed at entertaining as well as proselytizing. They actively sought radio time as a way of obtaining "live" engagements and enhancing their reputations. And the boom in gospel broadcasting came as quartets were riding their own rising wave of popularity, although the relationship was symbiotic, as radio exposure helped swell this wave. But other sacred material, although not as well documented, is also part of the story of broadcasting. Church services were broadcast at least from the 1930s, and a number of preachers, choirs and soloists were also heard over the air.

From Cleveland came the Wings Over Jordan Choir, which soon after its establishment in 1936 obtained a regular local program. This became so popular that it was syndicated as a national broadcast and led to a number of national tours during the 1940s, which, as Ray Funk points out, was "an unusual thing for a large choir in that time."[25] In Detroit, the New Liberty Baptist Church had a regular broadcast around 1946 which featured the church choir, the Moments of Meditation. (The pastor of New Liberty was Ernest Rundless, who sang tenor with the Soul Stirrers until the early 1940s when he left to preach; one choir member was his wife, Earnestine Rundless, who formed the popular Meditation Singers, initially from members of the choir.)[26] In Newark, New Jersey, the Abyssinian Baptist Church played an important role in the area's gospel music history, partly because of the great singers it produced (including Carrie Smith, Leon Lumpkin and the Banks Brothers, Charles and Jeff; Alex Bradford was the minister of music from 1960 until his death in 1978) and partly because of its weekly WHBI broadcast, which ran from 1948 until 1960.[27] In Los Angeles, the St. Paul Baptist Church Choir—one of the first ensembles in the city to sing the "new" gospel style developed in Chicago by Thomas A. Dorsey—was equally influential through its broadcasts.

Several of the African-American church's best-known preachers made extensive use of the radio to extend their ministry. One of the pioneers was Elder Lightfoot Solomon Michaux, from Newport News, Virginia. By 1933, he was preaching on radio, introducing each program with his theme tune, "Happy Am I"—a song which he made so popular that his billing became "The 'Happy Am I' Preacher." In 1933, the Victor recording company used Michaux transcription discs made by WJSV in Alexandria, Virginia, to produce two 78 rpm records—one of them featuring "Happy Am I." (On his broadcasts, Michaux turned the station's call letters into the acronym **W**illingly **J**esus **S**uffered for **V**ictory.)

Michaux's flamboyant style was already well developed on these early recordings,[28] and he went on to broadcast his Radio Church of God over the CBS and Mutual networks. His preaching trademark was to repeatedly address the congregation as "pilgrims"; with every repetition, the "pilgrims" would respond on cue "yeah yeah." He was a master of the grand gesture, as Savoy Record Company owner Fred Mendelsohn describes (writing in a style as extravagant as its subject) in notes to a 1962 Michaux album: "This man has performed acts that have made religious history. He has been responsible for bringing 600 gallons of water direct from the River Jordan, where JESUS was baptized, to baptize 150 converts at his revival meeting at Griffith Stadium in Washington DC where over 25,000 people attended. He was also responsible for flying in a chartered plane from Nome, Alaska . . . with a BIBLE in a sealed container which he dropped over Russian territory, six months later Stalin was dead which was certainly more than coincidence."[29]

Detroit's Rev. C. L. (Clarence LaVaughn) Franklin, achieved a national reputation for the power and eloquence of his preaching. The Chess record company, of Chicago, issued more than seventy records of Franklin preaching at his New Bethel Church, but he was also a regular on station WJLB in Detroit. Another very successful preacher and singer, Rev. Cleophus Robinson, gained a taste for broadcasting in 1948 when he left his home in Canton, Mississippi, for Chicago to meet his idol, Mahalia Jackson. During his eighteen months in Chicago, he sang with Jackson and the Roberta Martin Singers, and guested on the occasional radio show. He then went to live with his uncle, Rev. L. A. Hamblin, pastor of a Memphis church. There, at the age of seventeen, he started a weekly radio program, *The Voice of the Soul*, from Rev. Hamblin's church. In 1957, he went to St. Louis and became pastor of the Bethlehem Missionary Baptist Church. Every Sunday through the 1960s, he broadcast his *Hour of Faith* over KATZ, using a remote line from his church. (In 1964, Robinson started a national television show that ran for twenty-five years.)[30]

Historically, the best-known gospel station—although it has never been a full-time religious broadcaster—is WDIA in Memphis. Today, its gospel programming is overshadowed by the city's fulltime religious stations. But throughout the 1950s and into the 1960s, it was the South's premier outlet for broadcast gospel. It had the star DJs, the top artists, and the community involvement that helped it live up to the nickname it gave itself, "the goodwill station." WDIA was not the first Memphis station to air gospel music. KWEM, across the Mississippi River in West Memphis (in 1953, it moved to Memphis and became KWAM; it is now a full-time gospel station) and WCBR (later WLOK) did so when WDIA was still a white-oriented station, sliding towards bankruptcy on a diet of classical music and some occasional country. Its white owners, Bert Ferguson and John Pepper, bought the station in 1947; within months they were trying to sell it again. But buyers were scarce, and, in desperation, Ferguson and Pepper moved in 1948 to all-black programming, making WDIA the first station in the United States to do so. It was a decision based on economics rather than philosophy—about five hundred thousand African-Americans were within range of WDIA's 250-watt transmitter, 46.9 percent of the total radio audience[31]—but it was a success, and after a tentative start the station moved as quickly as it could to an all-black format.

One of the early problems was finding enough material to broadcast to the new audience. Gospel music was an ideal solution. It appealed to the audience, it was inexpensive to present, and a vast reservoir of it could be found in and around Memphis. Also, by using local performers, WDIA could forge links with its listening community. Eventually, around half of WDIA's programming was religious; much of the other half was rhythm and blues. Among the first gospel groups to appear, early in 1949, were the Spirit of Memphis, the Southern Wonders and the female Songbirds of the South, while Rev. W. Herbert Brewster's East Trigg Avenue Missionary Baptist Church provided the *Gospel Treasure Hour* at 7:15 on Sunday mornings. (As well as being a preacher and singer, Brewster was also one of the foremost gospel songwriters of the post–World War II era.[32] His influence extended even into the world of rock 'n' roll—Peter Guralnick notes that the young Elvis Presley would "sneak out" of services at his own church and "drive down to the colored church at East Trigg where the Reverend Brewster delivered his stirring sermons and Queen C. Anderson and the Brewsteraires were the featured soloists.")[33]

As well as giving exposure to gospel artists from Memphis and further afield, WDIA also created its own stars, the DJs who ran the gospel programs. The best known of these were Ford Nelson and Theo "Bless My Bones" Wade, who joined the station in 1949 and 1952 respectively. Nelson started as a pianist backing blues singer B. B. King during his daily fifteen-minute show, and made his announcing debut on the rhythm and blues show *Let's Have Some Fun*. Although he kept this show for a number of years, WDIA discovered that gospel DJing was his forte, and he moved increasingly into that field. Theo Wade, a school teacher who gained his nickname from the expletive he used when he spilled a cup of coffee while on air, came to WDIA after twenty years as manager and booking agent for the Spirit of Memphis. In 1954, the station upgraded to fifty thousand watts and starting broadcasting each day at 4 a.m. instead of 6:30. The extra hours were assigned to gospel music, DJ'd by Theo Wade. Despite the early hour, Wade's selling ability and the music made it one of WDIA's most popular shows with listeners and advertisers. Nelson and Wade also presented the 7–9 p.m. *Hallelujah Jamboree*, with Nelson doing the first hour and Wade the second. The show's ratings matched those of WDIA's R&B shows, especially on Saturday night, when Wade did the whole show, presenting a potpourri of "live" music, records and hard-sell advertising.

The change to fifty thousand watts sent WDIA's sound over much of the South, and brought a surge in bookings for performers featured on the station. Jethroe Bledsoe, of the Spirit of Memphis, recalled: "When WDIA went 50,000 watts, that's what blew the top! We were getting letters from all over, as far as the station would reach." Another group member, Robert Reed, said, "When the station got bigger, we got bigger."[34] Other groups whose careers flourished as WDIA expanded its reach included the Pattersonaires, the Jubilee Hummingbirds, the Sons of Jehovah, the Jordan Wonders, and the Dixie Nightingales, who first broadcast on the *Hallelujah Jubilee* as a teenage group called the Gospel Writer Junior Boys.

WDIA's involvement with Memphis gospel was not limited to on-air broadcasts. The music was prominently featured in the station's two annual charity revues, the *Star-Lite Revue* and the *Goodwill Revue*, both of which raised money for WDIA's independently run Goodwill Fund, set up to help crippled African-American children in Memphis. (It later also financed a number of other charitable activities, all aimed at helping black children.) As a spin-off from the *Hallelujah Jubilee*, WDIA set up the *Hallelujah Jubilee Caravan*, which about once a month would tour gospel acts in Mississippi and Tennessee. WDIA even briefly had its own record label. Around 1950, the station recorded two tracks by Rev. W. Herbert Brewster and the Brewster Singers, and issued them on the Tan Town label (*Tan Town Jamboree* was a long-running WDIA program). The station also recorded ten-inch acetates of several Memphis gospel acts for airplay. Many of these valuable disks were subsequently destroyed; those saved include the only recordings of some performers from the 1950s.[35]

Throughout the 1950s and into the 1960s, WDIA was the dominant station in Memphis. Ferguson and Pepper sold it in 1957 to Chicago broadcasting mogul Egmont Sonderling, although Ferguson stayed on as general manager. The format remained largely unchanged until the 1960s, when it was modified to match the style of other Sonderling stations in San Francisco, New York, and Washington. As social attitudes changed, the "blacks only" label became anachronistic, and today, while WDIA is still a leading Memphis radio station, only its history now differentiates it from the many other stations vying for a share of the listening audience and the advertising dollar.

But if WDIA's gospel programming has withered to a selection of records on Sunday morning, gospel radio in general is a bigger force in the 1990s than it has ever been, which is ironic considering that the market for gospel on stage has shrunk to the point where only a few artists can now make a living from their music. Gospel radio is a vital ingredient in the gospel record industry, both from the demand it generates and because of its own requirement for music to play. Said Richard Simone, head of gospel promotion and marketing in 1989 for the major Malaco label: "There are a lot of 24-hour and sun-up to sun-down stations that constantly demand more product. Radio has always been important; it's even more important now."[36]

Singers are also still aware of the importance of radio. A cynical view was expressed in 1985 by Clara Anderson, leader of the Memphis Harps of Melody: "Put your radio on and you can hear quite a few stations with gospel singing, gospel music for hours. So now you really don't have to go to church to hear gospel singing any more. . . . When they didn't used to have all these radio stations, people would go out more to hear it."[37] But Sandy Foster, leader of the 1990s incarnation of the Blind Boys of Mississippi, takes a more positive—and typical—view. In a 1992 interview, he explained how the group selected its repertoire for programs while on tour. Some songs, obviously, are standards associated with the group since the days of Archie Brownlee. Also, Foster said that "you sing what's being played in that area. And if you sing that', you gonna be a hit with the people. Usually, when you sing in an area, you've got to do a radio interview so people know you are in town. Then you've got to talk to the disc jockey and ask him what he's playing."[38] In 1981, Foster and the Blind Boys made an elaborate pitch to about two hundred disc jockeys in a bid to promote their album *I'll Make It All Right* (Jewel JC-0161). First, they recorded the secular song "Pilot of the Airwaves" for the album. The song contains the line "pilot of the airwaves, sweet personality," and Foster spent a day in the studio recording the names of the two hundred DJs, which were inserted into demo versions of the song to replace the words "pilot of the airwaves." The personalized disks were then sent to DJs. Said Foster: "That song would've done us no good no way by itself. But it helped [make] that disc jockey play us in that area."[39]

# Early Wright

*"Gospel and I go on about our business. . . ."*

In an era when radio disc jockeys go in and out of fashion as quickly as the clothes they wear, Early Wright is different. He's seventy-seven years old and dressed in a plain white shirt and casual trousers; on his feet are the polished black boots he wears winter and summer. He's a gospel and blues DJ on WROX, "1450 on your radio dial," in Clarksdale, in the heart of the Mississippi Delta. He's had the job since 1947. His five-days-a-week show has had different times over the years, but it's always been in the evening, and it's always been split evenly between gospel and blues. Now, it starts at 6 p.m. and finishes four hours later. For the first two hours, Early Wright is the "Soul Man," playing blues ranging from new hits by southern favorites such as Bobby Bland or Bobby Rush to classics from artists like Lightnin' Hopkins and one-time Clarksdale resident Muddy Waters. He answers the frequent telephone calls from listeners by saying "Soul Man speaking." But after the 8 p.m. syndicated news broadcast, it's gospel time. "No more Soul Man," he says, spinning "Now Is the Time (To Depend on the Lord)" by Memphis singer and preacher Leroy Liddell. "This is gospel. This is Early Wright."

*Early Wright in the studio at WROX, Clarksdale, Mississippi.*

"I've always been in gospel. I joined the church in my teenage years, when I came to be a member of the Mt. Olive Baptist Church. That was in Drew, Mississippi, in 1927. Rev. Galloway was my pastor. Ever since then, I've been a member of the church. And I haven't been a member of too many. I stay in a church until I move out of the community. I was at Mt. Olive Baptist Church until I moved to Council Spur, out from Dublin, about eighteen miles from here. I joined the St. Mary Baptist

Church and I stayed in that church until I came to Clarksdale. I moved to Clarksdale in 19 and 37, in the month of December. I joined the New Bethel Baptist Church, I joined there first Sunday in January of '38. And I've been a member of that church until now. We have lost our pastor and I stayed right there. Most people, when their church gets in a confusion, they jump up and go to another church. But it's there, too! So I stayed right there. We haven't had too many confusions; our church has had 'bout less confusions than any other church. ['Confusions' refers to any form of trouble or disruption, ranging from a simple misunderstanding to the civil rights struggle of the 1960s.]

"I was born in 1915, on a Monday morning at three o'clock, my mother said. My nickname was Puddin', because when I was a little boy crawling around, they cooked on a wood stove. And they had cooked a pudding. And I crawled up and got the stove open and went in there and got that pudding. I ate a large amount of that pudding. Then I lay down and went to sleep. I was layin' down 'side the pudding, and they named me Puddin'. But I've had it harder than any man . . . ain't a man that ever walked on concrete had it harder than me. I growed up the hard way. I had a stepfather, and he wouldn't allow me to go to school. That's why I don't have the proper education, because he wouldn't let me go. We moved to Missouri, and he had to let me go or go to jail. If I missed a day, the police was at his house wanting to know . . . he had to give an account of why I wasn't at school. So what learning I got, I got in Missouri mostly, because that's where I could go to school. I was under my stepdaddy, and he wouldn't let me go to school. He'd find something for me to do, have me working. He was lazy and triflin', and I had to get out . . . sometimes we couldn't get groceries unless I went and asked on my mother's behalf. They served us groceries out of a [plantation] commissary. Man said, 'We just gave y'all some flour the other day.' Well, there was ten of us in the family—there was ten children and one died—and my mother and stepdaddy, that made eleven of us. And a little sack of flour doesn't last long with eleven people. And I'd go to people's houses with a little bucket, just seeing if they'd let me have some meal. I'd get out and do things for hours and hours for twenty-five cents. I've been obedient. Never say anything to my mother, not one time."

*Early Wright is a tall man, well over six feet, and solidly built; his posture is still erect, and his hair is tinged with gray only at the temples. Most of his front teeth are gold-capped; he's self-conscious about them and is reluctant to smile for photographs. His broadcasting style is relaxed and unique. He seldom identifies the records he plays—if he names the artist, he usually doesn't give the title, and if he gives the title he doesn't name the artist. His assumption is that his audience knows these records. If he's out of the room when a record finishes playing, WROX will be silent until he returns—the broadcasting demon of "dead air" holds no fears for Early Wright. His programming method is simple. First, he collects a pile of records he thinks he might play that night. Then, while one is playing, he sifts through the stack looking for a suitable one to follow it. Some of the records he hears for the first time as he plays them on his show. "They come to my house. I just bring 'em on up and play 'em. Audition them on the air by playing them. I don't have time to do it at home. I don't know if the record's good or bad until I get it on the air." His technique for reading advertisements is almost stream-of-consciousness. Most of the advertisements booked for his show are unscripted; if a script is supplied, chances are he'll ignore it. "I'd like to tell you here in Clarksdale we got one of the finest shoe stores that I know about. That is Connerly's. Connerly's got one of the best shoe stores with the reasonable prices with best quality shoes that I know of. You buy good shoes at Connerly Shoe Store when you go there. They got all sizes—sizes up to thirteen wide for ladies, they got as large as I wear for men. I wear fourteen, fifteen, like that, you know. Sometimes I go there and they don't have my shoe. I put a couple of boxes on my feet and go about my business until my shoes or boots come in. That's from Connerly's. . . ."*

"I was a strawboss [foreman] on a plantation. And I was a jackleg mechanic. That was down at Council Spur. All the people brought their cars to me, and I worked on 'em when I had time. When I moved to Clarksdale, I got a job at Robertson Motor Company as a mechanic. Then I quit there and went to work for the railroad company because they were paying more money. And I stayed there a while. I worked at the freight house a while, then I worked on the track a while. Then I went to the engines—switching 'em, putting coal in 'em, put this one over here and that one over there. And I got pretty good. I learned how to drive a train.

"I used to be manager of a gospel group, the Four Star Quartet. And we were broadcasting in Helena, at KFFA. See, I went to WREC in Memphis, Tennessee, but they didn't allow Negroes to broadcast, although they didn't tell me that, just gave me other excuses.[1] And I couldn't pay them to let me broadcast with my group at WREC. So I went to broadcasting at KFFA, Helena, Arkansas, with my gospel group. I stayed there with KFFA until WROX opened up in Clarksdale. They started, like, this week, and next week I went to the manager and bought me some program time, bought fifteen minutes of time. And when I broadcast with my group there that Sunday, the manager of the station heard me, and he began to worrying me about being a DJ. I didn't know anything about being a DJ. But he kept on worryin' me and worryin' me about it, and I told him I'd let him know. He waited for two weeks, then he got other people to come to me and try to talk me into it.

"He said, 'Well now, if you take it, you're gonna have to play blues. I'd like for you to play blues if you could.' I told him I didn't think I could play the blues for him, because it might be difficult with the members of my church. But I went to my pastor, Rev. M. G. May, and talked to him. He said, 'Early, that's a job. And I don't see no reason in the world why anybody would have a complaint with you playing it because we know you're good in church.' So I went on then."

*Early Wright is uncertain of the date on which he started at WROX. In 1988, he told one interviewer how he used to tell people that he started later than he actually did to "try to keep from being so old."[2] But it was possibly 1946, certainly no later than 1947. And his appointment made him—as far as he knows—the Midsouth's first black announcer.*

"At the time, the black folks came in through the back door of the building. And the manager took me and showed me where we came up the stairs on the side from the alley. They didn't allow black folks to come in the front door of that building. I came up two times, then I said, 'Now, I don't have anything, but I'm as much as anybody to myself.' I didn't come in the back door no more. I came up there two times, then I went to coming in the front door. And I didn't have no confusion. I didn't have any problems at all. I have gotten along with white and black, I'm still getting along with them. I don't have no problems out of white or black. And when confusion came [the civil rights strife of the 1960s], I went on the radio asking people to pray. I didn't know I was doing so much good until some of the people told me, 'Early, you did more good than some of us out here marching, you did more good than some of us out here shedding blood.' They felt that I did more good with the radio program. I asked for peace, and I got peace.

"Since I've been on the radio, I've been treated real nice. But I don't take no side money, like for playing records. I'm honest with the station, I'm honest with you and with everybody else. I'm seventy-seven years old now, and I have never had an FCC [Federal Communications Commission] complaint. You know, folk come in . . . a man [he names a well-known R&B singer] walked in here one night, pockets stuck way out, and went to unrolling his money. I said, 'What are you doing?' He said, 'I'm gonna show you how we appreciate you. Every blues and gospel artist should appreciate you, and I'm gonna show you tonight how I appreciate you.' I said, 'Put your money in your pocket. I don't want a penny.' I have never taken a penny for playing records. Anything I want bad enough or need bad enough, the Lord give it to me. I ain't making no big buck on WROX, and I ain't got no racket. If I had a racket, everybody would know it overnight. I can't afford a racket. If folks catch me with a racket, that'd bring down my prestige. I couldn't afford that.

"The Lord will help you to do anything that you have the right spirit and heart to do. You don't have to worry about nothing but trusting him. Sometimes I get broke. I have taxes to pay. And when tax time came this past year, I didn't have any money. Well, tax time came, and my name never hit the paper [he was not publicly named as a tax defaulter]. I had the money. I paid my taxes. I don't know where my money came from. I just talked to the master. Sometimes things happen to me, I wonder 'how did it happen?' The Lord's good to me."

*In addition to his radio work, Early Wright has had a long involvement in presenting gospel music, starting with the Four Stars in the 1940s. In the 1950s, he promoted programs by several major groups, including the Soul Stirrers when they were at their peak and were led by one-time Clarksdale resident Sam Cooke.*

"The Four Stars started to splitting up, going this place and that. Two of them left together and went to Chicago to do better. One of them told me afterwards, he said, 'I don't know why I did it. I ain't did no good.' But there used to be a man here that run a barbershop and he had a group, too. And my group was whipping his every time they got in his presence. Every time they'd catch him on stage, my group would out-sing his. And he told my group, 'Why don't y'all go to Chicago where you can do much better.' Because when people see you doing real well, they'll come to you and say 'You're losing time here. Why don't you go to Chicago, where you can do so well at what you're doing. You'd be a big-time star, big as so-and-so, if you go to Chicago or Detroit or California.'

"But we were doing real good. We were locking the doors on some of the other groups because we were pretty good at that time. That was at singing contests. See who can sing best and upset the house. 'Cause we would make games with nobody. Fellows would get up and say different things, but we'd sit in the seat and pray. And when we got to the stage, the Lord was with us. I used to tell my group, 'I don't care how bad somebody make a mistake on a song, don't you snigger. Don't you grin. I don't care how bad a mistake one of the men in the band make on the song, give him a smile.' I used to be with my quartet, and there might be a group that's better than us. But if they were making a mistake in their singing, I would point it out and tell them that if they would correct it up, they would be better. And people would call me crazy. Because we'd all be in concert that day, waiting to hit the stage against one another. Singing against one another. But I just can't help it. If I can tell you something to help you, I'll do it. I couldn't sing myself, but I could make up the numbers. I tried singing bass and baritone, and if we didn't have the man, I'd get in there and make up the numbers. I could carry the part, but I had other men could sing well enough to cover up for me and we got by.

"I know practically all . . . a lot of the big-time groups like the Soul Stirrers and the Fairfield Four and all those groups, the early groups that used to broadcast over Nashville, Tennessee. I have promoted them here. I don't know so many of the later ones, you know, the ones that just came up in the last few minutes. But the older groups, I have brought them here. I don't do any promoting now because I've got a bad heart and all this jumping in and out of an air-conditioned car . . . when you promote, you work a little harder than you usually work. But the Soul Stirrers . . . that was Sam Cooke. Sam Cooke spent the night in my house, he stayed in my house at least five nights in his lifetime of being with the gospel Soul Stirrers, before he went to pop. And when he went to pop, he had a wreck and they brought him to Memphis hospital. I went and talked with him. I asked him about going back to gospel. He's out there in the blues field, but he said, 'Early, I don't want to be out here.' He said, 'I'm out here, but I don't wanna be. I'll give you a promise that I'll come back to gospel.' But he got killed.[3] It was a great loss, because Sam was a great young man.

"I've got a church, my church. It was a run-down building but I put my shoulder in and braced it up a little bit. It's called Mt. Zion Missionary Baptist Church. I haven't got a pastor there or anything— anybody can preach and anybody can sing. I get preachers there, I get singers there, we have a hallelujah time. Most times we have a good crowd and we just have a good time down there. There's a lot of gospel groups around Clarksdale. We have a lot of them broadcast on my station, then there's so many that don't broadcast but are still in the gospel field. I used to go out and record people and play them on the radio. I am the cause of a lot of preachers and people being heard that had never been heard. I've recorded at Rev. Willie Morganfield's church, recorded his service. [Rev. Morganfield was a member of Wright's Four Star Quartet before going on to a career as a singer and preacher. He now pastors the Bell Grove Baptist Church in Clarksdale.] I've got my own recording equipment, I don't have to use the station's."

*Early Wright's reputation outside Clarksdale is as a blues, rather than a gospel, DJ. An interview in* Living Blues *magazine4—with a photo of Wright on the front cover—covers his involvement with gospel in half a dozen lines. But Wright views himself as being firmly on the gospel side.*

"They call me 'the father of the blues' because I play the blues. But I had a man that called me long distance because he wanted to talk to me about gospel. He had heard that I knew a lot about gospel and I was still in church. He said, 'I feel you're playing the blues as a job, I don't feel like you're playing them from your heart.' And he's right! Indeed, right. See, when I leave my program, I leave the blues at the station. Then gospel and I go on about our business. I can play blues all the way through my program if I want to. They [WROX management] don't bother me if I play all the one music. If I play all gospel it wouldn't bother them, if I play all blues . . . they leave it to me, they don't interfere with me. But I try to be honest and right. I can play blues all the way through if I want to. But I'd get a feedback. I'd hurt too many people. People just wouldn't be able to see it that I didn't want to participate in gospel. I have never had any complaints because I play gospel and blues. I've played them together right from the start, and if there was a complaint they kept it to themselves. I interview preachers on my blues show. Preachers come up and I interview them. I am a Christian. You can be a Christian and listen to the blues, 'cause they don't affect me.

"Playing the gospel, maybe I'll play one record that you don't like, but then the next one you'll like. That's the way it goes. We've got people that love it all. All of those records have got information in them that'll be a help to you tomorrow if you take heed to them. Gospel to me is like an eraser and a pencil. It will correct a lot of things in you. The words of gospel music will tell you something if you listen to them. It can mean a lot to you. It will correct you up sometimes. The Devil, he's as busy as. . . . The evil spirit is as busy as the good spirit. And what gospel will do for you—I'll tell you what happened to me one time. I was thinking something to myself, and I was thinking wrong. I went to Rev. Willie Morganfield's church and he preached a sermon that day, and his text and his subject and his sermon, all of them were talking to me. It was talking directly to me. When I left him, I begged myself pardon. I was thinking wrong, and I was wrong."

*Early Wright is a prominent citizen in Clarksdale. A street in the north end of the town is named Early Wright Drive. He travels around the town to a constant stream of greetings, and his radio show rates highly with listeners and advertisers. He and his wife, Ella, live in a brick bungalow not far from Early Wright Drive; they have two grown children. Two recent but secondhand Cadillacs are parked in the driveway of their home—Early never buys new cars. "I could buy a new car, but it takes six months to get the bugs out of it. If you buy a used car, somebody else took all the bugs out." He uses the Cadillacs for longer journeys, but around Clarksdale he travels in a green Chevrolet pick-up truck that he's had for seven years and which has become part of his image—"I drove to the radio station in one of my Cadillacs one time. A lady saw me and said, 'Early, don't you feel out of place?' I said, 'Why?' She said, 'Get back in that pick-up so you look like Early Wright.' "*

"I'm a type of person like this—I'm not the best person in the world. I don't profess to be, I don't try to build myself up. I've been wrong like everybody else and I still get drunk. I'm open-spoken. Any time you leave me with a smile, you can rest assured that we're all right. 'Cause if I don't agree with you, can't get along with you, then I don't have anything to do with you. But that's happened only a few times in my life. I can hardly remember any person that I just really didn't want to have anything to do with. But I'd rather not have anything to do with a person than can't get along with them. I won't treat one person one way and somebody else another way. I just treat everybody the same.

"I don't know how long I'm going to keep on. I don't know. Three different years, I was going to quit at the end of the year. When it got to the end of the year, I'd stay on. So I don't think I'm going to quit now. I'm just going on."

# BROTHER JAMES CHAMBERS

*"It's a city of gospel music . . ."*

If WDIA's Theo Wade was "Mr. Gospel" in Memphis during the 1950s and 1960s, fifty-seven-year-old James Chambers inherited his mantle in the 1980s and 1990s. Chambers started his career as a gospel music radio announcer in the early 1970s, and is now general manager of Memphis's newest religious station, WBBP—"Bible believers, praising God twenty-four hours a day." As well as running the station and DJing his own program, he promotes gospel concerts, bringing artists to Memphis from all over the United States. He's the city's most in-demand gospel emcee, fronting everything from major concerts

*Brother James Chambers in the studio at WBBP, Memphis.*

to anniversary programs for local groups. And he owns Chambers' Total Gospel Center, a store selling religious material ranging from Bibles to gospel records and tiepins inlaid with rhinestones spelling out the name 'Jesus.' He's a deacon at his church, and sings in the choir. One wall of his WBBP office is covered with community citations and awards; he has many more at home. One in his office is a Certificate of Appreciation from the state governor for "outstanding service in the best interests and in the highest traditions of the State of Tennessee." His wife, Marva, has recently retired from school teaching. They have five children—Claudette, Veronica, Gerald, Edward, and Yuri (named for Russia's first cosmonaut)—three grandchildren and one great-grandchild.

"PRIOR to me, there was a gentleman who played gospel for years and years. Brother Theo 'Bless My Bones' Wade. He was the manager of the Spirit of Memphis for years. And I kinda came under him as a student. I admired him, and he used to take me with him, introduce me to his crowd of folks. He'd call me up and ask me if I wanted to go with him. He introduced me in crowds of people and sometimes let me bring a group on the floor—'You introduce this group.' So he kinda got me started.

"I got into radio about 1972, and I still enjoy it as much as I did the first day I came into it. I was born about twenty miles out of Memphis, at Eads, Tennessee, up on Highway 64. I moved to Memphis when I was about eight or nine and went to school here. I went to college for a year and a half, then got married and started a family. I've done various jobs. I was a city bus driver back in the sixties, then I moved to Detroit for about three and a half years, was a city bus driver there. I came back to Memphis and did various jobs until I went into radio. How that happened . . . I was in the armed forces from 1954 to 1957, in England. After I came out, I went to various schools. I had some more time left on the GI Bill, didn't know what I wanted to do with it, so I said, 'I'll go to broadcasting school.' Went to Columbia School of Broadcasting, that's a correspondence course out of Los Angeles, California. It's a two-year course, but by me having so much time, I finished it in nine months. I was working in a radio station before I finished it. I had a job that no one else had done—the only black announcer playing country music on the radio.

"I went to the station looking for a job. It was WMSO in Collierville, about twenty-three miles east of Memphis. It was a country and western station. They gave me a chance to play country music, and I really went over well. As a little boy, I used to listen to country all the time, but then I got away from it and listened to other kinds of music. But after playing it, it came back to me again and I started liking it again. I still like it, to this day I like country music. Most of it tells a good message, a good story. So I was playing country music for about two and half years. Then I asked the gentleman who owned the station if I could include some other music with the country. The hit records from the R&B side, black artists who had good records. I said that if I could mix it, it may bring a mixed listening audience. I figured if I could mix in some other kinds of music with the country music, that would get a lot of Memphis listeners, black, white, everybody. And he said, 'Yes, try it.' I tried it and it really happened. About six or eight months later, I asked him if I could play black gospel records every now and again. He said, 'Well, everything you've tried so far works, so try that.' And I played the gospel records. That's when things began to change. That's when I started to get phone calls from Memphis. There was no gospel music in Memphis in the middle of the day like there is now. Just early in the morning and some late at night. So when people heard these records, they wanted to know where in the world was this gospel coming from in the middle of the day? And I got calls from several radio stations, wanting to know if I was interested in coming in to Memphis to work part-time. Garland Markum, program director at WLOK, was one of the ones that called me, and I accepted a weekend position at WLOK. That was in 1974.

"I came in playing R&B. I was just sitting in for announcers who were out, especially on the weekend. They had a young man there who was playing gospel every Sunday. And one day, he had to go to his grandfather's funeral, so I played the gospel in his place. Garland Markum heard me, and asked me if I was interested in doing it every Sunday instead of the other guy. He called us both in and told us what's getting ready to happen. The other guy didn't like it. He'd been there for a few years, and he said, 'If I can't play the gospel, then I'm gone.' So that Sunday evening, he was to come back to work and relieve me. He never came back. He's in real estate now, doin' real well. WLOK at that time was playing R&B, with gospel on Sunday only. I was the only person playing gospel at that station. But from that one program, it progressed so well 'til we kept adding gospel, adding gospel, adding gospel. Today, it's a twenty-four-hour gospel radio station because of the impact of what the Lord allowed me to do at that station.

"I was with WLOK for seventeen years. Then my pastor, Bishop G. E. Patterson of the Temple of Deliverance, Church of God in Christ,[1] decided to buy this radio station [WBBP] when it became available. And by me being at the church—a deacon in the church—and in the radio business, he asked me if I would be interested in coming with him and running it. Naturally, it was a move up for me from WLOK. I was program director there. But to be the general manager of a radio station gave me a lot of avenues in which I could work and expand my horizon. At WLOK, I had gone my distance. I wasn't going to own the station and more than likely I wasn't going to be general manager, so program director was probably as high as I could go.

"When the bishop bought WBBP, it was a station that was filled with ministries—ministers of the gospel who preached. It was running services one after another all day. They were from around Memphis and out of Memphis, through to Chicago—we had ministers on from all round the country. Black, white, it was all mixed. And so I got with the bishop. . . . What I really wanted to do, I wanted to do both. I want to have good gospel music, along with some of the ministers and ministries. So now we have primarily music and ministries. We select the ministers and ministries that have a message, and play the best music there is. And people are listening. Rating-wise, we have done more in two years . . . the number one gospel radio station is WLOK, and we have just about split the listening audience with them already. Yeah, we're destined to be number one, and we're half way."

*For a city of about nine hundred thousand people, Memphis is well endowed with gospel music stations. The market leader is WLOK, which adopted the all-gospel format in 1984. In second place is WBBP, followed by the gospel pioneer KWAM. The other Memphis-based gospel station is WXSS, while WMPS broadcasts twenty-four hours a day into Memphis from Millington, about fourteen miles out of town. Another three or four stations, including WDIA, also play some gospel music, mainly on Sundays.*

"It's a city of gospel. We've got three or four thousand churches here. And if we've got, say thirty-five hundred, you've probably got two thousand black churches or more. Because Memphis is about 55 or 60 percent black. Every street you go on, there's a church on it. Some have three, four, five churches if they're long enough. Because we stay with the Founding Fathers—In God We Trust. We in Memphis, in the South, are very conscious of the fact that Jesus Christ lives and God is. So in almost every city in the South, you'll hear quite a bit of gospel music. And we still believe this is the right way to go. And lately, gospel has been so profitable. That's another reason why you see so many gospel stations— it's profitable. Gospel stations attract a lot of listeners, so you can attract advertisers too. WLOK proved it was profitable. Then stations came from everywhere. The number of stations sometimes makes it unprofitable, because everybody's got to go after that one market. But this station [WBBP] is doing very well.

"I really learned everything I know about how to play the music when I was at WLOK. I don't want to brag, but every station you listen to now, it came primarily from WLOK, from what I put together and started in the city. And even now when I listen to WLOK, I hear some things that I started which are now competition for me. But there's room for all of us, and I don't regret anything that I have done as far as leaving, coming here.

"We play some of all music on WBBP. But we realize that the choirs have more people in them. So if you play sixty/forty, seventy/thirty choirs as opposed to quartets, groups and soloists, you're going to reach more people, they'll listen to you more. And you go to church. . . . You have two thousand [black] churches, you got that many choirs. So it's always beneficial to a radio station with this many churches and choirs in its area to play music that more people like. So that's why you're more likely to hear choirs on WBBP than anything else. We play it all, but we make sure we reach the big crowd of folks with the music that we play. I used to be heavily quartet, personally, because I liked them—I still do. But I had to realize what I was doing. I was playing to a big city of people, and if you aimed at just what you liked the most, you'd miss the boat. You have to aim at who's out there, and make them listen to you.

"Theo Wade was known as a quartet man, and I learned from him. So I came on the radio with the same kind of program. Quartets. A lot of them, I'd play them in a row almost. And people labeled me as a quartet disc jockey. They still do, even now. I play more choirs than I do quartets, but they still label me as a quartet announcer because I play more quartets than the average person on the radio. I don't worry about it. I always believed in giving the quartets justice, giving them some airplay. I realize it's profitable to play more choirs because of the makeup of the city. But I still give the quartets more play than the average radio station. Sometimes, you play music because the artists are from your city, you see them all the time, you know them, and when they do an album, you want to try to help them. Some of the singers in Memphis get airplay because of the announcer knowing them. They're from Memphis, so 'it's my friend, and I can at least do this.' It may not necessarily be one of the best records in the world, but you just do it.

"I started out singing quartet when I was about fourteen, in high school. The guys I was with were older guys, out of school, in their early twenties. We named ourselves the Mount Pleasant Specials, after our home church. We used to travel with a gentleman named Gatemouth Moore.[2] He would go places and evangelize and preach, and we were the singing group with him. And we were on the radio at WDIA every Sunday morning at 10:15. Great big mike hanging down and we would stand around it. The engineer was in the next room, he would give us the cue. We had no music. You slapped your leg and sang in those days. We never did record. I wish I did have a tape of us in those days. But all the guys got called into the armed forces. Then when they came out, I went in. So we just never got back to singing again. But I sang with my church—I still do. I sing with a male chorus, every now and again I'll take a solo. I love singing. The only thing I love more than singing is basketball. I played a lot of that in high school and in the armed forces. And I still watch it religiously on TV and go to some of the games in the city."

*James Chambers's description of Memphis as "a city of gospel music" and "a city of churches" is indisputable. The churches range from imposing structures with congregations in the hundreds and more to run-down little buildings housing splinter denominations with only a handful of members. The gospel music covers the full range, from large choirs to soloists and duos. Choirs may dominate the airwaves, but Memphis's long-established quartet tradition continues to thrive.*

"Whoo! Well . . . I wouldn't know how many singing groups there are in Memphis. But there are many. Quartets—maybe two hundred. That's just a ballpark figure. And choirs? How many thousand churches have you got? That's how many choirs you've got. And more. Because there are community choirs, where people from different churches get together and form a choir, or some person forms a choir. I know at least fifteen of those in the city. Some are very successful. They have recordings on major labels, like O'Landa Draper and the Associates, that's a community choir. The Angelic Voices of Faith, they're on a major label. But Memphis is just so . . . we have a concert here, say, and we bring in the top artists in the country—choirs, preachers or quartet singers. And when they get to Memphis, they find the artists here are just as tough as the ones you're bringing in. Memphis has got some outstanding singers. And preachers. And churches.

"The quartets all have something in common. They love what they do. They love competition, so they don't fight about it. They love to come in to a program where there's five quartets to sing. And they love mingling and shaking hands, talking, and nobody's fighting about who can sing the best. I don't know what the chemistry is except they're Christian young men. Like everything else, you find some in the whole realm of quartet singing who do not live up to what they need to be living up to. But overall, it's a group of gospel-loving Christians who love what they do. Only the top four or five groups in the whole country are making enough money to live on—buy a home, maybe a car and support a family. Five groups out of thousands. Most of them do it for the love of the singing and the traveling. They work jobs, practice during the week and sing on weekends. They look forward to Sunday night somewhere. Sing three songs, be on stage twenty minutes, thirty minutes. That gives them another week, they go another week off that. Money-wise, they never get compensated. But they get so much satisfaction out of singing and playing gospel music. If they waited on money, they'd quit tomorrow."

*James Chambers was raised a Baptist, but moved to the Church of God in Christ in 1985 after his "home church," Mount Pleasant, was split when its pastor left to start his own church, taking half the membership with him. Chambers was "really attracted" to Bishop Patterson's church, and joined it. The COGIC is more rigid than the Baptists on the division between sacred and secular song, but despite being a senior member of the church, Chambers enjoys a wide range of music. He does so by drawing a difference between music and its lyrics.*

"I like all good music. I listen to all kinds of music and all kinds of songs for a reason—to learn more about what I do in my field. Music itself, I love it. Jazz, oh I love jazz. I listen to it a lot, because I can make the music say what I want it to say. Some people listen to music, 'That sounds like the blues,' or 'That's jazz,' or 'That's R&B.' But to me, music is nothing until you put some lyrics to it. You can classify it whatever you want to. And that's what I do. I listen to all kinds of music and I love it all. It's only the words that I might disagree with sometimes. My religious commitment to Jesus Christ, to the Lord, to gospel music confines me when it comes to what I listen to in the words. All music is fine to me. It's only when the words begin to convey a bad meaning, like some of the rap. . . . Then I turn it off. My commitment to what I do and who I am won't let me agree with that kind of lyric. So when you say 'blues,' I might disagree with the wording sometimes. But the music itself, the strings and the drums and the keyboards and all, I love it.

"I think it is true that gospel and blues are related, because of where they came from. It all came from the black man singing his kind of blues. As he worked on his job in the field, he sang the kind of songs he felt. His woman, his love life, even the food he ate and where he went and one lady didn't treat him right so he got another one . . . he sung what he felt. So gospel is about Jesus Christ, about the Lord, singing the word of God—but the rhyming and the background . . . well I don't know how to put it except that . . . gospel and blues are done by a specific group of people, black people. So that's how they mix. Because they're done primarily by the same people in the same way.

"Gospel music means so many things to me. It means satisfaction and peace of mind, whether I'm listening to it or playing it for somebody else. It means a word from the Lord, if it's really done tastefully in the right way. Or it may mean a prayer to the Lord. It may mean a comfort in time of bereavement, sickness. Gospel music can lift you out of the pits of sorrow. It will lead you to being saved if you're not already saved. If you're already saved, gospel music will tell you 'stay saved, and be a part of the church.' Or it tells you to get somebody else saved. Gospel music means all this to me. To see that people are living the right life, so that at the end of this life on earth, there is another life that you will live forever. Gospel leads from here to that life, if you take heed of it. Because it's singing about . . . gospel is not gospel if it doesn't sing the word of God, or lead you to biblical scripture, about Jesus, about God. If it's just words about . . . some songs I hear, I wonder if it's gospel. It's done by gospel artists. But they never say the word, they never say the name Jesus.

"They've named it 'urban gospel.' Or 'crossover.' That's a name record companies give music to sell it. But it's either gospel or it's not. Now they've got something called jazz gospel. Gospel blues. But there's just gospel. When you mix something else with it, it's not gospel any more. Some guys sing songs, [he mimics] 'He loves me,' and 'If I could only turn to him, He's my all and all.' 'He.' They never say 'Jesus,' never say 'God,' never say 'I love you Jesus.' Never say the name. That's not gospel. They're trying to sell it to both sides of the record-buying market. It's done primarily by songwriters who write for the record companies. The record company comes to them, 'I want you to write a song that I can sell to both markets.' So they write it. Now the good Christian gospel singer will refuse a song like that. But some get themselves in a bind after accepting a contract. When you accept it, you've gotta do what the company wants.

"Now I go along with the additions of music. I don't think a person can go wrong by adding synthesizers and keyboards and everything else. That gives gospel the same quality, the same listening power as all the other kinds of music and all the other artists. But you will never get completely away from the old traditional Mahalia Jackson, Sensational

Nightingales, Dixie Hummingbird kind of singing. It'll always be there. Those of us who were back there during that time, we appreciate it when we hear it. And some of the youngsters who never heard it back then, they hear it and they like it. So it'll always be there.

"I like some of all kind of gospel music. I like quartets, I like soloists, I like duets—it depends on who's doing it. I like some of all the music. But my favorite groups would be . . . well, gotta be the Williams Brothers, the Jackson Southernaires, the Mighty Clouds of Joy, the Canton Spirituals, the Gospel Warriors in Detroit. There are some I like that aren't on major labels, but they're good singers—there's about twenty of those. The Mighty Clouds, I would say, are the number one group. If I had to put 'em in order, they would be number one. Their record and their stick-to-it-ness down through the years would give them that credit. And they're good singers. They go all over the world. And when you say 'quartet', everybody will tell you 'Mighty Clouds of Joy.' They're well known in every state, every city, everywhere you go. Then there's the legendary groups. Dixie Hummingbirds, Sensational Nightingales, Spirit of Memphis Quartet. The Five Blind Boys of Alabama and Mississippi. They're legendary. The Pilgrim Travelers. During my quartet days, the Pilgrim Travelers and the Spirit of Memphis . . . I wanted to sing like Kylo Turner and I wanted to sing like Jet Bledsoe [leads with the Travelers and the Spirit respectively]. They were my favorite singers. So I had a mixture of those two when I tried to sing."

*Chambers's style on air and as an emcee is relaxed and casual, far from the high pressure torrent of some DJs, or the "Are you ready . . . are you REALLY ready" hype of some concert presenters. His technique on air or on stage is to draw listeners in, making them feel part of a family group. It's a casualness learned over years of experience, and only by specifically noting the way he keeps a program moving and involves the audience in the proceedings does one appreciate how professional and skillful he is.*

"I promote artists, bring them into the city so people can see them, hear them in person. And I emcee programs that other people put together. I'm always busy, going places—but I love it. I've been promoting for the last ten or twelve years. I promote two programs a year. And the people I've had . . . you name them, and I've had 'em here. Shirley Caesar, Rev. James Cleveland, Mighty Clouds of Joy, Jackson Southernaires . . . oh, wow! Everybody that you could name that has been here. If I wasn't bringing them or promoting them, I would be MC on the program. And I'm a member of the national organization Gospel Music Workshop of America, organized by Rev. James Cleveland. I'm a member of the announcers' guild, which is the nucleus of that whole organization. We meet once a year, in the second week in August, in various cities in the United States. We meet for a whole week, and it's all about music and radio announcers and every phase of music. And while the choirs and choir people and musicians are together every day in classes learning the music and talking about it, the radio announcers from all around the country are also meeting. And we're talking about the playing of the music on the radio all around the country, what we can do to better it, and who's doing what in what city. You learn what people are doing in other places, and when you go back to your city, you can bring back something brand new and start something that will be interesting to your listeners."

*Chambers's other business venture is Chambers' Total Gospel Center, in a shopping center on South Third Street, managed by his younger daughter, Veronica. It sells a wide range of religious material, but its core business is in gospel recordings—some of its trade comes from people looking for recordings they have heard on the radio.*

"I used to go around the record shops in this city, buying gospel records and tapes. And every record store that I went in, all the music I heard on the speakers was R&B. But we have all these churches in the city, and all these Christian people, gospel listeners. I said, 'Somebody needs to cater to these people. It shouldn't be necessary that everywhere you go to buy a gospel record, you got to listen to some other kind of music.' I talked to a few friends, and they said, 'Nope, it won't work, 'cause people can hardly make it selling all kinds of music.' And I said, 'But this is different because it's a different kind of music. It represents a different group of people, plus you're representing God, representing Jesus. It will work.' So I prayed about it and talked to my wife about it and . . . she was kinda reluctant, too. We didn't have any money. I think I went in with less than three thousand dollars of my own money. Opened the door with one stack of records. I sold those, ran across town and picked up some more. Sold those . . . sometimes I'd go three times a day to pick up some more records to bring to my shop. That was in 1985. And the Lord has proved himself. Even if I quit today, if it goes out of business today, I've already been convinced that being an all-gospel record shop in the city of Memphis—the first and still the only—works. We started with just records and tapes. And Bibles. We always had Bibles. And we just added other things that churches use. Like envelopes for collections and collection plates, crosses and different emblems that a church would use or an individual would wear. Everything that's Christian, gospel. We haven't gotten into robes and pews and those kind of things. But lately I've been thinking about maybe contracting pews for churches and robes for choirs and pastors and these kind of things.

"Gospel music is getting more exposure on records today because record labels, companies, found out it's profitable to do it. But they're still only using about one tenth of what's out there, one fiftieth of what's out there. Look at this city. We have thirty-two radio stations. We got six or eight that play gospel. It's usually the owners. I have a Christian, a Christian bishop, for my owner. But so many radio stations are owned by people who are not really Christians. They just own the radio station as a business. And gospel to them is a sideline, a backseat kind of music or singing. They feel intimidated by even talking about putting it on the radio station. It's the same thing in record companies. You very seldom have Christian owners, or church-going religious choir-listening-to persons. To a record company owner, it's always 'well, I got three gospel artists, I got forty R&B artists, so I'll just put these gospel artists on this little label over here.' They're not really committed.

"But I think those of us who are committed to gospel will see to it having a great future. It's going to be played and listened to on more radio stations. Magazines will be coming forth about gospel, TV . . . it's going to do nothing but go upward. In other words, God can't fail. He can't fail. It may look like gospel is going out because it's getting so thin in one particular city. But that does not diminish the power of God, even though it may not seem like it's happening where you are. But when you think of all the places where it is, and how strong it is in other places, you can be assured that it's going to continue, it's going to get bigger, it's going to spread over the earth and it's just going to . . . gospel's going to be everywhere. Sooner or later, it's going to be everywhere."

# REV. J. W. (JOHN) SHAW

*"There has to be a message . . ."*

A good case could be made for presenting Rev. John Shaw as the personification of the American dream. He and his wife, Opal, started singing together in response to a family member's request at a small country church; today, they are the Shaw Singers, recording artists who have performed in thirty states. When he suffered a racial slur while working at a Tennessee radio station, he resolved that one day he would buy the station; today, he and Opal own it. In 1980, he became pastor of the St. John Baptist Church in Stanton, just off Interstate 40 to Nashville, around forty miles northwest of Memphis. When

*Rev. John Shaw at his radio station, WOJG, in Bolivar, Tennessee.*

he took over the church, it had about one hundred members and an annual income of a little more than five thousand dollars; it now has more than four hundred members and is "well over a one hundred thousand dollar-a-year church."

The Shaws live in Whiteville, about fifty miles northwest of Memphis. But the core of their success is a small brick-and-wood building on East Jackson Street, in the Hardeman County seat of Bolivar, Tennessee, a rural town of about six thousand people ten miles on from Whiteville. An overhanging verandah protects the door from the fierce summer sun; on the roof is a satellite dish. The sign on the front wall says that this unpretentious single-story building houses "Shaw's Broadcasting Co., AM 1560, WBOL, Your Legendary Sound." But WBOL has not been the focal point of Shaw's Broadcasting since 1990, when the company received a Federal Communications Commission license to broadcast on the FM band. The Shaws used this to establish WOJG (the "W" is a federal requirement indicating that the station is east of the Mississippi River; the "OJG" stands for Opal, John, Gospel) as a twenty-four-hour-a-day gospel music station. WBOL, the company's original 6 a.m. to sundown station, still broadcasts, transmitting a syndicated southern (white) gospel program. Opal Shaw is the company's general manager. J. W. Shaw is company president and also DJs the morning show, coming off the air at 10 a.m. to start the rest of the day's work.

He is an ebullient man, outgoing and loquacious, elegantly dressed in a suit, white shirt and tie and wearing metal-rimmed eyeglasses. When speaking of himself, he sometimes uses the third person, talking of "J. W."; his record labels call him "J. W.," "John" or "Johnny." Opal is more reserved, and takes a back seat when the couple are together; she is obviously used to John's habit of finishing the sentences she starts. He is fifty years old, she is forty-seven. They have two adult sons, Reginald, twenty-seven, and Tracey, twenty-one, and a daughter, Rhonda, twenty-five. They have also adopted Tracey's five-year-old son, Jeremy.

**J. W.:** I was born in Laconia, Fayette County, Tennessee. I'm the baby, the youngest of a family of eleven brothers and sisters. I grew up on the farm. And I always was an ambitious person. I dreamed a lot, even in the cottonfields. And most of the things I dreamed of as a young person have become a reality. I finished high school, but I never went to college. At the high school level was where I met Opal and we got married. I started singing because it was a kind of therapy for me. We used to sing in the cottonfields, and we sang the blues most of the time, because we knew more about the blues than we did about gospel music. Mom didn't like it, but we got a chance to do that. That was always the old chants that came from the Negro spiritual, you know, like [sings] "If the Lord don't help me . . . ," you know, that type of thing. We'd do that, we'd sing some blues—we'd just sing. I never had an idea of making a career out of singing. It was just a thing to do. But once my mother knew I could sing, she decided "you need to do that in church." And of course I decided against that. But when I was eleven years old . . . my sister had already started singing a little bit, doing solos here and there. And . . . most of the black churches have an annual children's day. The young people are in charge, and they express their talent in every way. So one children's day, my mother said to me, "I want you to sing a duet with Peggy." I didn't want to, so she walked out to the edge of the church lawn and grabbed her a nice-sized little switch. She came back and said, "Whether you want to or not, you're gonna do it." So I did it. We sang "I Have So Much to Thank My Jesus

For." The people enjoyed it and we started singing that day, my sister and I.

In the black church, once people know you can do something, you'll get a request to do it. If you talk well, you get a request to do the response or the welcome. If you sing, you'll get a request to sing. So if you walk in and they know you sing, they say, "Well hey, J. W. Shaw's here, we're gonna request for him to sing a song." So my sister and I started getting these requests around our area, and we made a little name for ourselves. We were the Shaw Children. We kept singing until I got a little older and got in high school. Then I wasn't singing so much, just doing other things in church. I've always been involved in church. I started leading the prayer service in church early, and singing hymns and what have you. That was from about the time I was thirteen up until eighteen. I did do some singing, with the quartets. Guys in the community. We would always get together and we'd sing—we always were part of a group, even if we weren't doing anything. We'd come together on Wednesday or a Thursday night and have a little practice. And finally I met Opal.

**Opal:** My mother was a singer. Not so much publicly, but she sang around home. And that was inspiration to me, because I always wanted to do what my mom did. And I always wanted to play the piano, and I would go to church on Sunday and sit right beside the piano and watch Mrs. Miller. I was between five and six years old. Then I would get my bucket and go 'round the house in the chimney corner[1] and I would 'play my piano' and sing. My parents realized I really needed a piano, so my daddy bought one. My mother showed me the chords, and from that day on, if I heard a song, I could go to the piano and play it.

*Opal Shaw.*

I always liked to sing. It didn't matter where. I would just sing. Coming up in school, if singing needed to be done, I was there to sing, I was there to play. And I always wanted to marry someone who could sing. I always wanted to find somebody else that had somewhat of a style and a way of singing as I did. And, as time rolled on, I met this guy . . . I met him at his home church in Laconia, when I was there playing for their choir. He and his sister sang together as a duo. And that's where I met him. And I always tell him I taught him to sing after we married.

**J. W.:** After we met, we didn't see each other so much for a while. But her sister was playing for the Johnson's Chapel CME church at Vildo, a little community out from where we live now. And this particular Sunday, we were both at Johnson's Chapel, and her sister requested that the two of us do a number together. So we sang "Tell Him," and it was just like wildfire. From then on, it was always J. W. and Opal, the Shaw Singers. And we got married right out of high school . . . I think we were twelfth grade that year. We got married in June of 1963.

About a year or so after we got married, Opal saw an ad in the newspaper or some kind of magazine. "If you want to make a record . . . for $425 you can become a star." And she followed up on it. It was Style Wooten and Designer Records, in Memphis. We went to Style Wooten, told him we wanted to cut a record and gave him $425. He took us in the studio and we cut a single, thinking that the number one song was going to be "I Made a Promise." In fact, it was "This Old Life" that caught on. We cut the record and took five hundred copies home. They didn't last long. People in the community bought them, and we would sell them wherever we went to sing. And Brother Theo Wade, of WDIA, played it. I think what caught his attention was that people started asking for the song. He started playing it on WDIA, and we started getting calls from around the Midsouth, places we'd never been to, like Arkansas, Alabama, and Missouri and adjacent states where people could hear WDIA. They wanted the Shaw Singers. By this time, we'd made such a name for ourselves that Style wanted to do a contract—no more paying. "We want to get you in the studios, and don't worry about the four hundred and twenty-five bucks." So we went back to the studios and did another single, "Must Jesus Bear the Cross Alone" and "God Has Done So Much for Me." It did well, and the momentum just kept building. We started singing in Memphis and all around the Midsouth, and before we knew anything we just up and running.

*The Shaws' discography is difficult to establish. They recorded the single "This Old Life/I Made a Promise To the Lord" in 1968. John Shaw says he and Opal have made four singles, but at least thirteen have been issued on Wooten's Designer and Messenger labels, although some pair the same titles. Their first album,* Yesterday and Today,[2] *on Messenger, reissues six tracks recorded as singles between 1968 and 1973; the rest of the album was made*

*at an August 1975 session. Around 1979, the Shaws released another album,*
Special Prayer, *which was very successful and is now impossible to obtain.*
*Most of the songs they sing are their own. Opal is the main songwriter; she*
*also arranges the Shaws' versions of songs by other writers. Of the twelve*
*songs on* Yesterday and Today, *eight are by Opal, two are by John, and*
*the other two are "arranged by Opal Shaw." Their basic lineup consists of*
*the two of them singing to Opal's piano accompaniment; on their records,*
*other instruments are added—organ, bass, drums, and, on one occasion,*
*pedal steel guitar³ (the result is not as bizarre as might be imagined, but*
*neither is it an unqualified success). Even with the extra instruments, they*
*have a sparse sharp-edged sound with the same rough-hewn sincerity as*
*another husband-and-wife team, the better-known Consolers from Miami,*
*Florida. John Shaw accepts the comparison with the Consolers, but says it*
*is not deliberate. The Shaw Singers, he says, have no direct influences.*

**J. W.:** At the time we were growing up, it was hard to get the
communication in our area. So we didn't know a lot about the national recordings. We finally got the old battery-powered radio, and I
remember the Southern Wonders, the Pilgrim Travelers and a few others
that Brother Wade played on WDIA. But in our early stage, there wasn't
too much for us to get other than what we got out of our local churches.
So we just developed it. We've never tried to be like anybody else. You've
got to be yourself. To sing a song that has a meaning, you have to sing it
from the heart before it can touch someone else's heart. So I think that's
probably the reason why we get that different feel. As well, we're trying
to keep in mind that there has to be a message. Not just a beat, but a
message. We've found that the upbeat numbers do well on the radio, but
it's the slower tunes that really catch the audiences when we're singing.
The song that really has a meaning and is saying something. Some songs
that you won't ever hear us play on the radio are the ones that are most
effective when we're with an audience.

**Opal:** I feel that the kind of music we have, the generation before us
has carried it with them in their hearts, the generation with us has it in
their hearts, and it will grow on the generations to come. It just grows
on you. Because the more a person learns about the Word, about God,
the more they are traditionalized, so to speak. They want something
that will tell them something in a song. They want it to have a message,
something to say, something to give me a way to release my anxiety or
whatever it is I'm going through. Something to let me know there is a

way out, something that will help me to release all that is within me that needs to be released.

**J. W.:** I think the kind of music we do will always live. I think quartets will always be there, they're traditional. But I think choir music is very short-lived music. Choirs constantly put out songs, they're constantly before the public. The group doesn't die; the name stays there. It's their music that is so short-lived. They will have a hot tune today, and next month you don't hear much about it. I think it has to do with a feel more than a message. As well as what the words say, there has to be a feel to gospel music, it's got to be more than just words. And much of the choir music is just words. There is no feel. Choirs are a big thing just now, even with us [on WOJG]. Two thirds of our music load is choirs. But as a DJ, I notice that when a person really is down or depressed and wants a song, it's always the real downhome traditional stuff.

*J. W. Shaw's involvement with gospel music led him to his radio career. His first job was in a Whiteville business rewiring armatures from electric motors and generators, while Opal worked at a hospital. A group he was singing with bought time on WBOL and obtained sponsors to pay for it.*

**J. W.:** I was making the announcements for the sponsors, and the station manager heard me. Needing to satisfy Uncle Sam by putting some blacks on the staff, he called me up and offered me a job. I was hired as the station's first black. The racial tenseness was there, and I had problems within the station, because I was the only black there. I believe all racial problems stem from ignorance, in that we're not comfortable with each other because we don't know each other. And I think they felt real uncomfortable with me coming into the station. Things would happen, like they would sabotage my show or leave carts [tape cartridges] uncued or whatever, just to make me sound bad. I went in to get some training . . . I never shall forget it. It was a bright sunny Saturday afternoon, and the guy who was to train me sat with me for about ten minutes. Then he said, "Could you keep these records going while I run out to the store? I need some cigarettes, and I'll be right back." An hour went by and he didn't came back, hour and a half. . . . After about two and a half hours I decided, "You gotta do something other than just spin these records." So I opened up the mike, gave a station ID and started talking. Finally, he came back at sign-off and said, "I've been listening to you, you did real good. I

knew the only way you would do it was to let you do it." So that was
my start.

Then I wanted to get into production. I couldn't get anybody to teach
me anything. They never let me do any production. Finally one day I
walked in, and we had a little basket that said "production to be done." I
saw this ad in there and I thought, "This is my chance." I took the copy,
went back into the production room and I did the ad. It was a fairly
good job for my first production. But the manager came along and said,
"They don't want any blacks to do their ad. We'll have to do it over."
And something said to me at that very moment, "one day you'll own
this station. One day you will do what you want in this radio station."
And from that moment on, I always felt my chance would come. And
when I had almost given up the idea, it came. The station had financial
problems, and the owners needed to sell it. So they called us and said
we had a year [to raise the finance]. Less than a month later, they called
again and said, "If you want to buy it, you gotta buy it now." So we
put all our eggs into the basket and got our business plan together and
carried it to the bank. I gave it to the bank manager and he read it. Then
he looked up at me and said, "When do you want to start?"

That was in 1987, September 1987. At that stage, it was just the AM,
WBOL. Two hundred and fifty watts. With everything operating well,
good clear signal reached about fifteen or twenty miles. When we bought
it, it was a country music station. And part of the time it was disco. I
played disco for about nine years when the other owners had it, and I
got pretty popular locally as a radio man. But when we bought it, we
turned it into a gospel station. It was something different in the area.

The reaction from the white community out front was "Congratula-
tions, John." Underneath, they were saying, [he mimes talking behind
his hand] "You'll never make it." But the blacks! They'd never had this
before. It's our station and it's local. So it was a great success from the
viewpoint of listener participation. Very devoted, very loyal listeners.
The whites were not familiar with the power behind black gospel, and
what it means to black people. But we have been able to educate the
white business community—which is the sole financial support of this
thing—about what strength there is and what black gospel can do and
how devoted and dedicated black gospel listeners are. We had to educate
them on what we could do for them through our station. The first
question they would ask was, "Does anybody listen to a black gospel
station?" So I said to one guy I was trying to sell advertising to, "Have

you ever been to a black church?" He said, "A few times." I said, "Well, what did you see?" He said, "What do you mean?" I said, "Let's start with the parking lot. Some of the best-looking automobiles. On the inside, people who wear the best clothes. You see black guys with three-piece suits and the best kind of clothing. The black ladies wear the best dresses, nice jewelry, make-up . . . the list is endless." He said, "You know, I never thought of that." And these people have become aware of what black gospel can do. So now we're highly respected.

*A singing star and radio station owner, J. W. Shaw took up the other part of his life in 1980 when he was "called" to preach. Being "called" is a phenomenon of the Baptist, Methodist, and pentecostal churches, especially in the black tradition. A person "called" bypasses divinity school, becoming instead a minister of the Gospel through the "anointing" of God. John Shaw received his call in July 1980.*

**J. W.:** It comes through signs that God gives you. Most of the time, people think you get some kind of unusual revelation. But God can use a tree, a bird, any common thing that you see every day and give you some sign or revelation saying, "I want you to do more than what you're doing." I guess the best I can explain my call is . . . when I first started feeling there was something more for me to do than what I was doing, I had a real desire to read the Bible. Not just any part, but about the crucifixion of Jesus Christ. And I would read it and . . . I just got a real feeling that I had never gotten before. And finally I just started crying. I didn't want anybody to know it; I'd go off by myself and I'd just weep. It was something so special and dear to me. And I started saying, "Well, Lord, if there's something more you want me to do, then I'm willing to do that. Just show me." And it wasn't very long, about two days, before it came to me: "I want you to preach." But of course the Devil was very busy. He said, "Boy, don't you do that. You'll make a fool out of yourself. You don't go out and make this announcement. You realize that when you make this announcement, you're stuck with it. Don't do this." So I'm caught between him and making that decision. And I toyed with that and toyed with that. I'd jump up at night, get out of the bed—I almost drove Opal crazy. One night she said, "If there's another woman, why don't you just go on to her. I'm tired of you."

**Opal:** At the beginning, I didn't know what was on his mind . . .

**J. W.:** . . . but I knew. I just wasn't ready to say it. It was on my mind so much so 'til one Sunday I went to church and I spoke to my pastor. I told him, "Something's happening to me and I don't know what it is. I believe the Lord wants me to preach." He just looked at me and said, "If the Lord wants you to preach, you'll know it." That's about all he could say. And that Sunday we went through service, and it was just bearing heavily. Something just kept saying, [whispers] "Now's the time. Get up and say it. Get up and announce it." Because a revelation to preach . . . the process is the same as being saved. "Believe it in your heart, confess it with your mouth and thou shalt be saved."[4] We left church that Sunday and went over to Marianna, Arkansas, to sing. I really just had an urge to preach, rather than sing. But we sang and we sang 'til we got through. And during the gathering, the fellowship after the singing, this old couple, a man and a woman, walked up to me—he was around seventy, and the lady was his mother. He said, "I've long wanted to shake your hand. We've got your record. And we don't get out to church much, especially when it's cold. But when we don't get to church on Sunday, we put your record on and we have church at home." And he doesn't know, but he was my answer. The Lord said, "Now, if you can bless people like that through singing, why don't you just do what I say?" And coming home, I said to Opal, "I've got to preach. Got to preach." And when I said that, it felt like a million pounds came off my shoulders.

**Opal:** It didn't surprise me by then, no, it didn't. Every time we'd sing, people would tell him, "You know, you're gonna preach, the Lord wants you to preach." But I really wasn't looking for a preacher. I wanted a singer. [She laughs.] And I said to him, "If you ever preach, I'll leave you." But I got over it.

**J. W.:** She did say that to me. She sure did. And that, as well as what people said, was the cause of my reluctance to make the announcement. Thinking about what she said. And I'm thinking, "I'll miss you if you do that." But after I got started, everything was OK. And I've been preaching ever since I been called. I could've done a revival the week after I announced my calling. I turned it down because I felt I wasn't ready. But the second Sunday morning in November in 1980, I preached my first official sermon as pastor at the St. John Baptist Church where I am now.

Before I went there, the church was two Sundays a month. A lot of black Baptist churches used to be two Sundays a month, some were one.

And I got a call to go there. And right after, another church, at Whiteville, where I live, called me. So I had a choice, and the Lord made it real easy for me. I went back to St. John, and I said, "I don't want to be a part-time pastor. So if you guys aren't going to go every Sunday in the month, I will accept this other church. Preach two Sundays over there, and two Sundays over here." I didn't want to do that, because I didn't feel it could be a successful ministry—although I know some pastors do that, and I was going to do the very same thing if I had no other choice. But they said, "No, we don't want that. We would rather be a full-time church."

And our church has been very successful since then. We started with a little over one hundred people on the roll. And now we have about four hundred enrolled. The church has grown, membership-wise, financially-wise. The year I went there, in 1980, the church had raised five thousand dollars from January 1 up until the first of November. And from that second Sunday morning in November until the end of 1980, under my ministry, we raised another . . . well, they were inspired, and we raised another four thousand dollars. We ended the year with nine thousand dollars. And they were happy. They said: "Oh huh! This is . . . nine grand!" But from January 1 of 1981 until the end of that year, we raised fifty-two thousand dollars. From nine thousand dollars to fifty-two thousand dollars. Of course, God gets all the credit. But the Shaw Singers were a big part. "Rev. Shaw of the Shaw Singers and his wife pastors the church." "You mean the people that sing!?" And in that first year, we got a lot of spectators. And they leave donations. And we taught people the right way biblically to give and what they should do with the tithe and offerings and so forth. So now . . . I would have to go back and check the records, but we're probably well over a one hundred thousand dollar-a-year church now.

Being a pastor and devoting most of my time to the church, we cut back on the singing. But after about two or three years, the ministry took off, people started calling, and I started doing a lot of revivals. Because people knew that when they called us, they got more than just a revival preacher. They got me to preach, but they also got Opal. And they knew they would also get a song from Opal or from the Shaw Singers. So I have to admit that a lot of our calls, even to preach, stemmed from the fact that we were the Shaw Singers. But I am a preacher who sings—sometimes. I never try to mix the two or let the singing become some kind of a handle to my ministry. I'm a preacher. And I want to be identified as a preacher. When we go out to sing, I'm singing. But if I'm invited to preach, don't expect a whole lot of singing. The reason for that is . . . I think you take away from the message. If I plan a message to people's hearts and minds, and we get up and do a lot of singing, it's going to take something away. So I'm very careful not to do a whole lot of singing when I'm preaching.

*These days, the Shaws sing mainly at church-related functions. Opal is the St. John pianist, and when their children are at home, they play in the church band—Reginald on bass guitar, Tracey on drums, and Rhonda on organ. But the Shaw Singers' sound remains basically unchanged from the early days when they were recording artists whose popularity took them to venues as far away as Chicago, New York, and Detroit.*

**J. W.:** One thing that I believe has made us effective is that we've never changed our style of singing. We don't try to come out with something new and different like a lot of groups do. There's a Shaw Singers flavor. When you hear us, it's there. And most everyone will tell you that if you can get the Shaw Singers, you'll get a pretty good crowd. We've mostly been blessed with our singing ministry. Sometimes we lost money, sometimes we broke even, and sometimes we made money. But I don't think we ever really lost anything. Might have been a time when we didn't make anything, but then we made it up other times. I remember once, we went to Jackson, Mississippi, to play with Lucille Pope and the Pearly Gates and another major group . . . I forget who. We were the guest group. But for some reason, the promoter decided he wanted us to go on first. After we sang, about half the people in the auditorium got up and walked out. They didn't want to hear anybody else. So I went in to settle up with the promoter. Our part was thirty-six hundred dollars, after all the expenses were paid. But he started taking all the expenses out of my portion of the money. By the time he finished, he had me down to eighteen hundred dollars. And when I questioned that, he said, "Take that or leave." And I thought, "Well, that's better than nothing—I'll take it." But as I reached to take it, he drew a gun on me and said, "Put it back on the table." I said, "What?" He said, "You heard me. Put it back on the table." I put the money back on the table. And he said, "Just leave." At the point of a gun. And I went. But the Lord blessed us, because that very same night, we sold one thousand two hundred and forty dollars worth of our record. So we never lost. We lost that fee, but I think somehow or another he's the loser. But we've always made expenses. So I think we were well blessed. In fact, as I said, part of us getting into radio had to do with our singing ministry. It would be safe to say just about every aspect of our lives has been affected, even our marriage, by our singing ministry. I'm not even sure if we would have been together had it not been for our singing ministry. I would say it's probably had a greater impact on our lives than it has on the lives of the people who've listened to us.

*Although his life revolves around gospel music and the church, J. W. Shaw has not forgotten his old days of singing blues as a boy in the cottonfields. And he makes no secret of his non-gospel musical tastes.*

**J. W.:** Blues and jazz. My favorites. I realize that as a pastor I can't go out publicly promoting blues. I don't get in my pulpit and say, "Hey y'all, listen to the blues next week." But I don't have any problem saying to the people in my church, "I'm a blues lover." I love the blues. Because I think blues has a message. I don't think you can be a black gospel music lover without loving other kinds of music, because gospel is made up out of blues, country, jazz—that's the ingredients in gospel. Some of the greatest gospel singers were blues singers. If we didn't feel we would be so highly criticized by the public, you would see us in a lot of the clubs, listening to blues. People like B. B. King when he comes to town. But because I'm a pastor . . . they're rather narrow-minded . . . so we stay away for those reasons. Not because we don't like it—I don't think God cares about us loving the blues.

**Opal:** We were asked to do a blues album when we did our first album. I told him it wasn't even an interest. . . .

**J. W.:** No, it wasn't so much of an interest for us to do it. We knew we couldn't get away with that. What we would rather do is hear someone else sing the blues. Singing gospel is a fulfillment for me. Sometimes it's hard to explain, but I'm very devoted and dedicated to singing and I've always had an insight as to what a song could do. And it makes me feel good when I can sing a song, because it makes someone else feel good. And yet I'm being rewarded at the same time. I've always wanted to put all I had into a song every time I sing it. I think you sing to the audience based on your mood and their mood. I don't think you make a list of songs and say "this is what I'm gonna sing when I get there." When you get there, the Holy Spirit will tell you what to sing. And the strange thing is that we have never had any official rehearsals. We did it on the road. (**Opal:** Or in church.) Or while we're doing the concert. A couple of songs we've got came out while we were in concert. While we were singing. We've sung together for so long, and become so accustomed to what each other is going to do, that it all just came together.

Gospel music to me is a way out. An avenue. A fulfillment. A sense of direction. When I sing . . . I may have a foggy view of something, and I can sing and it looks like it all comes through. It's a part of me, a part of my soul. And it's something that if you took it away from me, I don't think I could survive.

# 5   THE PREACHERS

*"The Lord told me to tell you . . ."*

The African-American church was born as a direct rejection of segregation in established white churches. It had its origins in the late eighteenth century, when some white churches opened their doors to slaves—but restricted them to designated seating, or held separate services for them after the white services. From about 1770, slaves were allowed to hold their own chaperoned services, and, in 1773, slave preacher George Liele established the first African-American church, at Silver Bluff, South Carolina. Overt moves against white-imposed segregation in worship began in 1776, when blacks who had been attending the First Baptist Church in Petersburgh, Virginia, left to found their own Harrison Street Baptist Church.[1] In 1794, the African Methodist Episcopal Church was founded in Philadelphia after black worshippers at the St. George Methodist Episcopal Church refused to be segregated in the church balcony. In subsequent years, other congregations were established as African-Americans asserted their desire to worship free of racially based restrictions. This voluntary segregation of the black church continues to the present day. It has been criticized as an impediment to racial integration, but other observers see it as a symbol of ethnic identity and as a rallying point and a refuge.[2]

Whatever view is taken of America's religious apartheid, it has produced a striking African-American style of worship with a clearly defined identity, especially in the more fundamentalist denominations. These groups reject the formalized rituals of "establishment" churches such as the Roman Catholic, Episcopalian, or Presbyterian in favor of a joyous, extroverted, and sometimes unruly worship, which is as much a celebration of triumph over life's adversities as it is veneration of a supreme being.

Music is an important part of an African-American church service, but it is not the focal point. Those who perform it are vital in the church structure, but they are not the key figures. Both these roles belong to the pastor, the preacher, the minister. The clergy's prominent role is, of course, common to all churches, but it is more pronounced in African-American churches, where the pastor is not only a spiritual figurehead but an active moral and community leader. Exploring the supra-religious role of the African-American church, Mellonee Burnim quotes a 1933 study: "Not finding the opportunity that is given to members of other racial groups in civic and political life, in business enterprises and social agencies, the Negro through the years has turned to the church for self-expression, recognition and leadership."[3] This observation has not been rendered irrelevant by the passage of time, and means, says Burnim, that "the church ceases to be a mere religious organization," becoming instead "an alternative means of self-development."[4] It is hardly surprising that the leader of such an organization should assume—and be given—a dominant role. As a corollary, a strong and assertive person is required to fill such a role.

The Baptists are the largest African-American denomination and also the most loosely organized. A national association exists, but it exerts no control on individual churches, and a minister can simply set up his own church, relying on his ability to attract a "flock." When an established church requires a new pastor, it can approach a preacher already known to it, or it can in effect hold auditions, calling in several ministers to conduct services, then voting to select the one it wants. In either case, the decision is made by the membership of the church, uninfluenced by any outside body. The two other dominant churches, the Methodists and the Church of God in Christ, have central hierarchical organizations and appoint ministers to pulpits (although a pastor can build a church independently, then affiliate with the COGIC). In rural areas, a Methodist preacher can be appointed to a "circuit" of two or more churches, holding services at each in turn on successive Sundays; a Baptist pastor may also minister to more than one church in the same way.

The elected pastor deals daily with a paradox. While each church has an elected "board," the pastor is very much the managing director. He is expected to provide strong leadership, and can at times find himself trying to move the flock in a direction it may be reluctant to take. But at the same time, he holds office only as long as the members are happy with his leadership. Once dissension arises between pastor and congregation, it will usually not be long before a new round of auditions is being held. Appointed pastors have a more secure hold on their pulpits, but must be aware of the congregation's power to vote with its feet, by leaving to "unite" with another church. An unpopular pastor can also find himself the subject of complaints to his central organization and resistance to his leadership.

One point on which Methodist, Baptist, and sanctified churches agree is that formal theological study is not a prerequisite to becoming a pastor. In fact, seminary-trained pastors are not common in rural churches, and have been the target of derision in song. Washington Phillips's "Denomination Blues Pt. II," recorded in 1927, contains the lines:

> There's another kind of preacher is high in speech,
> They have to go to the college to learn how to preach
>
> But you can go to the college and you can go to the school,
> But if you ain't got Jesus, you're an educated fool.[5]

(Almost identical lines are in "That's All," Rosetta Tharpe's 1938 reworking of the song.) The pastors Phillips would endorse are those "called" to preach by direct divine intervention in a process descended from the way in which Saul, the persecutor of Christians, was transformed into Paul, the disciple of Jesus, by a blinding light and a heavenly voice on the road to Damascus (Acts 9:3–8). Such "calling" is common; each of the pastors interviewed for this book had a revelatory calling, with only one having any extensive theological training. A Church of God in Christ member called to preach must attend the church's Bible college for training in doctrine and procedures before being ordained and assigned to a pulpit. In the Baptist church, any minister can—with the approval of his church board—ordain a "called" person to the ministry, after which the newly created pastor is free to seek his own church. This is not always an easy task; the Baptist church has many more ordained ministers than pulpits, and a church needing a new pastor is likely to have a number to choose from as word of the vacancy spreads.

The mandatory skill for any pastor is the ability to preach. Baptist and sanctified services are basic, with a strong emphasis on music and prayer. But the sermon is the core. Ostensibly the part of the service in which the pastor expounds on a piece of Scripture, the traditional sermon is also a cathartic experience for congregation and pastor. Marion Joseph Franklin, one-time musical director for Marion Williams, describes African-American preaching as "a corporate venture between the pulpit and the pew. . . . The primary function of the Black sermon is to help the hearers. It serves to create in the believers the climate of faith and a haven for hope. Preaching in the Black context is never abstract. It deals with true life situations. . . . [It is] not designed so that the respondents may escape from reality, but [so they] can accept the demands and realities of life. . . ."[6]

A typical sermon starts with the pastor delivering his text and indicating the message he plans to extrapolate from it. As he opens, his speech will be slow—sometimes slower than normal conversation—and deliberate, often with long pauses. But as the sermon progresses so do the pace and power of the delivery. Two-thirds to three-quarters of the way through, it shifts gradually into a shouted or nearly shouted hoarse chant in a process known as "shifting gears," "tuning" or "moving to a higher gear." The logical sermonizing is over, replaced by a raw blast of emotion. At its peak, the preacher delivers his words in half-sung four-beat bars, often punctuated by heavy chords from the church musicians. Sometimes he will leave the pulpit and move to the floor in front of the altar. By this time, if the sermon is going well, most of the congregation will be standing, shouting and calling encouragement and endorsement. Some "fall out," shrieking ecstatically and collapsing comatose, to be tended by neighbors or church ushers. (The vocal responses can also indicate to a preacher that his sermon is *not* working, as Rev. Dr. David Hall explains in his interview.)

Today, some pastors are moving away from this traditional preaching, preferring a more restrained and conventional style with the message, rather than emotionalism, as the focal point. This low-key approach is common in what Horace Clarence Boyer has categorized as "intellectual" and "conservative" churches.[7] It is less common in "emotional" and "fundamentalist" churches, such as most Baptist and sanctified, where it is likely to be strongly resisted by congregations which reject the very concept of a sermon without a concluding peroration.

The traditional style of preaching was already well established by the 1920s, when recording companies discovered a market existed for mini-sermons, compressed to fit in the three minutes or so allowed by a ten-inch 78 rpm record. Despite this time limit, most recorded sermons were developed in a condensed version of the "shifting gears" style, or the related "straining" style, in which most of the message is declaimed in a tight-throated, hoarse, tense-sounding shout, sometimes punctuated by rasps of hyperventilating breathing. Paul Oliver has suggested that pulpit sermons of the period may have been "much shorter than the hour-long sermons often mentioned in the literature"—he says sermons of six to nine minutes may not have been uncommon, which means recorded preachers "may not have had to condense too much. . . ."[8] But in today's church, a sermon of six to nine minutes would satisfy neither pastor nor congregation, and when the long-play album was invented, preachers had no trouble filling both sides of a record with a single sermon. At a service attended by the author in Rocky Mount, North Carolina, in October 1994, Rev. F. C. Barnes told his congregation how God woke him the night before with the subject for today's sermon. He then preached for more than hour, although he afterwards said, "I don't usually preach that long." (He also lent support to those who feel that "shifting gears" can interfere with the message. "Many times when we go to church, we look for the preacher to get down," he told the congregation at the start of his sermon. "I mean, just get down and whoopin' and hollerin' and carryin' on. And I do that sometimes. But I'm getting away from that, [doing it] less and less now. Because my heart is going out for you, it's going out for the people. I'm trying hard to warn you. Because this is my job, and I'm concerned about it. So we're not going to get down today. The only getting down we're going to do is getting down to business.")[9]

One can only speculate as to why recording companies ventured into sermons. Spoken word recordings were common in the early days of the industry, and some minstrel and vaudeville artists had recorded comic sermon parodies. But there appears to be no precedent suggesting that the genuine article would be a money-spinner. The first company to test the waters was Columbia, which in January 1925, recorded ten sermons by Calvin P. Dixon, issuing all but two of them over the next eight months under the pseudonym Black Billy Sunday. Although he was not a dynamic preacher, Dixon used a number of themes that would later be successful for other preachers—"Dry Bones In the Valley," "As an Eagle Stirreth Up Her Nest," "The Prodigal Son"—and his records sold. But it was sixteen months before Columbia recorded another preacher.

In April 1926, the label sent a recording unit to Atlanta. Of the five acts recorded, four were religious, including Baptist preacher John M. Gates, who recorded four mini-sermons. As well as the preaching, all featured singing by Rev. Gates and two anonymous women, setting a style that would be followed by most subsequent sermon recordings. Some records were label-credited to the preacher " . . . and His Congregation," although the congregation could be as few as two people, usually female. Despite the attempt to create a "live" sound, these were studio recordings, and a few sound stiff and self-conscious, reflecting the artificial conditions confronting pastor and "congregation." But the best preachers (and their supporting voices) overcame this to produce spirited performances which suggest it was possible for the Holy Spirit to manifest itself in the studio. Their recordings used singing in a variety of ways. Some started with a song, led by the preacher, then moved into the preaching; some opened with the sermon, which led into the singing. Others alternated snatches of singing with brief bursts of preaching. Whichever technique was used, "sermon with singing" records found a ready market, and very few sermons were recorded without a leavening of song.

Columbia's advance pressing order for Gates's first Columbia record was a cautious 3,675.[10] One side was the pedestrian "Need of Prayer," but the other side, "Death's Black Train Is Coming," used an analogy already familiar to church-goers and was successful enough to raise the advance order for Gates's next record to 34,025, with another twenty thousand pressed after the initial release. But Columbia did not place Gates under contract, leaving the way open for Atlanta talent scout Polk Brockman, who moved quickly to sign the pastor to an exclusive arrangement. By the end of 1926, Gates had recorded another eighty-four tracks— including four more versions of "Death's Black Train"—with a variety of labels. During one visit to New York, in September 1926, he recorded forty-four tracks for five different labels.

Gates's success alerted other record companies to the potential of sermons, and most moved quickly to fill the newly perceived gap in their catalogs. Between 1926 and 1942, about seventy preachers recorded approximately seven hundred and fifty sermons. The field was dominated by J. M. Gates, whose two hundred and fourteen tracks accounted for nearly 30 percent of the total, but other stars also emerged. Columbia replaced Gates with Kansas City pastor Rev. J. C. Burnett, whose 1926 recording of "The Downfall of Nebuchadnezzar" sold more than eighty thousand copies.[11] Vocalion contracted the Chicago-based Rev. A. W. Nix, who recorded fifty-four sermons between April 1927 and March 1931. It has been suggested he was the same man as Professor W. M. Nix, who was a member of the committee which compiled the National Baptist Convention's *Gospel Pearls* and who inspired Thomas A. Dorsey with his singing at the 1921 National Baptist Convention in Chicago.[12] But in notes to a reissue of A. W. Nix recordings, David Evans cites a Dorsey interview in which the composer spoke of two brothers named Nix, one a singer and the other a preacher,[13] an explanation which resolves the puzzle of one man being prominent in two related fields under two similar but different names.

A. W. Nix's first record trod familiar ground, using a train analogy to detail the fate awaiting a variety of sinners. The two-part "Black Diamond Express to Hell," on which Nix was assisted by "His Congregation" —two or three women calling encouragement from the background— details the stops the Black Diamond Express will make on its way to Hell. With "sin the engineer, pleasure the headlight and the Devil the conductor," the train's stops include Drunkardsville, Liars' Avenue, Stealing Town, Dancing Hall Depot, and several others. An October 1927 Vocalion advertisement in the African-American newspaper the *Chicago Defender* hailed "Black Diamond Express to Hell" as "The biggest-selling record of today."[14]

Burnett and Gates—and probably Nix—were Baptists, and their recordings reflect the musical customs of that church. Most of the singing was unaccompanied; occasionally, a piano or organ would provide a backing. The Church of God in Christ and related sanctified denominations have always taken a more liberal attitude, allowing any instrument to be used in their music. (The COGIC attitude has over the years permeated other denominations, and today's Baptists are considerably more relaxed about instrumental diversity.) When Victor first recorded Chicago COGIC preacher Rev. F. W. (Ford Washington) McGee, in 1927, his accompaniment consisted of four female vocalists, plus piano, cornet, guitar, mandolin, and double bass.

McGee was introduced to recording by fellow COGIC member Arizona Dranes when he and his Jubilee Singers backed her on a session at the end of 1926. Six months later, he recorded two sermons for her label, Okeh. Within a month, he was snapped up by Victor and recorded forty-six tracks between June 1927 and July 1930.[15] On February 7, 1928, Elder Richard Bryant recorded two sermons for Victor; by February

28, he was recording for Okeh with a jug band backing of harmonica, mandolin, guitar, washboard, and jug. Bryant was not nearly as able a preacher as McGee, Gates or Nix, but his recordings had a lively vigor that made up for his sermonizing shortcomings. Rev. D. C. Rice, who had twenty-eight tracks issued between March 1928 and July 1930, was Alabama-born, and became a preacher after moving to Chicago. There, he took over a small church and built it up, aided by the eight- or nine-piece bands he used to accompany the church's singing.[16] He used similar line-ups on his records, with trumpet, trombone, tuba, mandolin, and assorted percussion all featured at various times.[17]

The recordings of J. M. Gates, A. W. Nix, J. C. Burnett, F. W. McGee, and D. C. Rice account for well over half the total sermons recorded in their era. (McGee, Bryant, and Rice also recorded songs without sermons, an option more readily available to them than to the mainly unaccompanied Baptist preachers.) Women do not feature large in the discography of recorded preaching, unsurprisingly, as many churches did not allow them in the pulpit. But about half a dozen did record. The most prolific was Rev. Leora Ross, of the Church of the Living God, who recorded eight tracks—of which four were issued—in 1927. All five of the fiery offerings of Missionary Josephine Miles, believed by some to be the "altar ego" of vaudeville blues singer Josie Miles, were released. The brass-throated Rev. Sister Mary Nelson recorded four tracks in Chicago in 1927. Three were a cappella songs, blasted out with two backing singers trailing in Sister Mary's wake; the fourth was a sermon delivered very much in the manner of the male "straining" preachers.[18]

The rise of small independent labels after World War II brought an increase in gospel recording. But despite the easier access to recording, fewer preachers recorded between 1945 and 1970 than between 1926 and 1942, and most of those who did made only one or two recordings. The exception was Mississippi-born Rev. C. L. Franklin, pastor of the 4500-member New Bethel Baptist Church in Detroit. His first recordings, in 1950, were made as a singer, but soon after he began recording sermons, issued initially by the Detroit-based JVB label of Joe Von Battle, then by the bigger Chicago-based Chess company. Unlike his prewar predecessors, Franklin was not limited by 78 rpm record time limits. His first seventeen sermons came out on 78 rpm records but in "albums" of three or four discs. From then on, he recorded on the new long-play album format, which gave him up to forty minutes or more of preaching time—although even then, editing was sometimes needed to fit his message onto the disc.

Franklin, father of soul star Aretha Franklin, was a larger-than-life character who in the early 1950s was earning up to four thousand dollars a sermon as a guest preacher. He enjoyed the material benefits his success brought him, and in 1967 was fined twenty-five thousand dollars for tax evasion. More than seventy of his sermons have been issued, all recorded during New Bethel services. He was a powerful and eloquent preacher in the "shifting gears" style, and his success can be gauged by the fact that several of his sermons are still in print thirty and more years after they were recorded. These include his most successful, "The Eagle Stirreth Her Nest," the same theme used by Calvin Dixon when he became the first recorded preacher in 1925.[19] In 1979, Franklin was shot in the head by an intruder in his house—some theorists have suggested a more sinister background to the incident—and remained in a coma until his death in 1984.[20]

No other postwar preacher has enjoyed the success of Franklin, but preaching records continue to sell. Mainstream labels virtually ignore sermons, but many of the larger independents have a number in their catalogs. The Jewel label, from Shreveport, Louisiana, had several of the better-known latter-day preachers, including Rev. W. Leo Daniels (eleven albums), Rev. Johnny "Hurricane" Jones (eight albums), and Rev. Jasper Williams (eight albums). Jewel is no longer recording, although much of its catalog is still in print. The Air (Atlanta International Records) label, which has a distinct bias towards traditional styles, had at the end of 1994 about twenty-five sermons in its catalog of 158 albums, including three by W. Leo Daniels and six by Jasper Williams. Others are on small local labels, some financed in the same way as many gospel music records, by the person whose talents are displayed.

The subjects covered in these recorded sermons vary widely, just as they do in the pulpit. Bible stories, parables and analogies are popular— Jonah in the belly of the whale, the wise and the foolish virgins, separating the wheat from the tares, the prodigal son—all are staples from which it is easy to extrapolate a message of relevance to the congregation. Many preachers use their pulpits to disseminate morality messages aimed at a wide range of sinners; the same applies to recorded sermons. Drunkards, drug addicts, gamblers, thieves, liars, and adulterers receive their share of castigation. Some recorded sermons from the 1920s and 1930s reached almost surreal heights in their efforts to make the message topical and attractive to the record buyer. One of the more unusual is Rev. W. M. Mosley's "You Preachers Stay Out of Widows' Houses": "My subject tonight is you preachers stay out of widows' houses. . . . Some of these mornings, some of these nights, you going to some widow's house, some grass widow, [where] you ain't got no business. They gonna find your body there, but they won't find your head. . . . When you go up to St. Peter and he'll ask you, 'Oh Mr. Preacher, where you from?' And you'll tell him, 'I'm from Atlanta,' 'I'm from Macon,' 'I'm from New York.' And he'll say, 'Where's your head?' And you can't find it. . . ."[21]

It may be hard today to find something as outré as Mosley's "Widows' Houses," but homilies on living right are common. F. C. Barnes's divinely inspired marathon referred to above was mainly on "the time is now," a "last days" theme, but he opened with a separate message: "You know what the Lord told me to tell you, this congregation today, all of you, whoever you are, wherever you come from? If you smoke, the Lord told me to tell you to stop. . . . He told me to tell you that cigarettes will shorten your life." Most of C. L. Franklin's sermons are on specific biblical themes, but a few of his later recordings address wider subjects, including "The Man On the Moon," "I Heard It Through the Grapevine," and "The Meaning of Black Power." All relate to topical events—"I Heard It . . ." is named for the 1968 Marvin Gaye soul hit of the same name. Other preachers also linked their sermons to current events or fashions. W. Leo Daniels's "The Answer to Watergate" was still in the Jewel catalog (J-0100) more than two decades after the event which inspired it; Rev. Walker Thomas has recorded a number of sermons named after television soap operas—"One Day at a Time," "The Young and the Restless," and "As the World Turns" (Air 655, 656 and 657). Many pastors attack drugs, especially "crack" cocaine, identifying them (with every justification) as the major scourge of the African-American community in the 1990s.

The mixture of singing and preaching found on sermon recordings reflects the close relationship between the two. Many pastors have enjoyed considerable success as gospel music singers; many gospel music singers have heeded the call and gone to pastoral roles. The interchange is not surprising, as preaching and gospel singing have much in common. Both are religious expressions with strong performance and presentation elements; each must seize the attention of its audience so the message is transmitted as effectively as possible. Preachers and singers share many of the devices which do this, most notably the building of a performance—song or sermon—to a fevered climax. Both often leave their performance areas—stage or pulpit—heightening the tension by moving among their audiences. Many gospel singers evangelize from the stage, using speech patterns modeled on those heard from the pulpit; many preachers move into a half-sung chant, often pitched to a preselected key, as the sermon reaches its climax. And the result of a successful sermon is the same as that of a successful song—an audience or congregation deeply "in the spirit," shouting its encouragement and joy.

Some gospel singers who carry the honorific "Reverend" do not pastor churches; in some cases, it is an honorary title, or it may be self-bestowed. But others combined singing careers with church duties. One of the best known is Rev. Cleophus Robinson, whose singing career started in 1949 and has continued into the 1990s. In 1957, he moved from Memphis to St. Louis, and soon after was called to become pastor of that city's Bethlehem Missionary Baptist Church. He has combined the two roles since, recording extensively but also maintaining his church work. His recordings are almost all songs, but they do include two sermons and a few "narrations." From Memphis came Oris Mays, who pastors a church and makes radio broadcasts as well as recordings; from Los Angeles came Rev. Lonnie Farris, who issued songs featuring his steel guitar playing on his own Farris label. Among the more flamboyant was Samuel D. Kelsey, pastor of Temple Church of God in Christ in Washington, D.C. His 1940s and 1950s recordings are credited to Rev. Kelsey, but when he recorded in 1965, for the first time since 1951, he had been elevated to Bishop Kelsey. (The most extravagant course of promotion, as charted through record labels, belongs to Louis H. Narcisse, a New Orleans Creole and uncle of gospel diva Bessie Griffin, who pastored Mt. Zion Spiritual Temple in Oakland, California. In 1950, he was Rev. Louis H. Narcisse; by 1953, he had become "Bishop." In 1960, he was King Louis H. Narcisse, and, by 1962, he was His Grace King Louis H. Narcisse.)[22]

Some singers called to the ministry give up singing, or at least reduce their involvement in music, seeing it as a conflict with their pastoral roles. F. C. Barnes, whose recording of "Rough Side of the Mountain" was the biggest gospel hit of 1984, also pastors the sanctified Red Budd Holy Church in Rocky Mount, North Carolina. During the early and mid-1980s, he spent a lot of time touring to perform his music. "But it hurt the church," he said. "It began to dwindle. People would come here and look for me and I'd be away in Texas or California, and they'd get discouraged. We lost a lot of members, and I had quite a bit of building up to do. So I quit extensive traveling."[23] Barnes still sings and records, but organizes his traveling so he will always be at church on Sunday. Rev. Percell Perkins, a leading 1950s quartet singer with the Swan Silvertones, the Blind Boys of Alabama and Mississippi and a number of other top groups, now pastors the small Galilee Missionary Baptist Church in Helena, Arkansas. Claude Jeter, famed lead and tenor singer of the Swan Silvertones, quit the group in the mid-1960s to become a minister in the Church of Holiness Science of Detroit.[24] Around early 1953, religious convictions forced another member of the Swan Silvertones out of the group. Rev. Robert Crenshaw upset other group members by "singing too long," "mixing preaching with singing" and "getting happy too quickly," all failings which the other group members felt were "killing us in person."[25] Ironically, Crenshaw was recorded again, in 1959, when folklorist Alan Lomax visited his New Browns Chapel in Memphis. Obviously seeking examples of traditional worship, Lomax taped examples of "lining" hymns and an impassioned prayer from Crenshaw, apparently without realizing that the source of this authentic old-time religion was once a member of one of gospel music's most sophisticated quartets.[26]

# REV. ARTHUR
# FITCHPATRICK, JR.

*"It's not an imitation thing . . ."*

Mt. Newell Missionary Baptist Church is a single-story red-brick building, on its own among the fields beside a narrow two-lane blacktop road in northeast Mississippi. It could be any community hall; only the white cross above the entrance porch proclaims its purpose. Mt. Newell is a location, not a settlement. The church's mail goes to Red Banks, a small cluster of buildings about ten miles back down the road. The nearest town is Holly Springs. But every Sunday, the grass and gravel parking area around the church fills with cars, as up to a hundred people gather to worship.

*Rev. Arthur Fitchpatrick preaching to Mt. Newell Missionary Baptist Church, north Mississippi.*

The worshipper who travels the furthest to reach Mt. Newell's services is the pastor, forty-three-year-old Arthur Fitchpatrick, Jr. Every Sunday—and at any other time he is needed at the church—he travels the forty-odd miles from Memphis, where he lives with his wife, Lorine, and son, Arthur III. Like most small rural southern churches, Mt. Newell cannot afford to pay its pastor a living wage, so Fitchpatrick works during the week in the laundry department of Memphis's main hospital, Baptist Memorial. His religious background is diverse. He was born a Baptist but was "called" to preach at age eighteen as a member of the Christian Methodist Episcopal church. Since then, he's had six pastorates, three Methodist and three Baptist.

He is a short man, stockily built. His conversation is not unlike his preaching style. He approaches each new topic carefully, speaking slowly and precisely until he warms to his subject. His home is a comfortable bungalow in south Memphis. In the lounge, a framed case on one wall commemorates his military service in Vietnam, displaying his service details, his nametag, a photograph of him in uniform and his campaign ribbons. On other walls are his certificate as a Boy Scout leader, and a brass plaque given to him as a Baptist Memorial Hospital "employee of the month." He installed the room's wood paneling himself, and also sewed its red drapes. "I used to do a little bit of sewing, so I made these," he says casually.

"I'VE been Methodist and Baptist. When I was born, my people were in the Baptist church. That was in Fayette County [Tennessee], between Collierville and Rossville. I was converted, joined the church, but I didn't go back any more. Then we moved from Collierville to Slayden, in [north] Mississippi, and we lived less than quarter of a mile from a church. And my two sisters and I, we got involved. I started Sunday school and I became the janitor, sang in the choir. . . . This was a Methodist church, Roberts Chapel. They used to say to me, 'Why don't you join?' and I'd say, 'No, I'm a Baptist.' I never had a good definition of the difference between the Baptist or the Methodist. The only thing I knew that the Methodists sprinkle you for baptizing and the Baptists immerse you. But they said 'You need to join this church. You come here every Sunday, you don't go anywhere else.' I told them 'I don't want to be sprinkled.' And they said, 'You don't have to be sprinkled.' The Methodist church will honor immersion, but the Baptists won't honor sprinkling. So I ended up joining the church, and about three years later, I started preaching.

"That was when I had just become eighteen. I had got involved with the church. I became the superintendent of the Sunday school, joined the choir. . . . I was in school, and I would study all the time. I was an A student. I loved to read. And I read the Scripture and became inspired in it. I could memorize the Scriptures better than I can now. But when I was seventeen, I quit going to church. I suppose some of it had to do with changing in age, and probably peer pressure. Wanting to take on habits like the other guys and be like them. But what was really happening was that I was in the church, but I wasn't of it. I was just there. What I was doing was imitating other people. It hadn't really become a part of me when I first started. It was an imitation—I was imitating some of the older people. If it had really been a part of me, I probably wouldn't have quit. Because now it has become a part of me. It's not an imitation thing.

"So I had been out of church for almost a year. Then one night I was trying to do an outline from my biology book for school. I knew how to do it, but it just wouldn't stick. Then I got restless. And I said to myself, 'Well, I'm gonna get my Bible.' I got my Bible and started reading. Then . . . it was just like when the light's on and you squeeze your eyes up and see the rays from the light. I didn't see an image or anything. It was just bright rays and my vision got strange. Next minute, my mother had me up in her arms, saying, 'Where do you want to go? You said you were going. You were ready to go.' My mama told the pastor. She came home and said, 'The pastor wants to see you.' So I went on up, and he says, 'Son, tell me what's happening to you.' And I told him how I felt and what had happened. He said, 'The Lord is dealing with you. You've been called into the ministry.' I said, 'No sir, no sir.' He said, 'I'll tell you what you do. Pray and ask the Lord to do something for you.' I went down in the woods and I asked the Lord if he would let it rain before that weekend. And the sun was shining so beautiful one day, then a cloud came over and a few drops of rain came. I went back to church and the pastor said, 'Did you ask the Lord? Did he do anything?' I said, 'Well, I asked him to let it rain. Didn't but a few drops fall. I don't call that rain.' He said, 'Son, what are you looking for?'

"Then he said, 'I'll tell you what you do. Third Sunday in March, I'm going to let you preach. Prepare yourself.' I said, 'No sir, I haven't been called to preach.' He said, 'Now our policy is, until you get your ordination, I will have to let you speak from the table.' I said, 'Well that's fine, because I don't think I'm worthy to be up in the pulpit, no way.' I got some notebook paper, and I started writing. When I finished, I had twenty-five pages. I got up in church, and I read about five pages. Then I just started to preach. The paper was all flying on the floor. I knew everything that was in it. Didn't need the paper. And people were just waving, waving, waving, waving.

"I got back in the church after I was called, and I stayed in that church where I had preached for four years. Each year I would go to the [CME regional] conference, hoping to be assigned to a church, and each year I would be disappointed. I was still in the last years of high school, because I got a late start in going to school. Most of the guys my age were ready for their first or second year in college, but I was ten years old before I started going to school. During the time when I was coming along, there were separate school seasons for the blacks and the whites. We would be in the fields while the whites would be riding along in the buses going to school. And a lot of parents weren't interested in their children going to school. They were more concerned about making a living, getting the field work out of them, than getting them an education. And my parents happened to be among them. They were doing farming work, sharecropping."

*At his fifth annual North Mississippi CME conference, Arthur Fitch-patrick was assigned to two tiny churches in Coldwater, Mississippi. "I guess there were about five people at each church when I went there," he says. A year later, in 1971, he was in the army, being trained to fight in Vietnam. Although he was an ordained minister, he lacked formal qualifications and was unable to avoid the draft, despite appeals from his bishop, his wife, and his parents that went as high as the president of the United States. His primary designation in the army was "infantry," but the military recognized his religious qualifications by giving him a secondary designation of "chaplain's assistant." He spent most of his time in Vietnam working with chaplains, spending only enough time in the field to satisfy an army requirement that he serve for a certain time in his primary designation. During his time as a chaplain's assistant, he learned to drink beer; during his time in the field, he swore off it for life.*

"When I first started working as chaplain's assistant, I had a Protestant chaplain. He was very strict. He didn't want any drinking. But after he left, we had a Catholic chaplain, and he believed in drinking. One night we were all sitting around and they were drinking beer. He said, 'Go on Arthur, why don't you take one?' And, oh, he keeps talking and I drink one. And at the time, I was smoking. And that drink, with the cigarette I had, it really went good. He said, 'Why don't you try another one?' The next morning, I got up, my head was hurting and they showed me all those cans I had drank and I . . . 'No, no, I didn't do it!'

"So after I had got started, I said, 'I'll try this again.' On this particular night we got attacked, it was New Year's Eve. We had to jump on the deuce-and-a-quarter, the Jeeps, and go out where we had gotten information from reconnaissance that the Vietnamese were supposed to be. I did it all right. It was exciting. But I'd had a couple of beers. I was feeling good, I wasn't afraid of anything. We got there, and it was at night. You don't see anything. And you start firing, tree limbs falling down and all that . . . everybody just cut loose when the squad leader says 'fire.' Nobody knows who hits who, or whether you got anybody 'til the next day. I guess it was about twenty seconds and it was over. But I was crying. I said, 'Oh, Lord, please. If I get out of this, I'll never drink another beer.'"

*On his return to the United States Fitchpatrick turned down the offer*
*of a sergeant's stripes to stay in the infantry, and returned to Memphis.*
*As a veteran, he hoped to find better-paying work than was available at*
*Baptist Memorial Hospital. But he was unable to get into the factories*
*"paying twelve, thirteen, fourteen dollars an hour," so he want back to the*
*hospital, moving from the housekeeping department where he had worked*
*pre-Vietnam to the laundry so he could have Sundays off—although he*
*did not intend to return straight away to the ministry.*

"This presiding elder was after me. He was short of a minister—one
died or something—and it was in the middle of the conference year.
But I said, 'I'm not going to do anything. I'm going to take a couple
of months break before I do anything in church.' And I was doing fine
until he spoke to my wife. I said, 'I'm not going.' My wife said, 'Oh yes
you are. I told the Lord what you was going to do.' So I ended up taking
the church. And it just so happened, it was in a circuit with the church
where I was called into the ministry, Roberts Chapel. The church he
assigned me to in the middle of the conference year was Berry's Chapel.
The next year he sent me back to Berry's Chapel and to Roberts Chapel."

*His return to Roberts Chapel was not a success. He was pastoring people*
*he had grown up with and people who remembered him as a child, and he*
*found it difficult to establish himself as their spiritual leader. "The worst*
*thing I ever remember was trying to pastor those people where I started*
*at," he recalls, shaking his head. "So I stayed there one year and I left—I*
*had to go." His next assignment was to a four-church circuit spread over*
*the rural area around Holly Springs. He held services one a month at three*
*of the churches; the other got two services a month. It was at this time that*
*his rising disenchantment with the CME came to a head—and he had to*
*face a revolt by some of his church members.*

"Methodism reminded me of sharecropping. You had your annual
assessment, a certain amount of money you have to bring in each year.
And if the people didn't come up with their assessment, I would have to
pay it at the end of the year. Out of my pocket. In the Baptist church, you
get together with your flock and decide what's best for the church. But
in the Methodist church, you've got to take orders from a higher level.
You have your bishop, then the presiding elder over your district, then
the minister, then the flock. And they were telling me the conference

came before anything else. If you needed to do some renovations in the church, they'd say, 'You pay your assessment first, then you fix the church.' So I had these ones over me and they would pressure me and I would take it out on the people. And if one church did something I didn't like, I would take it out on the other churches. Which was wrong. When the people said anything about it, the bishop told them, 'You have to take who we send you.' And for a long time they accepted this. But then they got smart. They said, 'If we can't get who we want, we don't pay no assessment.' And one of the churches called the presiding elder and said, 'You're gonna have to get him out from down here.' By the time the conference year ended, things were all right between us again, but I had made up my mind that it was best for me to go on over to the Baptists where I could be on my own. I said, 'I'm going on. I need more freedom.' As well, there were certain things . . . like christening babies and the sprinkling part. I had learned to deal with it pretty well. But the Baptist part never did come out of me, it never did leave me. I was Baptist-oriented from the beginning. I was preaching one thing and doing another as far as doctrine was concerned. So I went on and left. I had a cousin that had a small Baptist church, and he ordained me. I left the first of September, the last of September I was ordained a Baptist minister.

"After I got ordained as a Baptist minister, I said, 'I'm going to take a break. I don't want another church.' But there was a church on Highway 311 in Holly Springs, Strawberry Missionary Baptist Church, and its pastor was getting ready to leave. And . . . strange thing . . . the people at that church knew the members at one of the Methodist churches where I was, and they recommended me. I went there and talked to the pastor, then I preached for him that Sunday morning. Then the church asked me to come out and meet with them. And they asked me questions. One of the questions was . . . I never will forget it . . . the lady says, 'When you were in the Methodist church and you ran into a problem, you could turn to the presiding elder or the bishop. But what are you going to do if you run into a problem over here in the Baptist church?' I said, 'I'm gonna turn to the one above that has all power. I know someone who is higher than the presiding elder and the bishop.' They were pretty well pleased. And they elected me. Didn't anybody preach for that church. I was the only one.

"See, in the Baptist church, whenever a minister passes or something happens where he has to move on, the people take it through the same procedures that we use if we are going to elect a president. Whoever gets the most votes gets the church. If the minister dies, they have a procedure where they keep the pulpit vacant. They veil the chair and won't let anyone sit in it, because that church is without a leader. Most churches will go at least ninety days before they let anyone preach for the church. They have services in the meantime, but they have different ministers come in and speak. They don't have one minister as a pastor. After three months are up, they'll say, 'We're going to preach ministers, we're going to try ministers for a period of, say, two months.' And ministers come. There's so many ministers that have been called into the ministry but don't have churches. Younger guys. And they'll hear about it, and they'll go there. There may be ten or fifteen ministers. Then it becomes something like the Miss America pageant. The board will eliminate it down until they get to two ministers, then they bring it before the church and the church will say, 'Well, we feel this is the one we need.' Then they'll call that minister in and interview him and ask him about pastoring and how he feels and what he expects from the church and how he plans to lead them. And then if they feel this is what they want, they'll vote him in."

*Fitchpatrick stayed at Strawberry for eight years, until Baptist Memorial Hospital changed his working hours, requiring him to work a night shift on a roster that included Sundays. "I was going to work at night, then sitting in the pulpit sleeping." He transferred to another job in the hospital, but the move reduced his wages by one hundred and fifty dollars a week. Negotiations with Strawberry on an arrangement whereby he would preach an extra service in return for extra money collapsed in acrimony and he resigned, again vowing, "I don't want nothing else to do with church. I'm through." But again he was enticed back, this time to lead a small congregation in Memphis after its pastor died. He reorganized the church, putting its business affairs in order, renaming it New Genesis and eventually moving it from its "storefront" church ("next to a service shop and with a nightclub out in front of us") into a proper church building. Then Mt. Newell's pastor of twenty years died, and the members contacted Fitchpatrick. Initially, he turned them down, suggesting instead his ordained uncle for the job. But the church wanted Fitchpatrick, and eventually he decided he could juggle the two congregations by having his uncle take New Genesis's service on the one Sunday a month he was required to preach in Mississippi. The plan foundered almost immediately when Mt. Newell decided it wanted services on two Sundays a month. Fitchpatrick solved that by having his uncle take one of the Sundays at New Genesis, while on the other, he would hold a morning service at Mt. Newell and an evening service at New Genesis. But the split in their pastor's attention created tension at New Genesis, and eventually the members gave him a "them or us" ultimatum.*

"We had a meeting, and they talked to me so bad. So I went to Mt. Newell, said, 'I tried to be a city boy, but it looks like I'm back in the country.' But I told them I couldn't deal with just two Sundays a month. We had to go every Sunday. About two weeks after that we went every Sunday."

*The relationship between Mt. Newell and its new pastor has not always been smooth. The church is rural and probably the most old-fashioned and "traditional" in the area. Fitchpatrick is more progressive, wanting to make changes. He is having an effect on the church—but concedes it is also having an effect on him. One area of difference is in baptisms. Most churches now baptize converts in an indoor pool; Mt. Newell holds an annual outdoor baptizing in a local lake. Arthur Fitchpatrick wants it to install an indoor pool. Golden Stars singer (and former Mt. Newell member) Katie Davis Watson dismissively attributes this to his being "scared" of the snakes which inhabit the lake; Fitchpatrick's rationale is more practical.*

"The way we do it, it's a once-a-year thing. So if somebody comes and joins the church in the middle of winter and they haven't been baptized, they won't have the rights of the rest of the members because they've gotta wait until September. When you've got an indoor pool, you can go ahead and take care of it right away. Out in that lake, it's cold when you first go out there. But it warms up. And that particular lake is different. The first baptism service I did was about fifteen CME people. The bottom of that lake was soggy, so you could anchor down into the mud. But the bottom of this lake is hard, so each time you take someone down you slide. And they want the preacher to do all the dipping. I try to tell the officers, 'If you've got a lot of people, then when I dip, two of you can dip too.' But they're so traditional."[1]

*Preaching is another area of difference between church and pastor—one which it appears the church may be winning. Arthur Fitchpatrick would prefer to preach in the more restrained "intellectual" style, rather than in the traditional "shifting gears" style. His church adheres firmly to the old way. It's a style Fitchpatrick was raised with, and one he does well. He may want to modify it, but as well as overcoming church objections, he has to overcome his own upbringing. He talks of "coming off" the old style, but four years after he came to Mt. Newell, his finales still send the recorder he uses to tape his sermons soaring into distorted overload.*

"The old ministers in the church say, 'If God calls you, you don't need a manuscript [a written sermon]. You only need a Bible.' And if you come in [to church] without a Bible, that's really a disgrace. 'He doesn't even have a Bible! Who does he think he is?' But you can come in with a manuscript and place it inside your Bible and never read your text from the Bible. Read it from the manuscript—as long as it's on the inside of the Bible. They see the Bible there and they believe you're preaching from the Bible and they listen. But if you've got a manuscript in a folder and as you finish one sheet they see you turning to the next. . . . 'He ain't preaching from the Bible!'

"The basic part of a sermon is the text and the subject. The other stuff, you're just going over and over, trying to get them in the mode of it. Coming out of the pulpit . . . the thing I hate is that people run after you and grab you. I try to stand still. They got me a cordless [radio transmitter] mike, but I very seldom use it. I always say, 'I'll stand in the pulpit.' But once it gets on, it seems like the floorboards are better, and you come out of the pulpit. Sometimes in the shifting, when you start walking around, you may get into the spirit. I've gotten into it there. I've had certain things go over me where I've just blanked out and I didn't know what was going on. It's just like it was when I was called, when I saw this light. I don't know the last thing I did. The only thing I know was that I was up [preaching]. And when I listen to the tape recorder, I can't remember what I said.

"Ministers coming along now have a different style of preaching. It's not all that emotionalism thing. But at Mt. Newell, that's all they have ever known, so I'm having to gradually come off it. And it's harder for me to come off it at a church like Mt. Newell, because it is a very emotional church, so you've got to do it. It's a tradition. And once you do it somewhere, it becomes a part of you. In a way, it's just as hard for me to refrain and come off it as it is for me to get the people to accept me coming off it. Because once you do it so long. . . . See, I started with the old people in the rural. The Methodist preachers in the city area weren't doing this old style. Then when I got a chance to get away from the old ministers and go to a church on my own, I was sent to a rural area where there were other old ministers. But when I started going to workshops and being exposed to seminary people, I saw . . . this guy, he's doing a sermon. He barely raised his voice, he was so soft. And people weren't jumping, they were sitting in the pews, tears running down their eyes. And I said, 'Well, look at this!'

"If a minister preaches and he doesn't do any shifting, just teaches his message . . . if something comes up and he's running short of time, he closes out. No one never will detect that he didn't finish, that he didn't conclude his message. But if I get up and take the same message with my style and something comes up and I don't get to the part where you're shifting—I didn't preach. To them, I didn't preach. So really, they're not listening to what is being said, they're going with the emotions. Not the notion but the emotion. Say you're depressed. You need to make a decision on something and you come to the church. And I go through my sermon. Emotionally. You're gonna feel good. But when it's all over, you haven't got any information on what to do about your problem. So it's going out of style. In fifteen or twenty years, the preaching I'm doing won't work. I need to get out and get the young minds, tell them they need to come to church, come off the corner selling the drugs. And that preaching style won't work with the young minds."

*Despite his youthful choir membership at Roberts Chapel, Fitchpatrick's attitude to music in the church is ambivalent. He recognizes its place in the history and procedures of the church, but also believes it too often becomes an end in itself, rather than being a part of worship. It's another delicate area between pastor and congregation, because, as well as being traditional, Mt. Newell is also a very musical church, in which the choir plays a major role. When the church was holding full services only once or twice a month, it filled the intervening Sundays with singing sessions.*

"When they were doing this, the church became oriented more to singing than to the gospel. What you call a singing church. The music seemed to have a tendency to draw more people than the gospel. Because this is an emotional thing. They love that music. You can fill the church with the music easier than you can if a minister's preaching. And I found one thing about the people. Until I learned how to do a bit of singing,

I couldn't get a response from them. At first I said, 'I'm not going to sing. I'm not going to do it, because it's not a right thing.' Then after a while, I said, 'Well, maybe I could take this song and lure 'em into the church, then drop the gospel on them.'

"To me, the music of the black church is an offbranch of the blues. Blues is a way of expressing the things you're going through. I kinda like it because it's a cleancut thing. It's not like some of this music nowadays with its filthy lyrics. And when you get into the church in the country, the blacks have always had a rhythmic thing. There's not that much rhythm in the Methodist churches, especially in the city area. They sing it from the hymn books, and you can hear plainly what they're singing. But in the local Baptist church in the rural, they sing songs that identify with the spiritual songs, with the slavery aspect. Like in the book of Revelation, they have symbols—some things in Revelation are coded. And the black people used to do that with spirituals when they were in the slavery. Like, if the preacher wanted to get a message back to the congregation, and didn't want the white man to know what it was. And so this thing led up into the black church with the black preacher. Now they sing with more music [accompaniment]. It used to be that only certain denominations had music, like the Church of God in Christ. Twenty years ago, you wouldn't find a drum in Mt. Newell, because it is a Baptist church. [As recently as 1989, Mt. Newell's 'music' was a solo piano. It now has piano, drums, and an electric guitar.] Some of the deacons said, 'There'll never be a set of drums come in here,' but they got there.

"But it sometimes adds too much emotion. Sometimes it gets a little out of proportion. You don't know whether you're in the club or in the church. But it's music that's supposed to reach the soul. Now, you've got what they call contemporary music, people like the Winans Singers, and it's very hard to tell it from some of the rock music. If you don't listen to the words, you'd never know it was gospel. Some of it you couldn't call gospel. So I don't agree with it all—I think there should be some principles, some morals about it. You've got some gospel artists, well-known people who have made records, who never go inside a church until they get ready to sing. And a lot of times, people will come—like at Mt. Newell—on Sunday morning and they're not that much concerned about the gospel, they just want to sing. They're not really into the spiritual part of it, it's just a feeling good thing. But you can be listening to B. B. King and it'll make you feel good. So that's where a lot of people get it mixed up. To me, gospel singing has taken a shift away from the way it was when I started in Roberts Chapel. Now, when you see people singing it, you seem to detect showmanship, and that takes a little of the spirit out of it for people that are real. It seems to be leaning more towards an entertainment level. But the gospel is the savior. You must have that so you have a knowledge of why you're singing and the purpose of it."

# REV. WILLIE MORGANFIELD

*"When the Lord told me to come..."*

*Rev. Willie Morganfield in his office at Bell Grove Missionary Baptist Church, Clarksdale, Mississippi.*

As a singer, Rev. Willie Morganfield is one of gospel music's luminaries. His 1959 recording of "What Is This?" sold more than a million copies, and recordings he made in the 1960s are still in print. As a preacher, he is in demand all over the United States—he's been in pulpits from Florida to Los Angeles, from New Orleans to New York. But Willie Morganfield does not see himself as a singing star or a nationally known preacher. He is pastor of Bell Grove Missionary Baptist Church in the Mississippi Delta heartland center of Clarksdale. The invitations to preach come second to this role, the singing a distant third.

Clarksdale has a rich blues heritage, which it promotes to a steady stream of dedicated fans. Prominent in this legacy is Willie Morganfield's first cousin, McKinley Morganfield—better known by his childhood nickname, Muddy Waters. A display in the Delta Blues Museum attached to the town's library lists local blues stars; Muddy Waters gets top billing.

Gospel singers feature in another list, which highlights Sam Cooke and Rev. C. L. Franklin as one-time Clarksdale residents. Rev. Willie Morganfield's name does not appear. But Clarksdale is where he was raised, and it's been his home again since 1975. He lives in a large wooden house on a quiet tree-lined street in one of the older parts of town. At the front door is a gift from a church member, a black rubber mat with "The Morganfields" embossed on it in raised white letters. Not far away, across Highway 61 on Garfield Street, is his church. Clarksdale, like most southern towns, is well supplied with churches, "forty-eight Protestant churches, two Catholic churches and one synagogue," for its population of just under twenty thousand.[1] Bell Grove Missionary Baptist is one of the larger Protestant churches, a red-brick building with a wide flight of concrete stairs leading up to the front doors. The building is on two levels. Above is the sanctuary, its white-painted pews and pale-colored walls contributing to a feeling of airiness and spaciousness; underneath are the pastor's office and function rooms.

At sixty-five, Willie Morganfield is a leading citizen of Clarksdale. He carries a badge identifying him as a deputy sheriff, and is known and respected by blacks and whites alike. A bout of three heart attacks in 1991 forced him to lose weight and go on a course of exercise, but he is still a well-built man with the composed self-confidence of one secure in his beliefs and his position, and his commanding presence makes one remember him as taller than he is. He is aware that many of the tourists who come to his church want to see Muddy Waters's cousin, rather than Willie Morganfield, and his initial response to requests for an interview was one of noncommittal reluctance. Once it is established that he, rather than his cousin, will be the topic of discussion, and that the interview will not be done on a Sunday, he thaws slightly, but the opening minutes are still awkward as he rattles off his biography with the air of a man who has done it all before.

"I was born out here at Stovall, six miles out, and I stayed here until '45. I left here and went to Memphis and left there and went to New Orleans. I stayed in New Orleans '46 to '48. I was with a group there called the New Orleans Chosen Five. And we traveled. It was the old Soproco Singers. They had a contract with the Soproco Company that handled the detergent. After the contract was over, they went back to being the New Orleans Chosen Five. I was with them until '48. Then I went with the old original Kings of Harmony, who were stationed in

Baltimore and New York. They were from Bessemer, Alabama. I traveled with them until 1951. Then I moved to Cleveland, Ohio, and started work there, for a construction company. I trained a group there, the Delta Friendly Four. I had two brothers singing with them, Elvie Morganfield and Otis Howard, he's a half-brother. Then I came to Memphis in '59, and I wrote 'What Is This?' in 1959, and I recorded it in November 1959, twenty-seventh of November.[2] And the thirteenth of January 1960, it was number one across the country. It sold a million copies. I started going from there—'Serving the Lord,'[3] 'Lord Thank You Sir'[4] and many others that I wrote and recorded. In 1960 I got married. The twenty-seventh of June 1960, in Memphis. My wife [Jane] is from Metcalfe, Mississippi, twelve miles out of Greenville. In 1962, we moved back to Cleveland, Ohio, and that's where I accepted my calling into the ministry, in 1970. I started pastoring in 1972 in Fairmont, West Virginia. Morning Star Baptist Church. And I stayed there until 1975 and I moved back here. To Bell Grove. That's where I've been ever since."

*Missing from this succinct biography are Morganfield's first singing groups, Early Wright's Four Star Quartet and the Glorybound Singers. The Clarksdale-based Glorybound Singers made no recordings, but had a local reputation which led gospel researcher Ray Funk to describe them as "legendary."[5] They had a local radio show, and toured extensively through the Midsouth. Another Glorybound Singer was Percell Perkins, who was also in the New Orleans Chosen Five. Morganfield was recruited from the Chosen Five to join the Kings of Harmony as one of the double leads; the other was Walter Bugett, another ex-Glorybound Singer who went to the Chosen Five in the same year as Morganfield and moved to the Kings of Harmony a year before him. Morganfield stayed with the Kings until he was drafted into the army in October 1950.[6]*

*His pastorate in West Virginia was a full-time job, and he did well at it. But he gave up this relatively comfortable life to come to Clarksdale and Bell Grove, then a struggling church which met on only one Sunday a month.*

"Well, it's a thing that's hard to convince another person how it is. It's like . . . I feel sorry for my wife in having children. But I don't know what she goes through. The only person who knows that is the person who has gone through it themselves. So this is the way it is with preaching. It's a personal conviction. You don't have any money, but you say, 'My mind keep telling me to go to Clarksdale.' You don't know what's going to happen in Clarksdale, but you don't be satisfied until you go. So I was called. And chosen. When the Lord told me to come, I came here. I came here from a full-time church where I had everything at my disposal—parsonage, insurance. . . . I left all of that to come to this church, one Sunday a month. And so the Lord blessed me to make it full-time. Now we have about seven hundred members on the roll. It's been a struggle, but the people are beautiful. I've taught them the value of loving folk. By my traveling and having stayed in the northern cities, I've learned there shouldn't be hatred among white or black. We accept them, whoever they are, to come and enjoy the service. And that's the way folk treat me. The same way.

"The Scripture declares that Christians are sheep. And a sheep needs a shepherd. It's important that you have someone to lead you. Now, we know that when it comes to the worldly side of life, a lot of folk out in the audience are more equipped or more qualified than the preacher. But when it come to the spiritual aspects, the preacher is more qualified than the layman. A person maybe drives an 18-wheeler. And he's qualified to drive it, he's experienced. But when he comes into the church, he forgets about driving and learns what the Spirit is telling the preacher to tell the people."

*Willie Morganfield's father, Lewis Morganfield, was also in the ministry —"forty-three years he pastored in Memphis." Willie and his wife have four children, Reginald, Delores, Teresa, and Cassandra. Reginald works for a security firm in Houston, Texas, Delores lives in Hattiesburg, Mississippi, and has recently completed a master's degree in social studies, and Teresa works for General Dynamics in Fort Worth, Texas. Cassandra lives in Clarksdale, where she works for the welfare department. She plays piano and sings in the Bell Grove church, and teaches music to about thirty pupils. She also accompanies her father's singing—although, since he was called to preach, Willie Morganfield has largely abandoned his musical career; today he does most of his singing from the pulpit.*

"I do very little singing now. I recorded an album with the choir at the church.[7] It did very well. And I have recorded sermons. 'Love In Action,'[8] 'The Bible,'[9] and others. And they've sold well. They're widely known across the country. That's why I get a chance to go to so many places. Because folk know me everywhere. Of course after my heart attack, I had to cool down a little. I had three, at home. I never lost consciousness. I was going to drive my car to the emergency room, but my wife insisted I get one of my nurses from the church. She drove me over, then they flew me to Memphis in a helicopter. Now I walk every day, maybe a mile and half, two miles in the morning and maybe a mile and a half, two miles in the evening. I'm getting a lot of exercise. I really needed to lose some weight, and this is a way of doing it. It's hard, yeah, gee it's hard. But I know I need it. I feel better after walking and exercising and eating properly. And I guess I'm going just as strong as I was, in fact stronger in some areas, because once your blood circulates properly, that make all the members of the body function.

"Before I started my preaching, I was known as a singer. But I don't want to be known as a singer that can preach. I want to be known as a preacher that can sing. 'Cause preaching is first. It takes priority over singing. Singing is to preaching is like gravy is to steak. Steak is not gravy, and gravy's not steak. But gravy makes the steak taste better. And singing is not preaching. But singing can soften the heart, and while the heart is soft, you can inject the gospel in. So they combine, they work together—like bacon and eggs."

*Whether he's serving bacon or eggs, Willie Morganfield has a style of his own. He writes his own songs—including his most successful numbers—but also includes gospel classics in his repertoire. He sings in a full, relaxed, open-throated baritone, letting the song present its own message without histrionic adornment. His style has the same apparent simplicity as many of the great Chicago soloists, but with a more natural and easy sound, not dissimilar to that of Rev. C. L. Franklin or Rev. Cleophus Robinson, both also Mississippi-born singers; perhaps a case can be made for it being a southern style. It delivers the emotional feeling of gospel music, but with more subtlety than the "hard" end of the genre. To hear the passion and fervor that the crucifixion of Christ can arouse in a believer, listen to Sam Cooke singing the traditional "Were You There (When They Crucified My Lord)?"; for an insight into the stark reality of a man nailed to a cross, listen to Willie Morganfield sing the same song.[10]*

*His preaching is a skillful mixture of the old-style "shifting gears" and the more restrained "teaching" style. He builds to a climax, dropping into the four-beat patterns of the traditional style. But his delivery is regulated so that at the climax he is speaking loudly, rather than shouting. He also makes frequent use of a barbed sense of humor. To the Sunday school at*

*Bell Grove, he said, "They say now that homosexuality is all right, because they've passed a law saying it's OK. If that's the case, God owes Sodom and Gomorrah an apology." In his 1988 recorded sermon "Love in Action," he chastises people who "live in a ninety thousand dollar house, drive a sixteen thousand dollar automobile, wear a two hundred and fifty dollar suit . . . then come to God's house and leave one dollar or less in the offering plate." But if the suit means so much, he asks, "why is it that when you get in a tight situation, you don't pray, 'Suit, have mercy on me?' "*

"Preaching is an art. It's a gift, too. But then, preaching is teaching toned up. Teaching is preaching toned down. Preaching and teaching work together. They have to work together. Your teaching helps folk to further understand. And your preaching helps them to accept what they understand. When I prepare a sermon, I get the matter, the manner and the purpose. What it is, how it is, and why it is. Those are the three main things. And I may have subpoints that go along with those points to drive it home. I have a script. But I only use it at intervals. I look down to get my bearings, just like you do with a map. You know you're going on Highway 61 to Memphis. But every now and then you look at the map and say, 'Oh, I'm going through Tunica.' So you have it for this reason. You have to keep making new sermons. That's why I have books, books, books. [He gestures at the full bookshelves in his sitting room.] But I'll tell you what you can do. You can preach a sermon from one scripture, then turn it around and preach the same sermon from another scripture. But what you do is, you never preach it the same way."

*A discussion on families brings Muddy Waters into the conversation for the first time. "Muddy's dad and my dad are brothers. His dad was Ollie Morganfield, mine was Lewis. Muddy was not a church man, but he was devoted to his family and friends. I'd go up there and maybe stay with him two or three days, a week. And whenever he came to where we were, he would always contact us and we'd get together." From there, it's a short step to the blues and the constant temptation for gospel singers to "cross over" and perform secular material.*

"I was offered forty-six thousand dollars to sing two rock 'n' roll numbers. That was in 1961. I was in Chicago. I was in Muddy's house when I got the telegram. The man told me to call him collect, and I called him and he told me he had three companies wanted me. And I was going to do it. But after I thought about it that night . . . it worried me and I said, 'No, I'm not going to do it.' I had my mind made up to do it. I was trying to figure out a way to do it and keep my spiritual integrity. But you can't mix it. I said, 'I'll sing it and get the money, then I'll go back to gospel.' But something said, 'You may not be able to get back.' Then I said, 'Well, I'll sing it and change my name.' But something says, 'Somebody'll know your voice.' My daddy had written a song for me, 'I Can't Afford to Let My Savior Down.'[11] And that song stayed with me all night long. I just can't afford to let my savior down. The next morning I told the man I couldn't do it. He was on one of those fifty thousand-watt radio stations, and he quit playing my records. But after six months he saw I was determined, so he started playing them again.

"I don't have too much to do with blues. But I can't be a hypocrite. I won't refuse to listen. And there are some pop numbers I've gotten sermons from. 'Smiling Faces Tell Lies Sometimes,' that's one of the pop numbers. That comes from the scripture, where it says, 'You worship me with your mouth, but your heart is far from me.'[12] So you can use that. I've used the titles of the songs for sermons that will help people get along. They are songs that relate to the conditions of people, some things that they have gone through. And I don't fight that.

"But I know this. I know you can't be both. You can't be wet and dry at the same time. The Scripture says you can't serve God and Mammon. So if you're gonna serve God, then you serve God. And if you're gonna serve Mammon, you serve Mammon. And there's enough folk doing that without the Christian folk getting into it. Sam Cooke is a good example. Sam Cooke was making four hundred dollars a week as a Soul Stirrer. But he wanted to make more. So he went into the other field. Now, you can't tell me he's as a good a Christian as I'd be if I'm serving God with all I have. And he's drawing folk away from the church. The Staple Singers the same. They're good friends of mine, and we've traveled together. When they were singing gospel, I went to Chicago and did their anniversary for them. I've known them since they were children. But they've strayed away from what they had when they started. You don't mix it. That's the thing I give Muddy credit for. He stayed with what he started. He didn't try to cross the fence. He never sung a gospel song. Nothing but blues.[13] And you can respect a person for that. But if you're gonna change . . . sing the blues today and gospel tomorrow, then you're saying you really don't know what way you want to go.

"Al Green . . . there's nothing to it. It's a front. Because if he was really truly centered on right and righteousness, he would leave that other stuff alone. But he mixes it. And that's not good. That's wrong. [Green, a soul star of the 1970s, has his own church in Memphis, but also performs secular shows.] Aretha Franklin, a good friend of mine. . . . But that's their business. They have to live their lives. And if they feel like they're right, who am I to kick? You can't argue with success. But it's the way success is acquired, that's what you argue with. If you're in business and you scuffle and come on up and make it being fair to people, then glory to you. But if you come up and cheat folk, then there's not too much to you."

*His conversation is liberally sprinkled with Bible quotes, most carefully identified—"As it says in Hebrews 13:8 . . . You can see it in Isaiah 55 and 8. . . . But he laughs off any suggestion that he must know the Scripture by heart—and amplifies his answer with another quote.*

"Nooooo. . . . But I read a lot, and I know quite a bit of it. It'll come to you when you need it. He said: 'At that time, the Holy Spirit will bring these things to your remembrance.'[14] But you can't remember what you haven't read. So that's why I read. And maybe you forget what you read. But at the time you need it, the Holy Spirit will bring it to your remembrance. You go to school and you learn, you can't contain all you learn. You couldn't quote it all right now. But if something comes up that has something to do with what you learned, then you can remember. It'll come to you. It's the same with singing and preaching. I've sung songs on the stage and forgotten the verse and added another verse and nobody knew the difference. That comes from experience. I was in Atlanta, Georgia, with . . . oh . . . three or four thousand people. I was singing a song I wrote and I forgot a verse. But I added one. I made up one, while I was singing. And it worked.

"I'm aware of where my talent comes from. From God. All good and perfect gifts come from him. And I want my music to be . . . well, let me say it this way, I pray and ask God to give me a song. Not for myself, but to help somebody else. And this is what it means to me, is to help somebody else. If you are down, here's a song that will lift up your spirit. And most of my songs . . . they are always thoroughly understood, and they always make sense. Always. I don't sit down and write something just because I can write. I write something that has a meaning, something to help somebody else. And it helps me. Oh yeah. Most of my songs I wrote out of experience of an uplifting. 'He Works That Way.'[15] I wrote that in five minutes. I was laying in the bed and thinking about when Jesus talked to Nicodemus.[16] In essence, what he was saying was, 'You're asking one thing with your mind on something else.' And it came to me that. . . .

> God doesn't answer prayer the way we want him to.
> He has us to know there's some things we must do.
> He waits until we've done our best,
> Then he steps in and he do the rest.
> He works that way. . . .

"Then it goes on to say. . . .

> When your meal barrel is empty,
> It seems no friend's around.
> You begin to think,
> That the Lord has let you down.
> You don't know how,
> When or where.
> But when you look around,
> The Lord is standing right there.
> He works that way.

"That's the way he works. He operates that way."

*Not surprisingly, considering the success he has enjoyed, Morganfield sees gospel music as a lucrative field. It's an opinion that clashes with the views of most other gospel singers, who generally regard their art as a labor of love while gazing enviously or disdainfully at the rewards offered to secular singers. But his trenchant views on the effect money has on gospel singing, and on the merits of modern gospel music, follow a more orthodox "traditionalist" line.*

"I guess I started when singing was a part of an individual. Now, it's more of a money matter. A lot of gospel singers, man, they fight if they don't get a certain amount of money. But me, I've never charged anything yet. I don't tell 'em how much I have to have. I go to New York, go to California, I never tell 'em how much they have to pay me. But I've always made it. They pay me. Pay me well. I never suffered. They pay my plane fare, my hotel bill, and . . . you know . . . take care. But there are gospel people in it for the money. And there's more money in it than you'd think. There's guys making acres of money singing gospel. You've got guys making twenty-five hundred dollars a night, singing gospel. You've got a lot of big names out there making it. You got Shirley Caesar, you got [Edwin] Hawkins, the Mighty Clouds of Joy. . . . When James Cleveland was living, we went on the road. We went to Atlanta and had fifty-eight hundred folk. Fifty-eight hundred! At seven, eight dollars a head, you're not doing bad! So there's money in it. Good money. People may not make so much locally. But . . . oh, I wouldn't even try to name all the people that are out there making money. And some of them are under contract. They get money sent in advance. Now, they say they're Christian folk. But that's not a Christian attitude. I've known some people, supposed to be big-time Christians and they go there and curse and fight over their money. I couldn't do it. I've been mistreated out there. I've gone places and the guy didn't do what he promised. But I couldn't fight it. I just go on to the next place, and the Lord fixes it where the next place pays off for what he didn't pay. And then he got to reap what he sow.

"But [gospel] singers have really made some money. And now, it's becoming prevalent. People are making all kind of money singing. And they have a lot of contemporary gospel. Sad to say, but it's not going to last. Because it doesn't have the depth. People, even young folk, want something they can relate to. They want something that's standard. 'Amazing Grace' is standard, and you can't change that. Ain't no good, no use, trying to soup it up and make it fast and jitterbuggish. You leave it where it is. Because everybody needs to have something to relate to. My songs are mostly related to life, Christian life. And they're still going strong. They're playing them everywhere. Every now and then, even in the midst of all this contemporary, somebody comes out with something that's original. And it just takes over. Where contemporary stuff is just a thing that you just do right now and forget about it. So I think that whatever we have, we oughta stick with that, and it'll last. We need to be flexible, adaptable, adjustable. But we need to have a standard and stick to it. And that's what I've done.

"I can change or pick up the tempo on a song. I'm sixty-five years old and I can still make my voice do some things that the average person can't do. But I don't really get excited over singing out. I get excited over singing at the church. Maybe twice a year I'll go and do seven or eight songs on a program. But as far as auditoriums and so on . . . I don't have any desire for that. Preaching is just my thing. I love it. I'm just a plain man, and that's the way I've been all my life. You know, people look at my car and say, 'How come you don't buy a new one?' I say, 'For what? What am I going to do with a new car.' That one there [a 1980 Cadillac] has got one hundred and sixty thousand miles and I haven't used a quart of oil in a year. I don't go anywhere but to the hospital and the airport. That car carries me anywhere I want to go. So that's a blessing. I don't need to have a new car. You know, the average person doesn't even know I live in Clarksdale. They think I live up in New York somewhere. But I enjoy living here. The people are nice—that's white and black. I'm recognized and respected, and I respect them and . . . what else could you ask for?"

# REV. DR. DAVID HALL

*"It's an incredible feeling..."*

Temple Church of God in Christ, on South Lauderdale St. in Memphis, is special. It's not a particularly imposing building, a two-story red-brick rectangle in a seen-better-days inner-city neighborhood. White crosses are inlaid on either side of the front door, and the small hedges and patch of lawn in front of it are neatly trimmed. The new Pentecostal Temple, a few blocks away on Danny Thomas Boulevard, is Memphis's main Church of God in Christ; Mason Temple, also nearby, is the venue of the annual COGIC convention, the Holy Convocation. But Temple Church is "the mother church," started by church founder

*Rev. Dr. David Hall's "altar call" at Temple Church of God in Christ, Memphis.*

Charles Harrison Mason in 1910. Bishop Mason pastored the church for forty-five years, handing it over to his son, C. H. "Bob" Mason, Jr., in 1955. Bishop J. O. Patterson, Sr., first presiding bishop of the COGIC after C. H. Mason's death, is a former pastor, as is his son, Bishop J. O. Patterson, Jr., now prelate of the church's Headquarters Jurisdiction and pastor of the Pentecostal Temple. Obviously, Temple Church is a special pulpit, a step in the right direction for those destined to hold high COGIC office.

Rev. Dr. David Allen Hall has been pastor since 1991. A slender soft-spoken man of forty-five, he initially presents a reserved, almost judicial air, and it's easy to see him in an academic role. The impression is not wrong. Born in Kokomo, Indiana, and raised in Indianapolis, he has a bachelor of arts from Butler University in Indianapolis, a master of divinity from Mason Theological Seminary in Atlanta, and a doctor of ministry from McCormick Theological Seminary in Chicago. He has taught at New York Theological Seminary, and was editor of the COGIC

newspaper *The Whole Truth*. He has written a number of books on
COGIC theology, and was a member of the committee which produced
the church's revised hymn book, *Yes Lord!*, in 1982. He is now doing
research on C. H. Mason for a book on the history of Temple Church.
But he is also a rousing traditional "shifting gears" preacher who goes
into the streets and prisons of Memphis with his church choir to carry
the message beyond the church walls. He plays saxophone, and has a
sharp sense of humor which comes to the fore as he talks about the
pitfalls of preaching. He and his wife, Gloria, have two sons; David, Jr.,
aged nineteen, is studying law, and Thomas, fourteen, wants to be a
professional tennis player. His family has been involved in the Church
of God in Christ since 1912.

"My grandfather was brought from the sinful life into the Church of
God in Christ in 1912 under the preaching of C. H. Mason. And to his
dying day, he believed there were only three great men that ever walked
the face of this earth. Moses, Jesus, and Bishop Mason. That was my
grandfather. And from that time forward, my entire family has been a
part of the Church of God in Christ. As preachers, missionaries . . . all
of us. My father was a minister, all my uncles. They're ministers, but
they're also businessmen. Ministry is something we do, wholeheartedly,
as another career, involved with our regular careers. I didn't intend to
go into the ministry. What I intended to do was what my father told
me. He said, 'Go be our first lawyer.' But I lost a brother who was a
freshman in college, and the Lord changed all of that. So I went into the
ministry. Being a minister is fulltime for me. But I also write, and I'm
the secretary of Bishop Patterson's jurisdiction.

"C. H. Mason started the Church of God in Christ in Lexington,
Mississippi, and between 1897 and 1907, he and a gentleman by the
name of C. P. Jones were more or less partners in the ministry. In 1907
they split company due to the advent of Pentecost into Mason's way of
thinking. That was because he had been recipient of the baptism of the
spirit. After that, C. H. Mason came to Memphis, Tennessee, to begin
the Church of God in Christ as a pentecostal church. In 1910, he began
Temple Church. A few years after that, World War I came about. C. H.
Mason preached against violence. He was a pacifist. He didn't believe in
the shedding of blood at all. Consequently, the good white citizens of
Lexington, Mississippi, decided he had to go. So after being thrown in
jail and then set free, he was banished from the city of Lexington. After

that, this church became the forefront of all his ministerial activities and growth. They used to call this the Mother Church, many people still refer to it as the Mother Church. Because from 1910 until 1955, C. H. Mason literally carried forward the ministry of the Church of God in Christ from this spot of ground."[1]

*The building in which David Hall preaches is not the one Mason built; that was destroyed by fire in 1958, while Mason's son was pastor. COGIC history tells how the rebuilding project ran into difficulties and was faltering when Mason, then in his nineties and very weak, came to the site and "softly prayed that God would smile upon the labor of his son." The building was completed in 1961, the year of C. H. Mason's death at the age of ninety-five.*

*Today, the Church of God in Christ is a worldwide movement, with about four million members in fifty-three countries. All are ultimately governed by one central organization, based in Memphis, although the church makes an effort to place indigenous people in local senior positions. From its inception, the church has been adventurous in its music. At a time when other churches were singing sedate hymns accompanied by piano or organ, the COGIC was "making a joyful noise" with up-tempo songs accompanied by all the instruments used in secular music. It was part of C. H. Mason's philosophy, an attempt to make the new church attractive to potential converts. But at the same time, he set strict rules on the type of music acceptable to the church.*

"The church's philosophy on music is that there are two kinds of music—secular music and church music. And our tradition says that if it's not church, it's bad. Obviously that's erroneous. There are forms of music which are not expressly gospel church-oriented music and there's nothing wrong with them at all. But when C. H. Mason was preaching, he wanted to make the distinction plain, crystal-clear. He said blues was the Devil's music. God doesn't give you the blues. He gives you the spirit of rejoicing. Though, of course, gospel music, jazz and all of it come out of the Negro spirituals, the African traditions of black people, and was born and nurtured in the church. The basic blues and early jazz and big band musicians all had their origins in the church. They came from the church and went to the secular society. So the kinship is there; it's undeniable, it's a fact of history. But to make the difference clear, C. H. Mason said there's one kind of music that we do. That's church music.

But the instruments weren't classified as sinful. They used spoons and washboards, anything that could make noise. They considered it a part of a joyful noise. Anything that would make noise, they would use it. Jew's harps, harmonicas. . . .

"Other churches were modeling and fashioning their churches after mainline white Protestant institutions. They had a piano and an organ, and that was it. They had prepared literatures and other things. But the Church of God in Christ came out of African tradition, its call-and-response mode. So a lot of the songs in the Church of God in Christ are congregational call-and-response. [sings] 'I'm a soldier/ In the army of the Lord.' And you had maybe five or six basic melody lines, and then just different words in the call-and-response mode, for whatever would fit the lead. There is a definite COGIC style, and it has influenced the whole of gospel music. Mattie Moss Clark was the first lady of gospel music in terms of the big choir style. And it was her Southwest Michigan State Choir that recorded on the Savoy label back in the early sixties—the *Salvation Is Free* album, and 'Climbing Up the Mountain'²—that really put the big choir sound on the map. The Church of God in Christ led out all over. Edwin and Edward Hawkins and the North-west Jurisdictional Church of God in Christ Choir produced 'Oh, Happy Day.' Before the big choir sound, Rosetta Tharpe and all of those personalities, they all sang in the Church of God in Christ. Utah Smith with "Two Wings"? COGIC. The Church of God in Christ has always been in the vanguard of expressing music.

"One thing the Church of God in Christ understood very early on was that if you want to hold children in church, let 'em sing. If they're not saved, let 'em sing. They'll get saved. Let 'em hang around the church long enough, let 'em fall in love with singing. I don't know anybody that's a preacher in this church, a missionary in this church, that did not start off singing in the choir. If you were a child in this church, you sang. Even if you couldn't carry a note in a bucket. The choir is where I began. I blew saxophone—and every now and again I still do. I've blown alto, soprano, and tenor. But basically I did my blowing and my music in the church. And so I have my musical part that I played in the church. My brother was the organist for the church. My other brother, Nathan, is the organist here [at Temple Church]. He's minister of music for this church. And we have an adult choir, and a youth choir, and we have our Sunshine Band, little children. So singing plays a part, from the cradle to the grave.

"The Church of God in Christ is choirs. Quartets are by and large a product of the Baptist church. Baptist people have good choirs, but quartets . . . out of the Mississippi Delta, out of the backwoods of Alabama and every place else, you had four guys with a guitar and drums—that typifies their musical traditions. Whereas we've always leaned toward choirs and the big sound. There's no reason for it—just evolution. Although a lot of quartets carry a bad reputation with the Church of God in Christ. I've heard some preachers say, 'They're singing songs about their mama being dead and she's sitting on the front pew.' I don't make that a main part of my reflection when I deal with quartets. I enjoy some quartet music. But all that stuff had its origin with . . . guys sang quartet, same guys sang rock 'n' roll and blues. Guys like Little Johnny Taylor. He sang quartet, now he sings rock 'n' roll, blues—and he's also a preacher.[3] People in this church say, 'How can you do that?' Sam Cooke . . . I remember when I was a kid, Sam Cooke had not made the transition and he was singing in the quartet. And he's killing them. And he found his niche and also found his destruction out there singing secular music. Al Green is the same way. What's he gonna sing? 'I'm Still In Love With You' or 'Near the Cross'? What's he singing today? He's standing in both places. I guess he says God gave him the talent to sing both ways, and he's going to do it.

"The Church of God in Christ has always wanted to draw that line and make it clear. But we have faltered. We have people who sing rock 'n' roll and want to sing gospel at the same time. We have recording artists who are just that same way. Singing rock 'n' roll and singing gospel. I think it sends a confusing signal. It's erasing the line. The definite line. And with that erasing of the line, because music is so important for the drawing of young people, we are losing more young people. They don't know where they want to stand. They don't think they have to make a choice. They don't have to make a choice, and because they don't have to make a choice, they don't make a choice.

"So the Church of God in Christ doesn't deal with quartets, but music groups such as the Winans have a strong basis in our church. They lean towards the more pop contemporary-oriented music. And we draw lines there, too. Because sometimes that music can get too far out. There was a day when the world patterned its music after what the church was doing. Now, the church in many places is leaving what it has done well and has used to establish itself in the hearts of people, and has gone after rap and all other kind of nonsense. And as far as I'm concerned, it has no place in the church. It's all commercial. It's strictly money. It's not God's business, it's show business. It's strictly business. The lead songs on most of their albums will hardly ever mention the name Jesus. And if you listen to the lyrics, a guy could be singing the same lyrics to a girl. When you see the videos, they're mimicking pop stars in their presentation. And they're not doing any good. They're not doing anything that's of any true validity, except making a lot of money. And also confusing the youth of today. And sooner or later they are going to wake up to the travesty they have perpetrated on their own roots with this trashy commercially oriented so-called gospel music.

"A lot of them start out very sincere. But then somebody waves that first ten thousand dollar appearance contract in their face, they say, 'Hey, if we're going to maintain this kind of money, we're not playing for only church crowds. We're playing for all crowds.' And so they choreograph their presentations. They have people dancing behind them . . . they may as well be doing something that Marvin Gaye and the Temptations used to do. There's nothing sacred about it. It's secular. It's about CBS and Polygram signing them and distributing those albums and CDs. It's about money. If you wanted to get a major recording group to come and do your local church—they'll slap a contract on you that says I gotta have X number of dollars, I've got to have X number of seats, or seating capacity, I have to have a certain type of piano, I have to have a certain kind of sound system, I want X number of musicians and this and that to be done, I need to have this kind of food and that kind of soda in my room—the whole bit. It's pop music, it's a pop contract, it's pop production, the whole bit."

*During time spent with pentecostal churches while researching a doctoral dissertation, Mellonee Burnim encountered "a widely accepted axiom— 'Music gets 'em and preaching keeps 'em.' "4 The suggestion is that music will draw people to the church, and good preaching will keep them faithful. "Music is . . . viewed not as a threat, but as an aid to accomplishing the desired religious mission," Burnim concludes. David Hall is not so sure.*

"It's a common expression, and it may have some validity. But I don't buy it. Singing plays its part, but God didn't tell us through Christ Jesus to *sing* the Gospel. He said *preach* the Gospel. And preaching is the thing. There's not a gospel singer that was not influenced by the preacher's word, by the read word. It's the word of God. That's what's doing it. Not singing songs. Singing has its place, so we wholeheartedly support it and all the instrumentation that you want to apply to it. But preaching is the key. The motivating factor is the word of God. The words that you hear in gospel music were born out of the Scripture and out of the preaching that convicted people. They translated that into the rhythms and the expressions of the people—that African genre, that hand-clapping foot-stomping soul-driven thing. And in many ways, gospel music used to be preaching in song. But the stuff you're hearing nowadays has no true gospel value in terms of lyric."

*Preaching in the Church of God in Christ is firmly based on the fiery "shifting gears" style, or "tuning" as it is also called in the church. This is a reference to the half-sung cadence that brings the sermon to a climax and a pun on the fact that preachers orate in specific keys, often taking a pitch note from the choir musicians before starting the sermon.*

"It's not a formal requirement, that a minister has to be able to sing. But . . . you sing! You practice songs. Because the people expect you to lead songs. And of course our preaching style has its points of lecture and teaching, but there is always the endpoint, where it moves into the gear, where you wind your message up, with music. So most preachers know their key. Because we have sung, you know where you're strongest. I prefer G, unless my voice is a little bit rocky. Then I drop to F. The Baptist church is a B♭ church. Most Baptist preachers will be in B♭ or E♭ because of the way they start their cadence. Church of God in Christ, you'll find them in F and G. You take the note before you start because . . . if I'm gonna protect my voice, if I'm going to properly amplify, if I'm going to do this thing right, I need the pitch. I have to be on key, because the throat is my tool for creating what I want to have happen in terms of word delivery. So singing has a definite part to play, even in the delivery of the gospel. You can preach without getting into gear or going into a certain key and finishing like that. But for us, it's so much better if you do.

"You just know when it's time to move the people to a higher gear. It's when you want to really bring them in and make the preaching not only an intellectual process, but bring the spirit to envelop the entire person into what you say, to make the Word flesh and get not only the mind but the whole emotion and the whole energy of the person listening involved. And it's just something that at the right time you move into.

You pick your moment, you feel it and you move into it. The people will let you know when they're ready. They'll start tellin' you, 'Say it!' 'Preach!' 'Bring it on home.' Or whatever it is to let you know that, 'All right. We understand the proposition. We've received the scripture, you've made your sell. Now bring it home.'

"Sometimes I preach from manuscript, other times I just take my Bible to the pulpit, lay it there, read the scripture and kind of extemporize. But when I preach manuscript and I'm getting ready to move into the higher gear, I close my Bible and go from there, drawing on what I've said and tying things up. There are some who have their stuff written all the way down to the last 'amen.' If you want to go that way . . . fine. But you lose that spontaneity, which is what makes it so much alive. Because you're playing back off the feedback of the people, the raw power and the raw appeal of the Word coming back at you. It's an incredible feeling. And you just don't know where you're going a lot of times. You get totally out of yourself and the Spirit takes you into that. And that's why people say, 'He finally started preaching.' Though you have been preaching all the time.

"There are some who say you don't need to tune up, don't need any music. Sometimes I do it that way. I stand flatfooted and talk. In this church, you have the option to go as you want. The only thing people are critical of in this church is . . . if the word gets out that you can't preach. My dad told me when I started preaching, he said, 'Son, people will forgive a minister anything. If you mess up, do something wrong, you ask them for forgiveness. They'll forgive you. You ignore them, or do this or do that, they'll forgive you. But if you get up and you don't preach, they'll never forgive you.' Because the next time you take the pulpit, somebody'll lean over and say to their neighbor, 'You know he can't preach.'

"With preaching, it's like an Italian tenor. People in Italy know what an Italian tenor is supposed to do. If he's singing that aria way up high and he cracks, they boo him. If he's too cautious and he isn't bold and daring when he moves out on that thing, they don't want to hear him any more. If you're preaching and you mess up on the scripture, the people will say, 'Oh well, he's not well read, is he?' If you fumble and make a mistake and aren't careful how you deliver, or if you take 'em some place and don't finish the thought . . . they're listening. When you're winding up and falling back and singing, 'Say yeah' and all that . . . they're listening. And if the preacher's not saying anything, they let him know. 'He ain't saying nothing.' 'He's just hollerin', that's all he's doing.' 'That boy can't preach.' 'Help him, Lord.' Those mothers get to rocking. 'Oh, help him Lord.' 'Send your help, Lord.' It's in the inflection. You know where they're coming from, make no mistake about it. 'We need your help here, Lord.' 'Ohhh help him, Lord.' 'Ohhh Jesus.' 'Oh that poor boy. Help him, help him.' 'Help him, help him, Lord.' And when you hear that—[he laughs]—you start praying! 'Y'all gon' pray with me here?' 'Get up off me now. Don't sit on me. I'm trying. You praying with me? I'm gon' preach if you pray.' There's a way to make that connection, hook that train up so everybody's going the same way. They're always on your side. Just like that Italian tenor. They want him to sing. And they want you to preach. It's the same way with singers too. That person leading the solo in the choir? Man, they want 'em to throw their head back and wail. Deliver. Come across with it."

*People do change churches. Some switch allegiances when they move to an area where the church they came from is not active. Some become dissatisfied with a church—they don't like the pastor, or they quarrel with another member—and move elsewhere. But, generally, members are fiercely loyal to their denomination and their church. The church is not only a center of worship but a community center, for reasons that have as much to do with culture as with religion.*

"If you're COGIC, you're COGIC. Our members heavily identify with the Church of God in Christ. And Baptists do the same thing. There's the old expression: 'A Baptist born, a Baptist bred; when I die, I'll be a Baptist dead.' But it's the same with black people in general. Whatever the organization they are in, they have created a real sense of community. We know who we are and what we're in. In the church, I think it is a cultural phenomenon, because the church lends credibility to people who have been stripped of everything. My grandfather . . . his sister became a member of the Church of God in Christ first, influenced by C. H. Mason. My grandfather didn't care about being nothing, until his sister introduced him to the church. Just like most black men back in that day at the turn of the century . . . they were running for their lives, they were trying to eke out a living, they wanted to get from behind a plow, stop picking cotton, get a job in a factory. My grandfather went to Chicago, Illinois. Now, Chicago had an ordinance that the Irish voted in, that shops and the like had to serve everybody. Because when the Irish first came to this country, they were not received. They were classified as dumb micks. They were only one generation away from being acceptable, though. Because of white skin. Black people would never be acceptable. So he went from behind the plow into Chicago and found out he could go into any place he wanted. He took his new bride into a nice restaurant and sat down to eat. And they served him. Said, 'Wow!' Never in his wildest dreams. But when he went to pay the check, the guy said, 'We don't want your money.' Then he took the china they had eaten from and broke it in the middle of the floor. He said, 'We don't want your money, nigger. Get out!' And did that in front of his new bride. But when they got into the Church of God in Christ . . . he only finished the third grade, but he was a minister, he was a preacher, he was a pastor, he led people who followed. He could hardly read, but grandmother could. So he'd say, 'Read, mama,' and she'd read and he'd preach. He'd say, 'Read some more.' She'd read and he'd preach. And as a result of that, he established or helped build eight different churches. As a result of that, he owned his own property, traveled anywhere he wanted to go, and when he died, he'd educated twelve children. College-educated half of them. And he finished the third grade. But the church gave him . . . it made him somebody.

"I have an earned doctorate, simply because I chose to. But I can go out on the street corner and preach. A guy that's seeing me can drop his marijuana and his liquor, stop smoking his crack cocaine and come in here [to the church], live right, do everything he's supposed to do, and if he feels the Lord has called him to the ministry, and he's willing to subject himself to the training and everything within this church and meet the criteria of the bishop, that guy can be a preacher and never once set foot in a seminary. There is an internal system, a rite of passage from unlicensed minister to minister to ordained clergy. You have to go to our church Bible college so you have the basic understanding of scripture, church doctrine, discipline and those other things. But formal education—you might have only finished the third grade and you can become an ordained elder in this church. I finished college, graduate school, and then completed my doctorate studies. But if I had done none of that, I could still be sitting in this chair if the bishop decided to appoint me to this church."

*The core tenet of the Church of God in Christ's theology is the conversion experience—being "born again" through possession by the Holy Spirit, as happened to the Apostles in their upper room on the day of Pentecost (Acts 2:2–4). A person who has experienced this is "saved" or "sanctified" and can become a "saint," a member of the church.*

"Conversion starts within the heart. It is not a matter of education, cognitive process, catechizing. We don't believe in that. We catechize you after you get in here. In our church song, 'This Is the Church of God in Christ,' there is a line which says, 'You cannot join it, you have to be born in it.'5 As in 'born again.' We literally mean that. Someone comes in saying, 'I want to put my membership here at this church. Can I join and sign up the roll?' We don't do that. We have people here [at Temple Church] who are not formally members, but who attend. But are they truly members of this church? No. Not if they have not come to the altar and asked God to forgive them of their sin. And we then desire that they not only ask God to forgive them of their sin, but that they then practice their faith.

"We do things to help people in tough situations. This church expresses itself that way. So it's no big thing when I say to my choir, 'Let's go to prison. We're gonna sing.' When you see some guy on the street . . . people say, 'That nut's out on the street preaching.' Fifty per cent of the time he'll be COGIC. Street preaching. I do it. Sure I do it. Because you've got people who never come inside a church. So I go outside. Preach outside. Walk the street with a big sign. I go right where the drug dealers are selling their stuff, set up shop and start preaching. I say, 'The street doesn't belong to you. I've got a right to be out here, too.' One time, we went down and we were being harangued and harassed by some guys, man, we were all upset by the way these guys were treating us. Catcalls and hollering and threats at us. Then we did the altar call, and the ringleader came down and stood up there. When he stood there in front of me, I started to ask him, 'Why did you come down here?' But I caught myself and I realized, this man has come to the altar, and I said, 'What can I do for you?' He said, 'The Lord is saving me.' And his partners were having fits! But that's what it's about. The gospel has to leave the four walls."

*Temple Church has a membership of about four hundred people, and the four hundred and fifty-seat sanctuary is filled almost to capacity most Sundays. The main choir has about thirty members, the children's choir about twenty. Music in the church is organized with its own hierarchy*

*and structure (although the structure is looser in small churches, with less*
*formality and more spontaneous music from the congregation).*

"Most churches have a minister of music who is in charge of the
ministry in music. Selecting songs to be sung appropriate to the type of
service you're going to have, training the choir, playing the music. You
have your organist and other musicians, you have a choir president, you
have general officers over the choir. It is structured. Highly structured. It
goes along with what the Church of God in Christ hands down from the
national church in terms of its organization. So it's modeled, from up
top down to the local level. The choir has practices weekly for training
purposes, and it does other things to express its ministry. A big choir
should be doing more than singing in the sanctuary. It should do other
things. Our choir sings in prisons, and if I need 'em to sing out on the
street corner when I'm preaching outside . . . if I want my choir outside,
I want 'em outside.

"Our hymn book has traditional Christian hymns, plus all those call-
and-response songs of the Church of God in Christ. 'I'm a Soldier in
the Army of the Lord,' 'Glory Glory Hallelujah,' 'Jesus Is on the Main
Line. . . .' Some of these are songs that transcend denomination, and
that transcendence is because of the broad acceptance of what COGIC
is about. Other churches have adopted those songs because they know
what COGIC is about now. There was a time you never would've heard
'Jesus Is on the Main Line' in a Baptist church or in a Methodist church.
But now the Church of God in Christ has been accepted for what it has
brought to the mix. It's had an influence everywhere. In the Catholic
Church, they now do gospel masses. It comes right back down to C. H.
Mason's original philosophy. Bringing the totality of our experience in
song, so that you have songs to make merry in your heart and to live
and get by."

# 6  BACK IN CHURCH

*"I'm gonna get me religion . . ."*

The grainy videotape shows an elderly man seated on a plain wooden chair and holding a steel-bodied National resonator guitar, the sort prized by 1930s blues players for their volume and durability. Before he plays it again, the old man has a message for the mainly young, mainly white audience watching him out of the range of the camera:

> I was brought up in church from a little boy on up. And I didn't believe in no blues. I was too churchy, and I didn't believe in that. And I talked against it. And I really was called to preach the gospel. That's why I knowed it so good. I didn't have to read the book so much, it came from above. . . . I'm sitting here playing blues and I play church songs, too. But you can't take God and the Devil along together, because them two fellows, they don't communicate so well together—they don't get along so well together. Now you've got to separate those two guys. . . . You got to follow one or the other. You can't hold God in one hand and the Devil in the other. You got to turn one of 'em a-loose. . . . You're a friend or an enemy 'twixt God and the Devil. You can't sit straddle of the fence—you got to give up one side or the other.[1]

The speaker is Eddie "Son" House, one of the early giants of Mississippi blues, who in the mid-1960s found a second musical career playing to mainly white audiences. His homily is delivered in soft-spoken, halting, and heavily accented tones to an audience which, judging by its impassive reaction to his attempts at humor, understands little of what he is saying. He is addressing one of the perennial issues of African-American folk music—the relationship between blues and religion. The conclusion he reaches—"you can't straddle the fence"—is a commonly used analogy; the incongruity of House's espousal of it is heightened by the fact that before his soliloquy, he performed an unaccompanied religious song, and after it came a blues.

Blues and religion is a topic which has been extensively discussed in books and articles, usually from a secular perspective. Finding examples of cross-pollination between the two is not difficult. Religious references abound in blues lyrics; blues phrases are not uncommon in gospel tunes. A number of gospel singers have "crossed over" to sing secular music; a number of blues singers have turned to sacred music. Most observers see blues and sacred music as antipathetic, citing blues singers' jibes at religion and church-goers' rejection of the blues as "the Devil's music." But community feeling on the subject covers a wide range. At one end of the spectrum is rejection of all nonreligious music. This is part of Church of God in Christ doctrine, but other congregations can also take a disapproving line. Blues singer Jessie Mae Hemphill, who belongs to the New Salem Baptist Church near her home outside Como, Mississippi, says, "People look at me, you know, when I go to church. They think it's so terrible for me to go to church because I sing the blues. They say I ought not to go to church. I say, 'Well, I ain't doing no badder than nobody else.' I said, 'I ain't had no woman's husband and I ain't killed nobody. But somebody in here will be doing worse than me. Somebody in here now is going with some woman's husband, and that's just as bad as me playing blues.' And I tell them, 'God knows everything. God knows why I'm doing this. He know I needs to pay my bills.' They say you can't serve the Devil and the Lord, too. But my belief about it is that God spared me and brought me this far."[2] Most Baptists are not as hardline as those Hemphill describes. Writer Mark Humphrey singles out the denomination as having a theology which makes it easy for performers such as Son House (and Jessie Mae Hemphill) to mix sacred and secular: "House was a Baptist, and an important tenet of Baptist faith is 'once in grace, always in grace.' A believer 'fully saved' in this denomination might believe that a little blues singing wouldn't jeopardize his soul, while members of 'hardshell' holiness and pentecostalist churches would find such liberality untenable."[3]

Son House was only one of many musicians who made a living from blues, but who also performed religious songs. The recordings of many well-known blues artists include religious selections. But the influence of religion on blues extends beyond injecting sacred songs into the repertoires of secular musicians. In the era when blues was firmly rooted in its folk origins, it took much of its lyric substance from the day-to-day lives of its practitioners and their audience. Religion was a pervasive part of that life, and as such became a resource from which blues singers drew. Some used religious references to make distinctly non-religious points, as did Texas pianist Andy Boy in his "Jive Blues":

> Now the good book say thou shall not break the ten commandment law
> I'm gonna break the ten commandments on your jaw.[4]

Others suggested quite plainly that while they may be singing blues, religion was also a part of their lives. Another Texas artist, T-Bone Walker, attended church as a child, and there is no note of insincerity when he sings, "Sometimes I sing the blues when I know I should be praying."[5] In a 1941 Library of Congress interview, Muddy Waters told Alan Lomax of composing a blues after "I was just walking along the road and I heard a church song that kinda 'minded me of it."[6] The song was "I Be's Troubled," which as "I Can't Be Satisfied," was Muddy Waters's first commercial success, in 1948. Unfortunately, Lomax did not ask him what the "church song" was.

The ubiquity of religion in black life is also illustrated by the existence of parodies and wordplay. Such maneuvers can be successful only if the sources being burlesqued are familiar to the listener, which presumably would be the case if they were issued on recordings intended for wide distribution. Jim Jackson and Ben Covington recorded versions of "I Heard the Voice of a Pork Chop,"[7] drawn from Rev. Horatius Bonar's hymn "I Heard the Voice of Jesus Say." Winston Holmes, who as an entrepreneur first recorded Rev. J. C. Burnett, and guitarist Charlie Turner recorded the two-part "Death of Holmes's Mule,"[8] which included parodies of Isaac Watts's "Am I a Soldier of the Cross" and Sankey and Moody's "Hark From the Tomb."[9] Even Georgia Tom Dorsey, before he became gospel music doyen Thomas A. Dorsey, indulged himself in a moment of whimsy when he sang:

> Dark was the night, cold was the ground
> When you caught me kissing Miss Lizzie Brown.

This was in his 1930 blues "You Got Me in This Mess";[10] the first line is the title and opening line of the widely known crucifixion hymn by

Thomas Haweis—"Dark was the night and cold the ground/On which the Lord was laid."

Many other examples of religious references in blues lyrics have been cited, most extensively by Paul Oliver in *Songsters and Saints* and *Screening the* Blues,[11] and also by Jon Michael Spencer in *Blues and Evil*, a study of the relationship between blues and religion.[12] More recent blues artists do not delve into the spiritual side; as Spencer suggests, this is due to the diminishing influence and impact of the church on the day-to-day lives of singers and audiences, rather than to any change in the underlying philosophy of blues singing.[13] However, where blues remains in touch with its community, rather than being primarily a commercial undertaking, religious songs and references are so plentiful, and apparently so accepted by singers and listeners, that one could wonder whether blues versus sacred is an issue of more concern to researchers and musicologists than to those involved. But the equanimity is not universal. Some singers do balance their secular and sacred sides; for others, the tension between "God and the Devil" can create pressures.

Son House was one such artist, and his ambivalence on the subject is not surprising. Many singers have turned from gospel to secular music; House is probably the only one who stepped from the pulpit to play blues. Born in Lyon, Mississippi, in 1902 (other dates as early as 1886 have also been suggested), he was raised in a religious family, and preached his first sermon when he was fifteen. He discovered the blues around 1926, and two years later started learning to play the guitar, captivated by the slide playing of unrecorded Delta bluesman Willie Wilson, who gave him a few lessons.[14] He continued preaching, but the conflict between his two roles increasingly concerned him. "I began to wonder, now how can I stand up in the pulpit and preach to them, tell them how to live, and quick as I dismiss the congregation and I see nobody ain't looking and I'm doing the same thing."[15] This conflict is also reflected in "Preachin' the Blues," a song which he recorded in 1930 and which stayed in his repertoire throughout his performing life. Superficially, it may be seen as antireligion; it is in fact a condemnation of hypocrisy and a statement of House's own dilemma:

> Oh, in my room, I bowed down to pray,
> But the blues came along and drove my spirit away.
>
> Oh, I'd've had religion on this very day,
> But the women and the whiskey, well they would not let me pray.[16]

House continued to straddle the fence throughout his life. In the 1930s, he made sporadic returns to preaching; in the 1960s, his repertoire included a cappella "church songs." David Evans nominates him as an "originator of soul music, . . . not so much in its modern form of blues secularism poured into a gospel framework, but in an older form in which the holy fervor of gospel music infuses the blues. It's all there in his music, the moaning and groaning and pleading, the catch in his voice like the preacher in mid-sermon, the effortless leap into falsetto, the melismatic endings of his lines and the content of the songs themselves, with their frequent invocations of God and their messages of burning love."[17] Evans also suggests that House used blues as an "intermediary force" which enabled him to deal with his sacred/secular dilemma. "Through the personification of this force and his close identification with it, he was able to address God, to stay in touch with God." Implicit in this is support for the concept that the religious bluesman need not be—and is not—a contradiction in terms.

Charley Patton, a Delta contemporary of House, was another whose religion was as much a force in his life as his blues, although his biographers are at odds over the subject. In *King of the Delta Blues*, Stephen Calt and Gayle Wardlow dismiss Patton's claim of once being a preacher, suggesting that it was nothing more than an attempt "to impress others with his piety." Yet on the same page, they tell of Patton's "inexplicable habit" of breaking into religious songs while playing for dances.[18] In a virtually rival biography, David Evans describes a man who had a thorough religious education from his church deacon father, who sometimes performed in church programs, and whose fifty-two issued recordings include ten religious pieces.[19] Also, says Evans, Patton "for most of his life wrestled with what he thought was a calling to be a preacher." Family members recall Patton preaching at a church on the outskirts of the Delta township of Renova,[20] and, in a detailed account of her uncle's last days, Bessie Turner described to Evans how a bedridden Patton declared, "I've got to preach the text of the Revelation," and did so for a full week before his death of heart failure, in April 1934.[21]

Whatever the conflicts created in their lives by the clash between blues and religion, House and Patton remained blues singers. Several artists felt the call of religion strongly enough to quit their worldly music forever. Some, such as Rubin Lacy, Ishmon Bracey, Roosevelt Darby, Walter Davis, Robert Wilkins, Gary Davis, and Dwight "Gatemouth" Moore, became ordained preachers. Thomas A. Dorsey's decision to renounce blues had far-reaching effects on the world of gospel music. Roebuck Staples, raised in the same area of Mississippi as Charley Patton and Son House, played blues in his youth, but went on to create with his children one of gospel's best-known groups.

For many of these people, conversion came dramatically. Gatemouth Moore tells how his career as an urban blues singer came to an end one night when he was due to sing at a nightclub in Chicago. After twice missing his cue to sing, he says, "when I opened my mouth, I started singing 'Shine On Me.'"[22] Rubin Lacy, raised by his Methodist preacher grandfather, returned to religion in October 1932, after being badly injured when a loose brake shoe from a passing train struck him in the leg while he was working at a Mississippi sawmill. "When he hit the ground, he heard a voice saying, 'The next time it will be death.'" Once he had recovered from his injury, Lacy went to a nearby Baptist church and "confessed his calling to preach."[23] For Robert Wilkins, the change came as suddenly, but not as dramatically. "In the early part of '36, I was playing for a ball in Hernando, Mississippi, one Saturday night," he told Pete Welding. "And it just came to me to quit." Wilkins was not a regular church-goer at the time, but his wife was a Christian "and I didn't want to raise my children up under the blues life."[24] He was ordained a minister in the Church of God in Christ in 1950, and remained in the church until his death at the age of ninety-one in 1987.

A common factor in the background of most of these singers was a childhood exposure to religion, so they were returning to something they knew, rather than stepping into a new world. And although they stopped playing blues, many were not prepared to completely deny their former music. In an interview with David Evans, Rubin Lacy recounted how in one of his sermons, "I tell the people that . . . I used to be a famous blues singer and I told more truth in my blues than the average person tells in his church songs."[25] He also suggested that "sometimes the best Christian in the world have the blues quicker than a sinner do, 'cause the average sinner ain't got nothing to worry about. But a Christian is obligated to do certain things and obligated not to do certain things. That sometimes cause a Christian to take the blues."[26] In 1977, Thomas A. Dorsey—with nearly fifty years of gospel music behind him—defended blues as an integral part of African-American culture, as important to it as religious music (although there is an irony in his "vulgarity" qualification, given his role as a leading figure in the double entendre "hokum" blues vogue of the late 1920s): "I don't see anything wrong with the blues unless you use vulgarity in it. But the blues, the music itself? It can't hurt. It can do more good than it can do harm. . . . Blues is as important to a person feeling bad as 'Nearer My God To Thee.' I'm not talking about popularity, I'm talking about inside the individual."[27]

Robert Wilkins rebuffed friends urging him to "make two or three records of the blues" for the money he would earn by quoting Mark 8:36, "What shall it profit a man if he shall gain the whole world and lose his own soul?" He was also concerned at the example a blues-singing pastor would set his flock, and said his conscience would not allow him to sing secular songs. But he conceded: "Now I don't think singing a song like 'John Henry' is harmful very much. If I was in the Baptist church, I could play those songs and be accepted, but they won't accept me in the church I'm in."[28]

Wilkins did not entirely abandon his secular repertoire when he joined the Church of God in Christ. The tune of one of his best-known blues, "That's No Way To Get Along," became the vehicle for a nine-minute retelling of the parable of the prodigal son; another piece, "Old Jim Canan's," lost its lyrics—dealing with a particularly rough barroom in Memphis—to become the instrumental "I'm Going Home To My Heavenly King."[29]

The practice of using secular tunes to support religious lyrics is not uncommon. On a 1993 anthology of Chicago singers, Gladys Beamon Gregory performs "I've Got a Song" with what album compiler Anthony Heilbut describes in his notes as "bluesy grandeur." This ambiance is considerably aided by the fact that the tune she sings is that of the blues standard "See See Rider."[30] Sister Wynona Carr's "I Heard the News (Jesus Is Coming Again)" is a reworking of Roy Brown's much-copied 1947 recording "(I Heard the News, There's) Good Rockin' Tonight."[31] The change is also made the other way, with sacred songs being remodeled into secular. Among the better known is C. A. Tindley's "Stand By Me," reworked to become a secular hit for Ben E. King in 1962. Bluesman B. B. King sings a secularized version of Thomas A. Dorsey's "I'm Going to Live the Life I Sing About In My Song." In the 1960s, brothers Curtis, Robert and Andrew Kelly, from Chicago, sang gospel as the Kelly Brothers, and R&B as the King Pins, producing one of the more singular examples of tailoring the song to the market. Their 1960 recording of "He's All Right" has the first verse:

> He's all right, Jesus is all right.
> He's been with me day and night,
> Know the man makes my burden light,
> I can say Jesus is all right.[32]

Two years later, they joined forces with Johnny Otis to record "She's All Right." To the same tune as "He's All Right," they sang:

> She's all right, my baby's all right.
> She's been with me day and night,
> Don't you know the girl makes my burdens light,
> Well I can say, she's all right.[33]

One of the best-known artists to adapt sacred techniques to secular songs is Ray Charles. Even before his own music made him an international star, he arranged Eddie "Guitar Slim" Jones's million-selling hit of 1953, "Things That I Used To Do." The song's core lyric—"The things that I used to do, I don't do no more"—also occurs in the gospel song "Great Change Since I've Been Born," recorded by artists as disparate as Bessie Johnson and Rev. Gary Davis, and Charles's arrangement reinforces the lyric with a strong gospel "feel." The following year, Charles recorded "I Got a Woman," which introduced what was to become his trademark fusion of gospel and blues stylings. "I'd been singing spirituals since I was three," he explained, "and I'd been hearing the blues for just as long. So what could be more natural than to combine them?"[34] The gospel influence was especially overt in some songs—"This Little Girl of Mine" is a secularized "This Little Light of Mine," and "Hit the Road, Jack" reflects the "church song" call-and-response style to the extent that in 1961, the Angelic Choir, of Nutley, New Jersey, completed the circle by used the song's tune, structure and performance style for a song called "It's the Holy Ghost."[35]

Some blues artists see little musical difference between sacred and secular. Rev. Gatemouth Moore, is succinct on the subject: "I'm facetious when that question is asked, 'Moore, tell me, you sing religious songs now and you sang the blues. What's the difference?' And I say one word and smile. Lyrics. No other difference."[36]

Leland, Mississippi, singer James "Son" Thomas told William Ferris that "it's no difference in the music. It's in the words, you see. You're making the same chords. Some blues you play, you could turn right around . . . you can play a church song on that same blues music you had over there."[37] Thomas did, however, draw a distinct line between the overall philosophies of religious songs and blues, and felt it was wrong for a singer to "cross" between the two styles: "If I go to church and pray and sing church songs, and then time I leave there go to a jook house and play blues, I think that's where the wrongness comes in. You ain't supposed to cross them that way. I'd be afraid to do that, 'cause something bad can happen to you. That's what you call going too far wrong. You can't serve the Lord and the Devil too."[38] (At a 1989 concert in Greenville, Mississippi, attended by the author, Thomas was reluctant to perform until he was assured that, while the venue was church property, it was used only as an auditorium and was not a consecrated area used for religious services.)

A few singers simply ignore any division between sacred and secular, "crossing" at will. Solomon Burke, one of the top soul stars of the 1960s, is also founder of the House of God for All People in Los Angeles. Otis Clay has had gospel and soul albums on the market simultaneously. Rock 'n' roll star Little Richard Penniman has many times announced his intention to quit secular music and devote himself to the church: "I used to sing rock 'n' roll; now I'm standing on the rock and my name is on the roll." Each retirement has been followed by a comeback, but Penniman has recorded a number of religious albums. Texas blues pianist and disc jockey Dr. Hepcat was also Lavada Durst, associate minister at the Olivet Baptist Church in Austin and, he said, uncredited author of the Bells of Joy's "Let's Talk About Jesus," which reached *Billboard*'s secular "race" hit parade in 1952. He believed he was never acknowledged as the song's writer "because I was in the blues business, and people might not like it."[39] Durst, who died in 1995, saw no conflict between his two musical talents. "There's no harm when you want to hit a blues tune. As long as it's not harming my neighbor or hurting anybody, I can play blues all night long. Blues is a way of expressing your inner feeling, a soothing balm to your feelings. . . ."[40]

Al Green travels the United States and Europe singing the soul music with which he made his name in the 1970s. He does not keep his travels secret, but in Memphis, his hometown, he's Rev. Al Green, pastor of the Full Gospel Tabernacle, which he founded in 1976. His double life doesn't meet with universal approval. "He goes to California or Texas and sings that stuff," one Memphis gospel veteran said disdainfully. "He doesn't do it around here where his church is." But a member of his congregation defends him—"The pastor told us he has to make a living."[41] (Green has very occasionally sung soul music in Memphis.)

Sometimes, the two lives overlap. During a service attended by the author, Green addressed the congregation as "ladies and gentlemen"—then, flustered, stopped briefly. The phrase is not used in churches. On a "live" recording made in 1981, Solomon Burke reversed the faux pas. Singing in a Washington, D.C. nightclub, he inserted a heartfelt "Thank you, Jesus" between lines of the soul standard "What Am I Living For?"[42] The phrase is not one used in nightclubs.

Al Green, Solomon Burke and Lavada Durst are all better known for their secular music. Rev. Jessy Dixon is best known for gospel singing and his work with the Chicago Community Choir, but he spent eight years, from 1972 until 1980, touring as back-up singer and break-out soloist with singer Paul Simon, and has worked as coperformer, songwriter, or back-up singer for a number of other mainstream pop artists. This work spread his name to a wider constituency, and, by 1990, he was performing gospel music in countries as diverse as Poland, England, Russia, Sweden, and New Zealand—and hardly ever to African-American audiences in the United States. He has a ready answer to other gospel singers who would tell him he cannot be a star in two worlds:

> Usually, people who tell you that have never had the opportunity to do the other. And so they become very adamant about it. They say, "You must do one or the other"—but no one's ever asked them to do the other. They're not the ones called to do it. I have had many experiences with singers who've said to me, "You shouldn't do it"—then when they've had the opportunity to do it, they haven't been able to. They've been so fearful and so ill at ease singing to a secular audience. . . . But God's smart. God knows what he's doing. If you're called to do something, God prepares you to do it. He will not send you out any place unprepared. When I got the call to go with Paul Simon, we were all in God's plan. Paul Simon was being used to help further the gospel. I was too. And we knew it.[43]

Solomon Burke and Al Green would probably approve of this rationale. Robert Wilkins would not. Neither would Huebert Crawford or James Holley.

# HUEBERT CRAWFORD

*"I'm much satisfied . . ."*

At fifty-four, Huebert Crawford has the raffish good looks—not unlike an amiable Chuck Berry—and the style of the archetypal middle-aged playboy. Divorced for thirteen years, he lives in a modern and painstakingly neat apartment on the south side of Memphis. His collection of handguns is in his bedroom; the latest in a series of powerful motorcycles he has owned is in a rented storage space a few blocks away from his home. He is a musician, and has played his guitar behind many of the big names in soul music— Joe Tex, Curtis Mayfield, and Isaac Hayes are just some of the names on his musical

*Huebert Crawford at his home in Memphis.*

resumé. But despite the trappings, Huebert Crawford stepped out of the fast lane in 1975. For two years he stayed away from music, working only at his regular day job. Then he got the musical offer he'd always wanted.

"I WAS walking down the street one day and a guy named Fred Howard, the baritone singer of the Spirit of Memphis, says, 'Man are you still playing guitar?' I said, 'Well, sometime.' He says, 'We need a guitar player with the Spirit of Memphis.' All my life I wanted to get with the Spirit of Memphis. He said, 'Well, be at rehearsal on Saturday.' At that time I used to drink beer. That Saturday, I had two six-packs and I forgot all about the rehearsal. The following Saturday he contacted me again. I put the beer down. Just like that. Just stopped. I went to the rehearsal and talked to them. They wanted to know if I could play. So I played a few things for 'em and . . . see, once you're a Spirit of Memphis guitar player, you've got to sound like the rest. You have to have the same Spirit of Memphis sound. And this guy named Clarence [Clarence

Smith, guitarist and part-time singer with the group from the late 1950s]
was the guitar player, and I had to sit down and listen to what he was
doing. He would play chords, and I would play those chords. When
I ran across one and I didn't know exactly what it was, I would call
[bass singer, manager and singing trainer] Earl Malone on the phone.
He would sing the sound, and I would make it into the phone with the
guitar. And that's the way I learned to play with the Spirit of Memphis. I
tried to play identical to what Clarence was doing, and I picked up some
from Howard Carroll, guitar player for the Dixie Hummingbirds—he's
one of the greatest. And I put it all together with the little stuff I got . . .
it was really hard to play with the Spirit of Memphis because they sing
so many chords. We have had guys come in when we need a musician
and they can't play the chords.

"I was born and reared in Eads, Tennessee. When I was four or five,
I learned to drive a car so I could take my grandmother to church. It
was a '38 Chevrolet. They had these big old thick covers, and I would
put them on the seat of the car to raise it up, and I would take my
grandmother to church every Sunday. To change gear or stop, I'd slide
down off the seat so I could reach the pedals. Slide off the seat, down,
just holding the steering wheel at the top, and I could see through the
steering wheel and stop the car. And I had to go all the way round
the back roads—the church was right down the road, but I'd go all the
way round the back roads to dodge the policemen. Everybody used to
stand outside the church, just waiting til I got there. To see this little
kid driving the car. I was raised up in church. And when I got up, I
couldn't wait to stay away because I'd never seen a thing in the world.
Then when I went out in the world, I found out it wasn't anything out
there. So I went back to church. That is the best place to be. And all my
friends, associates or whatever that's of the world now . . . we might be
the same age, or some of them are much younger than I am. But they
look much older. See, you can't keep up with this world out here. You
cannot do it. That's why I say I'm much satisfied being like I am. I'm
much satisfied.

"I started in music when I was about four or five years old. The
Spirit of Memphis used to come out and do programs at our church.
And when they finished, my grandmother would take them home and
cook for them. They would do a rehearsal in the house, and I'd be in
the next room listening and trying to catch the voices. That's where I
started. When we were kids, we just wanted to sing. So we got a group

together and we sang Spirit of Memphis songs. I started playing guitar after we moved to Memphis, when I was in sixth grade [aged 12 or 13]. I bought me a guitar. It cost twelve dollars. I would go on the school ground, down the bottom, and I would play this little guitar. And the guys would come by and laugh at me. I had a friend, and he said, 'You won't never play that thing.' I said, 'One day, you're gonna pay to see me.' It was fun to them, but it gave me the ego to go on. When I started playing it, I took all the strings off but the top two. I could play them, the others were in the way. But as I learned a little bit, I'd add a string until I had all six of 'em back on it. And you know, one Friday night I was playing the Flamingo Room—that was the biggest club in Memphis— and I saw this guy standing in line to get a ticket. I just walked up to him and said, 'See. I said you'd pay one day to see me.' "

*As he became more proficient on the guitar, Crawford joined a local gospel group, the Melodyaires, and also started playing rhythm and blues. But his ambition was to join the Spirit of Memphis. "One day, I said, 'I'm going to the Spirit of Memphis rehearsal.' I went out to where they were rehearsing and walked up on the porch. And they were sounding so good, and the guitar player was sounding good—and I turned around and left! That was in 1958."* At the time, he was newly married, to Carrie, with a baby son. He was working as a truck driver and honing his guitar skills with his gospel group and with a fledgling R&B group—"we didn't even have a name." His musical path for more than fifteen years was charted when the firm he was working for went out of business, leaving him jobless—and the R&B group landed a paying engagement.

"I didn't have any money, and I was wondering how I was going to buy groceries. Then I played that Friday night and they paid me eight dollars. Eight dollars! I said, 'Is all this mine?' The bandleader says, 'Yes. What's wrong with it?' I said, 'Not a thing.' Next day, I went and bought enough groceries for a family of three. With eight dollars, and had about seventy-five cents left. So the guys with the gospel group say, 'Man, are you coming to rehearsal?' I said, 'No, they want me to play Saturday night.' Saturday night they paid me ten dollars. That did it. I stayed out there for years and years. I started playing with the big bands, then they started calling me in the studio to record. And I started playing sessions, and a session then paid you $156. I was a millionaire! Then I joined a band called Freddy Woods and the Thrillers. They paid fifteen dollars a night. We started traveling, and then we ran into a gig with Bill Black's Combo. . . . And we played behind Curtis Mayfield and the Impressions and all these guys. . . ."

*The Thrillers, led by keyboard player Freddy Woods, became proficient enough to work as backing band for a number of soul stars when they visited Memphis. Artists Crawford backed include Jimmy Hughes, Joe Tex, Smokey Robinson, and Muddy Waters. It was hard work; at one stage he was working six days a week as a truck driver and playing music seven nights a week.*

"That was in the sixties, before we had this integration thing, and when the band got through playing, we had to sit in the kitchen. You couldn't mingle with the people or anything. [In the 1950s and 1960s, Memphis and West Memphis had a number of white-only clubs which hired black bands.] Well, we were working three nights a week at one club, and we used to just leave our instruments on the stage when we got through. But one Saturday night we got there to play and all the instruments were gone. I mean, they stole everything. We came to find out it was the club owner. We didn't have money to buy things, so they [the club] said 'Well, we'll buy y'all this and buy you this.' And then we had to repay them. So this guy [the club owner], he paid for my instrument and the bass player's instrument. One night we were playing at another place over on 78 Highway. That man was out there drinking and dancing and I noticed he kept looking up at the bandstand. I think I owed him about fourteen dollars. So he got drunk enough to come up on the bandstand. And he walked up there and he stopped the band. I won't say what he called me, but he said, 'You gonna pay me my money for that instrument.' Wasn't but fourteen dollars, I was going to give it to him as soon as I got through playing. So he said it again, and this time the drummer said, 'Why don't you get off the bandstand, and we can take up all this stuff after we get through. We're gonna pay you the balance of your money.' Oh! He called him that name too! I pulled my guitar off and set it down, and I laid one on him, right there. Integration or no integration! I laid him out. And the drummer says, 'Huebert! You hit that white man!' I said, 'That's not the worst of it.' I'm stomping him . . . he was, like, 'please don't hit me no more.' I just beat the stuffing out of him, right there on that bandstand. Later, he came back to me and said, 'I was drunk.' I said, 'No, you had just enough in you for me to find you out.' And I said, 'I'm going to have you investigated. You got my instrument in the first place.' And boy, from there he said, 'You don't owe me a thing!' And we kept those instruments forever.

"Now one guy . . . I really wanted to join his band so bad 'til I sat down one day and wrote to his enterprise—I never heard from 'em— was James Brown. I wanted to play with him, because what his band was playing, I could play all of it. Every time I went out to perform, I would do his songs. I would sit down and just study him. His steps, I had them. And I did something once I would never do again; I didn't have sense enough to realize what I was doing. We went away down in Mississippi to do a show and I posed as James Brown. They had heard him, but they'd never seen him. And the way it happened . . . James Brown's name was not on the poster, but when they called me on the stage, I came out doing this dance and I started singing, and they just *gave* me the name. They thought I was James Brown. And I just said, 'Well, oh, thank you, OK.' But I coulda got in trouble. So I did it, then we hurry up and got out of there."

*Crawford left the Thrillers to join songwriter and musician Gene "Bow-legs" Miller's band after turning down an approach from young Memphis soul band the Bar-Kays (which went on to become the "road" backing band for soul star Otis Redding; all members but one died in the 1967 plane crash which also killed Redding). Around the mid-1960s, he formed his own band, Huebert Crawford and the Soul Setters, with, at one stage, his son Huebert, Jr., on drums. "He's a professional drummer now, and he was playing professionally at ten—with me, in my band. He was so little we had to smuggle him into nightclubs and sneak him out." The Soul Setters worked extensively around Memphis and throughout the Midsouth, and made a 45 rpm single record on the local J'Ace label, although it seems the disc did not appear until after the band broke up.[1] That happened in 1975. Part of the reason for the breakup was simply that Crawford was tired of spending his days on the road in a truck and his nights on the road in a band. But he was also experiencing a growing spiritual unease, which he summarizes as "I just wasn't satisfied."*

"I never was completely away from church. I would go some time, or go to hear quartet singing, but never really just to membership with the church. But I was back in church before I went with the Spirit of Memphis. When I say I wasn't satisfied, what I mean . . . a lot of people call it luck, I call it blessings. Blessings come after blessings. And I was being blessed, and I was throwing it away by going ahead playing of the world. There's a certain thing I call 'of the world.' If you're 'of the world,' you're doing everything the world is doing. But if you're not of the world, you are staying back, and your blessing is back here. And you stay humble. So I just like to stay humble and . . . I'm satisfied now with gospel. And in gospel, you don't look for a lot of money. In rock, you do.

"We don't make that much money in the Spirit of Memphis. We cover our costs, but we don't make that much. And the little money we make, we keep it in a treasury. So if we need something, we can take it out. We don't give it to each individual. We don't make enough to do that. That's the difference between gospel and rock. Guys in rock, they're not gonna take their instruments out until they get paid. But gospel is all about love. Most everybody you see in gospel . . . some have a bad attitude, but most of them are living it. I know we are, we try to. These rock groups, they're just out there for the money, that's it. The gospel people know there's not a lot of money in it. But there are some groups that don't ever go to church until they get ready to sing. They don't have a church home. A church home is a membership where you go when you are not singing. You have a special church you go to. Everybody in the Spirit of Memphis has a church home. But these groups that don't, well, they might as well be out there . . . they're the type of people that couldn't make it in rock. So they sing gospel, because nobody wants 'em in rock. And a lot of the musicians playing for these groups would rather be playing rock. But they can't. See, if you're playing gospel music and that's all you ever played, you can't play blues. But if you start in blues, you can play anything. That's why I started in blues. Then I started playing gospel. I like gospel music better, but I still listen to blues and I take my guitar sometimes and play a little of it, just to stay up on it.

"Gospel music means to me . . . you can have a feeling inside of you. People call it the spirit. You can feel the spirit playing blues. You get a certain feel inside of you. But gospel music means something has happened to you and you are really testifying about it and it comes direct from the heart and it brings tears from your eyes. It's really a testimony. Blues is a different feel. Anybody can have the blues. You can get up one morning and don't have any money and you got a bill due today—you got the blues. A little baby can be in the cradle and can't get the milk, well, he's got the blues. The blues is just real words of things that have happened to you. And gospel is the same. Gospel songs are supposed to come from the Bible. But a song really comes from whatever is happening in the world. Just like you can take any rock 'n' roll song and turn it into a gospel song by taking out 'baby' and putting in 'Jesus.' People dance to this music on a Saturday night, then they shout to it on a Sunday. It's the same music. But what I look at is *where* you are playing it. I sing from my heart. I don't care if people don't even applaud, I really don't. Because I'll be the one feeling what I'm doing. If you feel it first, they will feel it. In gospel, it's heart to heart. You can get up and sing a song, and a person sitting out in the audience that really feels your singing is going to reach heart to heart."

*As minister of music for the Spirit of Memphis, Crawford is responsible for the instrumental accompaniments to the group's songs. Soon after he joined the group, then-manager Earl Malone appointed him his "assistant," and suggested Crawford should succeed him as manager. "But I told him, 'I'm not a big talker like Melvin. Let Melvin have it, he can do a better job.' So he started training Melvin, and now Melvin's the manager." Mosley and Crawford work closely together, and the line between their designated roles sometimes becomes blurred, with Crawford helping shape the singing parts and Mosley working with the musicians. "We fall out sometimes," says Crawford, "but we don't go to the extreme." In the mid-1980s, however, they did go to an extreme, with an argument that led to Crawford quitting the group for two years, during which time he made another secular recording.*

"I wanted to play keyboards. Melvin said, 'We don't need keyboards.' I said, 'We need to change the sound. The group has been going all this time with the guitar, we need keyboards.' He said, 'Who's gonna play 'em?' I said, 'I am.' He said, 'You can't play 'em.' I said, 'I can learn.' I bought a little keyboard with miniature keys and took it to rehearsal one night. He said, 'Play it.' I played it, even though I couldn't play in but one key, and that was E♭. Melvin said, 'We don't need a keyboard. We're not gonna use a keyboard. It doesn't fit.' I say, 'OK.' Bang. I quit. They didn't ever vote me out—you know, we're voted in and out. I quit the group. I sat down with the keyboard and my guitar and worked out the chords from the guitar to the keyboard until I learned to play it. Then I took that keyboard and went and recorded a single. I just got mad and decided to show them. I went into the studio and wrote the stuff out, got two more musicians and cut it. It's called 'King Rider Boogie.'[2] The

King Riders were a motorcycle club—it wasn't no gang, it was a club.[3] I was with it for a long time. I've been into motorcycles for a long time. I still have one; I used to have four.

"So I was out of the group, and I said, 'Well, I'll go and do this and do that . . .' you know, and just go and start making some more money. But I wasn't satisfied, so I dropped it and came back to the group. I went back to the group with my keyboards. I walked into the rehearsal and said, 'Here I am, I'm back, whether you like it or not, Melvin. This is my group, I'm back with keyboards and I'm gonna play 'em—forget the guitar.' And that was it. Now, he doesn't want me to play guitar. I've been back ever since. And I'm not gonna leave again. Because now, we've got a law says that if you quit, you don't come back. We got one guy, Jack Stepter, he quit. Now he wants to come back, but they're not going to accept him. And I can see why. He didn't have any reason to quit. But I quit to try to advance. And when I came back, I advanced the group. I had come to a standstill—if they didn't want me to play keyboards, I'd never learn to play. So I had to quit."

*Crawford's keyboards were quickly integrated into the Spirit of Memphis sound, and he played them on an album recorded soon after his return to the group.[4] Although it was made in 1987, the album is the group's most recent release, and Crawford would like to do more recording. But he does not want the Spirit to have to pay for it, and he is cynical about the chances of getting radio exposure in the group's hometown.*

"Memphis is the type of town where radio stations don't do anything. They just sit and stare at each other. Our records are being played somewhere else, but we very seldom hear them here. I think it's mostly a payola thing. 'You pay me this and I'll play it.' They got a lot of hit records down at these radio stations laying up on top shelves, saying 'don't play.' Why? It sounds good. Why don't they play it? Because they didn't get enough money. Even the gospel stations. You got to deliver 'em some money. You can tell who's paying what, because they play it all the time. Any time you cut a record and you promote this record and put money behind it, it's gonna play. And it'll catch, it'll turn out to be a hit. Because you can't cut a hit record. Money makes a hit. You got to pay the DJ, take him to dinner and this type of thing. And we just don't do it. We don't do it because . . . if you got a record company that's gonna stand with you, it's up to them to promote you. It's not for you to go out there and do it. A lot of guys cut records and then they have to walk around and sell 'em. I don't like that. They'll pay so much, like twenty-five hundred dollars, to record a record. But when they get it done, there's no record company gonna promote them. They have to do their own thing—get out there and sell your record. But the Spirit of Memphis, we go with a regular company. [The group does not have a recording contract, although Crawford regards it as being "with" the University of Memphis's High Water label, which released an album in 1984.[5]]

*Crawford's "church home" is the small Lemoyne Truevine Missionary Baptist church, pastored by Rev. Jimmy Lee King, a former quartet singer whose son, James King, was one of the Bar-Kays who died with Otis Redding. Crawford is the church organist, the drummer is Robert Stewart, also in the Spirit of Memphis, and the guitarist is former and would-be Spirit member Jack Stepter. Crawford's role in the church's music appears to have been a factor in his decision to rejoin the Spirit of Memphis. While he acknowledges that some people can, in apparently clear conscience, combine performing sacred and secular music, he is not one of them.*

"I won't do it. I won't do it. Straddling the fence, we call it. You're doing one thing over here for the Devil, and one thing for the Lord on the other side. If someone can do it . . . then he's got to give an account of himself. I tried it and it didn't work. I would play in church on Sunday, and on Saturday night I'd been playing a nightclub. And man, I couldn't function right. I knew it was wrong. I had to stop. I had to make a choice. I had to say, 'Well, either I do this or I do that.' And I said, 'But the money's over here.' Then I thought, 'Money's not everything.' So I came back and I just stick with what I'm doing. I'd rather stay like I am. I've had a lot of offers, like . . . I can do it. I'm qualified. But I just don't do it. I think you should choose one and just stick with it.

"When you get into [a church] service, well, it's something, it's a feeling. And God can put something on you. If somebody's shouting from the heart and the spirit is on them, they can fall over and never get hurt. We were singing down in Mississippi one night and it was really cold. They had this big old heater lit, and a lady knocked that heater over. She didn't get burned nowhere. There was a girl [a friend of Crawford's] who was driving one night and she went to make a left turn. A tractor-trailer ran over her. Running top speed. Spun her car round and round. The truck went off in a ditch. I started right for her and man . . . out of all four doors on that car, there wasn't but one you could open. She didn't get a scar. Not one scratch! She was a good church member. Suppose she had been of the world. Tractor-trailer? At full force?"

*An accident in 1988 forced Crawford to give up his truck driving job. Since then, his main occupations have been church, the Spirit of Memphis and working in a voluntary program with the Memphis sheriff's department. "It's to do with the older people. A lot of guys are in it, and we go and check on them, see if they're all right and try to keep protection around them."*

"When I had my accident, I fell off a truck at work. I fell about fifteen feet on to concrete. I broke this [left] wrist in four places. If my head hadda hit the concrete, I would have splattered my brains. But my body's messed up for life now. I have to wear a back brace. I never will be able to play guitar like I was playing, because sometimes this wrist will lock up on me. And my fingers and my legs, they lock up. I guess we're all going to have some kind of thing we won't be happy with. But as far as happiness . . . I get by on being happy every day. I'm happy—in a way. But in a way I'm not. Because sometimes it seems as though there's part of me closing in on me. . . . But I guess I am happy. I get the short end sometimes, but I just get on my knees and pray for the one that gave it to me. They wonder, how do I make it? I steady go on, I just steady go on. You've got to be careful the way you treat people, because everybody, I don't care what color, they're still people. And I think the same of everybody. They say, 'Don't let the sun go down on you with hatred in your heart for your brother.' Don't care what color, it's still your brother or your sister. And when I get in my bed each night, I haven't done anybody wrong. But most times I get in there, somebody's done me wrong. I don't care. I just go right on."

# JAMES HOLLEY

*"I came off the road . . ."*

The Full Gospel Tabernacle, off Elvis Presley Boulevard on suburban Hale Street, is
a Memphis tourist attraction. The city has
other religious attractions, mainly related
to the Church of God in Christ, which
has its world headquarters and some of its
oldest churches there. But the Full Gospel
Tabernacle's focal point is its pastor, Rev.
Al Green—still more widely known outside his hometown for his soul music than
for his church or his later gospel recordings. Every Sunday, the congregation includes a sprinkling of visitors, American
and foreign, present not for the worship
but to see the man who recorded "Let's
Stay Together," "I'm Still in Love With You" and other hits in the 1970s.
The regular worshippers easily identify the tourists and generally ignore
them—as does the pastor, who after Sunday services protects the passage
leading to his office with a steel grille and two ushers to guard it. The Full
Gospel Tabernacle is a large single-story building, much of it given over
to offices and activity rooms. The sanctuary, at the front of the building,
is semicircular, with natural wood pews arranged in four banks, wide at
the back and narrow at the front near the altar and pulpit. At the back
of one of the pew blocks is a professional sound-mixing desk. Beside the
choir stalls, on the pastor's left, is the band area, dominated by a grand
piano, a Hammond organ, and a drum kit.

*James Holley sings at his home
in Memphis.*

The choir and Rev. Green are accompanied in song by a five-piece
band, made up of piano, organ, guitar, bass guitar, and drums. It's
a polished and professional-sounding unit that can lay down a solid
modern sound and cope quickly on the occasions when the pastor
launches into song without telling anyone the title or the key. Prominent
in the band is the guitarist, a stocky barrel-chested man in a blue suit

who plays sitting down, but often leaps to his feet in religious fervor during songs and sermons. His name is James Holley. At forty-four, he's two years younger than his pastor. Like Green, he is a former soul musician who was raised in a religious family and returned to the faith after a spiritual upheaval. Unlike Green, he has renounced all contact with secular music, a decision which has taken him from a life of glamour in which he performed with many of Memphis's most popular singers to the tough manual labor of rigging for a crane company. He is not an educated man, but he talks fluently and candidly, stumbling only when overcome by the depth of his religious feeling. He and his family live in a small suburban house; it's rented and is a bit run-down, but "at least it's a roof over our heads." His car, a big 1970s Oldsmobile, is parked outside. He bought it for seven hundred dollars while he was in Tucson, Arizona, after God came to him in a dream and told him where to find it.

"I WAS born down there in New Albany, Mississippi, in 1948. There's eleven children in my family. We didn't go to church that much, but Mama put it in us to fear God. She was some kind of special woman. She always told us about Jesus and she always got us and put us on our knees and made us believe there is a God—and you know, there *is* a God. Mama never worried about nothing. She would always go on her knees and ask God. And things would happen when she'd go on her knees and put us children on our knees and call upon Jesus. Way back in the fifties, we used to clear the cottonfields, chop the cotton, and we would sing. Sometimes mama and them would get so happy out there in the cottonfield that the Spirit of God would come in and some of the ladies would start crying and falling out. They were singing some old songs, sorta like spiritual songs.

"I knew I was going to be a guitar player, because it was in me back then. My daddy was a guitar player. His name was Ben Holley. He died when I was real young. But it seems like I can remember a time when we were in church and Daddy used to play his guitar. He played with two of our kin, Uncle Bill and Aunt Lucy Mae. They were playing violins. And they could play real good. They played in church, then they would play around the house and they would play blues and stuff. They were great. When we would come back from the cottonfields, we would have a little time around the house in the evening. And I would take some wire and some nails and an old brick—we didn't have a hammer. I'd nail about six, maybe eight nails upside the house, then I'd take my wire and wrap it around those nails. I'd tighten it up and I would take my little thumb and play it to make sounds. The first guitar I had . . . a fellow named Robert Evans used to come over. He had a box [acoustic] guitar. He didn't know how to play, but we started to learning. And then my sister got married, to a fellow named George Gates. And George was a great guitar player. He'd sit down and show us things. And there was another fellow, named Troy Starch. Troy was playing guitar, he could play a little bit better than I could. But I didn't let that stop me. I knew that if I kept on trying . . . if you keep on trying, you'll learn how to play or learn how to be whatever. And I used to play Mr. Leon Pinson's guitar. He used to be at our elementary school, singing some of those old . . . I didn't know the names of the songs he was singing. And sometimes he'd get tired of playing, so he would put his guitar in my arms. I'd play chords and things, and he used to tell me that I was coming on pretty good.

"I wasn't playing too much around New Albany, but then we moved to Blue Mountain, and that's where I started to playing. I started to know my G chords and my A chords and the minors and the majors, the sevenths, the sixths. . . . I dropped out of school in the fifth grade. I was about sixteen—a sixteen-year-old in the fifth grade! [Fifth grade-children are usually about eleven years old.] I think I could've done better in school if I just woulda left the guitar alone. But my heart would burn for the guitar, for the chords and things that I wanted to learn. Music was so soothing and it was so beautiful, so sweet, that I would cry at night. I just wanted to learn. I prayed a whole lot, and I asked God, I said, 'Lord, let me learn how to play the guitar. I want to play a guitar.'"

*James Holley's brother, Sonny, was also musical—he is a recording artist still active in Memphis—and when the family moved from Blue Mountain to the nearby larger town of Ripley, the brothers joined three other local musicians to form a band which performed at local functions and clubs. When he was "about eighteen or nineteen," Holley moved to Memphis—and into a new level of music. For three years, he didn't play anywhere, but as his confidence and skills grew, he started working with a variety of bands, eventually becoming one of the musicians working for the Hi record label and its influential producer, Willie Mitchell. Mitchell, a trumpet player and bandleader, had his first production success for Hi with a soul record by former gospel quartet singer O. V. Wright[1] in 1966, and over the next fifteen years produced artists ranging from Bobby "Blue" Bland to Al Green. In the process, he established Hi as a national label, and when in 1970 he was offered a job with Atlantic, Hi owner Joe Cuoghi moved quickly to protect his interests by making Mitchell his vice president. Months later, Cuoghi died of a heart attack, and Mitchell became head of the company.[2] The core of his studio band was the Hodges brothers—guitarist Tennie, bassist Leroy and keyboard player Charles—but outside this was a group of musicians not contracted to the studio but available to tour behind Hi artists, record demos and do other studio sessions as required. James Holley was a member of this group.*

"When I came to Memphis, I thought I wasn't good enough to play with the musicians here. So I practiced about three, maybe four years on my guitar. I just had to know it, because when you play with the musicians here, you have to know exactly your notes, you have to know your keys. There were some great musicians here. And I would go to church. I was playing with a gospel group, the Friendly Harmonizers, from out in Collierville. I was helping them out, playing guitar with them, and trying to play the other kind of music too. And I finally got with a group here in Memphis, a group named the Right Combination. I was playing with them, then on Sunday I would play my guitar in church behind the Friendly Harmonizers.

"At the time, I was working at Wonder Products. They made rocking horses. Yeah, we made rocking horses, we made football pads and things, and I learned how to run those machines. We'd take a bag of plastic and pour it in a mold to form what it was going to be. But I quit the job because the music was still messing with me. I just wanted to be a professional guitar player. Then I got with a band called the Trickers. That was in the late sixties. I played with them for a while, and they changed their name to the Thumping Gizzard band. I got good experience with that band. We played disco and rock songs, and we started backing people up. After that, I played with a group called High Voltage. Willie Mitchell's stepson, Horace Turner, was the drummer. We played together about a year, maybe a little bit better than a year. We got a whole lot of clubs, we made maybe thirty, forty dollars a man a night and we played maybe two nights a week. That was a little money back then. I didn't have a job, and that sixty, maybe eighty dollars a week, that was it. The group finally broke up, and that's when I got with Hi Recording Studio Band. That's when I started doing the big stuff. Things didn't start to really booming until I got with Willie Mitchell's band. It was more professional, you had great musicians. Willie didn't play out with us, but he would play with us in the studio to show us exactly how it's supposed to go. He would teach us, like, Ann Peebles stuff, Syl Johnson's stuff and O. V. Wright's stuff. Al Green had his own band. I didn't get a chance to play with Al until I went to church with him.

"I wasn't involved with the church at this time. But I was still praying. See, Mama always told us to pray, and to believe God with all our hearts. Maybe I wasn't going to church. I don't know, is that right or wrong? But the church is in your heart anyway. And when I would go out and play in clubs or wherever, I would always pray. And I guess that's why I was so relaxed when I got up there. I didn't have to have drugs, alcohol . . . I just believed God, and God was always with me."

*Holley also rejoined Thumping Gizzard, which worked clubs around Memphis and backed solo artists. Between this and his work for Hi, he had well and truly fulfilled his ambition of becoming a top professional guitarist. He toured behind many soul artists, including Smokey Robinson, Syl Johnson and Ann Peebles, and played on recording sessions for a number of lesser known soul and pop performers. They were heady days for the young guitarist from New Albany—and they ended dramatically when he was arrested, tried and sentenced to three years in jail.*

"On the paper, it said assault and battery, intent to rape. What happened was . . . I was staying with this woman, and she had one daughter who always used to play with me too much. I used to tell her, 'You stop playing with me like that.' But she kept it up. She wouldn't pay no attention to what I was saying, and she . . . she really came on to me real tough. And I made love to her and . . . she was young. She was thirteen. And I got some time. That was about the year of '77. . . . The incident happened about the last of '76, and I got locked up in '77. On a Sunday. I went to jail on a Sunday. I always thought they locked you up during the week. Now since I've repented, and believing on the name of Jesus, I know it was wrong—I knew it was wrong when I done it. But that was in the Devil's way, and I'm looking to the Lord now. Because when I got locked up . . . I don't know, was I feeling self-pity when I got locked up? . . . but I got to calling on the name of the Lord. And the power of God came in my life that night, and he filled me with the Holy Ghost. I've looked down on myself for what happened in the past, but the Lord does forgive me for all of those things that I did. I cleaned my life back up, I'm in the church and I'm a minister in the church. And God is doing some great things in my life. We started a group in the place, a gospel group called the Holy Light. The warden even trusted us to go out to other places, to the federal places and to different churches, and sing. That lasted for about a year, then when everybody got out we went our separate ways.

"I got out in the year of '79. And I went back on the road with Ann Peebles. Played with her one year. In '80. Then we were in a hotel—I think we were down in Florida somewhere—and God was reminding me of what I had done in jail. We had to play that night, and I went in the hotel and laid on the bed. The Bible was laying there and the pages just flipped over. Wasn't nobody in there. Just flipped over. And I went over and I looked at it, and it was on a chapter of Matthew. I read all of Matthew, the whole book of Matthew. And the power of God came in and touched me back over again. And I cried, I wept, I wept, I repented back over. And I came off the road. That was in '80. In '81 the Lord called me to be a preacher. He showed me that I was a minister. I had a vision and I saw the Lord in Heaven, walking on the clouds. He had on a white robe, had his arms open and I was laying down on the clouds. And he said, 'Arise! You're a preacher.' When he said that, it just ran all through me. A cold chill came all over me and I started speaking in tongues, just like I did that night when I got locked up. And I know God saved me and filled me with the Holy Ghost. I got up and I was crying . . . I mean I had joy, but I was crying. The way I was thinking was that I didn't have enough education to preach the gospel. But sometimes it don't take education—you just know something. You know God has saved you, that the spirit of God is in your life.

"I started out in the Church of God in Christ, over in north Memphis, True Vine Church of God in Christ. I was a minister, but . . . back then, Church of God in Christ preachers, they wouldn't hardly put you up [to preach]. They think you ain't got enough knowledge, so they set you back for a long time. But I believe if God is in you, you've got something and folks shouldn't hold you back like that. I think they should put you up, because if God lives in you, you've always got something to say. Because he's gonna speak for you. And I think I've been set back a whole lot because I'm a musician. But I'm a preacher too. You got to respect me as a preacher too because . . . I know I play my guitar, but

I'm a preacher. Some preachers and elders think, 'you play your guitar and I'll do the preaching'. But that burning desire is in me to preach. I want to preach any time, I don't care if it's out on the street. That's the way God has given it to me."

*In 1981, he married Clara, daughter of his pastor at True Vine COGIC. They have four children, James, ten, Anthony, nine, Tony, seven and Kim, six (Holley also has two teenage children from previous relationships). The early years of their marriage were difficult. Holley had renounced secular music, but work outside the music world was hard to find, especially for someone whose only job skills were musical.*

"I wasn't playing my guitar much, just in the church. In the Church of God in Christ, they feel you should do one thing. If you're on this side, on the Lord's side, you've got no business going over there and playing in the nightclub. If you're in the church, you can't go out and play a blues and make you some money. But I wonder sometimes, if you've got a gift of playing the other stuff, would that hurt you? I believe if that's a gift God has given you, God knows where your heart is. He knows your heart is not in the blues thing, you're just there to make some money and come back and take care of your family. You can work in a liquor store, selling liquor. But you don't have to drink it. I hear church folks say, 'I wouldn't work in a liquor store. That's the Devil's job.' I don't know if they're right or I'm right. But what if you've got a family and they need food and stuff and that's the only job you can get? Where you gon' work? I got locked up for about three days for not paying child support. But there was no work. It's not that you don't want to pay it. You can't pay it if you've got no work. I think the judges should be tried for taking people and locking them up 'cause they don't have a job."

*Through the 1980s, he worked where he could. He eventually found a steady job as a handyman for a white Presbyterian church, doing everything from gardening to preparing the church for weddings. His father-in-law died, and his church went into decline, so Holley joined another, becoming assistant pastor and minister of music. He stayed there until around 1989, when he left to work with another preacher, Elder Donnell Johnson, who spent much of his time proselytizing on the streets. In 1991, he joined a group headed by a white evangelist and took Clara and their family to Tucson, Arizona, to evangelize. They were away only a few months when Elder Johnson contacted Holley and asked him to return. The reunion was not a success.*

"I went back with him and stayed about three months and tried to hold out with him and tried to work with him. But I sensed it wasn't gonna . . . we love one another, but he's got his own ministry, and I got mine too. So we split up. And the drummer at Al Green's church . . . his name's George Williamson, and we played together just about all our lives. He used to beg me, 'James, come on over there, we ain't got no guitar player.' And finally I did. I came over there. That was in September of '91. And Al was smiling and waving at me, glad to see me. I hadn't seen Al . . . back in '76 was the last time I saw him. Al is a very great person, and I always loved him. I loved his singing. He was one of my idols, you know, back when I was . . . Jesus is my idol now. But when we were out doing that other stuff, Al was one of my idols. I used to sing a whole lotta Al's songs. Now I play at church . . . our choir rehearsal is on a Thursday, Friday night regular service and then Sunday regular service. And Al pays all the musicians seventy-five dollars a week. It's a little cheap, but I appreciate it. It's better than a lot of places. A whole lot of places don't want to give you anything at all. They let me preach sometimes on a Friday.

"I am an evangelist. God showed me that. He showed me my calling. I love being in church, but I love going out there and playing my guitar to the lost souls. We have to put ourselves out there. I think we're supposed to go to the lost sheep of the family. We're supposed to go get that lost sheep and bring him on in. I will go out on the street myself, my one guitar and a little microphone and I will sing and preach. That's real good to me. That's doing something. That's working in the kingdom. I was out in the street preaching, late at night, one, two o'clock at night, and a man told me, after I had prayed for him and he came to the Lord, he said he had been going to go and kill himself.

"To me, gospel music means a revival in my heart. Gospel music to me is something that is so touching it can prick anybody's heart. It can touch anyone, I don't care how hard your heart. Gospel music can break through. I've got songs of my own. I write songs. I have some songs that Pastor Green said he's gonna let me record. But that takes money, and I ain't got no money."

*Holley's songwriting is strongly influenced by the soul sound of Willie Mitchell and Al Green, with intricate melody lines and extensive sections of almost ad-libbed vocals. As he sits in his little kitchen playing and singing, he interrupts himself to describe how the song would be arranged with a full band. "I hear horns, I hear strings." "I'm singing the background part." "Now this is where the backing voices go . . . then you have some more way up high."*

"I'm gonna get a whole lot of voices to sing on this stuff. If I can get them, I want a hundred voices. I want 'em to sound like angels. I think I have some beautiful songs. The Lord blesses me to write those songs. And when I take them out, they touch folks, they really do. I want to go places, because everywhere I go, the spirit of God just reaches out and touches folks. You can see the tears. I want to be used by God. And God has shown me that just by the hearing of my music, people are gonna get saved and come to the Lord. God showed me that I'm gonna be preaching before big crowds of people and all I have to do is just say a couple of words in the name of Jesus and the anointing will be there, folks just gonna fall out. I've had dreams. I sure have. And I want these dreams to come true. I know they're gonna come true."

> I'm going to put my trust, trust in you, Lord
> That's what I'm gon', gonna do
> I'm going to put my trust, trust in you
> That's what I'm going to do
>
> If it means loving my brother
> Lord, that's what I'm gon', gonna do
> If it means treating my neighbors right
> That's what I'm gonna do

# EPILOGUE

It was a cool fall Sunday evening when I traveled to Tunica, Mississippi, for the anniversary of the Tunica Harmonizers. I'd heard the program advertised on a gospel radio station, with the added promise of "mystery guests from Chicago." The Pilgrim Jubilees, from Chicago, were somewhere in Mississippi, so maybe I would be in luck. I had never been in Tunica, although I had driven through its outskirts on Highway 61 several times. But a building called the Tunica Auditorium shouldn't be hard to find in a town of about fourteen hundred people. Up and down the main street. No sign of anything resembling an auditorium or a gospel program crowd. The only lights came from a videotape rental shop. At first, the two middle-aged men in the shop were nonplused. They knew of no Tunica Auditorium. Then one had a thought. "Is that a colored place?" he demanded, making one syllable of the adjective— "cuhled." I allowed that it might be. "Go on up there a way 'til you come to a church. There'll be someone hanging around outside. I guess they'll be able to tell you." His sudden lack of interest in me and my destination wrestled with his curiosity as to why I wanted to go there; lack of interest won.

Turn right at the church, go one block, turn left . . . the Tunica Auditorium is small, plain and rather down-at-heel. Inside, rows of metal folding chairs are lined on the bare concrete floor. About forty people are there, children chasing each other around the aisles, adults chatting as they wait for the music to start. The reverberation from the children's calls makes it obvious that the acoustics are going to be dreadful—and they are. The Harmonizers aren't rivals to the Mighty Clouds of Joy—although their young tenor lead could hold a place in any group—but they produce competent performances of some standards and some other songs which I don't recognize and presume are the group's own compositions. The rest of the artists are all seated in the audience, rising to sing a song or two when summoned by the Harmonizer emcee. They range from children to an elderly woman who sings unaccompanied. None is a professional or even semiprofessional singer. No order of appearance has been drawn up; sometimes the emcee simply asks, "Who's next?" and another person rises to sing. The atmosphere is of a family gathering where uncles, aunts, cousins, nephews, and nieces entertain each other with performances made no less enjoyable because they are familiar. The Pilgrim Jubilees never come—belated logic tells me a "name" group would not be camouflaged as "mystery guests." Perhaps the mysterious Chicagoans are the visiting friends or family of someone in the audience; it is never made clear. But as I drive away from the auditorium, I reflect that, while the bigger programs in Memphis may offer more polished and skillful performances, I have seen and heard in Tunica the heart of gospel music.

# SUGGESTED LISTENING

This section lists recordings by people featured in this book, and other related recordings, mainly of artists discussed in the chapter introductions. African-American gospel music is not always easy to find in mainstream record stores, but many larger cities in the United States have stores which specialize in it; outside of these, a developing interest by collectors has led specialty mail order companies to stock it. Record companies such as Air, Jewel, and Malaco/Savoy also supply direct. In the United States, secondhand record stores are a valuable source of recordings.

The listing is mainly of recordings which were still in print at the time of compilation, in late 1995. The change from vinyl to CD format has removed many gospel recordings from the market, and CD issues do not yet provide a comprehensive survey of all facets of the music—note the imbalance between vintage quartet recordings and those by choirs or preachers of the same era. Recordings by artists featured in the book are listed unless they have been out of print for some time and are effectively impossible to obtain. For other artists, the listing is confined to CDs—many reissuing analog recordings—with vinyl albums listed only if they contain material of particular significance not available on CD. Such albums are likely to have been deleted by their manufacturers, but may still be available through retail outlets. It is also worth noting that much gospel music, especially on cassette tape, is distributed only in limited areas and limited quantities. None of these issues is listed here, but readers able to seek out such recordings will find some gems among them.

All recordings listed are compact discs unless otherwise noted. If the issue is not American, the country of origin is given after the title, as is the format if it is not CD. Some issues may be available in other formats; many CDs are also available as cassette tapes. Much of the 1920s and 1930s material listed is on the Document label. These issues are produced in Austria, but are available elsewhere in Europe and in the United States. They contain the complete available output of the artists named unless otherwise specified.

## THE GOSPEL EVANGELISTS

### Elder Roma Wilson

**Arhoolie ARHCD-429,** *This Train.* Contains all six Joe Von Battle tracks and fourteen recorded in 1994. Two are with the congregation of Johnson's Chapel, Church of the Living God, in Aberdeen, and two are vocal duets with his wife.

**Global Village C-228,** *The Deep South Musical Roots Tour* (cassette tape). Six 1990 tracks, four with Rev. Leon Pinson. Rest of tape by the Birmingham Sunlights (a cappella quartet) and Lynn August and the Hot August Knights (zydeco).

### Rev. Leon Pinson

**Global Village C-228.** See Elder Roma Wilson.

### Boyd Rivers

**L+R 42.041** (anthology), *Country Gospel Rock* (Germany; vinyl), six tracks. 1980.

**L+R 42.030** (anthology), *Introduction to the Living Country Blues U.S. Series* (Germany; vinyl) one track. 1980.

### Others

**Brown, Rev. Pearly.** Rounder 2011, *It's a Mean Old World to Live In* (vinyl). 1975.

**Clayborn, Rev. Edward W.** Document DOCD-5155, *Rev. Edward W. Clayborn (1926–1928).*

**Davis, Gary.** Document DOCD-5060, *Complete Recorded Works, 1935–1949.*

————. Smithsonian/Folkways SF-40035, *Pure Religion and Bad Company.* 1957.

————. Original Blues Classics OBCCD-547, *Harlem Street Singer* (Germany). 1960 Bluesville recordings.

**Johnson, Willie.** Columbia C2K-52835, *The Complete Blind Willie Johnson* (2 CDs).

**Taggart, Joe.** Document DOCD-5153/4, *Blind Joe Taggart Vols. 1 and 2.* Vol. 2 also has tracks by Edward W. Clayborn and Gussie Nesbitt.

**Tharpe, Sister Rosetta.** Document DOCD-5334/5, *Vols. 1 and 2 (1938–44).*

**Various artists.** Columbia CK-46779, *Preachin' the Gospel: Holy Blues.* Willie Johnson, Washington Phillips, Joshua White, Gary Davis, Sister O. M. Terrell, and others.

———. Document DOCD-5054, *Storefront and Streetcorner Gospel (1927–1929).* Blind Mamie and A. C. Forehand, Luther Magby, Washington Phillips.

———. Document DOCD-5072, *Memphis Gospel.* Bessie Johnson, Lonnie McIntorsh, Elders McIntorsh and Edwards, Rev. Sister Mary Nelson.

———. Document DOCD-5101, *Guitar Evangelists.* Blind Benny Paris and Wife, Rev. I. B. Ware, Blind Willie Harris, Eddie Head and Family, Mother McCollum.

———. Document DOCD-5222, *Slide Guitar Gospel.* Rev. Utah Smith, Rev. Lonnie Farris.

———. Document DOCD-5300, *Sanctified Jug Bands.* Elder Richard Bryant, Rev. E. S. (Shy) Moore, Holy Ghost Sanctified Singers, Brother Williams Memphis Sanctified Singers.

———. Heritage HTCD-09, *Gospel Evangelists: God's Mighty Hand* (U.K.). Rev. Utah Smith, Sister O. M. Terrell, Willie Mae Williams, Elder R. Wilson and Family, and others.

**Wilkins, Rev. Robert.** Genes GCD-9902, *Remember Me.* In U.K. on Edsel EDCD-380. 1971.

**Williams, Connie.** Testament TCD-5024, *Philadelphia Street Singer.* 1961.

Q U A R T E T S   A N D   G R O U P S

Spirit of Memphis

**Abec ALP-7005**, *New Horizon* (vinyl).

**Gospel Jubilee RF-1404**, *When Mother's Gone* (Sweden; vinyl). 1949–1954 recordings, including a WDIA radio show.

**Gusto/King/Starday K-5020-X**, *Original Greatest Hits* (vinyl). 1949–1952 King recordings.

**High Water LP-1005**, *Traveling On with the Spirit of Memphis Quartet* (vinyl).

**Nasha 001**, *Lord Jesus* (vinyl and cassette tape). Includes early recordings.

NB: Only High Water LP-1005 was in print at time of publication; no Spirit of Memphis albums were available on CD.

Shaw Singers (Opal and J. W. Shaw)

**Messenger MLP-2001**, *Yesterday and Today* (vinyl).

Others

**Birmingham Jubilee Singers.** Document DOCD-5345/6, *Vols. 1 and 2 (1927–1930)*.

**Birmingham Sunlights.** Flying Fish FF-70588, *For Old Time's Sake*. Young a cappella group formed in 1979.

**Canton Spirituals.** Blackberry 1600, *Live in Memphis*. 1993 concert. See videotapes.

**Chosen Gospel Singers.** Specialty SPCD-7014-2, *The Lifeboat*. In U.K. as Ace CDCHD-414. 1952–1955; personnel includes Lou Rawls.

**Consolers.** Ace CDCHD-425, *Give Me My Flowers/Heart Warming Spirituals* (U.K.). Reissues two Nashboro albums, 1955–1963.

**Dixie Hummingbirds.** Gospel Jubilee RF-1405, *In the Storm Too Long* (Sweden; vinyl). 1939–1949.

————. Mobile Fidelity/MCA MFCD-771, *Live*. 1976 concert recordings.

————. MCA Special Products MCAD-22043, *The Best of . . .* 1950s.

**Fairfield Four.** Nashboro 4003, *Standing on the Rock*. In U.K. on Ace CDCHD-449. 1950–1953.

**Five Blind Boys of Alabama.** Elektra 7559-61441-2, *Deep River*. 1992.

————. Flyright FLYCD-946, *Five Blind Boys of Alabama* (U.K.). 1948–1951.

————. P-Vine PCD-1830/31, *The Complete Specialty Sessions* (Japan; 2 CDs). 1953–1957.

————. Specialty SPCD-7041-2, *The Sermon*. Mainly previously unissued Specialty tracks. In U.K. as Ace CDCHD-479.

**Five Blind Boys of Mississippi.** Mr R&B RBD-1402, *You Done What the Doctor Couldn't Do* (Sweden). 1948–1959.

————. Charly CPCD-8086, *Jesus Is a Rock* (U.K.). 1950s.

**Four Eagles.** Global Village C-227, *Traditional Gospel Singing From Alabama* (cassette tape). 1992.

**Golden Gate Quartet.** Columbia CK-47131, *Swing Down Chariot*. 1941–1950.

————. RCA Heritage 66023-2, *Travelin' Shoes*. 1937–1939.

**Gospelaires (of Dayton, Ohio).** Mobile Fidelity/MCA MFCD-763, *Bones in the Valley/Can I Get a Witness*. 1961, 1968 Peacock albums.

**Harmonizing Four.** Heritage HTCD-29, *Harmonizing Four* (U.K.). 1950–1955.

————. Charly CPCD-8112, *I Shall Not Be Moved* (U.K.). 1950s.

**Heavenly Gospel Singers.** Document DOCD-5452-55, *Heavenly Gospel Singers, Vols 1–4 (1935–41)*.

**Highway QCs.** Charly CPCD-8113, *Count Your Blessings* (U.K.). 1950s and 1960s.

**Jackson Southernaires.** Malaco MAL-6012, *Live and Anointed*. 1992 concert. See videotapes.

**Mighty Clouds of Joy.** MCA Special Products MCAD-2045 and MCAD-2050, *The Best of . . . Vols 1 & 2*. 1950s and 1960s.

————. Word 7019202608, *Pray For Me* (also on cassette tape ET-48547). 1990 concert.

**Norfolk Jazz/Jubilee Quartet.** Document DOCD-5381-5386, *Vols. 1–6 (1921–40)*.

**Paramount Singers** Arhoolie CD-382, *Work and Pray On*. 1990s recordings by a cappella group founded in the 1940s.

**Pilgrim Jubilee Singers.** Malaco MCD-6016, *In Revival*. 1994 concert.

————. MCA/Mobile Fidelity MFCD-756, *Walk on/Old Ship of Zion*. 1962, 1964, first two Peacock albums.

**Pilgrim Travelers.** Specialty SPCD-7030-2, *Walking Rhythm*. In U.K. as Ace CDCHD-463. 1947–1951.

————. Specialty SPCD-7053-2, *Better Than That*. In U.K. as Ace CDCH-564. 1951–1956.

**Radio Four.** Ace CDCHD-448, *There's Gonna Be Joy* (U.K.). 1955–1965.

**Sensational Nightingales.** MCA Special Products MCAD-22044, *The Best of . . .* 1950s with Julius Cheeks, lead.

————. Mobile Fidelity MFCD-767, *Heart and Soul/You Know Not the Hour*. Peacock albums from 1973 and 1974, with Charles Johnson, lead vocal.

**Soul Stirrers.** Specialty SPCD-7013-2, *Shine on Me*. In U.K. as Ace CDCHD-415. 1950, with Rebert Harris, lead vocal.

————. Specialty SPCD-7031-2, *Jesus Gave Me Water*. In U.K. as Ace CDCHD-464. 1951–1956, with Sam Cooke, lead vocal.

————. Specialty SPCD-7052-2, *The Last Mile of the Way*. In U.K. as Ace CDCHD-563. 1953–1957.

**Staple Singers.** Stax (Fantasy Inc) CDSX-006, *Respect Yourself* (England/Germany). 1970s "inspirational" recordings.

————. Charly CPCD-8087, *Uncloudy Day* (U.K.). 1955–1960. Also on P-Vine PCD-1404 (Japan).

**Swan Silvertone Singers.** Specialty SPCD-7044-2, *Heavenly Light*. In U.K. as Ace CDCHD-482. 1950s, including concert recordings.

————. Charly CPCD-8089, *Singin' In My Soul* (U.K.). 1950s and 1960s.

**Various artists.** Clanka Lanka CL-144001/002, *Birmingham Quartet Anthology* (Sweden; vinyl). Pre-1943 recordings by Birmingham Jubilee Singers, Famous Blue Jay Singers, Dunham Jubilee Singers, Ravizee Singers, Bessemer Sunset Four and others.

————. Document DOCD-5061, *The Earliest Negro Vocal Quartets 1894–1928*. Standard Quartette, Dinwiddie Colored Quartette, Apollo Male Quartette, Polk Miller and His Old South Quartette.

————. Global Village GVM-206, *New York Grassroots Gospel* (vinyl). 1980s recordings by New York community-based groups; companion to Ray Allen's *Singing in the Spirit*.

————. Heritage HTCD-08, *Glad I Found the Lord; Chicago Gospel 1937–1957* (U.K.). Golden Eagle Gospel Singers, Famous Blue Jay Singers, Norfleet Brothers and others.

————. Nashboro 4002, *It's Jesus, Y'all*. Soul-influenced groups, mainly 1970s. In U.K. on Ace CDCHM-381.

————. Spirit Feel CD-1001, *Fathers and Sons*. Early recordings of Soul Stirrers, Five Blind Boys of Mississippi, Sensational Nightingales.

————. Zu-Zazz ZCD-2019, *The Assassination* (U.K.). Memphis quartets, 1963–1983. Dixie Nightingales, Revelators, Harps of Melody, Gospel Writers.

WOMEN'S VOICES

Leomia Boyd

**Air 10105,** *I Am Ready* (vinyl).

**Air 10122,** *That's the Way the Lord Works* (vinyl). 1988 album, nominated for a Grammy award.

**Jewel JC-0182,** *I'm Depending on You, Lord* (cassette tape). Originally on Jewel J-182 (vinyl).

**Jewel JC-0185,** *Changed* (cassette tape) Originally on Jewel J-185 (vinyl).

Others

**Andrews, Inez.** Spirit Feel SF-1006, *The Two Sides of Inez Andrews* (vinyl).

**Angelic Gospel Singers.** Heritage HT-CD-11, *Touch Me Lord Jesus* (U.K.). 1949–1955.

————. Nashboro 4509, *The Best of . . .* 1950s and 1960s.

**Caravans.** Charly CPCD-8088, *Amazing Grace* (U.K.). 1960s with Shirley Caesar, Albertina Walker.

**Carr, Sister Wynona.** Specialty SPCD-7016-2, *Dragnet for Jesus*. In U.K. as Ace CDCHD-411. 1950–1954.

**Caesar, Shirley.** Savoy 14202, *The Best of Shirley Caesar.*

**Davis Sisters.** Savoy 7017, *The Best of the Davis Sisters* (cassette tape). Mid to late 1950s.

**Dranes, Arizona.** Document DOCD-5186, *Arizona Dranes (1926–29).*

**Franklin, Aretha.** Atlantic 2-906-2, Aretha Franklin with James Cleveland and the Southern California Community Choir, *Amazing Grace.* 1972 concert.

————. Charly CDCD-1164, *Gospel Roots* (U.K.). First recordings, made at the age of fourteen in her father's New Bethel Baptist Church, Detroit, in 1956.

**Gospel Harmonettes** (with Dorothy Love Coates). Specialty SPCD-7017-2, *Get on Board.* In U.K. as Ace CDCHD-412. 1951–1956.

————. Charly CPCD-8115, *Love Lifted Me* (U.K.). 1960s.

**Gospel Harmonettes of Demopolis, Alabama.** Global Village C-224 (cassette tape). 1992.

**Griffin, Bessie.** Spirit Feel SF-1009, *Even Me* (vinyl). 1952–1987.

**Ingram, Maggie.** Nashboro 4516, *The Best of . . .* 1960s.

**Jackson, Mahalia.** Columbia C2K-47083, *Gospel, Spirituals, and Hymns* (2 CDs). Columbia recordings, mainly 1954–1963.

————. Pair PCD-2-1332, *The Apollo Sessions.* Includes her best-known early recordings.

**Martin, Sallie** (Sallie Martin Singers). Specialty SPCD-7043-2, *Throw Out the Lifeline.* In U.K. as Ace CDCHD-481. 1950–1952.

**Meditation Singers.** Specialty SPCD-7032-2, *Good News.* In U.K. as Ace CDCHD-465. 1953–1954 and 1959.

**Pace-Rhodes, Shun.** Savoy 14807, *He Lives.* 1991.

**Pope, Sister Lucille** (w. The Pearly Gates). Nashboro 4511, *The Best of . . .* 1970s.

**Smith, Willie Mae Ford.** Savoy 14739, *I Am Bound for Canaan Land* (cassette tape). 1970s.

**Tharpe, Sister Rosetta.** Document DOCD-5334/5, *Vols. 1 and 2 (1938–44).*

————. Rosetta RR-1317, *Sister Rosetta Tharpe* (vinyl). 1943–1969, with Lucky Millinder, Sammy Price, and Marie Knight.

**Various artists.** Shanachie 6004, *The Great Gospel Women.* Sixteen artists, including Mahalia Jackson, Willie Mae Ford Smith, Marion Williams.

————. Specialty SPCD-7056-2, *Women of Gospel's Golden Age.* In U.K. as Ace CDCHD-567. Ten 1950s soloists and groups.

————. Spirit Feel SF-1008, *Stars of the Gospel Highway* (vinyl). Roberta Martin

Singers, Gospel Harmonettes, Famous Davis Sisters; 1947–1954.

———. Spirit Feel SF-1010, *Mother Smith and Her Children* (vinyl). Willie Mae Ford Smith, Martha Bass, Edna Gallmon Cooke.

**Washington, Sister Elizabeth.** Document DOCD-5462, *Sister Ernestine Washington (1943–1948)*.

**Williams, Marion.** Shanachie SH-6011, *My Soul Looks Back*.

———. Spirit Feel SF-1013, *Strong Again*.

PREACHERS

Rev. Willie Morganfield

**Jewel JCD-3052,** *Serving the Lord*. Singing.

**Jewel JCD-3065,** *The All-Powerful Name*. Sermon.

**Jewel JCD-3125,** *Bell Grove Baptist Choir*. Singing.

**Jewel JCD-3154,** *The Bible*. Sermon.

**Paula LPS-837,** *While I Can* (vinyl). Singing.

**Paula C-104,** *Willie Morganfield's Gospel Favorites* (cassette tape). Singing.

**Testament T-5001,** *Love In Action* (vinyl). 1988 sermon.

NB: Jewel/Paula issues are of material recorded in the 1960s and 1970s; at time of publication the label was converting its back catalog to CDs.

Others

**Daniels, W. Leo.** Air 10072, *Down in the Dumps With the Blues* (vinyl/cassette tape). Also on cassette tape Paula P-1107.

———. Air 10090, *Put Down Your Whiskey Bottle* (vinyl/cassette tape). Also on cassette tape Paula P-1109.

**Franklin, Rev. C. L.** Jewel JCD-3083, *The Eagle Stirreth Her Nest*.

———. Chess CH-9131, *The Prodigal Son* (vinyl).

NB: These are among the best known of Franklin's sermons. Many others were also issued on Chess albums; they are also on other labels through licensing deals.

**Gates, J. M.** Document DOCD-5414, 5432–33, 5442, 5449, 5457, 5469, 5483–84, *Vols. 1–9.* 1926–1941.

**McGee, F. W.** Blues Documents BDCD-6031/2, *Vols. 1 and 2* (Austria). 1927–1930.

**Nix, A. W.** Document DOCD-5328, *Vol. 1 (1927–1928)*.

**Rice, D. C.** Document DOCD-5071, *1928–1930*.

**Various artists.** Document DOCD-5326, *Singing the Gospel.* Elder Solomon Lightfoot Michaux, Elder Oscar Sanders, Professor Hull, Elder Otis Jones; 1933–1936; mainly singing.

———. Document DOCD-5329, *Elder J. E. Burch and Rev. Beaumont (1927–1929).*

———. Document DOCD-5363, *Rev. Johnny Blakey and Rev. M. L. Gipson (1927–1929).*

———. Global Village C-203, *The Storm Is Passing Over* (cassette tape). Rev. Samuel Kelsey, Rev. R. A. Daniels, Rev. Rimson, Elder Brodie; 1940s singing and preaching.

MALE SOLOISTS

**Banks, Willie** (and the Messengers). Malaco MCD-4460, *The Best of Willie Banks.* See videotapes.

**Barnes, Rev. F. C.** and Rev. Janice Brown. Air 10059, *Rough Side of the Mountain.* Originally on vinyl, with same issue number.

——— and Company. Air 10194, *I Can't Make It (Without the Lord).* See videotapes.

**Bradford, Alex.** Specialty SPCD-7015-2, *Rainbow In the Sky.* In U.K. on Ace CDCHD-413. 1953–1958.

———. Specialty SPCD-7042-2, *Too Close.* In U.K. on Ace CDCHD-480. 1953–1958.

**Clay, Otis.** Bullseye CD-BB-9536, *On My Way Home.* Compilation of gospel recordings by a singer better-known for his soul music.

**Fountain, Clarence** (see also Five Blind Boys of Alabama). Jewel JC-0055, *Alive in Person* (cassette tape; also issued on vinyl). Early 1970s concert recordings.

———. Jewel JCD3143, *Golden Moments in Gospel.* 1970s.

**Green, Al.** Myrrh MSB-6702, *Precious Lord* (vinyl). 1982.

**Jeter, Rev. Claude** (see also Swan Silvertones). Shanachie 6010, *Yesterday and Today.* 1969, plus 1954 Swan Silvertones recordings.

**Johnson, Willie Neal** (and the New Keynotes). Malaco MCD-6017, *Lord Take Us Through.* 1993 concert. See videotapes.

——— (and The Gospel Keynotes). Nashboro 4501, *The Best of . . .* 1970s.

**May, Brother Joe.** Specialty SPCD-7033-2, *Thunderbolt of the Middle West.* In U.K. as Ace CDCHD-466. 1950–1955.

———. Specialty SPCD-7054-2, *Live, 1952–1955.* In U.K. as Ace CDCHD-565. Concert recordings, including with the Sallie Martin Singers, Annette May.

**Ramey, Troy** (and the Soul Searchers). Nashboro 4505, *The Best of . . .*

**Robinson, Rev. Cleophus.** Specialty SPCD-7055-2, *Someone to Care.* In U.K. as Ace CDCHD-566. 1962–1963.

——— (with Swan Silvertones). Savoy 14668, *The Lord Is My Light.*

**Various artists.** Shanachie 6005, *The Great Gospel Men.* Nine artists, including J. Earle Hines, James Cleveland, Norsalus McKissick, Robert Anderson, J. Robert Bradley.

**Williams, Melvin.** Blackberry 5434, *In Living Color.* 1992 concert. See videotapes.

**Williams Brothers.** *The Best of and More. Live*, Blackberry 5437. c. 1993 concert. See videotapes.

## Choirs

**AARC Choir** (African-American Religious Connection). Savoy 7106, *I'm Going Through.* With Revs. Clay Evans, Cleophus Robinson, Oris Mays, James Lenox, Milton Biggham. c. 1991 concert. See videotapes.

**Abyssinian Baptist Gospel Choir** (dir. Alex Bradford). Columbia CK-47335, *Shakin' the Rafters.* 1960; originally on Columbia CS-8348 (vinyl).

**Chicago Community Choir** (dir. Rev. Jessy Dixon). Ambassador AMB-47005-2, *We Give You Praise.* 1993.

**Clark, Mattie Moss** (directing Greater Williams Temple COGIC Choir). Gos-Pearl 16004, *Mattie Moss Clark Presents . . .* (cassette tape).

**Cleveland, James** (and the Northern and Southern California Choirs of the Gospel Music Workshop of America). Savoy 7097, *Breathe On Me.* See videotapes.

———— (and the Southern California Community Choir). Savoy 7099, *Having Church.*

———— (and the Angelic Choir of First Baptist Church, Nutley, N.J.). Savoy 14076, *Peace Be Still* CD reissue of 1963 album.

**Draper, O'Landa and the Associates.** Word 7019277608, *Above and Beyond.* 1991.

**Georgia Mass Choir.** Savoy 7102, *I Sing Because I'm Happy.*

**Hawkins, Edwin** (Edwin Hawkins Singers). Savoy 7077, *The Best of . . .*

**Los Angeles Community Choir** (Harrison Johnson, dir.). Nashboro 4524, *Harrison Johnson and the Los Angeles Community Choir.* 1970s.

**Mississippi Mass Choir** (dir. Frank Williams). Malaco MCD-6003, *The Mississippi Mass Choir: Live In Jackson, Mississippi.* 1989. See videotapes.

**Thompson Community Singers** (dir. Rev. Milton Brunson). Word/Epic 7019269605, *My Mind Is Made Up.* 1992.

————. Nashboro 4530, *The Best of . . .* 1970s.

**Various artists.** Smithsonian/Folkways SF-40072, *African-American Spirituals: The Concert Tradition.* Florida A&M University Concert Choir, Fisk Jubilee Singers and others.

ANTHOLOGIES

**Ace CDCHD-537,** *Get On Board Little Children: The Modern Gospel Recordings* (U.K.). Artists recorded for the Modern label, 1947–1952.

**Alligator ALCD-2801,** *In the Spirit.* Blue Jay Gospel Singers, Carolina Kings of Harmony, Brother Hugh Dent, Argo Gospel Singers. P-Vine PCD-2187 (Japan) is virtually identical.

**Cascade CDROP-1017,** *20 Gospel Greats* (U.K.). Specialty artists; 1950s.

————— **CDROP-1019,** *20 More Gospel Greats* (U.K.). Nashboro artists, mainly 1950s.

**Chess/MCA CHD-9336,** *None But the Righteous: Chess Gospel Greats.*

**Columbia CK-57160,** *The Gospel Sound* (2 CDs). 1920s to 1960s.

————— **CK-57163,** *The Essential Gospel Sampler.* Mainly groups, 1940s to 1960s.

————— **CK-57164,** *Precious Lord—The Great Gospel Songs of Thomas Dorsey.* Marion Williams, Alex Bradford, R. H. Harris and others sing songs by Dorsey.

**Document DOCD-5312,** *Negro Religious Field Recordings 1934–1942.* Library of Congress recordings, including Silent Grove Baptist Church, Turner Junior Johnson and others.

**Global Village CD-225,** *Of One Accord.* Ring shout-style "singing and praying bands" from Tidewater Maryland and Delaware.

**Heritage HTCD-01,** *Get Right With God* (U.K.). Mainly 1940s groups and guitar evangelists.

————— **HTCD-04,** *The Best of Gotham Gospel* (U.K.). 1940s and 1950s.

**Memphis Archives MA-7012,** *Rock and Roll Sermon.* 1947–1956 tracks by fifteen artists, including Elder Beck, Utah Smith, Two Gospel Keys, Rev. A. Johnson, Elder Lightfoot Solomon Michaux.

**Nashboro 4001,** *The Best of Nashboro Gospel.* Mainly quartets, with some soloists. In U.K. on Ace CDCHD-373.

**P-Vine PCD-2828,** *Heaven Bound Train: Southern Gospel 1949–1950* (Japan). Mainly quartets, including first two Spirit of Memphis tracks.

————— **PCD-2829,** *Rock the Church: Delta Gospel Anthology* (Japan). Mainly quartets, 1962–1974.

————— **PCD-3016,** *Jesus Is Listening: Modern/Kent Gospel Masters Vol. 1* (Japan). Echoes of Zion, Swanee River Quartet, Smith Jubilee Singers, and others.

————— **PCD-3017,** *Go Devil Go: Modern/Kent Gospel Masters Vol. 2* (Japan). Lillie Mae Littlejohn, Prof. J. Earle Hines and His Goodwill Singers, and others.

**Rhino R2-70288 & R2-70289,** *Jubilation! Great Gospel Performances Vols. 1 and 2.* Mainly 1950s.

**Shanachie 6008,** *The Soul of Chicago.* The Gay Sisters, Gladys Beamon Gregory, Delois Barrett Campbell, Robert Anderson, and others.

**Spirit Feel SF-1012,** *The Gospel Sound of Spirit Feel.* Includes quartets, male, and female soloists, choirs.

**Smithsonian/Folkways SF-40073,** *African-American Congregational Singing:*

*Nineteenth Century Roots.* Ring shouts, lined hymns, and call-and-response songs.

———— **SF-40074,** *African-American Gospel: The Pioneering Composers.* Songs written by C. A. Tindley, Lucie Campbell, Thomas Dorsey, Herbert Brewster, Roberta Martin, and Kenneth Morris.

———— **SF-40075,** *African-American Community Gospel.* Groups, soloists and choirs from Alabama and Washington, D.C.

**Specialty SPCD-7045-2,** *The Great Shrine 1955 Concert.* In U.K. as Ace CDCHD-483. Concert recordings; Soul Stirrers, Pilgrim Travelers, Brother Joe May, Gospel Harmonettes.

**Vee Jay NVG2–501,** *Black Nativity: Gospel on Broadway.* Alex Bradford and the Bradford Singers, Marion Williams and the Stars of Faith. 1962.

V I D E O T A P E S

All videotapes listed are produced in the United States. Material on most is also available on CD; issue numbers are noted in parentheses, and some are also listed above.

**AARC Choir** (dir. Rev. Clay Evans). Savoy SAVV-9516, *I'm Going Through* (Savoy 9516).

**Banks, Willie** (and the Messengers). Malaco Mal-V-9009, *In Concert.*

**Barnes, Rev. F. C.** (and Company). AIR 10194, *I Can't Make It* (Air 10194).

**Canton Spirituals.** Blackberry BBV-3000, *Live In Memphis* (Blackberry BBC-1600). With James Chambers, MC.

**Cleveland, Rev. James.** Savoy SAV-9500, *Down Memory Lane.* With Inez Andrews, the Barrett Sisters, Albertina Walker and others.

———— (and the Northern and Southern California Choirs of the Gospel Music Workshop of America). Savoy SAV-9506, *Breathe On Me* (Savoy 7097).

**Dixie Hummingbirds.** AIR 10184, *Live in Atlanta* (*In Good Health*) (Air 10184).

**Jackson Southernaires.** Malaco MAL-V-9018, *Live and Anointed* (Malaco MCD-6012).

**Johnson, Willie Neal** (and the New Keynotes). Malaco MAL-V-9020, *Lord Take Us Through* (Malaco MCD-6017).

**Mississippi Mass Choir.** Malaco MAL-V-9006, *Live in Jackson, Mississippi* (Malaco MCD-6003).

**Pilgrim Jubilees.** Malaco MAL-V-9008, *Live From Jackson, Mississippi.*

**Ramey, Troy** (and the Soul Searchers). Air 10173, *Live In Atlanta* (*Earth Has No Sorrow*) (Air 10173).

**Sensational Nightingales.** Malaco MAL-V-9010, *Ministry in Song.*

**Various artists.** Malaco MAL-V-9003, *Homecoming.* Robert Blair and the Violinaires, Willie Neal Johnson and the Gospel Keynotes, Jackson Southernaires, Williams Brothers.

**Williams, Melvin.** Blackberry BVD-5434, *In Living Color* (Blackberry 5434).

**Williams Brothers.** Blackberry BVD-5437, *Live/Best of and More* (Blackberry 5437).

BLUES

The following albums are by blues artists who also recorded religious material or who abandoned blues for sacred music.

**Dorsey, Thomas A.** (Georgia Tom). Blues Documents BDCD-6021/2, *Vols. 1 and 2, 1928–1934* (Austria). Sacred material on second disc.

**House, Eddie "Son."** Columbia C2K-48867, *Father of the Delta Blues* (2 CDs). 1965 recordings.

————. Capitol CDP 7243-8-31830-2-9, *Delta Blues and Spirituals.* 1970 concert recordings. Reissues Liberty (U.K.) LBS-83391, *John the Revelator.* (See also Document DOCD-5002 below.)

**Hurt, "Mississippi" John.** Yazoo YAZCD-1065, *1928 Sessions.*

**James, Nehemiah "Skip."** Yazoo YAZCD-2009, *Complete Early Recordings, 1930.*

**Jefferson, Blind Lemon.** Document DOCD-5017-5020, *Vols. 1–4, 1925–1929.* Sacred material on first two discs.

**Fuller, "Blind Boy"** (Fulton Allen). Document DOCD-5091-5096, *Vols. 1–6, 1935–1940.* Sacred material on Vol. 6.

**McGhee, Brownie** (Walter Brown McGhee). Columbia 4757002. *The Complete . . .* (2 CDs).

**McTell, "Blind" Willie.** Document DOCD-5006-5008, *Vols. 1–3, (1927–1935).* Sacred material on Vol. 3.

————. Blues Documents BDCD-6001, *1940* (Austria). Library of Congress recordings.

**Patton, Charley.** Document DOCD-5009/10/11, *Vols. 1–3, 1929–1934.*

**Various artists.** Atlantic 7824962, *Sounds of the South* (4 CDs). Alan Lomax field recordings from 1959–60. Includes sacred, blues and country.

————. Document DOCD-5002, *Son House and the Great Delta Blues Singers (1926–1930).* Son House, Rube Lacy and others. No sacred material.

**White, "Bukka"** (Booker T. Washington White). Travelin' Man TMCD-03, *The Complete Sessions, 1930–1940* (U.K.).

————. Arhoolie ARHCD-323, *Sky Songs.* 1963.

**White, Joshua ("Josh").** Document DOCD-5194/95/96, *Vols. 1–3, (1929–40).*

**Wilkins, Robert.** Document DOCD-5014, *Memphis Blues (1928–1935).* No sacred material.

ADDRESSES

Mail Order

In the United States: Roots & Rhythm, P.O. Box 837, El Cerrito, California 94530.

In Britain and Europe: Red Lick Records, P.O. Box 3, Porthmadog, Gwynedd, Wales, United Kingdom LL48 6AQ.

These outlets are able to supply most of the collector-oriented issues, including those on Document, Specialty, Ace, Columbia, P-Vine Special (from Roots & Rhythm) and others.

## Record Companies

The mail order outlets tend not to carry albums on labels selling primarily to the African-American gospel audience. The three such labels most frequently mentioned above are:

Air: Atlanta International Records, 881 Memorial Drive S.E., Atlanta, Georgia 30316 (also handles GosPearl and Tyscot labels).

Jewel: Jewel/Paula Records, P.O. Box 1125, Shreveport, Louisiana 71163–1125.

Malaco/Savoy: Malaco Records, P.O. Box 9827, Jackson, Mississippi 39286 (also handles Blackberry recordings and videotapes).

# NOTES

## MUSIC IN THE AIR: AN INTRODUCTION

1. One researcher who has examined the phenomenon of being "in the spirit" is Ray Allen, in *Singing in the Spirit: African-American Sacred Quartets in New York City* (Philadelphia: University of Pennsylvania Press, 1991). He notes that "most researchers in this area fail to take seriously the beliefs and supernatural explanations of those who actually engage in spiritual practices" (p. 159), and quotes several singers describing the sensation of being in the spirit (pp. 162–63).

2. Both views are presented by Mellonee Victoria Burnim in *The Black Gospel Music Tradition: Symbol of Ethnicity* (Ph.D. diss., Indiana University, 1980), p. 179. Ms. Burnim, an African-American Methodist, opts firmly for the same-culture view, saying: "It is crucial to view the gospel tradition as a medium created by Blacks, for Blacks and subject only to meaningful criticism and analysis from the vantage point of a Black aesthetic" (p. 6). Obviously I have reservations about such a restriction. Joyce Marie Jackson also discusses the "insider as researcher," without expressing any preferences, in *The Performing Black Sacred Quartet: An Expression of Cultural Values and Aesthetics* (Ph.D. diss., University of Indiana, 1988), p. 19.

3. Studs Terkel, *Race: How Blacks and Whites Think and Feel About the American Obsession* (New York: Anchor, 1992).

4. Ibid., p. 136. The quoted speaker is Chicago insurance broker Joseph Lattimore.

5. In *Conversation With the Blues* (London: Cassell, 1965; New York: Horizon Press, 1965), p. 19, English researcher Paul Oliver reports a similar experience, noting that his "European origin was a help rather than a handicap" as he conducted interviews.

6. Kip Lornell, *Happy in the Service of the Lord: Afro-American Gospel Quartets*

*in Memphis* (Urbana: University of Illinois Press, 1988; 2nd ed. Knoxville: University of Tennessee Press, 1995), pp. 3–4. David Evans's observations are in "The Roots of Afro-American Gospel Music," *Jazzforschung* 8 (1976), pp. 119–35.

7. Marion Joseph Franklin, *The Relationship of Black Preaching to Black Gospel Music* (D.Min. diss., Drew University, 1982): 90.

8. Alan Freeman, author's interview, Atlanta, Georgia, October 14, 1994. The album is Rev. F. C. Barnes and Rev. Janice Brown, *Rough Side of the Mountain*, Air 10059 (issued on vinyl, 1984; reissued on CD, 1989).

9. Anthony Heilbut, *The Gospel Sound: Good News and Bad Times*, rev. 3rd ed. (New York: Limelight Editions, 1975).

10. Viv Broughton, *Black Gospel: An Illustrated History of the Gospel Sound* (Poole, England: Blandford House, 1985).

11. Lornell, *Happy in the Service of the Lord*.

12. Allen, *Singing in the Spirit*.

13. Paul Oliver, *Songsters and Saints: Vocal Traditions on Race Records* (London, New York: Cambridge University Press, 1984).

14. Laurraine Goreau, *Just Mahalia, Baby: The Mahalia Jackson Story* (Waco, Texas: Word Books, 1975). Jules Schwerin, *Got To Tell It: Mahalia Jackson, Queen of Gospel* (New York: Oxford University Press, 1992).

15. Michael W. Harris, *The Rise of Gospel Blues: The Music of Thomas Andrew Dorsey in the Urban Church* (New York: Oxford University Press, 1992).

16. Bernice Reagon Johnson, ed., *We'll Understand It Better By and By: Pioneering African-American Gospel Composers* (Washington: Smithsonian Institution Press, 1992).

17. All Bible quotes are from the King James version.

18. Doug Seroff, "Polk Miller and the Old South Quartette," *78 Quarterly*, no. 3 (1988): 27–41.

19. *The Earliest Negro Vocal Quartets 1894–1928*, Document DOCD-5061 (Austria; CD; 1991) reissues five of the six Dinwiddie Colored Quartet tracks and one by the Standard Quartette. *The Earliest Negro Vocal Groups Vol. 2 1893–1922*, Document DOCD-5288 (CD; 1994) includes one track by the Unique Quartet, one by the Standard Quartette, and the sixth Dinwiddie track. All Document issues quoted below are Austrian-produced compact discs.

20. R. M. W. Dixon and J. Godrich, *Recording the Blues* (London: Studio Vista, 1970), p. 37.

21. Ibid., p. 38.

22. *Sanctified Jug Bands (1928–30)*, Matchbox MSE-222 (England; vinyl; 1986), contains the complete recordings of Elder Richard Bryant, Brother Williams's Memphis Sanctified Singers and the Holy Ghost Sanctified Singers. For more on early soloists, preachers and jug band-style groups, see Oliver's *Songsters and Saints*. Bruce Bastin's *Red River Blues* (Urbana: University of Illinois Press, 1986) includes discussion on some blues-styled soloists.

23. *Gospel Pearls* (Nashville: Sunday School Publishing Board, National Baptist Convention, U. S. A). This hymnal was published in 1921, and has remained in print since; reprints are not dated.

24. This aspect of Dorsey's influence is examined by Harris in *The Rise of*

*Gospel Blues* and in his essay "Thomas A. Dorsey: Conflict and Resolution," in *We'll Understand It Better By and By*, ed. Bernice Johnson Reagon.

25. Opal Louis Nations, notes to Rev. Cleophus Robinson, *Someone To Care*, Specialty SPCD-7055-2 (U. S.; CD; 1993).

26. Broughton, *Black Gospel*, p. 63, quoting an interview by Doug Seroff. Parts of the interview are also in Seroff's *Gospel Arts Day 1989* booklet (Nashville: Fisk University, 1989), p. 9.

27. Harris's role in revising the role of lead singers is examined by Anthony Heilbut in notes to *Fathers and Sons*, Spirit Feel CD-1001 (U. S.; CD; c. 1992), which contains early recordings by the Soul Stirrers, the Five Blind Boys of Mississippi and the Sensational Nightingales.

28. Broughton, *Black Gospel*, p. 64.

29. Ray Funk, notes to the Dixie Hummingbirds, *In the Storm Too Long*, Gospel Jubilee RF-1405 (Sweden; vinyl; 1991).

30. Broughton, *Black Gospel*, p. 68.

31. From an early 1970s interview in *Radio World*, quoted by Ray Funk in "Let's Go Out to the Programs," *Rejoice*, 2, no. 4 (summer 1990): 16–25.

32. Neil Slaven, "We Sang Like We Did Down South," *Blues & Rhythm* 69 (May 1992): 4–5.

33. Horace Clarence Boyer, "Kenneth Morris: Composer and Publisher," in *We'll Understand It Better By and By*, ed. Bernice Reagon Johnson, pp. 309–28.

34. Broughton, *Black Gospel*, p. 112.

35. Heilbut, *The Gospel Sound*, p. 214.

36. Jessy Dixon, author's interview, Auckland, New Zealand, June 15, 1995.

37. Anonymous informant, author's interview, September/October, 1992.

38. Broughton, *Black Gospel*, p. 122.

39. *The Mississippi Mass Choir*, Malaco MCD-6003 (U. S.; CD; 1989); *God Gets the* Glory, Malaco MCD-6008 (1991); *It Remains To Be Seen*, Malaco MCD-6013 (1993).

40. Pepper Smith, "Two Generations of the Jackson Southernaires," *Rejoice* 3, no. 6 (December 1991–January 1992): 15–18. Frank Williams was also executive gospel producer and director of gospel promotions for the Malaco label. He died in 1992.

41. Heilbut, notes to anthology *The Soul of Chicago*, Shanachie 6008 (U. S.; CD; 1993).

42. *Yes Lord! Church of God In Christ Hymnal* (Memphis: COGIC Publishing Board, 1982); *The New National Baptist Hymnal* (Nashville: National Baptist Publishing Board, 1977).

43. Edwin Smith, "Catching Up With Andrae Crouch," *Rejoice* 4, no. 4 (August–September, 1992): 7–9.

44. Bill Carpenter, "The Shirley Caesar You've Never Met," *Rejoice* 4, no. 5 (October–November 1992): 3–5.

45. See note 43.

46. The influence of southern churches and gospel music on other regions is examined by Allen in *Singing in the Spirit*, pp. 186–204.

CHAPTER 1 THE GOSPEL EVANGELISTS

1. James Rooney, *Bossmen: Bill Monroe and Muddy Waters*, rev. ed. (New York: Da Capo, 1991), p. 107.

2. The development of this market is described in Dixon and Godrich's *Recording the Blues*.

3. Bastin, *Red River Blues*, pp. 167–68.

4. Taggart's thirty-two issued recordings, made between 1926 and 1934, are on *Blind Joe Taggart, Vols. 1 and 2*, Document DOCD-5153-54 (1993). They include one Blind Joe Amos track; the other was never issued.

5. Oliver, *Songsters and Saints*, p. 206.

6. Clayborn's issued recordings are on *Rev. Edward W. Clayborn (1926–1928)*, Document DOCD-5155, and *Blind Joe Taggart, Vol. 2*, Document DOCD-5154, which includes Clayborn's 1929 tracks (both 1993).

7. *Storefront and Streetcorner Gospel (1927–1929)*, Document DOCD-5054 (1991), includes the complete recordings of Blind Mamie and A. C. Forehand (seven takes of four songs), and Luther Magby. *The Songster Tradition*, Document DOCD-5045 (1991), includes all William and Versey Smith's recordings.

8. All recordings of Blind Benny Paris and Wife, Rev. I. B. Ware, Blind Willie Harris, Eddie Head and Family and Mother McCollum are on *Guitar Evangelists*, Document DOCD-5051 (1992). Lonnie McIntorsh's are on *Memphis Gospel*, Document DOCD-5072 (1991); Sister Cally Fancy's are on *Gospel Classics, Vol. 2*, Document DOCD-5313 (1994).

9. Guido van Rijn and Hans Vergeer discuss the construction and history of the dulceola in notes to anthology *Trouble Done Bore Me Down*, Agram AB-2011 (Netherlands; vinyl), which includes one Phillips track.

10. Phillips's issued recordings (plus two not issued on 78 rpm) are on *I Am Born To Preach the Gospel*, Yazoo YAZCD-2003 (U. S.; CD; 1992).

11. Johnson's recordings are on *The Complete Blind Willie Johnson*, Columbia C2K-52835 (U. S.; 2 CDs; 1993).

12. Rev. Charles Walker, "Lucie E. Campbell Williams, a Cultural Biography," in *We'll Understand It Better By and By*, ed. Bernice Johnson Reagon, p. 132.

13. Blind Connie Rosemond's eight recordings (all with keyboard accompaniment) are on Document DOCD-5313 (see note 8).

14. Chris Albertson, *Bessie, Empress of the Blues* (New York: Stein and Day, 1972; London: Sphere, 1975), pp. 113–14.

15. Portia K. Maultsby, "West African Influences in U. S. Black Music," in *More Than Dancing*, ed. Irene V. Jackson (Westport, Conn.: Greenwood Press, 1985), pp. 25–57.

16. David Evans, notes to *Atlanta Blues 1933*, JEMF 106 (U. S.; vinyl; 1979).

17. Bastin, *Red River Blues*, pp. 220–21.

18. Gary Davis's 1935 recordings (including one unissued on 78 rpm) are on *Complete Recorded Works, 1935–1949*, Document DOCD-5060 (1991). The album also has one track from 1945 and two from 1949.

19. Bastin, *Red River Blues*, p. 221.

20. Smith's New York recordings are on *Gospel Evangelists: God's Mighty Hand,* Heritage HTCD-09 (U. K.; CD; 1992). His issued Checker sides are on *None But the Righteous,* MCA CHD-9336 (U. S.; CD; 1992). All four songs, plus the Two Wing Temple tracks, are on *Slide Guitar Gospel,* Document DOCD-5222 (1994).

21. *The Singing Reverend,* Stinson SLP-56 (U. S.; vinyl).

22. *Harlem Street Singer,* Bluesville BVLP-1015 (also on compact disc Original Blues Classics OBCCD-547), *A Little More Faith,* Bluesville BVLP-1032 (no CD issue at time of writing), *Say No To the Devil,* Bluesville BVLP-1049 (OBCCD-519). Original vinyl issues U. S.; reissue CDs Germany.

23. *Philadelphia Street Singer,* Testament TCD-5024 (U. S.; CD; 1995). Reissues Testament T-2225 (U. S.; vinyl; 1974). Notes by Pete Welding.

24. *Georgia Street Singer,* Folk-Lyric FL-108 (U. S.; vinyl; early 1960s); *It's a Mean Old World to Live In,* Rounder 2011 (U. S.; vinyl; 1975).

25. Originally on *Negro Church Music,* Atlantic SD-1351 (U. S.; vinyl); reissued as part of *Sounds of the South,* Atlantic 7824962 (U. S.; 1993), a four-CD set of Alan Lomax's secular and sacred 1959–60 recordings from white and black traditions.

26. *Sorrow Come Pass Me Round,* Advent 2805 (U. S.; vinyl; 1975).

27. Broughton, *Black Gospel,* p. 84.

28. David Evans, "Ramblin'," *Blues Revue 14* (Fall, 1994): 18–20.

29. Sister Terrell's eight recordings (two from 1948, six from 1953) are on *Country Gospel: The Post-War Years (1946–1953),* Document DOCD-5221 (1994). Willie Mae Williams's two tracks are on Heritage HTCD-09 (see note 20).

30. Lonnie Farris's recordings are on Document DOCD-5222 (see note 20).

31. Rev. Charlie Jackson, *Louisiana Dynamite,* Curlew 1001 (Scotland; cassette tape; 1988).

## Elder Roma Wilson

1 *Negro Religious Music, Vol. 1,* Blues Classics BC-17 (U. S.: vinyl; 1968); notes by Pete Welding.

2. *God's Mighty Hand—Gospel Evangelists,* Heritage HTCD-09 (U. K.: CD; 1992); notes by Bob Laughton.

3. While Wilson is disparaging about the old tunes, "Lost John" is a folk harmonica standard which made its recording debut about the time he was learning it—in New York on Wednesday, August 20, 1924, by Stovepipe No. 1 (Sam Jones), who played it on guitar and harmonica (see note 6).

4. Bush harbors (also known as "brush/bush arbors") date to antebellum days when slaves used them as a venue for clandestine services held as an alternative to the censored version of Christianity offered by slave owners. They are discussed by, among others, Wyatt T. Walker, *Somebody's Calling My Name* (Valley Forge, Pa.: Judson Press, 1979), pp. 30–31, Harris, *The Rise of Gospel Blues,* p. 245–51, and Julius Lester, *To Be a Slave* (London: Longman, 1968), p. 104–105.

5. Farming "on a share" (sharecropping), meant that Wilson grew cotton on usually white-owned land for a share of what the crop fetched at market, minus

"expenses" and advances. When he "rented," he paid a set fee for the use of a block of land and took the full return from the crop, minus the rent. A concise examination of the sharecropping system and its economic and social impact is in James C. Cobb's *The Most Southern Place on Earth* (New York: Oxford University Press, 1992).

6. Sam Jones's issued recordings are on *Stovepipe No. 1 and David Crockett (1924–1930)*, Document DOCD-5269 (1994).

7. Blind Roger Hays's two tracks are on anthology *Sinners and Saints (1926–31)*, Document DOCD-5106 (1992).

8. Four tracks by Turner Junior Johnson are on anthology *Negro Religious Field Recordings 1934–1942*, Document DOCD-5312 (1994). The same tracks are also on *Negro Religious Songs and Services*, Library of Congress AFS-L10 (U. S.; vinyl).

9. Alan Lomax, *The Land Where the Blues Began* (New York: Pantheon Books, 1993; London: Methuen, 1993), p. 32.

10. Joseph Von Battle ("Von" was his middle name) was a black entrepreneur who, as well as selling records from his Hasting Street shop, also ran a recording studio there. He had his own JVB and Von labels, and also sold recordings to other labels. He issued mainly blues, but also recorded several religious performers, including Detroit preacher Rev. C. L. Franklin.

11. *Harp Suckers—Detroit Harmonica Blues 1948*, St. George 1002 (Germany; vinyl; 1983). The tracks are also on Elder Wilson's 1994 CD, *This Train Is a Clean Train*, Arhoolie ARHCD-429.

12. In notes to the Meditation Singers, *Good News*, Specialty SPCD-7032 (U. S.; CD; 1993), Ray Funk says: "The Meditations were initially recorded by Joe Von Battle at his record store in Detroit; unbeknownst to the group, he leased their one record to Deluxe Records. They had come in to use his studio for rehearsal, and suddenly found they had a record out."

13. *The Deep South Musical Roots Tour*, Global Village C-228 (U. S.; cassette tape; 1992, recorded 1991). The tour was sponsored by the Southern Arts Federation in Atlanta.

14. Standard discographies and album notes list the personnel for these tracks as Roma singing, backed by the harmonicas of Robert Lee, Clyde and Sammy Lee. Roma does do all the singing, but also plays the lead harmonica.

15. "Just As Well Get Ready, You Got to Die" is a traditional song performed by, among others, Blind Willie McTell, who recorded it for the Library of Congress in 1940 and commercially in 1949. The version Roma Wilson sang for Joe Battle is a variant of the traditional form, and does not include any his self-composed lyrics. These verses, which alter the form of the song, were presumably written after the Battle recordings were made.

16. The song is on Arhoolie ARHCD-429, recorded after this interview.

17. Luke 6:38.

18. Acts 2:41–45 tells how about three thousand people were baptized in one day, then gave up their possessions "and parted them to all men as every man had need."

REV. LEON PINSON

1. Pinson's "we never did put out any records" qualification is necessary to separate his group from the many Silvertone groups which did record. The name seems to have been a popular choice after World War II; Cedric J. Hayes and Robert Laughton's *Gospel Records 1943–1970* (England: Record Information Services, 1992) lists nine groups with "Silvertone" in their names; other non-recorded Silvertones also existed. R. M. W. Dixon and J. Godrich's *Blues and Gospel Records 1902–1943*, 3rd ed. (Chigwell, England: Storyville, 1982) lists three "Silvertone" names, although two were pusedonyms for groups appearing on the Silvertone label.

2. The purchase puts Pinson among the earlier folk-style guitarists to change to an electric instrument, although established jazz and blues performers had been using them since the late 1930s. The instrument he bought in Racine was a Gibson, the same "top-of-the-market" brand he uses today.

3. This is the tour that produced Global Village C-228, *The Deep South Musical Roots Tour* (see Roma Wilson, note 13).

4. The Northeast Mississippi Blues and Gospel Folk Festival, held annually at Rust College in Holly Springs since 1979.

5. Named for English hymn writer Dr. Isaac Watts (1674–1748), whose music has been a force in African-American religious music since the 1730s. As Pinson's use of the term "a Doctor Watt" shows, Watts's name has become a generic term, used for old hymns sung in "meter," usually in "lining-out style" in which one person speaks or chants a line and the congregation repeats it, singing very slowly with individual ornamentation. One well-known example sometimes cited as a "Doctor Watt" is *Amazing Grace*—written not by Watts but by John Newton.

6. "There's a Hand Writing On the Wall" is based on the incident described in Daniel 5, in which a phantom hand writes the prophetic message "Mene mene tekel upharsin" on the wall of the banquet hall as the Babylonian king, Belshazzar, is drinking from vessels taken by his father, Nebuchadnezzar, from the temple at Jerusalem. Daniel translates the message, which predicts Belshazzar's downfall, and as a reward is made "third ruler in the kingdom." That night, Belshazzar is slain. Various tellings of the incident have appeared on record, the earliest being "The Handwriting On the Wall," a sermon recorded by Calvin P. Dixon (Black Billy Sunday) in New York in January 1925. A song version, "There's a Hand Writing On the Wall," was recorded by Blind Joe Taggart in Chicago in 1928. The time limitation of a 78 rpm record means Taggart is unable to finish the story, so he ends abruptly with a verse telling how Belshazzar grew worried.

BOYD RIVERS

1. David Evans provided information about this tour and some other details.

2. Homemade instruments are a common starting point in the careers of black rural guitarists. For the single-string variety which Rivers describes, a wire is strung between two nails driven a yard or so apart into a flat surface such as a wall, porch post or board, and tightened by blocks wedged in at each end.

The player strikes the wire with a stick or a finger, and obtains a melody by sliding a bottle or similar hard object up and down it, producing a main note and the simultaneous sound of the harmonic running in the opposite direction. Multistring versions were also made, as described by James Holley in chapter 6. See David Evans, "Afro-American One-Stringed Instruments," *Western Folklore* 29, no. 4 (1970): 229–45.

3. The arrival of the Holy Spirit in a convert usually provokes ecstatic shouts and movements; hence his grandmother's injunction on Rivers not to move unless he genuinely felt the Spirit. Rhythm-and-blues singer Ruth Brown has recalled that she and her brother were punished by their grandmother for simulating conversion (Arnold Shaw, *Honkers and Shouters* [New York: Macmillan, 1978], p. 401). As a corollary, prominent Memphis preacher and gospel song writer Rev. William Herbert Brewster told Bernice Johnson Reagon how his conversion was not accepted because the Holy Spirit did not impel him to "cut up and stand on my head and jump benches" ("William Herbert Brewster: Rememberings," *We'll Understand It Better By and By*, ed. Bernice Johnson Reagon, pp. 189–90).

4. In interviews with David Evans, Rivers first told of meeting Jackson in Canton, but later denied it, saying he met the blues player in California in the early 1970s. "Rivers was on a package tour arranged by Worth Long and went to see Jackson at a club on an off night or after a concert. Perhaps both stories are accurate" (David Evans, correspondence with the author, July 1995). It should be noted that the later meeting would have occurred well after Rivers rejected blues and nightclubs in favor of gospel music and church.

5. Six tracks are on anthology *Country Gospel Rock*, L+R 42.041. The other is on anthology *Introduction to the Living Country Blues U. S. Series*, L+R 42.030 (both Germany; vinyl; 1980).

6. David Evans, "Ramblin'," *Blues Revue* 14 (fall 1994): 18–20.

7. Rev. Cleophus Robinson, "Wrapped Up, Tied Up, Tangled Up." Recorded in Nashville, 1969; issued on single Nashboro 969; reissued on *Wrapped Up, Tied Up, Tangled Up*, Nashboro 4009 (U. S.; CD; 1995).

8. Boyd Rivers, "I'm Tangled Up." Recorded at his home, Pickens, Mississippi, Saturday, October 25, 1980; issued on L+R 42.041.

9. The Fairfield Four, "Tree of Level." Recorded in Nashville, c. February 1949. Issued on singles Delta JB210 and Dot 2003; reissued on *The Gospel Sound of Spirit Feel*, Spirit Feel SF-1012 (U. S.; CD; 1991).

10. The Golden Gate Quartet, "Jezebel." Recorded in New York, Friday, April 18, 1941. Issued on OKeh 6204; reissued on *Swing Down Chariot*, Columbia CK-47131 (U. S.; CD; 1991).

CHAPTER 2 THE QUARTETS

1. Lornell, *Happy in the Service of the Lord*, p. 16.
2. Lynn Abbott, "Play That Barber Shop Chord: A Case for the African-American Origin of Barbershop Harmony," *American Music* 10, no. 3 (fall, 1992): 289–326.

3. J. B. T. Marsh, *The Story of the Jubilee Singers* (London: Hodder and Stoughton, 1886). Doug Seroff has also researched the Fisk Jubilee Singers—see "On the Battlefield: Gospel Quartets in Jefferson County, Alabama," in *Repercussions: A Celebration of African American Music*, ed. Geoffrey Haydon and Dennis Marks (London: Century, 1985), pp. 30–53, *Gospel Arts Day* (Nashville; Fisk University, 1988), pp. 2–9; and *Gospel Arts Day* (Nashville: Fisk University, 1989), pp. 2–9. The *Gospel Arts Day* booklets were published as programs and background information for commemorative quartet performances at Fisk University.

4. Jackson, *The Performing Black Sacred Quartet*, p. 53, quoting research by Seroff.

5. Seroff, *Gospel Arts Day* (1988), p. 3.

6. Jackson, *The Performing Black Sacred Quartet*, p. 61.

7. Ibid., p. 65.

8. The activities of the white pharmacist-turned-banjo-player Polk Miller and the African-American groups he organized are documented by Doug Seroff in "Polk Miller and the Old South Quartette," *78 Quarterly* 3 (1988): 27–41.

9. *The Earliest Negro Vocal Quartets*, Document DOCD-5061 (Austria; 1991; CD) has tracks by the Standard Quartet (one), the Apollo Male Quartet (two), the Dinwiddie Colored Quartet (five) and Polk Miller and the Old South Quartette (seven).

10. Biddle University, in Charlotte, North Carolina, is now known as Johnson C. Smith College.

11. The Norfolk Jazz/Jubilee Quartet's recordings are on Document DOCD-5381-5386 (Austria; six CDs; 1995).

12. Lornell, *Happy in the Service of the Lord*, p. 19, quoting Thurman Ruth of the Selah Jubilee Singers.

13. For more on the Alabama tradition, see Seroff, "On the Battlefield," in *Repercussions*, pp. 30–53, and notes to *Birmingham Quartet Anthology*, Clanka Lanka 144001/002 (Sweden; vinyl; 1980).

14. Dixon and Godrich, *Recording the Blues*, p. 74.

15. Heilbut, *The Gospel Sound*, p. 79.

16. Seroff, *On the Battlefield*, p. 42.

17. Bessie Johnson's 1929 recordings are reissued on *Memphis Gospel (1927–1929)*, Document DOCD-5072 (1991).

18. Examples of the "clanka lanka" style, including some from the Famous Blue Jay Singers, are on Clanka Lanka CL-144001/002 (see note 13).

19. Heilbut, *The Gospel Sound*, p. 38.

20. Heilbut, notes to the Pilgrim Travelers, *Walking Rhythm*, Specialty CD-7030 (U. S.; CD; 1991).

21. The Fairfield Four, *Standing in the Safety Zone*, Warner Alliance WBD-4137 (U. S.; CD; 1992).

22. Willie Neal Johnson and the New Keynotes, *Lord Take Us Through*, Malaco MCD-6017 (U. S.; CD; 1993), recorded in concert in Fayetteville, North Carolina.

23. The Canton Spirituals, *Live in Memphis*, Blackberry BBC-1600 (U. S.; CD; 1993). A videotape of the concert is on Blackberry BBV-3000.

24. For more detailed discussion on the organizational structure of quartets, including the full text of the "bylaws" for two Memphis groups, see Lornell, *Happy in the Service of the Lord*, pp. 85–88.

25. Maultsby, "West African Influences and Retentions in U. S. Black Music," *More Than Dancing*, p. 47.

26. Robert Barr, "Joe Ligon on Working a Gospel Crowd," Associated Press interview, London, September 12, 1993.

27. Ray Allen explores divine involvement in gospel songwriting, and quotes several quartet songwriters, in *Singing in the Spirit*, pp. 62–65.

28. Harvey Watkins, Jr., the Canton Spirituals, *Live in Memphis*, Blackberry BBV-3000 (U. S.; videotape; 1993).

29. Jessie Mae Hemphill, author's interview, Como, Mississippi, September 16, 1992.

30. Sensational Nightingales, "At the Cross," on *Jesus Is Coming*, ABC Peacock PY-59232 (U. S.; vinyl; 1978).

31. Clarence Fountain, "Just a Closer Walk With Thee," on *In the Gospel Light*, Jewel LPS-0033, (U. S.; vinyl).

32. Arsenio Orteza, "Standing Room Only: Catching Up with Sandy Foster and the Five Blind Boys of Mississippi," *Rejoice* 4, no. 6 (January 1993): 6–9.

33. Pilgrim Jubilee Singers, "A Child's Blood," issued on single Peacock 3087 and album Peacock PLP-133 (U. S.; vinyl). The 1994 version is on *In Revival*, Malaco MCD-6016 (U. S.: CD).

34. Mighty Clouds of Joy, "Pray for Me," on *Live*, MCA Special Products MCAD-22022 (U. S.; CD; 1990).

35. Mighty Clouds of Joy, "Pray For Me," Word 7019202608 (U. S.: vinyl; also on cassette tape ET-48547); recorded at the Mt. Ephraim Baptist Church, Atlanta, Georgia, on July 23, 1990.

36. Drexall Singers, *View the City, Pts. 1 and 2*, issued on single Songbird 1045 and anthology album Songbird SBLP-206 (U. S.; vinyl; 1965).

37. Barr, "Joe Ligon On Working a Gospel Crowd."

38. Performances by ring shout-style "singing and praying bands" from Tidewater Maryland and Delaware can be heard on *Of One Accord: Singing and Praying Bands*, Global Village CD-225 (U. S.; CD; 1992).

39. Morton Marks, "Ritual Structures in Afro-American Music," in *Religious Movements in Contemporary America*, ed. Irving I. Zaretsky and Mark P. Leone (Princeton, N. J.: Princeton University Press, 1974), pp. 60–134.

40. This is discussed by Allen in *Singing in the Spirit*; on p. 151, he criticizes "the popular misconception that demonstrative gospel quartet singers are constantly raging out of control." Allen also discusses techniques of quartet performance.

41. Jackson, *The Performing Black Sacred Quartet*, p. 88, quoting Lynn Abbott. The full story of the Humming Four/Hawks conversion is told by Jackson, pp. 88–89.

42. Ibid, p. 91, quoting Abbott.

43. Clarence Fountain, *Alive in Person*, Jewel J-0055 (U. S.; vinyl) recorded in the early 1970s. The observation can be heard on other "live" recordings by Fountain and the Blind Boys of Alabama, and is obviously part of his established stage routine.

44. The Dixie Hummingbirds, "Keep Holding On," on *Every Day and Every Hour*, Peacock PLP-127 (U. S.; vinyl; c. 1965).

## MELVIN MOSLEY AND THE SPIRIT OF MEMPHIS

1. "We Are the Spirit of Memphis Quartet," written by Melvin Mosley, on *Traveling On with the Spirit of Memphis Quartet*, High Water LP-1005 (U. S.; vinyl; 1985).

2. The group's early and prime years are discussed by Lornell in *Happy in the Spirit* and in notes to *When Mother's Gone*, Gospel Jubilee RF-1404 (Sweden; vinyl; 1991), a collection of Spirit of Memphis recordings and airshots from 1949 to 1954. Other writing on the group is by Broughton in *Black Gospel*, pp. 67–68 and by David Evans in notes to High Water 1005.

3. The group recorded "Happy in the Service of the Lord" and "How Many Times" at radio station WJLD in Birmingham, Alabama, in May 1949. They were issued on a small local label, Hallelujah Spirituals TWX1/2. Soon after, the De Luxe company, of New Jersey, issued a different version of "Happy in the Service" backed by "My Life Is in His Hands," on De Luxe 3221. An element of mystery continues to surround these two tracks. Laughton and Hayes's *Gospel Records 1943–1969* (p. 697) quotes Jethroe Bledsoe as saying De Luxe bought tracks recorded at the WJLD session, which suggests that its "Happy in the Service" is on another take from that session, and "My Life Is in His Hands" is a third track recorded at the same time. However, it is possible that the De Luxe recordings were made at a separate session prompted by the success of the Hallelujah Spirituals record. The Hallelujah Spirituals songs are reissued on *Heaven Bound Train: Southern Gospel 1949–1950*, P-Vine PCD-2628 (Japan; CD; 1994).

4. The 1992 lineup of the Spirit of Memphis has not recorded. The remade "Happy in the Service of the Lord" is on the group's most recent recording, *Lord Jesus*, Nasha 001 (U. S.; vinyl and cassette tape; 1987). Personnel on this is Melvin Mosley, Huebert Crawford, Jimmie Allen, Earl Malone, Robert Reed, Jack Stepter and Brown Berry, although the album also contains the early Spirit tracks "Lord Jesus" (1952) and "The Day Is Passed and Gone" (1949) with overdubbed guitar and keyboard.

5. " . . . I know this group is not singing in vain" paraphrases a Spirit of Memphis song, "Singing Won't Be in Vain," recorded for Peacock in the early 1960s and again in 1984 for High Water (with Mosley as lead singer). Gospel singers often use lines from songs in their speech; instances appear in other interviews in this book.

## ODELL HAMPTON AND THE TRUE LOVING FIVE

1. The term "world fair" is sometimes used as a generic description for a large occasion; the True Loving Five played in 1986 at New Orleans's annual Jazz and Heritage Festival.

2. Golden Gate Jubilee Quartet, "Jonah," recorded in Charlotte, North Carolina, on August 4, 1937; reissued on *Jubilee to Gospel*, JEMF 108 (U. S.; vinyl; 1980).

3. The Trumpeteers' "Milky White Way," recorded in Baltimore on September 12, 1947, reputedly sold more than a million copies. *Milky White Way*, Mr. R&B RBD-1401 (Sweden; CD; 1991), reissues eighteen Trumpeteers tracks recorded between 1947 and 1954. (RBD-1401 is a CD reissue of Gospel Jubilee RF-1401 [Sweden; vinyl; 1988].)

4. " . . . see what the end's gonna be" is another gospel song quote (see Spirit of Memphis note 6) indicating determination to complete the journey through life and gain a heavenly reward. It occurs in a number of songs; examples include the Sensational Nightingales, "To the End," on *Songs of Praise*, Peacock PLP-101 (original issue only) (U. S.; vinyl; 1960), the Spirit of Memphis, "See What the End's Gonna Be" on *New Horizon*, Abec ALP-7005 (U. S.; vinyl; 1979) and Troy Ramey and the Soul Searchers, "Run On," on *Singing the Gospel*, Musicor MS-3258X (U. S.; vinyl; 1974).

## THE WATSON FAMILY SINGERS

1. Lornell's *Happy in the Service of the Lord* (p. 133) notes the Jordan Wonders as being founded in 1953. He dates its demise as a semi-professional group to 1960, but it continued singing after then; W. C. Watson joined it in the late 1960s and stayed until the mid-1970s.

2. For more on the role of quartet trainers, see Lornell, *Happy in the Service of the Lord* (pp. 88–93); Jackson, *The Performing Black Sacred Quartet* (pp. 201–26); Allen, *Singing in the Spirit* (pp. 53–54).

3. In 1994, Angela Watson received an offer from "an R&B producer," and was enthusiastic about the possibility that it would lead to recording work.

4. David Evans, *Big Road Blues: Tradition and Creativity in the Folk Blues* (Los Angeles: University of California Press, 1982), p. 58. Evans quotes other blues singers expressing similar views; more can be found in Oliver's *Conversation With the Blues*.

5. " . . . live the life that I sing about" quotes Thomas A. Dorsey's *I'm Going to Live the Life I Sing About In My Song*, published in 1941 and performed by many gospel artists.

6. " . . . I feel like I've been picked out to be picked on" quotes Troy Ramey and the Soul Searchers, "I've Been Picked Out To Be Picked On," the title track of AIR 10079 (U. S.; vinyl; 1984).

## CHAPTER 3 WOMEN'S VOICES

1. Nat Hentoff and Nat Shapiro, *Here Me Talkin' To Ya* (London: Peter Davies, 1955), p. 227, quoted by Oliver in *Songsters and Saints*, p. 189.

2. Oliver, *Songsters and Saints*, p. 189.

3. Eileen Southern, *The Music of Black Americans* (New York: W. W. Norton, 1971), p. 31.

4. Horace Clarence Boyer, *An Analysis of Black Church Music With Examples Drawn from Services in Rochester, New York* (Ph.D. diss., University of Rochester, 1973), p. 14.

5. Oliver, *Songsters and Saints*, p. 189.

6. Malcolm Shaw, notes to Arizona Dranes, *Barrelhouse Piano With Sanctified Singing*, Herwin 210 (U. S.; vinyl). Dranes's complete recordings are also on Document DOCD-5186 (1993).

7. Heilbut, notes to *The Gospel Sound of Spirit Feel*, Spirit Feel SF-1012 (U. S.; CD; 1991).

8. Westminister WP-6089 (U. S.; vinyl), reissued as *Gospel Singing in Washington Temple*, Collector's Issue C-5529 (Austria; vinyl; 1991).

9. Rosetta Tharpe's 1938–1944 recordings are on Document DOCD-5334 and 5335 (1995). Lection 841–143-2 (France; CD; 1994) reissues twelve recordings from 1956 originally on vinyl album Mercury 20201. A number of vinyl albums have been issued, although none is now in print. *Sister Rosetta Tharpe*, Rosetta RR-1317 (U. S.; 1988) contains tracks with Lucky Millinder (including "Trouble In Mind") and with Sammy Price and Marie Knight. *Gospel Train*, MCA MCA-1317 (U. S.; 1980) has 1946–48 tracks with Price, including "Strange Things Happening Every Day."

10. In notes to Rosetta RR-1317, Rosetta Reitz says Tharpe's wedding ceremony, on Tuesday, July 3, 1951, was "financed by a Washington chain of retail record shops" and included a five thousand dollar fireworks display. It was recorded by Decca, which issued four 78 rpm records (48265/6/7/8) of the service and its music; these were also issued in England on Vocalion. No reissue known.

11. Broughton, *Black Gospel*, p. 51.

12. Heilbut, notes to *Mother Smith and Her Children*, Spirit Feel SF-1010 (U. S.; vinyl; 1989).

13. Ibid.

14. Broughton, *Black Gospel*, p. 52.

15. Harris, *The Rise of Gospel Blues*, p. 258.

16. Schwerin, *Got To Tell It*, pp. 66–67.

17. In notes to Mahalia Jackson, *The Apollo Sessions 1946–51*, Pair PDEC-2-1332 (U. S.; CD; 1994), Charles Wolfe identifies James Lee as the pianist on "Move on Up"; earlier sources credit Mahalia Jackson's long-time accompanist, Mildred Falls.

18. Broughton, *Black Gospel*, p. 76.

19. Heilbut, notes to Dorothy Love Coates and the Gospel Harmonettes, *Get on Board*, Specialty SPCD-7017-2 (U. S.; CD; 1991).

20. The Memphis groups are discussed by Lornell in *Happy in the Service of the Lord*.

21. Opal Louis Nations, notes to *The Best of Maggie Ingram*, Nashboro NASH-4516-2 (U. S.; CD; 1995).

22. Nations, notes to *The Best of Sister Lucille Pope and the Pearly Gates*, Nashboro NASH-4511-2 (U. S.; CD; 1995).

23. Shun Pace-Rhodes, *He Lives*, Savoy SC-14807 (U. S.; CD; 1991). She has also recorded with a number of choirs, including the Gospel Music Workshop of America and the Central Georgia State Choir, and with a family group, the Anointed Pace Sisters.

24. Pepper Smith, "Look Out For Shun Pace-Rhodes," *Rejoice* 4, no. 4 (August–September, 1992): 15–16.

### RITA WATSON

1. "I Forgot to Remember to Forget" was recorded by Elvis Presley in Memphis in July 1955. Although Rita Watson describes it as a blues, it is a country song.

### LEOMIA BOYD

1. *I'm Depending On You, Lord*, Jewel J-182 (U. S.; vinyl). No longer available on vinyl, but at the time of writing, cassette tape Jewel JC-0182 was still available.

2. *That's the Way the Lord Works*, Air 10122 (U. S.; vinyl; 1988).

3. The album was still unreleased early in 1995.

4. "I'm a Country Girl," on *I Am Ready*, Air 10105 (U. S.; vinyl; 1985).

5. "Holy Ghost Fire," on Air 10122.

6. "I've Been Dipped in the Water," on Air 10105. See also "Been Dipped in the Water, Pts. 1 and 2" by the Hardeman Singers, Peacock 3067 (45 rpm vinyl; no reissue known) and "I've Been Dipped in the Water" by Brother Joe May and Rev. James Cleveland, Nashboro 7039 (45 rpm vinyl), reissued on *The Great Brother Joe May*, AVI 50024 (U. S.; vinyl; 1981).

7. Schwerin, *Got To Tell It*, p. 68.

### KATIE DAVIS WATSON AND THE GOLDEN STARS

1. Katie Davis Watson is referring to a custom devised when slaves were forbidden to hold their own church services. Secret services were held in secluded areas, and when people attending wished to call out in religious ecstasy, they put their heads into a large cooking pot to muffle the sound. In *The Rise of Gospel Blues* (p. 245), Michael Harris notes that "numerous accounts correlate on the fact that slaves had to use various devices such as an inverted pot to dampen the sound." These sources include Lawrence W. Levine's *Black Culture and Black Consciousness* (New York: Oxford University Press, 1977), p. 42.

2. "Crawlin' King Snake" was a hit for Mississippi singer-guitarist Big Joe Williams, who recorded it in March 1941. In June 1941, another Mississippi artist, Tony Hollins, recorded a markedly different version, which influenced John Lee Hooker's 1949 recording.

3. The songs the Golden Stars quote are blues hits first recorded in the late 1930s and early 1940s (although most have been re-recorded since by a number of artists). "Good Morning Little School Girl" and "Sugar Mama" are by Tennessee-born harmonica player and singer John Lee "Sonny Boy" Williamson, and were

both recorded on May 5, 1937; "Baby Please Don't Go" was recorded by Big Joe Williams on March 27, 1941. The verse "Mama caught a chicken, she thought it was a duck . . ." is from "Bottle It Up and Go," recorded by another Mississippi singer-guitarist, Tommy McClennan, on November 22, 1939—although the same verse occurs in other songs and was recorded as far back as 1928, by pianist and singer James "Stump" Johnson in "The Duck's Yas-Yas-Yas."

## CHAPTER 4 ON THE AIR

1. "Happy in the Service of the Lord," the Spirit of Memphis, on *Lord Jesus*, Nasha 001 (U. S.; vinyl and cassette tape; 1987).

2. "Jesus Is on the Main Line," The Brown Singers, on *Jesus Is Good News*, E&J EJ-71792C (U. S.; cassette tape; 1992).

3. Southern, *The Music of Black Americans*, p. 433.

4. Allen, *Singing in the Spirit*, p. 25.

5. Lornell, *Happy in the Service of the Lord*, p. 22.

6. Ibid., p. 116.

7. Seroff, notes to *Birmingham Quartet Anthology*, Clanka Lanka 144,001/002.

8. Brenda McCallum, notes to *Birmingham Boys: Jubilee Gospel Quartets from Jefferson County, Alabama*, Alabama Traditions 101 (U. S.; vinyl; 1982).

9. Allen, *Singing in the Spirit*, p. 29.

10. Lornell, *Happy in the Service of the Lord*, p. 22.

11. Heilbut, notes to *Fathers and Sons*, Spirit Feel CD-1001.

12. Ron Wynn, "Rebert H. Harris," *Rejoice* 3, no. 3 (June–July 1991): 22–24.

13. Chris Smith, notes to the Fairfield Four, *Standing on the Rock*, Ace CDCHD-449 (U. K.; CD; 1992).

14. Ray Funk, notes to *The Five Blind Boys of Alabama*, Heritage HT-315 (U. K.; vinyl; 1987).

15. Jackson, *The Performing Black Sacred Quartet*, p. 16.

16. For more on the Golden Gate Quartet, see notes by Peter A. Grendsya to albums *The Golden Gate Quartet*, RCA CL-42111 (Germany; vinyl; 1977) and *Swing Down Chariot*, Columbia CK-47131 (U. S.; CD; 1991), and Ray Funk, notes to the Southern Sons, *When They Ring Them Golden Bells*, Gospel Jubilee RF-1406 (Sweden; vinyl; 1990).

17. Allen, *Singing in the Spirit*, p. 30.

18. Jerry Zolten, "Don't Let Nobody Turn You Round," *Rejoice* 3, no. 6 (December 1991–January 1992): 3–11.

19. Jackson, *The Performing Black Sacred Quartet*, p. 74.

20. Lornell, *Happy in the Service of the Lord*, p. 118.

21. Ibid., quoting Lornell's February 5, 1983, interview with Walton.

22. Funk, "The Kings of Harmony," *Rejoice* 3, no. 2 (fall 1990): 10–13.

23. Lee Hildebrand and Opal L. Nations, notes to Swan Silvertones, *Heavenly Light*, Specialty SPCD-7044-2 (U. S.; CD; 1993).

24. Robert Reed, interviewed by Doug Seroff in Memphis, June 1979; quoted by Lornell in *Happy in the Service of the Lord*, p. 107.

25. Funk, notes to anthology *Cleveland Gospel*, Heritage HT-316 (U. K.; vinyl; 1987).

26. Funk, notes to the Meditation Singers, *Good News*, Specialty SPCD-7032-2 (U. S.; CD; 1992).

27. Leonard Goines, notes to the Abyssinian Baptist Choir, *Shakin' the Rafters*, Columbia CK-47335 (U. S.; CD; 1991).

28. Elder Lightfoot Solomon Michaux's 1933 recordings are on *Singing the Gospel*, Document DOCD-5326 (1995).

29. Fred Mendelsohn, notes to Elder Lightfoot Solomon Michaux, *The 'Happy Am I' Preacher*, Savoy MG-14058 (U. S.; vinyl; 1962).

30. Opal Louis Nations, notes to Rev. Cleophus Robinson, *Someone To Care*, Specialty SPCD-7055-2 (U. S.; CD; 1993).

31. Louis Cantor, *Wheelin' On Beale: How WDIA Became the Nation's First All-Black Radio Station . . .* (New York: Pharos Books, 1992), p. 21. Much of the information on WDIA is drawn from this book and from Lornell's *Happy in the Service of the Lord*.

32. Brewster's career and influence are examined in *We'll Understand It Better By and By*, ed. Bernice Johnson Reagon, pp. 185–234.

33. Peter Guralnick, *Last Train to Memphis: The Rise of Elvis Presley* (Boston: Little, Brown and Co., 1994), p. 75.

34. Lornell, *Happy in the Service of the Lord*, p. 50.

35. A number of these recordings are reissued on *Bless My Bones*, P-Vine PLP-9051 (Japan; vinyl; 1982), with notes by Doug Seroff.

36. Ron Wynn, "Malaco/Savoy," *Rejoice* 1, no. 4 (winter 1989): 9–11.

37. Jackson, *The Performing Black Sacred Quartet*, p. 92.

38. Arsenio Orteza, "Standing Room Only," *Rejoice* 4, no. 6: 6–9.

39. Ibid.

## EARLY WRIGHT

1. Despite Early Wright's allegation of mid-1940s racism at WREC, the station aired the first broadcast of African-American gospel in Memphis, in 1928 when it presented the I. C. Glee Club quartet (Lornell, *Happy in the Service of the Lord*, pp. 70, 116).

2. Andy McWilliams, "Night Time Is the Wright Time," *Living Blues* 82 (September–October 1988): 16–19.

3. Sam Cooke, lead singer for the Soul Stirrers from late 1950 until mid-1957, was shot in an altercation with a Los Angeles motel owner on December 10, 1964.

4. See note 2.

## BROTHER JAMES CHAMBERS

1. Bishop Gilbert Earl Patterson is also prelate of the Church of God in Christ's Fourth Jurisdiction, in Tennessee. His brother, Bishop James Oglethorpe Patterson, Jr., is prelate of the Headquarters Jurisdiction and pastors Memphis's largest COGIC church, the Pentecostal Temple. Their father, Bishop J. O. Patterson, Sr.,

was the church's first presiding bishop after the death of its founder, Bishop C. H. Mason, in November 1961.

2. Dwight "Gatemouth" Moore was a Memphis-born blues singer who became a preacher. He was a DJ on WDIA from 1949 until 1951.

## REV. J. W. (JOHN) SHAW

1. The "chimney corner" is a right angle formed by the wall of a house and the side of an exterior chimney. It was a popular place for children because it was sheltered, warm in winter and cool in summer, and usually secluded.

2. The Shaw Singers, *Yesterday and Today*, Messenger MLP-2001 (U. S.; vinyl; c. 1976).

3. *Trying to Do Thy Will/After While*, Messenger 45/6942 (45 rpm vinyl; 1971).

4. This often-used church expression paraphrases Romans 10:9: "That if thou shalt confess with thy mouth the Lord Jesus, and shalt believe in thine heart that God hath raised him from the dead, thou shalt be saved."

## CHAPTER 5 THE PREACHERS

1. Boyer, *An Analysis of Black Church Music*, pp. 12–14.

2. Burnim, *The Black Gospel Music Tradition*, pp. 54–61. She also briefly discusses the early years of the African-American church.

3. Ibid., p. 66, quoting Benjamin Mays and Joseph Nicholson, *The Negro's Church* (New York: Institute of Social and Religious Research, 1933).

4. Ibid.

5 Washington Phillips, "Denomination Blues Pt. II," recorded in Dallas, December 5, 1927, and issued on Columbia 14333-D.

6. Franklin, *The Relationship of Black Preaching to Black Gospel Music*, p. 82.

7. Boyer, *An Analysis of Black Church Music*, pp. 2–4.

8. Oliver, *Songsters and Saints*, p. 146.

9. Rev. F. C. Barnes, sermon at Red Budd Holy Church, Rocky Mount, North Carolina, Sunday October 23, 1994.

10. Columbia pressing figures from Dan Mahony's, *Columbia 13/14000-D Series* (Stanhope, N. J.: Walter C. Allen; 1961).

11. Rev. J. M. Gates's first recordings are on *Rev. J. M. Gates, Vol. 1 (1926)*, Document DOCD-5414 (Austria; CDC; 1995), the first in a series which will reissue all his recordings. Only a few Rev. Burnett tracks have been reissued, and most are out of print; "The Downfall of Nebuchadnezzar" is on anthology *Songsters and Saints, Vol. 2.*, Matchbox MSEX-2003/2004 (U. K.; vinyl; 1984).

12. See Harris, *The Rise of Gospel Blues*, p. 68. Harris accepts that A. W. Nix and W. M. Nix are the same man, and analyzes the preaching style of A. W. Nix to show influences on Dorsey. In *Songsters and Saints* (p. 150), Oliver tells how A. W. Nix "electrified" the National Baptist Convention with his singing in 1921; he makes no mention of W. M. Nix.

13. David Evans, notes to *Rev. A. W. Nix, Vol. 1 (1927–28)*, Document DOCD-5328 (1994), which contains Nix's first twenty-four sermons.

14. Jeff Titon, *Early Downhome Blues: A Musical and Cultural Analysis* (Urbana: University of Chicago Press, 1977), p. 211.

15. Rev. F. W. McGee's recordings are on *Rev. F. W. McGee (1927–1930)*, Blues Documents BDCD-6031-32 (Austria; CDs; 1992).

16. Oliver, *Songsters and Saints*, p. 180.

17. D. C. Rice's recordings are on *Rev. D. C. Rice (1928–30)*, Document DOCD-5071 (1991).

18. Rev. Sister Mary Nelson's recordings are on *Memphis Gospel (1928–29)*, Document DOCD-5072 (1991); Missionary Josephine Miles's are on *Gospel Classics, Vol. 3 (1924–42)*, Document DOCD-5350 (1994); one track of Leora Ross is on anthology *Songsters and Saints, Vol. 1*, Matchbox MSEX-2001/2 (U. K.; vinyl; 1984).

19. At the time of writing, "The Eagle Stirreth Her Nest" was available on Jewel JCD-3083 (U.S.; CD). It was also issued on Chess albums 9129 and 91528 and originally as three JVB/Chess 78 rpm records collectively cataloged Sermon 2.

20. For more on Franklin, see C. L. Franklin, *Give Me This Mountain: Life History and Selected Sermons*, Jeff T. Titon, ed. (Urbana: University of Illinois Press, 1989).

21. Rev. W. M. Mosley and His Congregation, "You Preachers Stay Out of Widows' Houses." Recorded in Atlanta on November 2, 1931; issued on 78 rpm Columbia 14635-D; no reissue known.

22. Hayes and Laughton, *Gospel Records 1943–1969*, pp. 527–28.

23. Rev. F. C. Barnes, author's interview, Red Budd Holy Church, Rocky Mount, North Carolina, Sunday, October 23, 1994.

24. Heilbut, *The Gospel Sound*, p. 120.

25. Hildebrand and Nations, notes to the Swan Silvertones, *Heavenly Light*, Specialty SPCD-7044-2 (U. S.; CD; 1992).

26. Rev. R. C. Crenshaw and Congregation of New Browns Chapel Memphis. Reissued on four-CD boxset *Sounds of the South*, Atlantic 7824962 (U. S.; 1994).

## REV. ARTHUR FITCHPATRICK, JR.

1. In *Blues People* (New York: William Morrow, 1963; Apollo edition, 1968), p. 37, Amiri Baraka (LeRoi Jones) suggests that baptism by total immersion was a major reason for the antebellum popularity of the Baptist church among slaves because "in most of the religions of West Africa, the river spirits were thought to be among the most powerful of the deities, and the priests of the river cults were among the most powerful and influential men in African society."

## REV. WILLIE MORGANFIELD

1. Church and population numbers from a c. 1990 Clarksdale Chamber of Commerce map of the town and surrounding Coahoma County.

2. "What Is This?" was issued on 45 rpm Jewel 757 and album Jewel LP-0002; its most recent issue is on *Willie Morganfield's Gospel Favorites*, Paula C-104 (U. S.; cassette tape). Hayes and Laughton's *Gospel Records 1943–1969* lists it as being recorded c. 1965, but adds that it was one of four tracks probably bought by Jewel from the Acquarian [*sic*] label, which issued Morganfield's first

four solo recordings. Morganfield's precise recollection of the recording date is undoubtedly more reliable than the *Gospel Records* estimate.

3. "Serving the Lord" was recorded c. 1967 and issued on 45 rpm Jewel 145 and album Jewel LPS-0016. Its most recent issue is on *Serving the Lord,* Jewel LPS-0052 (U. S.; vinyl), also available as compact disc JCD-3052.

4. "Lord, Thank You Sir" is another of the Acquarian tracks bought by Jewel. It was issued on 45 rpm Jewel 756 and album Jewel LP-0002; its most recent issue is Jewel LPS/JC-0052. A concert recording of the song is on Paula C-104.

5. Funk, notes to Archie Brownlee and the Five Blind Boys of Mississippi, *You Done What the Doctor Couldn't Do,* Gospel Jubilee RF-1402 (Sweden; vinyl; 1989).

6. Funk, "The Kings of Harmony," *Rejoice* 3, no. 2 (winter 1990): 7–12.

7. *Bell Grove Baptist Choir,* Jewel LPS-0125 (U. S.; vinyl); also as compact disc JCD-3125.

8. "Love in Action," Testament T-5001 (U. S.; vinyl; 1988).

9. "The Bible," Jewel LPS-0154 (U. S.; vinyl); also as compact disc JCD-3154.

10. Cooke's version of "Were You There?" is on Specialty SPCD-7009-2, *Sam Cooke With the Soul Stirrers* (U. S.; CD; 1992); Morganfield's is on *While I Can,* Paula LPS-837 (U. S.; vinyl).

11. "I Can't Afford to Let My Savior Down," on Jewel LPS-0052/JCD-3052.

12. The Staple Singers' 1972 Stax recording "I'll Take You There" includes the line " . . . no smiling faces, lying to the races." It is reissued on *Respect Yourself: The Best of the Staple Singers,* Stax CDSX-006 (U.K.; CD; 1987). Rev. Morganfield's Bible quote paraphrases Mark 7:6: "This people honoreth me with their lips, but their heart is far from me."

13. Muddy Waters did record two religious songs, "You Got to Take Sick and Die Some of these Days" and "Why Don't You Live So God Can Use You," for the Library of Congress in 1942. Both are on *The Complete Plantation Recordings,* Chess/MCA CHD-9344 (U. S.; CD; 1993). He later used "You Got to Take Sick" as the basis for his 1956 recording, "Diamonds At Your Feet," Chess 1630.

14. The quote paraphrases John 14:26: "But the Comforter, which is the Holy Ghost, whom the Father will send in my name, he shall teach you all things and bring all things to your remembrance, whatsoever I have said unto you."

15. "He Works That Way" was the B side of "What Is This" on Jewel 757. Its most recent issue is on Jewel LPS-0052/JCD-3052.

16. John 3: 1–21.

### Rev. Dr. David Hall

1. The site on which Bishop Mason built Temple Church was bought from Memphis preacher Rev. Sutton Griggs, who recorded six sermons in September 1928.

2. Southwest Michigan State Choir of the Church of God in Christ, *Salvation is Free,* Savoy MG-14120 (U. S.; vinyl; 1965). "Climbing Up the Mountain" is on the album.

3. Johnnie Taylor came from the Highway QCs to the Soul Stirrers in 1957 to replace Sam Cooke. He became an ordained Baptist minister during his time

with the Soul Stirrers, and left the group in 1960 to concentrate on his ministry. But by 1961, he was recording pop music for Sam Cooke's SAR label after Cooke "made me an offer I couldn't refuse" (Hildebrand and Nations, notes to the Soul Stirrers, *Heaven Is My Home*, Specialty SPCD-7040-2 [U. S.; CD; 1993]).

4. Burnim, *The Black Gospel Music Tradition*, p. 126.

5. "This Is the Church of God in Christ," author unknown, No. 57 in the COGIC hymnal, *Yes Lord!* The text of the song is:

> This is the Church of God in Christ,
> This is the Church of God in Christ.
> O you can't join it, you have to be born in it.
> This is the Church of God in Christ.
>
> I love the Church of God in Christ. (2x)
> O you can't join it, you have to be born in it.
> I love the Church of God in Christ.

Other verses can be extemporized.

## CHAPTER 6  BACK IN CHURCH

1. Son House, 1960s concert at unidentified venue. Copies of the film circulated among collectors for years; it is now on commercial videotape *Masters of the Country Blues*, Yazoo 500 (U. S.; 1991).

2. Jessie Mae Hemphill, author's interview, Como, Mississippi, September 16, 1992.

3. Mark A. Humphrey, "Holy Blues: The Gospel Tradition," in *Nothing But the Blues*, ed. Lawrence Cohn (New York: Abbeville Press, 1993), p. 128.

4. Andy Boy, "Jive Blues," recorded at San Antonio on Wednesday, February 24, 1937; reissued on *Texas Piano Styles (1929–1937)*, Wolf WSE-132 (Austria; vinyl).

5. Aaron "T-Bone" Walker, "I Got the Blues," recorded in Los Angeles in 1951; reissued on *T-Bone Walker: Classics of Modern Blues*, Blue Note BN-LA-533-H2 (U. S.; vinyl; 1975) and on *The Complete Recordings of T-Bone Walker 1940–1954*, Mosaic MR6-130 (U. S.; 6 CDs; 1990).

6. Muddy Waters, interviewed by Alan Lomax and John Work for the Library of Congress, at Stovall, Mississippi, August 1941. Issued on *The Complete Plantation Recordings*, Chess MCA CHD-9344.

7. "I Heard the Voice of a Pork Chop," recorded by Jim Jackson in Memphis, January 30, 1928, reissued on *Jim Jackson, Vol. 1*, Document DOCD-5114 (1992), and by Bogus Ben Covington in Chicago, c. September 1928, reissued on anthology *Alabama: Black Country Dance Bands (1924–1949)*, Document DOCD-5166 (1993).

8. Winston Holmes and Charlie Turner, "The Death of Holmes' Mule, Pts. 1 and 2," recorded in Richmond, Indiana, June 21, 1929; reissued on *Kansas City Blues*, Document DOCD-5152 (1993).

9. Parodies are discussed in more detail by Oliver in *Songsters and Saints*, pp. 134–37.

10. Georgia Tom, "You Got Me In This Mess (I Ain't Gonna Do It No More),"
recorded in Chicago, Thursday, April 10, 1930; reissued on *Georgia Tom, Vol. 2*,
Blues Documents BDCD-6022 (1991).

11. Oliver, *Screening the Blues* (London: Cassell & Company, 1968; New York:
Da Capo, 1989).

12. Jon Michael Spencer, *Blues and Evil* (Knoxville, Tenn.: University of
Tennessee Press, 1993).

13. Ibid., p. 111.

14. David Evans, notes to Son House, *Delta Blues and Spirituals*, Capitol CDP-
7243-8-31830-2-9 (U. S.; CD; 1995).

15. Oliver, *Screening the Blues*, p. 49.

16. Son House, *Preaching the Blues, Part 1*, recorded Chicago, May 28, 1930;
reissued on *Son House and the Great Delta Blues Singers (1928–30)*, Document
DOCD-5002 (1990). House also recorded the song in 1965 and 1969.

17. See note 14.

18. Stephen Calt and Gayle Wardlow, *King of the Delta Blues: The Life and
Music of Charlie Patton* (Newton, N. J.: Rock Chapel Press, 1988), p. 29. (Patton's
forename is variously spelled "Charlie" and "Charley." The latter was used on
his record label credits, and is more widely used today.)

19. Evans, "Charley Patton—The Conscience of the Delta," *The Voice of the
Delta: Charley Patton and the Mississippi Blues Traditions*, ed. Robert Sacré
(Belgium: Presses Universitaires de Liège, 1987), p. 137.

20. Ibid., pp. 138–39.

21. Ibid., pp. 170–71.

22. Peter Lee and David Nelson, "From Shoutin' the Blues to Preachin' the
Word," *Living Blues* 86 (May/June 1989): 9–19.

23. David Evans, "Rubin Lacy," in *Nothing But the Blues*, ed. Mike Leadbitter
(London: Hanover Books, 1971), pp. 239–45.

24. Pete Welding, "Reverend Robert Wilkins, Pts. 4 and 5," *Blues Unlimited*
54 (June 1968): 14; 55 (July 1968): 8–9.

25. Evans, "Rubin Lacy," *Nothing But the Blues*, p. 244.

26. Ibid.

27. Harris, *The Rise of Gospel Blues*, pp. 98–99.

28. Welding, "Reverend Robert Wilkins, Pt. 5," *Blues Unlimited* 55 (July
1968): 9.

29. Robert Wilkins's 1920s and '30s blues recordings are reissued on *Memphis
Blues*, Document DOCD-5014 (1990). "Prodigal Son" and "I'm Going Home to
My Heavenly King" were recorded in Washington, D. C. in February 1964, and
issued on *Memphis Gospel Singer*, Piedmont PLP-13162 (U. S.; vinyl; 1964). An
excellent concert version of "Prodigal Son," recorded at the 1964 Newport Folk
Festival, is on *Blues at Newport*, Vanguard VCD-115/16 (U. S.; CD; 1989).

30. *The Soul of Chicago*, Shanachie 6008 (U. S.; CD; 1993).

31. Sister Wynona Carr, "I Heard the News (Jesus Is Coming Again)," recorded
in Philadelphia, August 1, 1949; reissued on *Dragnet For Jesus*, Specialty SPCD-
7016-2 (U. S.; CD; 1992). Roy Brown recorded "I Heard the News" in New

Orleans in September 1947; it was issued on DeLuxe 1107. An even more successful version was recorded by Wynonie Harris as "Good Rockin' Tonight" in Cincinnati on December 28, 1947, and issued on King 4210.

32. Kelly Brothers, "He's All Right," recorded in Chicago, June 1, 1960, issued on King LP-810 (U. S.; vinyl).

33. King Pins with Johnny Otis, "She's All Right," recorded 1962, issued on King 5606.

34. Ray Charles and David Ritz, *Brother Ray: Ray Charles' Own Story* (New York: The Dial Press, 1978), quoted by Peter Guralnick in *Sweet Soul Music* (New York: Harper and Row, 1986), p. 63.

35. Angelic Choir, Savoy MG-14049 (U. S.; vinyl; c. 1962).

36. See note 22.

37. William Ferris, *Blues From the Delta*, rev. ed. (New York: Da Capo, 1984), p. 79.

38. Ibid., p. 81.

39. Alan Govenar, *Meeting the Blues* (Dallas: Taylor Publishing Co., 1988), p. 213.

40. Ibid., p. 216.

41. Author's interviews, Memphis, September 1992.

42. Solomon Burke, double album *Soul Alive*, Rounder 2042–2043 (U. S.; vinyl; 1983).

43. Jessy Dixon, author's interview, Auckland, New Zealand, June 15, 1995.

HUEBERT CRAWFORD

1. Huebert Crawford, *Love Affair With You/When a Man Is Weak*, J'Ace 45/3112 (U. S.; 45 rpm vinyl; 1977). The J'Ace label was owned by Style Wooten, who also issued gospel music on his Designer and Messenger labels.

2. Huebert Crawford and the King Riders Band, *King Rider Boogie, Parts 1 and 2*, High Water 426 (U. S.; 45 rpm vinyl; 1986).

3. In notes for High Water 426, David Evans writes: "The King Riders are one of the South's largest motorcycle clubs, founded by Mose Mumphrey in 1972. They have seven chapters in the Tri-State area, including Memphis, Blytheville, Arkansas, and Hernando, Pickens, Jackson, Columbus and Caledonia, Mississippi. . . . The King Riders Band is the official band of the Memphis Chapter. . . ."

4. *The World Famous Spirit of Memphis*, Nasha 101.

5. *Traveling On with the Spirit of Memphis Quartet*, Highwater LP-1005.

JAMES HOLLEY

1. O. V. (Overton Vertis) Wright sang with the Sunset Travelers in the 1950s, recording with them on Peacock. In 1956, he joined the Spirit of Memphis; two years later, at the urging of Peacock owner Don Robey, he quit gospel music for pop. Wright died in 1980, aged forty-eight.

2. Guralnick's *Sweet Soul Music* examines Willie Mitchell's career (pp. 300–307) and other aspects of the Memphis music scene of the 1970s.

# INDEX

Abbott, Lynn, 53, 66
Abyssinian Baptist Church (Choir), xxiv–xxv, 147
African-American church: first church, xxi, 186; early churches, 106, 186; segregation, 106, 186; women's role in, 106; service hours, 116; worship style, 139, 186–87; slave services, 186; social role, 186, 187, 229–30. *See also* Baptist church; Christian Methodist Episcopal church; Church of God in Christ; Pastors; Preaching
Air (record company). *See* Atlanta International Records
Alexander, J. W., 58–59
Allen, Jesse (Spirit of Memphis), 67, 70, 71, 76
Allen, Jimmie (Spirit of Memphis), 67, 70
Allen, Ray, xxi, 143
Allison, Margaret (Angelic Gospel Singers), 114
Amos, "Blind" Joe. *See* Taggart, "Blind" Joe
Anderson, Robert, xxiv, 112

Andrews, Ed, 4
Andrews, Inez, 92, 112, 113, 126
Angelic Choir (of First Baptist Church, Nutley, N.J.), xxx, 240
Angelic Gospel Singers, 111, 113–14
Anniversaries, xxxiv, 61, 71, 137
Armstrong, Vanessa Bell, 114
Arnold, John Henry "Big Man," 5, 8
Atlanta International Records (Air), xx–xxi, 113, 124, 194

Baker, Cassietta (née George), 112, 113
Ballen, Ivin, 21, 26
Banks, Willie (and the Messengers), 60
Baptist church: influence on rural musicians, 4; attitude to secular music, 9, 168, 234, 239; bars female preachers, 106; baptism, 138; structure, 187, 202; musical style, 192, 208; quartet links, 225; also, 6, 82. *See also* African-American church; Pastors; Preaching
"Barbecue Bob." *See* Hicks, Robert
Barber, Keith (Pilgrim Travelers), 58, 59

# SONG AND SERMON INDEX